University of Cumbria

SCULPTURE TO WEAR
THE JEWELRY OF MARJORIE SCHICK

TO JIM FOR HIS SUPPORT, TO PROFESSOR EIKERMAN FOR HER INSPIRATION,
AND WITH SPECIAL THANKS TO MY MOTHER.

MARJORIE SCHICK

SCULPTURE TO WEAR

THE JEWELRY OF
MARJORIE SCHICK

With contributions by:

Tacey Rosolowski

Glen R. Brown

Paul Derrez

Helen Williams Drutt English

Fritz Falk

Elizabeth Goring

Suzanne Ramljak

Marjorie Schick

Helen Shirk

Paul J. Smith

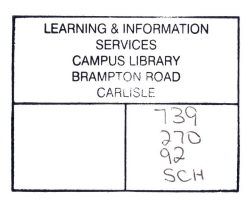
ARNOLDSCHE Art Publishers

© 2007 ARNOLDSCHE Art Publishers, Stuttgart and the authors

AUTHORS
Tacey Rosolowski
Glen R. Brown
Paul Derrez
Helen Williams Drutt English
Fritz Falk
Elizabeth Goring
Suzanne Ramljak
Marjorie Schick
Helen Shirk
Paul J. Smith

TRANSLATION
Joan Clough, Castallack (German-English, essay Fritz Falk)
Uta Hasekamp, Bonn (English-German)

DESIGN
nalbach typografik, Silke Nalbach, Stuttgart

OFFSET-REPRODUCTIONS
Repromayer, Reutlingen

PRINTING/DRUCK
Leibfarth & Schwarz, Dettingen/Erms

This book has been printed on paper that is 100 % free of chlorine bleach in conformity with TCF standards.

Bibliographic information published by Die Deutsche Bibliothek
Die Deutsche Bibliothek lists this publication in the Deutsche Nationalbibliografie; detailed bibliographic data is available on the Internet at http://dnb.ddb.de.

ISBN 978-3-89790-258-9

Made in Europe, 2007

ARNOLDSCHE art books are available internationally at selected bookstores and from the following distribution partners:
USA – ACC/USA, Easthampton, MA, info@antiquecc.com
CANADA – NBN Canada, Toronto, lpetriw@nbnbooks.com
UK – ACC/GB, Woodbridge, Suffolk, sales@antique-acc.com
FRANCE – Fischbacher International Distribution, Paris, libfisch@wanadoo.fr
BENELUX – Coen Sligting Bookimport, Amsterdam, sligting@xs4all.nl
SWITZERLAND – OLF S.A., Fribourg, Information@olf.ch
JAPAN – UPS United Publishers Services, Tokyo
THAILAND – Paragon Asia Co., Ltd, Bangkok, info@paragonasia.com
AUSTRALIA / NEW ZEALAND – Bookwise International, Wingfield, customer.service@bookwise.com.au

For general questions, please contact ARNOLDSCHE Art Publishers directly at art@arnoldsche.com, or visit our homepage at www.arnoldsche.com for further information.

PHOTO CREDITS:

The copyright in the designated photographs of Marjorie Schick's work belongs to the photographer
Joel Degen
42 Dinerman Court, 38–40
Boundary Road
UK – London NW8 0HQ
Telephone: 020 / 76 24 60 63

For further photo credits, see respective illustrations.

© Artwork by Marjorie Schick

COVER ILLUSTRATION:
GRASS, necklace, 2005, back view (see cat. no. 463)
FRONTISPIECE:
Marjorie Schick, 1984–85, with necklace cat. no. 280
Photo: Dr. James B. M. Schick

CONTENTS

ACKNOWLEDGEMENTS

Before there were cell phones and before I had a telephone in my office at the university, Jim would say, "You passed the test, Marj. Miss Eikerman telephoned you at home last night and you were at school in the studio working." My mentor, Professor Alma Eikerman, and I stayed in contact for all the years after I finished the Indiana University graduate jewelry program. Eikerman wrote frequently and sometimes called. Although I did not like to miss her calls, it was good that I was working. Along with teaching aesthetics, drawing, techniques, and jewelry history, she taught us about self-discipline and the importance of hard work. As graduate students, we kept time sheets of when we were in the studio and she checked them often. In a newsletter from 1975, she wrote, "Your main purpose in existence as a craftsman is to produce as much as you possibly can each year, each month." For her, if I missed the phone call because I was in the studio working, it was a good indication that I was living my life the right way.

For many years, Jim would pass by the telephone at home, and although it had not rung, he would pick it up and say "yes, Miss Eikerman, she's been working hard" or tell the imaginary caller that I had not been doing so.

Eikerman also taught her students how to live well. As a reward for their efforts, she regularly invited her first-semester students to her home for dessert after they had soldered the bases onto their silver bowls. Having designed her ultra-modern house herself, she filled it with contemporary art in all media, objects from her travels, beautiful books, and details such as sets of flatware from Scandinavia where she had studied metalsmithing. Elegant, stylish, energetic, adventurous, and loving a challenge, she advised us to save money for travel because it is "an investment for research – and a better life."

LIBERTY TORCH,
BROOCH, 1997
(SEE CAT. NO. 395)

With his brilliant mind and kind heart, Jim, University Professor of American History at Pittsburg State University, has resolutely supported me in so many ways from giving me ideas for pieces such as *Liberty Torch* brooch and *50 States* body sculpture, to taking photos, driving me places, writing for me and editing my writings, teaching me to use a computer and buying me a new one for this book project, and planning vacations around museum visits for me. How fortunate I have been to have a husband who has guided and advised me, as well as supported and encouraged my work no matter what, and a mentor for whom I am still working. This book is dedicated to Dr. James B. M. Schick and to Professor Alma Eikerman because without them, I believe that this body of work would not exist.

Special thanks go to my Mother, Eleanor Curtin Krask, who set the example of a hardworking, dedicated art teacher. She did everything for me and gave me all that she had, including this book, her extraordinary last gift.

Dirk Allgaier made the long, out of the way trip to Pittsburg, Kansas, to council me in choosing images and guide me through the book. Making hundreds of decisions, award-winning graphic designer Silke Nalbach created stunningly beautiful pages that make one eager to see what is next. With her keen eye, copy editor Julia Vogt studied all the written sections to make certain that everything is perfect. Helen Williams Drutt English supported the project with Arnoldsche Art Publishers from the very beginning. Because of their superb quality, their creative spirit, and their distinguished record of accomplishments, I am thankful that Arnoldsche and the publisher, Dieter Zühlsdorff, agreed to this project.

The principal writer, Dr. Tacey Rosolowski, and the other contributing writers Dr. Glen Brown, Paul Derrez, Helen Williams Drutt English, Dr. Fritz Falk, Dr. Elizabeth Goring, Suzanne Ramljak, Helen Shirk, and Paul J. Smith, each were generous in adding special insights and perceptions to this book.

Through their lenses, the photographers Joel Degen, Tom DuBrock, Rod Dutton, Carmen Freudenthal, Jud Haggard, Eva Heyd, Peter R. Leibert, Larry Long, James Mueller, Gary Pollmiller, James B. M. Schick, Martin Tuma, Malcolm Turner, and Hogers Versluys, presented my work professionally, clearly, and with fresh eyes.

Style, grace, spunkiness, and patience were provided by each of those who modeled the pieces: Kathlene Allie, Petra Blaisse, Elizabeth Hake, Cora Hardy, Beth Neubert, Annie Pennington Parthasarathy, and Jared Webb. The gift of mannequins from Ted Monsour also contributed to the display of the pieces.

In the late 80s, the first time I over-worked my right hand, I hired a student to help me. It was necessary to let my hand heal yet I had to continue finishing pieces. Since then, I have hired many who either had been or were currently students at Pittsburg State University. These invaluable assistants helped with the creation of pieces, gave advice, and helped me to meet due dates. Among other things, they cut, stitched, sanded, gessoed, sawed, pegged, painted, and built boxes for

FIFTY STATES, COMMEMORATIVE BODY SCULPTURE WITH EARRINGS, 2000 (SEE CAT. NO. 423)

shipping. I have learned from them, and have enormously enjoyed their company, their ideas, and their help. I thank each one of them: Keegan Adams, Kathlene Allie, Carl Barnett, Melanie Buckler, John Cohorst, Walter Delp, Jana Dunn, Randy French, Anna Friederich-Maggard, Matt Frost, Kristan Hammond, Ukiko Honda, Cherlyn Ingram, David Ingram, Hong Kim, Craig Krug, Janet Lewis, Kelley Losher, Linda Allee Maggio, Jillian Palone, Annie Pennington Parthasarathy, Connie Rogers, Curtis Wakeman, and Jared Webb. If I have inadvertently omitted anyone, I offer my apologies.

I have never made a studio at home but rather have always used my classroom nights and weekends as my studio. I appreciate the patience and tolerance of my students who have never bothered the work, not even when I left 32 painted rings on pedestals (for *Bands of Rings*) on a shelf in the classroom for a year. They have both challenged and encouraged me to work harder.

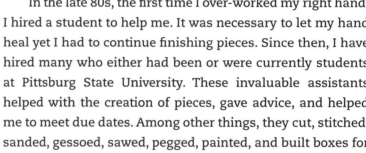

Teaching at Pittsburg State University has enriched my life and the school has been supportive in numerous ways including awarding Jim and me four sabbatical leaves and time for travel during the semester when necessary. My chairmen and colleagues, whom I have admired, have been loyal friends and have given advice and even aesthetic help when asked.

In the state of Kansas, I appreciate the support and recognition provided by the Kansas Arts Commission for giving

IT'S A BOY NAMED ROB, BODY SCULPTURE AND HOUSE, 2005 (SEE CAT. NO. 461)

me a Governor's Arts Award and an Artist Fellowship Award in Crafts. The KAC and the Kansas Artist Craftsman Association both make craftsmen in the state feel that we are part of a larger group and not alone in our endeavors.

It was Tacey Rosolowski who approached International Arts and Artists in Washington, D.C. and persuaded them to organize and promote a traveling retrospective exhibition of my work, a show very different from their usual direction. That exhibition spurred the creation of this book.

Watching Jim's total commitment to his university teaching, and having experienced Eikerman's dedication to her students, I recognize the importance and value of effective teaching. There have been many inspiring and amazing teachers in my past from Evanston Township High School to the University of Wisconsin, Indiana University, and the Sir John Cass School of Art in London. Still today, I continue to draw upon their lessons and am thankful for their contributions. In particular, Indiana University has generously supported my work by giving me two exhibitions that go well beyond the realm of classroom experiences.

The body sculpture *It's A Boy Named Rob* celebrates the birth of our son. Covered with safety pins inserted through colored circles, it references the birth announcements I made for friends. The form hangs from the image of a blue house because the piece is about family and home. Rob allowed Jim and me to see the joy of experiencing life through his eyes and he has remained an inspiration. The baby photo of Rob holding a new armlet destined as a present for Eikerman illustrates his sense of awe and wonder at everything in his world (see page 202).

In a newsletter to her students, the incredible (the word she used so often) Eikerman wrote "My best wishes to you. I am hoping Health and Happiness, and Time for your creative efforts will shine on you…." How fortunate I have been to have had good "Health," an abundance of "Happiness," and because of the amazing and unflagging support of Jim, have been blessed with the gift of huge amounts of "Time" for my creative efforts. This has been an enormous joint effort. I thank you all.

Marjorie Schick

SELF-PORTRAIT, BROOCH AND WALL RELIEF, BROOCH, 1996 (SEE CAT. NO. 458)

MARJORIE SCHICK: CROSSING BOUNDARIES, EXPANDING THE REACH OF FORM

Tacey A. Rosolowski

When Marjorie Schick is overseas, she hears, "Your work is so American"; in the United States, the jewelry and craft communities agree that her work has a distinctly European flavor.[1] Both observations are, of course, accurate. Over the years Schick has moved easily between the continents, teaching, lecturing, taking courses, contributing to and taking energy from a wide-flung jewelry community. Schick is thoroughly American, born in Illinois and living for most of her life in Pittsburg, Kansas. A product of the country's heartland, a pioneering spirit informs her distinctive artistic endeavors. Though trained as a metalsmith and jeweler, she is known for her large and brilliantly colored mixed-media body sculptures. The European tinge to Schick's work arises from her utterly unconflicted beliefs that jewelry is an art form and that the body is integral to completing a sculptural object. For over four decades her aim has been to alter the understanding of sculpture by bringing the human body into direct tactile and kinesthetic contact with form. Her works defy classification. They expand sculpture's expressive range and activate the artistic qualities of the human body itself.

Schick emerged into professional life during the sixties, having absorbed lessons from Viking, Celtic and African ornament, as well as the work of jewelers such as Alma Eikerman and Margaret De Patta. But she had (and has) always looked to sculptors for concep-

FIG. 1 TUBES, BODY SCULPTURE, 1974 (SEE CAT. NO. 107)

tual inspiration: David Smith, Alexander Calder, Julio González, Barbara Hepworth, and ceramicist Hans Coper, among others. Eclectic in perspective, Schick was poised to enter the vibrant conversation about the nature of art that engaged artists on both sides of the Atlantic. Traditional boundaries between the arts blurred as new forms of creative expression emerged. Schick's contemporaries in the jewelry world were such figures as Emmy van Leersum, Gijs Bakker, Caroline Broadhead, Wendy Ramshaw, and David Watkins – a loose community of "New Jewelers" who experimented with size and body location, rejected precious materials, and innovated techniques and forms for an expanded material palette.

In the seventies Schick carved out her own niche within the avant-garde in Europe and America. She was the guest artist for "Choreographing the Object: An Evening of Visual Art and Dance," an exhibition organized by Mary Ann Bransby that offered a unique arena to exemplify Schick's experimental approach. At each of the five performance venues, visitors entered an empty room adjacent to a gallery space and sat on the floor. Dancers would appear, one by one, to interpret pieces by Bransby, Schick and others: angular gestures brought Schick's geometrical armlets and body sculptures to life; swaying hips turned her large metal belt into a musical instrument. When finished, each dancer mounted his or her piece in the gallery for viewing after the performance. Sculpture became a "happening" – an event of perception – as Schick intends with all of her work. Direct physical experience of a form transforms how the sculpture is understood when it is displayed independently of the body (fig. 1). Schick also recalls how another dancer swooped and spun, setting the heavy fibers of a long body sculpture in motion. She watched, fascinated, as dust motes drifted upward from the piece, as if the sculpture – and the dancer's movements – were materially occupying the entire space.

The astonishing range of Schick's work has drawn on the subtleties of this artistic sensibility. Schick sculpts, but to activate space beyond localized mass or line. She paints, but to bestow on form the expressive gestures of movement and mood. She creates ornament, but exceeds anything defined as decorative. She crafts her objects laboriously but does not want her labor to show or to detract from the overall aesthetic impact of her work. Even when displayed off the body her work catalyzes many types of aesthetic response: experiential understanding of form; awareness of complex spatial relations; heightened perceptual awareness of an artistically crafted environment.

The story of Schick's career can be broken into two main periods. The first encompasses her graduate school training at Indiana University and extends into the eighties. During this time Schick established her visual vocabulary, putting her own stamp on the lessons of Modernist abstraction: exploring first principles of volume, line, space and mass. Equally critically, Schick established a solid platform from which she could move confidently beyond her training. This she accomplished in the second period of her career, when she gave herself freely to artistic interests that had been percolating latently for many years.

Schick was born in Taylorville, Illinois, in 1941. Her mother, Eleanor Krask, was a career woman who returned to school when Schick was a child to earn her Bachelor's and Master's degrees. Raising young Marjorie as a single mother, Krask provided an invaluable role model in the traditional climate of post-war America. An art educator, Krask filled the house with art materials, as well as books and periodicals that exposed her daughter to artists and jewelers, past and present. Krask taught her daughter to sew, collage and paint. Young Marjorie honed hand skills and familiarity with a wide range of media. When her mother took a job in Evanston, Illinois, just north of Chicago, Marjorie enjoyed the enriched art program at Evanston Township High School, taking art history, enameling and fashion design. She dreamed of becoming a dress designer. On Saturdays she would travel into Chicago to take courses in watercolor and fashion design and illustration at the School of Art at the Art Institute of Chicago.[2]

Schick went on to receive her B.S. in art education at the University of Wisconsin, Madison. Then, newly married to a doctoral student in history, James B. M. Schick, she decided to try for her M.F.A. With her wealth of experiences and skills, it is not surprising that Schick had difficulty deciding on a specific concentration in the applied arts. Serendipity often plays a role in forming an artist's life, and Schick admits she selected a jewelry concentration on Jim's advice. (Now, like Marjorie, a University Professor at Pittsburg State University, James Schick has always provided support in the form of time, energy, ideas and the occasional jolt of critique that every artist needs.)

FIG. 2 TEXTURED BRASS ARMLET, 1967 (SEE CAT. NO. 046)

Jewelry would provide an ideal arena to further develop her interest in form, materials and the ritual aspects of an object's experience and presentation.

During her graduate program at Indiana University, Schick worked under the mentorship of Alma Eikerman, who spurred her to explore jewelry form and conceptual content. *Textured Brass Armlet* (1967, fig. 2) studies the relation of texture to mass while the *Wheatfields* necklace (1968, cat. no. 59) packs lines densely to form a mass (in homage to Van

Gogh's brushstrokes in a painting of wheatfields). These interests would continue throughout Schick's career. *Shoulder Sculpture* (1968, cat. no. 60) explores a form's relation to body topology: a system of planes anchors against the clavicle, swooping upward in response to changes in angle from the chest and shoulder to the rise of the neck. A different sensibility appears in *Bracelet* (1975, cat. no. 113), *Finger Sculptures* (1967, 1968, 1972, cat. nos. 33, 62, 91), and *Hair Sculpture* (1975, cat. no. 112). Line lifts free of mass in these abstract studies, but one also can't help but ascribe

FIG. 3   SMALL AND MIGHTY, PIN, 1964
(SEE CAT. NO. 009)

a personality and emotions to their exuberant curves. They are reminiscent of Calder's wire caricatures and the expressive sculptures of Julio González.

In graduate school, Schick's sense of form strained against jewelry conventions. In 1966 she read an article about sculptor David Smith and imagined what it would feel like to put her hand or head through an opening in one of his forms. Earlier she had made a small brooch with protruding black wires (fig. 3) that, in her words, "gave me the nerve to extend forms out from the body into space." These two artistic discoveries would prove

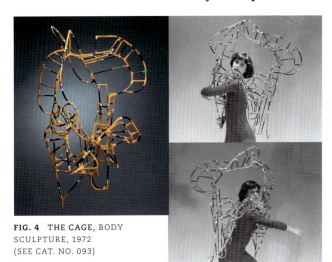

FIG. 4   THE CAGE, BODY
SCULPTURE, 1972
(SEE CAT. NO. 093)

crucial. However, for her experiments with volume, line and scale to truly break free, she needed to draw on a current of influence from beyond the metalsmith's training.

"My real love," Schick confirms, "has always been with alternative materials." Fresh from graduate school, she taught herself papier-mâché and discovered a new plastic freedom in her experiments with mass, form and, equally important, color. These resulted in a series of papier-mâché bracelets (which led to her first meeting with Paul Smith, Director of the American Craft Museum). Throughout the seventies Schick would make and display work in both metal and papier-mâché as well as other non-traditional materials, though she always thought of her alternative work as "less important." (The term "closet art" captures artists' complex attitudes toward these secondary or secret bodies of work.) In the sixties, lightweight and malleable materials enabled Schick to widen her artistic project. With *Blue Eyes* (1969, cat. no. 68), *Linear Shoulder Sculpture* (1969, cat. no. 67) and *The Cage* (1972, fig. 4), floating lines capture volumes and surround the human form. Schick wrapped the wire of many such forms in papier-mâché, adding the color that had "hooked" her as she worked on her exploratory bracelets.

Schick's experiments with line culminated in the *Dowel-Stick* series of the 1980s. These works captured international attention and inspired Hiroko Sato to comment that Schick was the greatest American influence on European jewelers.[3] They also demonstrated the artist's conceptual kinship with contemporaries Pierre Degen (UK) and Noam Ben Jacov (the Netherlands), other creators of moving personal and aesthetic environments. Schick's *Directional Forces* (1986, cat. no. 285) is a masterful example of constructiv-

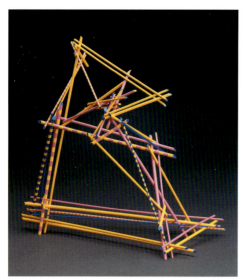

FIG. 5 ARZO ORANGE, NECKLACE, 1986
(SEE CAT. NO. 281)

ist form cast in her idiom. It is abstract, enlivened by its bonds to the body, and integrated by a sculpturally significant use of color, which guides the eye about the composition and adds a sense of vital movement. The piece has a compelling presence. As Michael Dunas observes, all the works in the series "extend the space of the body and establish an energized field where jewelry and wearer interact."[4]

Schick notes that there is 30-year jewelry and 3-hour jewelry. Then there is the 30-second jewelry she creates. The briefest contact with a form generates profound awareness: of changes in posture in movement, of the play of shapes and spaces around the now-altered body perimeter, and of the wearer's sense of self presentation in a social space. *Arzo Orange* (1986, fig. 5) seems to arrest a structure in the process of collapsing or re-organizing itself. When worn, it frames the face and fills in the zone of privacy that we take for granted around our necks. Perhaps the sculpture represents a wearer's shifting moods as her/his movements become more formal and deliberate. Perhaps each orange line is a comment about these feelings, the blue tips of each stick marking the beginning and ends of wearer's sentences.

The *Dowel-Stick* series expressed Schick's conceptual concerns with formal abstraction in a particularly pure form. Nevertheless, it represented only a small part of her overall perspective. Rudolf Arnheim notes that in art "there is no direct transformation of experience into form, but rather a search for equivalents."[5] Schick's mind is attuned to impressions drawn from dust motes rising from fiber, from landscapes and language, from architecture and even cosmological events. From the eighties on, during the second, fully mature period of her work, Schick enlivened her conceptual interests with such inspirations. Teapots would become brooches, disassemble into a series of bangles, or explode to frame the shoulder and neck. A Mies van der Rohe apartment building would transform into a body-conforming sculpture. Clouds of color would solidify, shifting and translucent, into a cocoon for a spiral necklace. Schick gave herself free rein to explore glowing color. She created forms inflected by atmosphere, humor, and a sense of playful juxtaposition or dislocation.

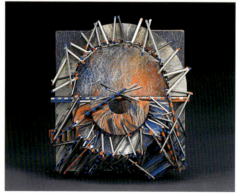

FIG. 6 WALL RELIEF WITH BRACELET, 1988
(SEE CAT. NO. 322)

Wall Relief with Bracelet (1988, fig. 6) and *Painting with Three Necklaces* (1988, cat. no. 331) were Schick's first wall installations. During the six weeks that she worked on the necklaces' painting, compelled to paint even the back of the form, she experienced one of those moments when an artist startles her/himself with a new idea. She recalls thinking, "Oh, what am I doing? I'm not a painter." She had been painting objects for years but, with this new turn, assimilated painterly techniques more directly to her own artistic project. She began to create "paintings in the round," as Glen Brown refers to them, applying color to disrupt the notion that even a flat work of art must be examined from one side only.[6] Such installations offer jewelry objects parallel aesthetic lives: when an armlet or necklace is worn, it unites with the body; when mounted on its relief, it blends fully into that structure. Color intensifies the physical merging and also defines each element's unique integrity. The wall relief of *Transition* (1992, cat. no. 344) has tendrils that flow from the lower left hand corner and undulate fluidly beyond the upper right. They seem to fuel the armlet's movement as it coils in the opposite direction. When the armlet is removed, both pieces work as independent expressions, the armlet sweeping its colored circles, the relief enticing the viewer to come close and examine the painted declivity in its center.

FIG. 7   FOR THE KUNST RAI, COLLAR AND ARMLET, 1992 (SEE CAT. NO. 347 AND 348)

These "paintings in the round" blur the boundaries between craft, ornament, painting and sculpture. (Schick has created explicit homages to painters: e.g. *In Henri's Garden* [2003, cat. no. 448] for Henri Rousseau and *Double Dutch Artists* [1998, cat. no. 413] for Mondrian and Van Gogh.) The hybrid forms do not result from a theoretical program, but emerge from Schick's working process. She rarely sketches ideas, preferring to begin with her hands on her material, working out the sculptural form and the evolving color patterns in a direct and laborious process. The free standing armlet, *Edged Wave* (1995, cat. no. 378), for example, took over sixty hours to paint, only in part because of the many layers of color Schick applied. "The majority of the piece is made up of edges," Schick explains (an interest retained from her jeweler's training to manipulate the thickness and conformation of edges for aesthetic and technical purposes).[7] She labored to work out a system of color patterns that would link one rippling edge to the next and to the central organic opening. Color is always her greatest challenge, "a monster," as she describes it. *For the Kunst Rai* (1992, fig. 7) uses a moiré color pattern to integrate the planar and curved edges of two sculptures. The result is a visually and formally active display: the angular sculptural neckpiece adjusts its balance gingerly while, at its feet, the armlet seems to roll and coil convulsively.

Like the armlets and necklaces on reliefs, these paired forms expand the arena for studying relationships in space. Schick admires sculptor Barbara Hepworth's exploration of sculptural relationships among groupings of sculptural objects. Schick describes her own pairs as "a sculpture and a friend," invoking a mood of affinity and conversation – appropriate, since this charged aesthetic space will open its boundaries to a wearer as well. *For Perth: Sculpture with Two Collars and One Armlet* (1992, cat. no. 345) and *LA:DC Suite* (1996, cat. no. 391), even *Spiraling Discs* (2006, cat. no. 467), a suite of thirty-two necklaces and armlets, multiply the aesthetic play of positive and negative relationships among objects whose arrangements can be infinitely shifted. Not surprisingly, Schick embraces Richard Serra's belief that an understanding of sculpture is kinesthetic, relying not merely "on image or sight or optical awareness, but on physical awareness in relation to space, time, movement."[8] Schick relocates (and redefines) the viewer so s/he experiences this flux of space through direct physical contact from within the sculptural form itself.

A small but critical paradigm shift enabled Schick to further expand the scale of her communities of sculptural forms. In 1998 she began creating multiples from modular units. The viewer wonders what it would be like to play chess with *Deception* (2003, cat. no. 445), whose pieces mark out a game space of Escher-like illusion. *Bands of Rings* (2006, cat. no. 470) and *Orbiting Rings: Balancing Act* (2004, cat. no. 457) call to the viewer to plunge his/her hands into sensually curved forms – there are many, more than enough, to satisfy a hunger for delight. Expanding the scale of work creates another range of emotional responses. *For Pforzheim* (1989, cat. nos. 334–338), a suite of five folding collars, each nearly two feet in diameter, can be displayed flat, the elements opened and closed like the pages of a book (fig. 8). Partially opened, they slip around a neck. Fully opened they can be suspended for display and contemplation as a system of gyroscopes. Progression (2007, cat. no. 441), a series of sixty-six square necklaces, each representing a year of the artist's life,

FIG. 8 FOR PFORZHEIM,
FOLDING COLLAR #1, 1989
(SEE CAT. NO. 334)

dramatizes the passage of time as it snakes across the floor. *Much Ado About Twenty Bracelets* (2006, cat. no. 475) brings the viewer into relationship with angles. Sections of the massive folding screen angle across fifteen linear feet. The imposing form and the bracelets it supports draw the viewer into the worlds-within-worlds of angular relations painted on every surface.

In the context of such work, the installation *Eclipse of the Moon: Earth's Shadow* (2004, fig. 9) may seem strangely out of place. These large veils of entangled fibers, one dark, one light, are designed to be wall-mounted as overlapping pools to represent the bright, reflected light of the moon and the shadow of the earth. They also drape, as light and shadow pour fluidly over a body. The majority of Schick's work uses rigid materials and expresses her interest in mass and contained volumes. However, *Eclipse* demonstrates her persistent interest in fiber's sculptural and kinetic possibilities. Schick made body sculptures and masks of string and rope in the seventies. She created drawings of paper and thread that led to construct a series of jewelry pieces in these materials in the eighties. She has worked with clothing forms: two Egyptian-inspired collars for *Amenhotep I* (2002, cat. no. 438), a semi-fluid scarf and belt *For Sonia Delaunay* (2003, cat. no. 447), and two large wearable forms to celebrate Elsa Schiaparelli in the fashion designer's signature shocking pink. Long fibers suspend geometrical forms that quiver and sway with the slightest movement in *Purple Swing* (1988, cat. no. 326), and a "black rain" (Schick's term) extends the aesthetic environment of the book necklace, "Connections" (2006, fig. 10).

Such fluidity and responsiveness to the body are reminders of Sartre's observation that the perception of even a remote object can become as immediately sensible as a caress. "[T]he warmth of air, the breath of the wind, the rays of sunshine," Sartre says, "all are present to me ... and reveal[ ] my flesh by means of their flesh."[9] Whether rigid or fluid, Schick's work invites viewers and wearers alike to fully embrace an object, transforming sculpture and the human form: both come

FIG. 9 ECLIPSE OF THE MOON: EARTH'S
SHADOW, VEILS, 2004
(SEE CAT. NO. 453)

alive through the piece's mood, atmosphere and moment of play. In addition to these focused moments of aesthetic perception, each piece demands a confrontation with assumptions about scale, the boundaries of jewelry and ornament, and what it means to work sculpturally.

FIG. 10   CONNECTIONS, BOOK NECKLACE
(124 PAGES) WITH STAND
NECKLACE STARTED IN 1999, NECKLACE AND
STAND: 2006
(SEE CAT. NO. 468)

Schick's work has always been controversial. Her contribution to contemporary jewelry and to craft emerges from her ability to cross boundaries of genre and materials, to link body with form, to bridge sensibilities across continents. Schick describes herself as "quietly rebellious." In person she offers a surprising contrast to her work, possessing a soft voice and mild manner. She also has a reservoir of tenacity that has enabled her to "go her own way" for five decades, propelled by her mission to "make jewelry into a fine art form." In 1966 the young Marjorie Schick asserted that "My jewelry may surprise and if necessary disturb the viewer, but above all it must be aggressive – it must be notable."[10] In 2002, the mature artist re-affirmed this commitment: "I want my work to be fearless." It has been and is, in its scale, its color and its relentless centrifugal push into space. Schick's work encloses a wearer, takes control and redefines the human body and perceptions in spatial and aesthetic terms. When work achieves such assertiveness, however, it is only because it draws on the fearlessness of the artist herself.

1   Anecdote reported by Marjorie Schick. Unless otherwise noted, quotations are taken from interviews I conducted with the artist between 1999 and 2006.

2   Marjorie Schick, interviewed by Tacey A. Rosolowski, April 4–6, 2004. Nanette L. Laitman Documentation Project for Craft and Decorative Arts in America. Archives of American Art, Smithsonian Institution. Website: www.aaa.si.edu/collections/oralhistories/transcripts/schick04.htm: see 12–15 (access date: 12/7/06).

3   Hiroko Sato and Gene Pijanowski. "Marjorie Schick: Drawing to Wear/Sculpture to Wear," in *Four Seasons of Jewelry* (Japan), Vol. 67 (June 1986): 56–63, 59.

4   Michael Dunas. "Marjorie's Schtick," in *Metalsmith*, Vol. 6, no. 3 (Summer 1986): 24–31, 28.

5   Rudolf Arnheim. *Toward a Psychology of Art* (Berkeley: University of California Press, 1966), 266.

6   See Glen R. Brown. "Absence and Self-Awareness: Inverting the Space of Sculpture," in this volume, 67f.

7   Marjorie Schick. Artist Statement addressed to Elizabeth Goring, November 1999.

8   See Lynne Cook. "Richard Serra: *Torqued Ellipses*." Website: http://www.diacenter.org/exhibs/serra/ellipses/essay.html.

9   Jean-Paul Sartre. *Being and Nothingness*, trans. Hazel Barnes (New York: Pocket Books, 1956), 506.

10 Marjorie Schick. "Thesis Statement." M.F.A. Thesis Exhibition, Jewelry and Metalsmithing, Indiana University, May 12–May 20, 1966.

SELECTED WORKS

009 SMALL AND MIGHTY, PIN, 1964, BRASS,
STERLING SILVER, AND IRON, CONSTRUCTED
H. 2" × W. 2 ½" × D. 1 ½"
PHOTO: JOEL DEGEN

023 DOUBLE FINGER RING WITH BLACK OPAL, 1966,
STERLING SILVER WITH BLACK OPAL DOUBLET, CONSTRUCTED AND FORGED
H. 2 ½" × W. 4" × D. 2 ⅛"
PHOTO: JOEL DEGEN

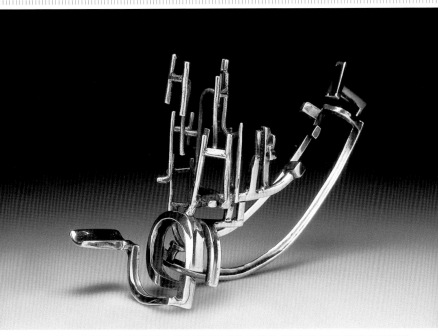

033 FINGER SCULPTURE, 1967, STERLING SILVER, FORGED AND CONSTRUCTED
H. 3 ⅝" × W. 4 ¼" × D. 1 ⅝"
PHOTO: JOEL DEGEN

"MOTHER, I MET THIS YOUNG MAN, JIM SCHICK. HE PLANS TO BE A HISTORY PROFESSOR." AFTER MARRIAGE IN 1963, HE WOULD BEGIN A PH.D. PROGRAM THAT FALL, SO I APPLIED FOR AN ADVANCED DEGREE.

THE QUESTIONS ON THE APPLICATION FOR GRADUATE SCHOOL APPLICATION PROVED DIFFICULT: FOR WHICH DEGREE WOULD I APPLY? I CHOSE M.F.A. BECAUSE IT HAD THREE LETTERS OF THE ALPHABET WHILE THE OTHER DEGREES HAD ONLY TWO. NEXT WAS TO SELECT AN EMPHASIS. NOT KNOWING WHICH OF THE ART SUBJECTS IN SCHOOL I PREFERRED, I ASKED JIM, THE PERSON WHO HAS GUIDED MY LIFE. WATCHING ME THROUGH FOUR YEARS OF COLLEGE, HE THOUGHT I LIKED JEWELRY BEST SO I CHOSE JEWELRY DESIGN AND METALSMITHING. SIMPLE AS THAT, HE DECIDED MY FUTURE. I AM FOREVER GRATEFUL.

NEWLY MARRIED AND HAVING ARRIVED AT INDIANA UNIVERSITY, I WROTE MY MOTHER, "I AM SO SCARED. WHAT AM I DOING HERE?" THE FIRST TIME MEETING ALMA EIKERMAN, PROFESSOR OF JEWELRY DESIGN AND METALSMITHING, I WAS "QUAKING IN MY BOOTS." I'VE GAINED MORE CONFIDENCE OVER TIME, BUT PLEASING HER REMAINS PART OF MY LIFE.

034 TIGER PRINT EARRINGS, (FIRST PAPIER-MÂCHÉ JEWELRY),
1967, PAINTED PAPIER-MÂCHÉ, FORMED AND PAINTED
H. 3 ¾" × W. 1 ¾" × D. 1 ¾"
PHOTO: JOEL DEGEN

A FABULOUS TIGER PRINT DRESS BOUGHT WITH MONEY FROM MY NEW JOB AT THE UNIVERSITY OF KANSAS IN 1967 INSPIRED ME TO MAKE HUGE EARRINGS TO MATCH IT, SO HEAVY THEY WERE SUPPORTED WITH MONOFILAMENT OVER MY HEAD. CHOOSING TO USE PAPIER-MÂCHÉ, I EXPERI-MENTED AND ASKED OTHERS HOW TO DO IT. THE LABORIOUS PROCESS WAS APPEALING. EVEN BETTER WAS THE FACT THAT I COULD COVER ANY SORT OF STITCHED, GLUED, WIRED, OR SOLDERED METAL OR CARDBOARD IN THE UNDERSTRUCTURE WITH PAPER STRIPS AND GLUE. BEST OF ALL, I COULD PAINT THE FORMS.

SIX BRACELETS FOLLOWED. ACRYLIC PAINTS WERE NEW AND I BEGAN WITH A STARTER SET FROM THE UNIVERSITY BOOKSTORE AFTER SEEING A LAVENDER PAINTED PILL BOTTLE IN A STUDENT'S TOOL BOX. TO PAINT WAS CHALLENGING AND FELT RIGHT. OBVIOUSLY, MY INTEREST IN COLOR HAD TAKEN HOLD, EVEN IF FOR THE MOMENT I WAS USING ONLY BLACK PAINT ON BROWN PAPER.

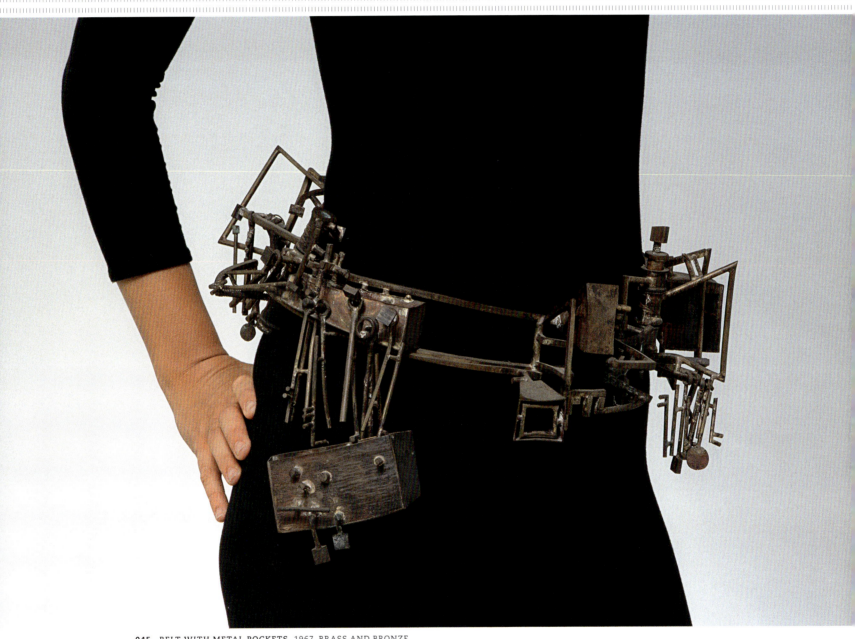

045 BELT WITH METAL POCKETS, 1967, BRASS AND BRONZE,
FORGED AND CONSTRUCTED
H. 9 ½" × W. 17" × D. 14 ½"
LOST
PHOTO: GARY POLLMILLER

046 TEXTURED BRASS ARMLET, 1967,
BRASS AND BRONZE, CONSTRUCTED AND
REPOUSSED
H. 5 ½" × W. 4 ½" × D. 4 ½"
INCLUDED AS PART OF THE 1968 INDIANA
UNIVERSITY EXPERIMENTAL METAL-
SMITHING CARNEGIE GRANT PROJECT
PHOTO: GARY POLLMILLER

061 OPEN POT FORM, 1968, STERLING SILVER, FORGED AND CONSTRUCTED
ESTIMATED: H. 8 ½" × W. 8 ½" × D. 8"
DONE AS PART OF THE 1968 INDIANA UNIVERSITY EXPERIMENTAL
METALSMITHING CARNEGIE GRANT PROJECT
COLLECTION: INDIANA UNIVERSITY ART MUSEUM, USA, 1969
PHOTO: LARRY LONG

INITIATION

Helen Shirk

Marjorie Schick completed her M.F.A. degree at Indiana University in 1966. The jewelry/metals studio was still reverberating with her presence when I arrived there as a new grad in 1967. I remember stepping off the second floor elevator and seeing this fierce accretion of metal wire and hammered forms in the jewelry showcase. The piece exuded an audacity and energy disproportionate to its actual scale and I was drawn to it in fascination. Who made this? I found out later that it was the jewelry of Marjorie Schick – a daring amalgam of the body with sculptural form that was to become her territory for the future.

Professor Alma Eikerman's program at Indiana provided training in traditional metalsmithing techniques, material experimentation, and form manipulation in combination with the study of historical objects and contemporary art. This rigorous curriculum immediately connected with Marjorie on many levels. She readily acknowledges that Professor Eikerman's guidance laid the foundation for her achievements in the arena of art jewelry. Both were Midwesterners, Marjorie from Illinois and Alma from Kansas, and both stayed in this geographical region for their long teaching careers. However, their visions encompassed the world and all the inspiration and potential that existed there. Eikerman had studied painting, design, art history and metalsmithing at Columbia University in the late 1930s and later traveled to Denmark and Sweden to further her technical skills in holloware. Throughout her life, museum collections and master craftsmen enticed her to travel abroad for study and inspiration, the results of which she generously shared with her students. Eikerman was an example of someone immersed in her art, passionate about learning, making, and teaching, and committed to a contemporary vision in her work. During the 1960s and 70s her female students, Marjorie was one of them, saw her as a model of a high-achieving professional woman, and one of only a very few women professors teaching in the predominately male field of metals. Today, in part because of Eikerman, the scales have tipped the other way.

The influence of Eikerman's commitment to three-dimensional form was clearly present in Schick's work in 1967. The forged and constructed armlet (cat. no. 46), shoulder piece, and rings she did during this early period reflect raw energy and boldness in the handling of material and construction of form. Each piece utilized the whole terrain of the body site chosen including the space around it, whether it was the finger, the shoulder, or the arm. Form was Schick's primary concern in visualizing a piece and all views were considered for their ability to interact with the human body. Texture, layers of color and pattern, and changes in material were used to expand the potential of the basic form. This attention to the complete three-dimensional form remains a constant in Schick's work today.

Shortly after her graduation, Schick was invited by Professor Eikerman to participate in a project involving the development of experimental metal forms, funded by a grant received from the Carnegie Foundation. Each of the nine grant participants was to develop three holloware forms, one each in copper, brass, and silver (cat. no. 61). I was also involved in this project and remember the animated discussions that arose surrounding the work Schick submitted in 1967. Schick's first two forms had an immediacy and spontaneity in approaching the metal that was the antithesis of the prevailing Scandinavian coolness and precision. Her third form, in silver, was seemingly a container but had no bottom – what commentary that evoked! Was this legitimate? All her grant pieces reflected a confidence and willingness to exploit the potential of material and to question the boundaries of what holloware could be. Since then, Schick's unique work with sculptural forms for the body in a wide range of materials has gained international recognition. Eikerman's mentorship of the young artist Marjorie Schick during the early years of her development contributed in a fundamental way to the evolution of this extraordinary body of work that consistently challenges the conventions and materials of adornment.

051 STRIPED SHOULDER SCULPTURE, 1967,
PAINTED PAPIER-MÂCHÉ, FORMED AND PAINTED
H. 12 ½" × W. 24" × D. 20 ½"
PHOTOS: GARY POLLMILLER

THANKFULLY, EIKERMAN, A METALS PERSON, LIKED THE NEW PAPIER-MÂCHÉ BRACELETS SO MUCH THAT SHE SUGGESTED I SHOW THEM TO PAUL SMITH AT THE AMERICAN CRAFT MUSEUM ON OUR TRIP EAST. I SAT ACROSS FROM HIM AT HIS DESK NERVOUSLY AND PULLED THE SIX PAPIER-MÂCHÉ BRACELETS FROM A BAG. INSTANTLY, HE TOOK SEVERAL IN HIS ARMS AND CARRIED THEM OUT OF THE ROOM. WHEN HE RETURNED, HE SAID THEY WERE PLANNING A "MADE WITH PAPER" EXHIBITION AT THE MUSEUM AND WOULD LIKE THREE FOR THE SHOW. WONDROUSLY, HE SUGGESTED THAT I KEEP HIM INFORMED OF FUTURE PAPIER-MÂCHÉ PIECES.

AFTER NEW YORK, JIM AND I CONTINUED TRAVELING TO VIRGINIA WHERE HE DID RESEARCH. WHEN WE ARRIVED, HE IMMEDIATELY TOOK ME TO A HARDWARE STORE TO PURCHASE METAL SHEARS, CHICKEN WIRE, AND WALLPAPER PASTE. WHILE HE WENT TO LIBRARIES, I STAYED IN THE MOTEL ROOMS TO BUILD FORMS AND PAPIER-MÂCHÉ.

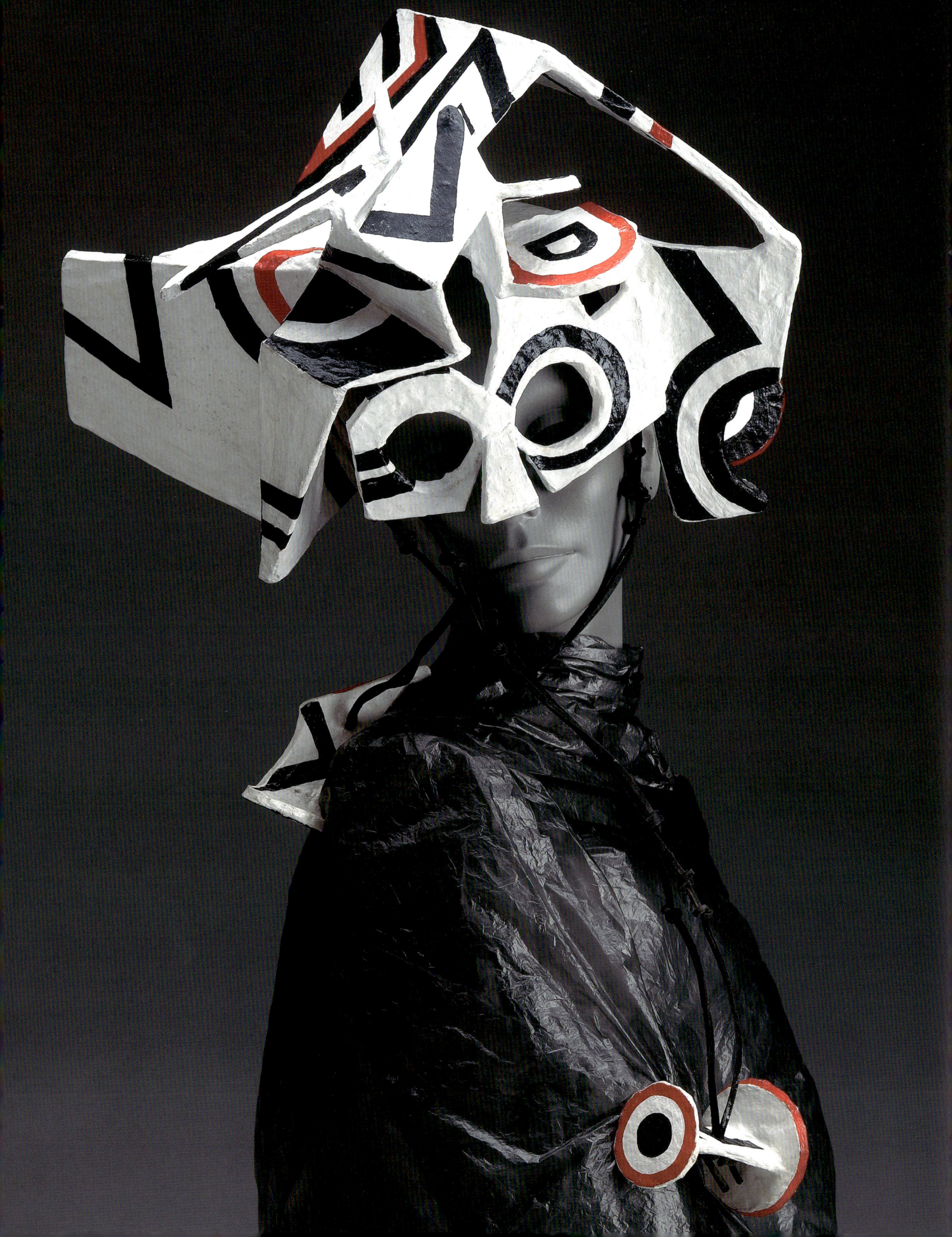

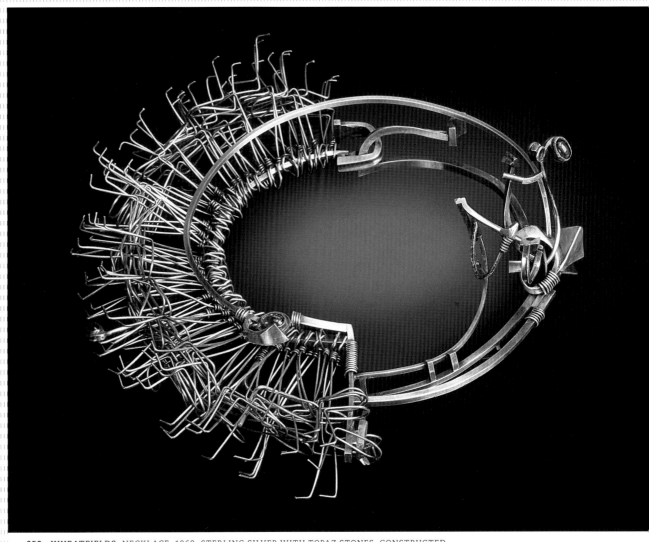

059 **WHEATFIELDS,** NECKLACE, 1968, STERLING SILVER WITH TOPAZ STONES, CONSTRUCTED
H. 9 ½" × W. 9 ⅛" × D. 2 ¼"
(MADE IN A SIMILAR WAY TO ONE CREATED IN 1965 THAT IS IN THE COLLECTION OF THE
INDIANA UNIVERSITY ART MUSEUM, GIFT OF THE FINE ARTS JEWELRY DEPARTMENT, USA, 1985)
PHOTO: GARY POLLMILLER

056 **HELMET MASK,** 1968, PAINTED PAPIER-MÂCHÉ AND
LEATHER, FORMED AND PAINTED
H. 26" × W. 16 ½" × D. 12 ½"
PHOTO: GARY POLLMILLER

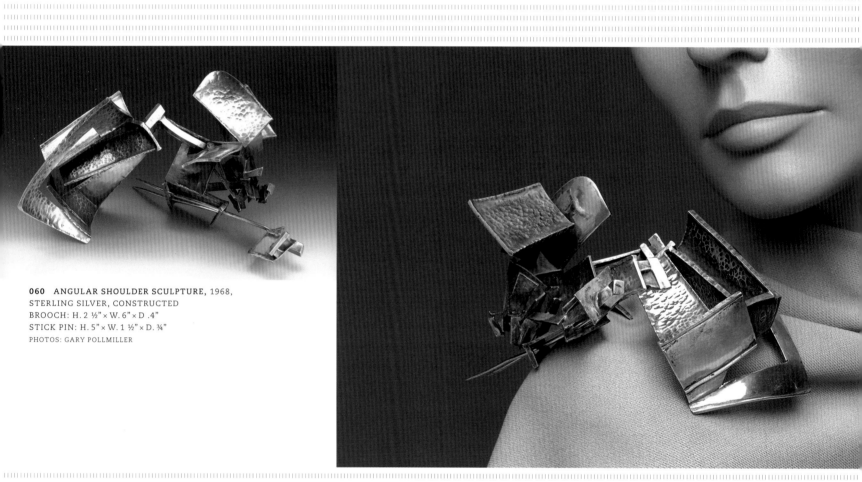

060 ANGULAR SHOULDER SCULPTURE, 1968,
STERLING SILVER, CONSTRUCTED
BROOCH: H. 2 ½" × W. 6" × D .4"
STICK PIN: H. 5" × W. 1 ½" × D. ¾"
PHOTOS: GARY POLLMILLER

049 TORSO SCULPTURE, 1967, PAINTED PAPIER-MÂCHÉ,
FORMED AND PAINTED
H. 20" × W. 14" × D. 11 ½"
PHOTO: GARY POLLMILLER

062 FINGER SCULPTURE, 1968,
STERLING SILVER, CONSTRUCTED AND FORGED
H. 2 ½" × W. 3 ⅝" × D. 1 ⅝"
PHOTO: GARY POLLMILLER

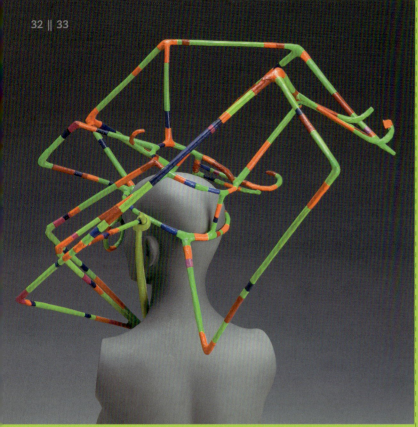

065 OPEN HEAD SCULPTURE, 1968, PAINTED PAPIER-MÂCHÉ AND LEATHER,
PAINTED PAPIER-MÂCHÉ OVER SOLDERED STEEL RODS
H. 25" × W. 25 ½" × D. 16"
WITH LEATHER STRAPS EXTENDED: 39 ½" LONG
PHOTO: GARY POLLMILLER

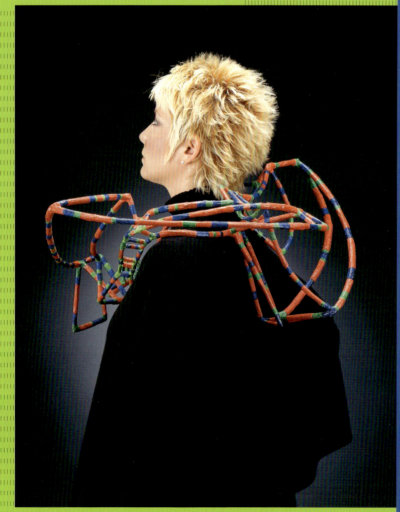

067 DRAWING TO WEAR: ORANGE, BLUE, AND GREEN, 1969,
PAINTED PAPIER-MÂCHÉ OVER SOLDERED RODS, CONSTRUCTED AND PAINTED
H. 11 ½" × W. 26" × D. 23 ¼"
PHOTO: GARY POLLMILLER

HAVING DONE A NUMBER OF PAPIER-MÂCHÉ PIECES THAT CONSISTED ENTIRELY OF PLANES, JIM ASKED, "IS THERE A WAY TO DO LINEAR PAPIER-MÂCHÉ?" AT THE SALVATION ARMY I PURCHASED A STACK OF OLD COAT HANGERS. THESE I STRAIGHTENED ON THE ANVIL, CUT, CURVED INTO NEW SHAPES, AND SILVER SOLDERED TOGETHER. WHEN THE LINEAR STRUCTURE WAS COMPLETED, I WRAPPED THE RODS WITH STRIPS OF PAPIER-MÂCHÉ AND THEN PAINTED THE FORM. THE DOWEL STICK PIECES OF THE 80S RELATE TO THE EARLIER LINEAR PAPIER-MÂCHÉ FORMS BUT ARE MORE DIRECT IN THEIR METHOD OF CONSTRUCTION.

068 BLUE EYES, HEAD SCULPTURE, 1969, BRASS,
BRONZE, AND PLEXIGLAS, CONSTRUCTED AND FORGED
H. 36 ¼" × W. 17 ¼" × D. 16"
PHOTO: GARY POLLMILLER

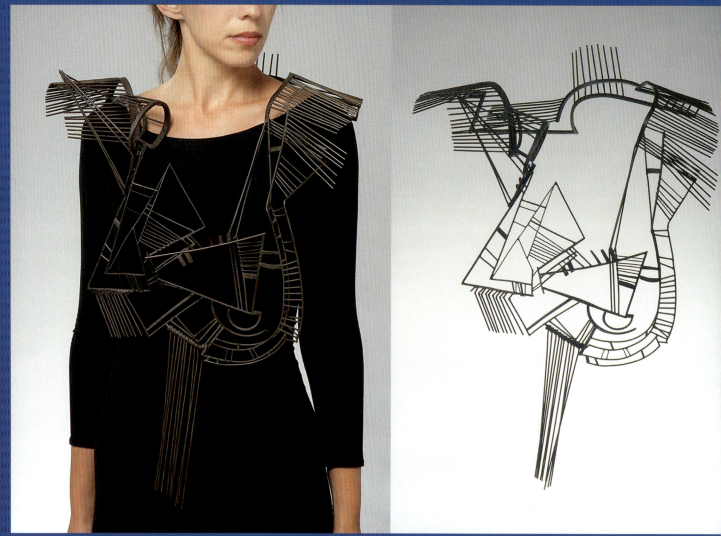

072 PECTORAL, 1968–9, BRASS AND BRONZE, CONSTRUCTED
H. 25" × W. 17" × D. 17 ½"
LOST
PHOTOS: GARY POLLMILLER

091 FINGER SCULPTURE, 1972, STERLING SILVER,
CONSTRUCTED
H. 6 ½" × W. 5" × D. ¼"
PHOTO: GARY POLLMILLER

081 HELMET WITH PROPELLAR, 1970, PAINTED PAPIER-MÂCHÉ
AND WOOD, FORMED AND PAINTED
H. 14" × W. 14" × D. 7"
PHOTO: GARY POLLMILLER

088 PARALLEL MOVEMENT, PAIR OF ARMLETS, 1971,
PAINTED PAPIER-MÂCHÉ, FORMED AND PAINTED
H. 11 ½" × W. 12" × D. 10"
H. 11" × W. 11" × D. 9 ½"
PHOTO: GARY POLLMILLER

093 THE CAGE, BODY SCULPTURE, 1972, PAINTED PAPIER-MÂCHÉ,
PAINTED PAPIER-MÂCHÉ OVER SOLDERED STEEL RODS
H. 46 ½" × W. 27" × D. 34"
PHOTOS: GARY POLLMILLER

106 GREEN DOT, NECKTIE, 1974, CARDBOARD,
WOOD DOWELS, AND LEATHER, CUT, PEGGED, AND TIED
H. 18" × W. 6 ½" × D. 2"
PHOTO: GARY POLLMILLER

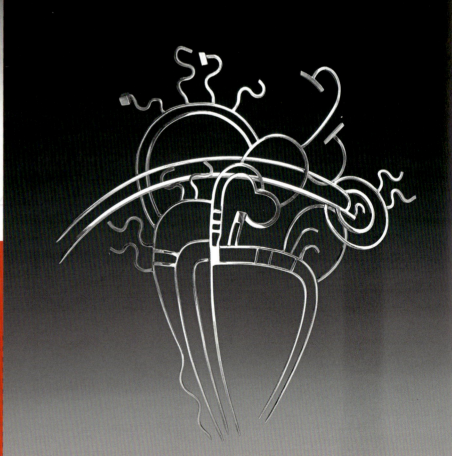

112 HAIR COMB, 1975, STERLING SILVER, CONSTRUCTED
H. 10 ¾" × W. 6 ½" × D. 1"
PHOTO: GARY POLLMILLER

119 BRASS NECKLACE, 1976, BRASS, CONSTRUCTED
H. 16" × W. 11" × D. 2 ½"
PHOTOS: GARY POLLMILLER

118 "BLACK, WHITE, AND READ ALL OVER," PONCHO, 1975,
NEWSPAPER AND COTTON STRING, LOOM WOVEN AND TIED
ONE-HALF OF TOTAL LENGTH: H. 62" × W. 27"
PHOTOS: GARY POLLMILLER

125 MOPPED: BEIGE, BODY SCULPTURE, 1977,
STRING AND REASSEMBLED MOP, LOOM WOVEN, RYA KNOTTED, AND DYED
ESTIMATED: H. 55" × W. 32" × D. 24"
PHOTO: GARY POLLMILLER

129 THE CONCEALER, MASK, 1978, STRING AND
PAPER-COATED WIRE, LOOM WOVEN AND RYA KNOTTED
H. 16" × W. 14 ½" × D. 11"
PHOTO: GARY POLLMILLER

A TRIBUTE

Paul J. Smith

Marjorie Schick has been a pioneer in creating unique body sculpture that transcends all traditional categories. Throughout her illustrious career since the late 1960s, Marjorie has produced an impressive collection of work that is not only unique in the United States, but holds a significant place in the context of international art jewelry.

With the human body as the central focus, she has explored creating a wide variety of dramatic theatrical forms combining graphic imagery with elaborate constructions. An important aspect of her work is innovative use of non-precious materials with a rich palette of color resulting in conceptual statements to be placed on the body, or displayed as independent objects.

Having represented her in several major exhibitions, I consider Marjorie an exceptional artist who has elevated body adornment and sculpture to a new level of achievement. In addition to her impressive credentials of awards, exhibitions, and representation in museum collections, she has generously shared her talent through teaching and workshops. This timely exploration of Marjorie Schick's work serves as an appropriate tribute to her important contribution to the arts in America.

145 SUMMER EXPERIMENT, NECKLACE, 1980, PLASTIC, CAST AND CONSTRUCTED
H. 15 ¼" × W. 18 ½" × D. 1 ¼"
COLLECTION: DR. JAMES B. M. SCHICK, USA
PHOTOS: GARY POLLMILLER

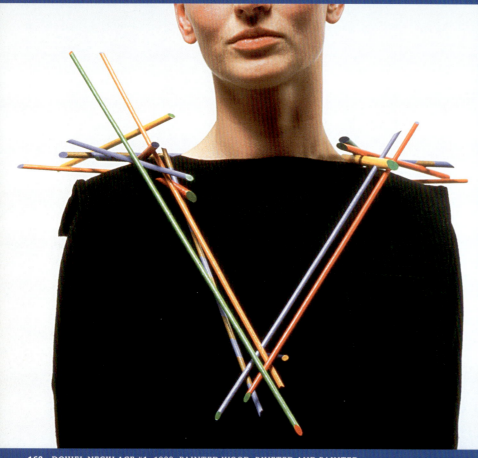

163 DOWEL NECKLACE #1, 1982, PAINTED WOOD, RIVETED AND PAINTED
H. 19" × W. 19" × D. 9"
COLLECTION: MIDDLESBROUGH INSTITUTE OF MODERN ART, MIDDLESBROUGH, UK
PHOTO: HOGERS VERSLUYS, COURTESY GALERIE RA, AMSTERDAM

165 GALERIE RA POSTER, 1983
PHOTO: HOGERS VERSLUYS, COURTESY GALERIE RA,
AMSTERDAM

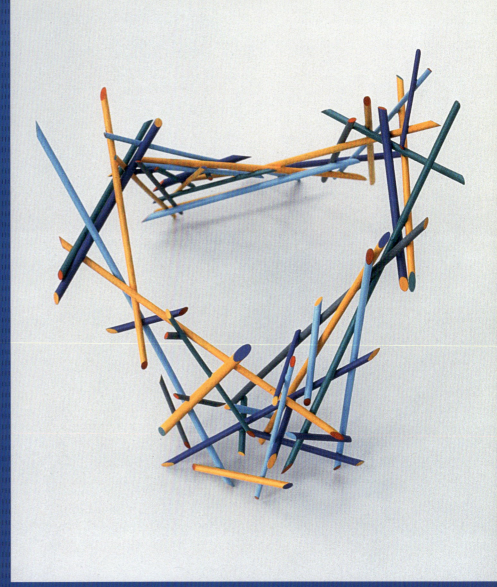

167 DOWEL NECKLACE #4, 1982, PAINTED WOOD,
RIVETED AND PAINTED
ESTIMATED: H. 13" × W. 16" × D. 14"
PRIVATE COLLECTION, UK
PHOTO: DR. JAMES B. M. SCHICK

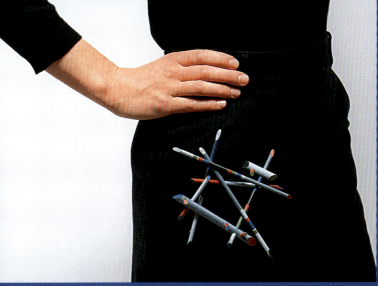

168 BROOCH, 1982, PAINTED WOOD WITH NICKEL PIN STEM,
RIVETED AND PAINTED
H. 5" × W. 5" × D. 1 ½"
PRIVATE COLLECTION
PHOTO: HOGERS VERSLUYS, COURTESY GALERIE RA, AMSTERDAM

170 BROOCH, 1982, PAINTED WOOD WITH NICKEL PIN STEM,
RIVETED AND PAINTED
H. 5" × W. 5" × D. 1 ½"
PRIVATE COLLECTION
PHOTO: HOGERS VERSLUYS, COURTESY GALERIE RA, AMSTERDAM

173 CELEBRATION, NECKLACE, 1983, PAINTED WOOD,
RIVETED AND PAINTED
H. 23 ½" × W.19 ½" × D. 6"
PHOTO: GARY POLLMILLER

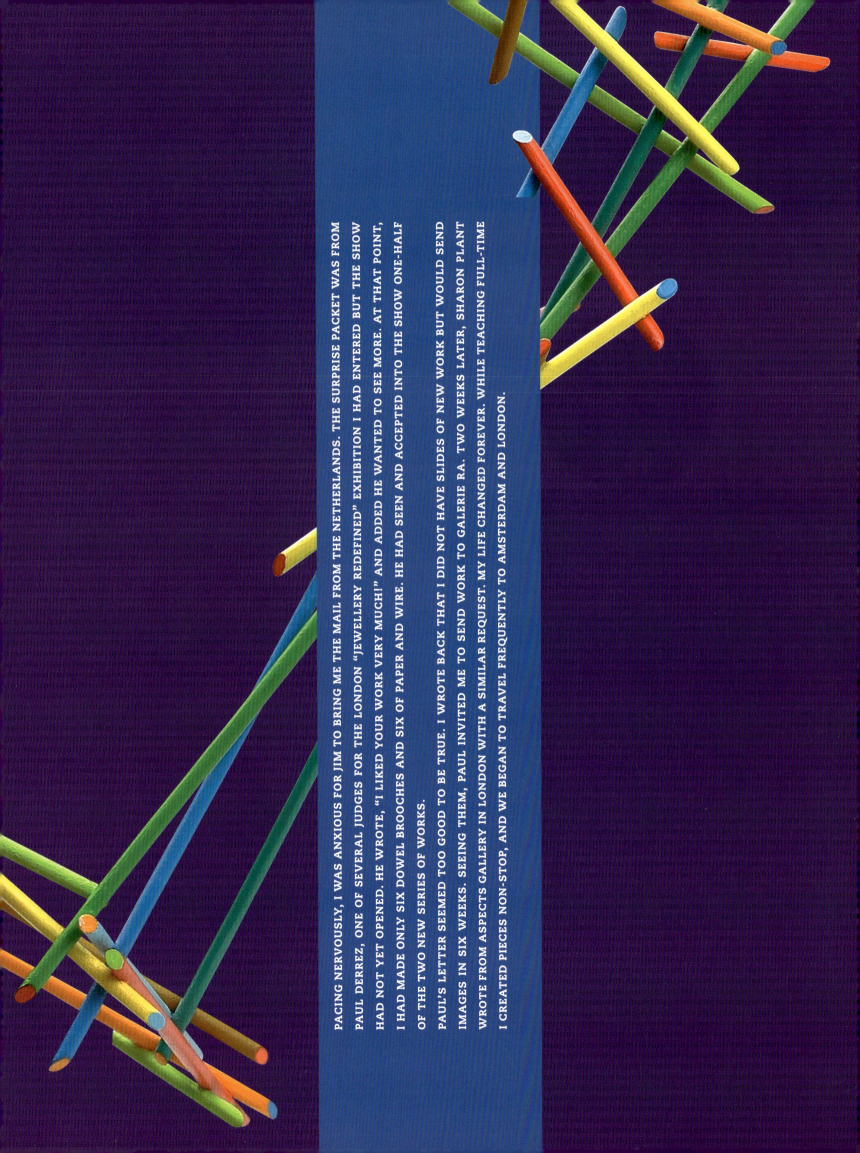

PACING NERVOUSLY, I WAS ANXIOUS FOR JIM TO BRING ME THE MAIL FROM THE NETHERLANDS. THE SURPRISE PACKET WAS FROM PAUL DERREZ, ONE OF SEVERAL JUDGES FOR THE LONDON "JEWELLERY REDEFINED" EXHIBITION I HAD ENTERED BUT THE SHOW HAD NOT YET OPENED. HE WROTE, "I LIKED YOUR WORK VERY MUCH!" AND ADDED HE WANTED TO SEE MORE. AT THAT POINT, I HAD MADE ONLY SIX DOWEL BROOCHES AND SIX OF PAPER AND WIRE. HE HAD SEEN AND ACCEPTED INTO THE SHOW ONE-HALF OF THE TWO NEW SERIES OF WORKS.

PAUL'S LETTER SEEMED TOO GOOD TO BE TRUE. I WROTE BACK THAT I DID NOT HAVE SLIDES OF NEW WORK BUT WOULD SEND IMAGES IN SIX WEEKS. SEEING THEM, PAUL INVITED ME TO SEND WORK TO GALERIE RA. TWO WEEKS LATER, SHARON PLANT WROTE FROM ASPECTS GALLERY IN LONDON WITH A SIMILAR REQUEST. MY LIFE CHANGED FOREVER. WHILE TEACHING FULL-TIME I CREATED PIECES NON-STOP, AND WE BEGAN TO TRAVEL FREQUENTLY TO AMSTERDAM AND LONDON.

182 BROOCH (ONE OF FOUR), 1983, PAPER, THREAD,
SCREEN, AND PIN BACK, PIERCED, THREADED, AND GLUED
H. 4 ⅝" W. 4 ⅝" × D. ⅜"
PHOTO: JOEL DEGEN

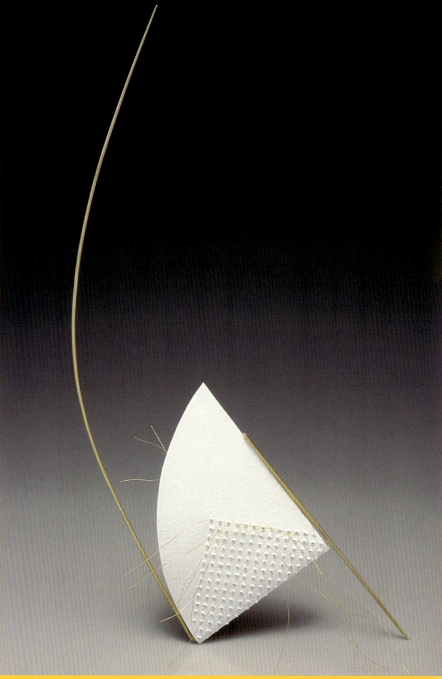

210 STICK PIN, 1984, BRONZE, PAPER, AND THREAD,
CONSTRUCTED, PIECED, GLUED, AND THREADED
H. 12 ¾" × W. 3 ⅛"
PHOTO: JOEL DEGEN

178 EXTENDED BROOCH, 1983, PAINTED WOOD AND NICKEL WIRE,
RIVETED AND PAINTED
H. 18" × W. 5 ¾" × D. 2"
PRIVATE COLLECTION, GERMANY
PHOTO: JAMES MUELLER

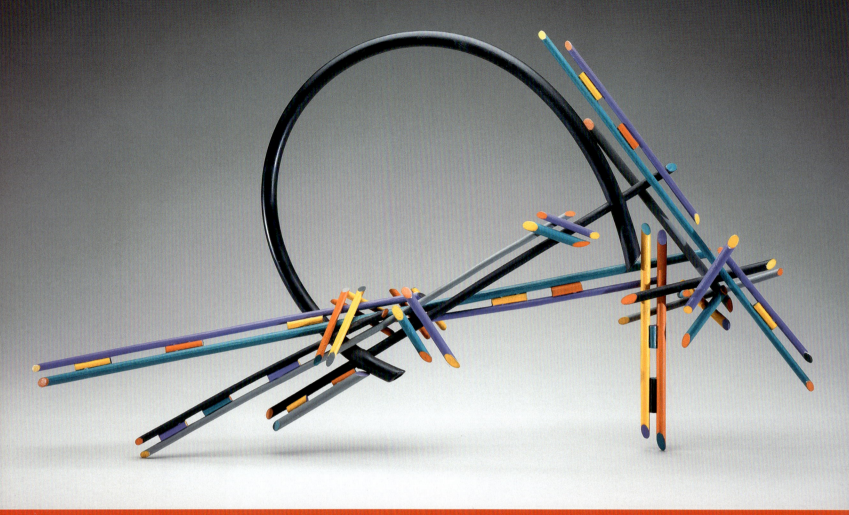

235 NECKLACE, 1984, PAINTED WOOD AND RUBBER,
RIVETED AND PAINTED
H. 21 ⅝" × W. 12" × D. 1 ¹⁵⁄₁₆"
COLLECTION: MUSEUM OF FINE ARTS, HOUSTON, HELEN WILLIAMS DRUTT COLLECTION,
GIFT OF THE MORGAN FOUNDATION IN HONOR OF CATHERINE ASHER MORGAN
PHOTO: TOM DUBROCK

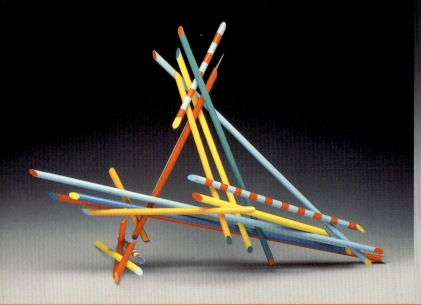

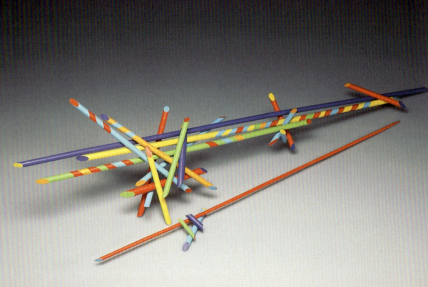

221 BROOCH WITH DETACHABLE STICK PIN, 1984,
PAINTED WOOD AND NICKEL WIRE, RIVETED AND PAINTED
H. 12 ¾" × W. 9" × D. 1 ¾"
PRIVATE COLLECTION, USA
PHOTO: JOEL DEGEN

222 BROOCH WITH TWO STICK PINS, 1984,
PAINTED WOOD, RIVETED AND PAINTED
H. 14 ½" × W. 2" × D. 1"
COLLECTION: MUSEUM OF ARTS & DESIGN, NEW YORK,
GIFT OF DONNA SCHNEIER, 1997
PHOTO: JOEL DEGEN

"MOM, DO YOU REALIZE THAT IN EVERY PHOTO OF THE FAMILY WE TOOK THIS SUMMER, YOU HAD A PAINT BRUSH IN YOUR HAND?" THIS WAS ROB'S COMMENT AFTER OUR SUMMER IN LONDON IN 1984. WHAT A LUXURY; SO MANY HOURS DEVOTED TO WORKING, GOING TO MUSEUMS, AND MEETING PEOPLE.

WHILE ARTIST-IN-RESIDENCE AT THE SIR JOHN CASS THAT SUMMER, I WORKED ON A SERIES OF BROOCHES THAT BECAME STUDIES IN METHODS OF FASTENING. AN ASTUTE TUTOR MADE ME CONSCIOUS OF AN IMPORTANT ASPECT OF MY WORK; IT IS PREFERABLE FOR THE VIEWER OF THE BROOCH TO SEE IT FIRST AS AN OBJECT AND THEN TO REALIZE THAT IT IS WEARABLE. IF ONE ENVISIONS THE OBJECT FIRST AS A BROOCH, THE MAIN CONCERN BECOMES HOW IT IS TO BE WORN. ALTHOUGH THIS IDEA APPEARS INSIGNIFICANT, IT IS HUGELY IMPORTANT AND FORCED ME TO CONSIDER BETTER AND SOMETIMES LESS OBVIOUS WAYS OF ATTACHING THE BROOCH.

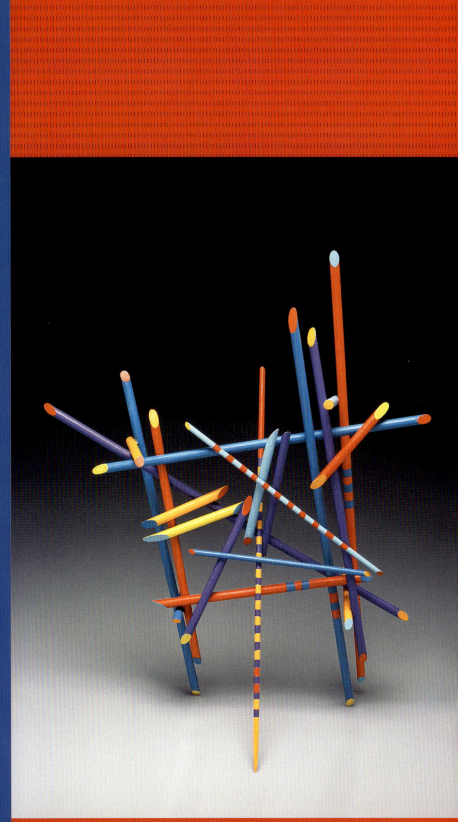

214   BROOCH WITH STICK PIN, 1984,
PAINTED WOOD, RIVETED AND PAINTED
H. 11" × W. 9" × D. 2 ¾"
PRIVATE COLLECTION
PHOTO: JOEL DEGEN

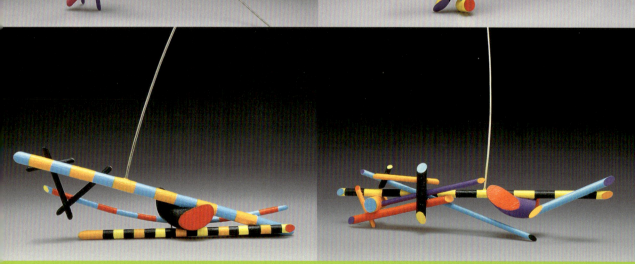

256 STICK PINS ON BASES, 1985, STICK PINS:
PAINTED WOOD, NICKEL WIRE, RUBBER, BASES:
WOOD AND BRASS, RIVETED AND PAINTED
STICK PINS:
A. H. 7" × W. 7 ½" × D. 1 ⅜"
B. H. 8" × W. 6 ½" × D. 1 ¼"
C. H. 7 ½" × W. 6 ⅞" × D. ¾"
D. H. 7 ⅜" × W. 7 ¼" × D. 1 ¼"
E. H. 7 ⅜" × W. 8 ⅜" × D. ⅝"
F. H. 7" × W. 10 ⅛" × D. 1 ⅛"
GROUP PHOTO: GARY POLLMILLER
INDIVIDUAL PHOTOS: JOEL DEGEN

251 BROOCH WITH BARK, 1985, BARK, AND PAINTED WOOD,
RIVETED AND PAINTED
H. 6 ¾" × W. 8 ¼" × D. 1"
COLLECTION: GENE AND HIROKO-SATO PIJANOWSKI, USA
PHOTO: JOEL DEGEN

252 BRACELET/BROOCH, 1985, BIRCH WOOD,
DOWELS, PAINT, AND THREAD, RIVETED AND TIED
H. 5 ⅝" × W. 8 ½" × D. 1"
PRIVATE COLLECTION
PHOTO: JOEL DEGEN

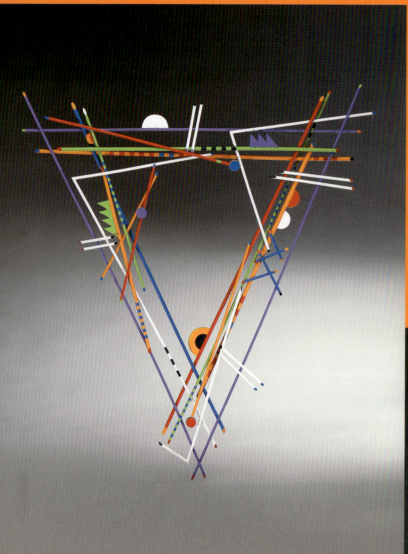

268 NECKLACE, 1985, PAINTED WOOD, RIVETED AND PAINTED
H. 31 ½" × W. 27" × D. 2"
PRIVATE COLLECTION, USA
PHOTO: GARY POLLMILLER

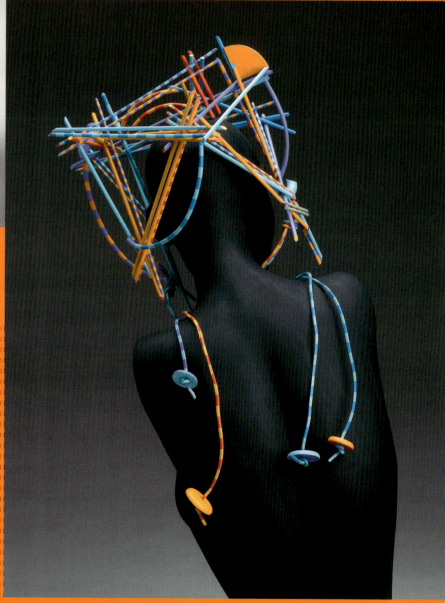

269 HEAD SCULPTURE, 1985,
PAINTED WOOD AND LEATHER, RIVETED AND PAINTED
H. 11 ½" × W. 12 ¾" × D. 10"
WITH TIES: 33 ¾" LONG
PHOTO: GARY POLLMILLER

270 NECKLACE, 1985, PAINTED WOOD, RIVETED AND PAINTED
H. 28 ¾" × W. 24 ½" × D. 7"
COLLECTION: INDIANA UNIVERSITY ART MUSEUM PURCHASE
IN HONOR OF ALMA EIKERMAN, USA, 1989
PHOTO: GARY POLLMILLER

280 NECKLACE, 1985, PAINTED WOOD, RIVETED AND PAINTED
H. 26" × W. 28" × D. 20"
COLLECTION: RENWICK GALLERY OF THE SMITHSONIAN
AMERICAN ART MUSEUM, WASHINGTON, D.C.
PHOTO: GARY POLLMILLER

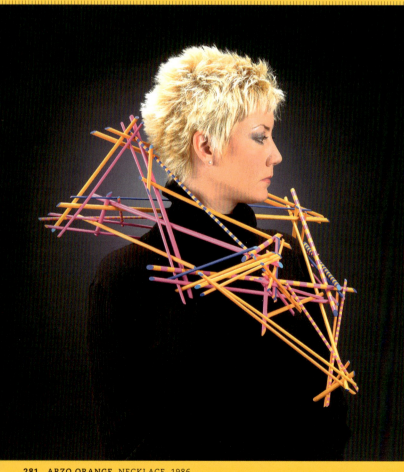

281 ARZO ORANGE, NECKLACE, 1986,
PAINTED WOOD, RIVETED AND PAINTED
H. 20 ¾" × W. 23" × D. 10"
PHOTO: GARY POLLMILLER

284 A PLANE OF STICKS, SCULPTURE FOR THE NECK, 1986, PAINTED WOOD, RIVETED AND PAINTED
H. 27" × W. 36" × D. 6"
PHOTOS: GARY POLLMILLER

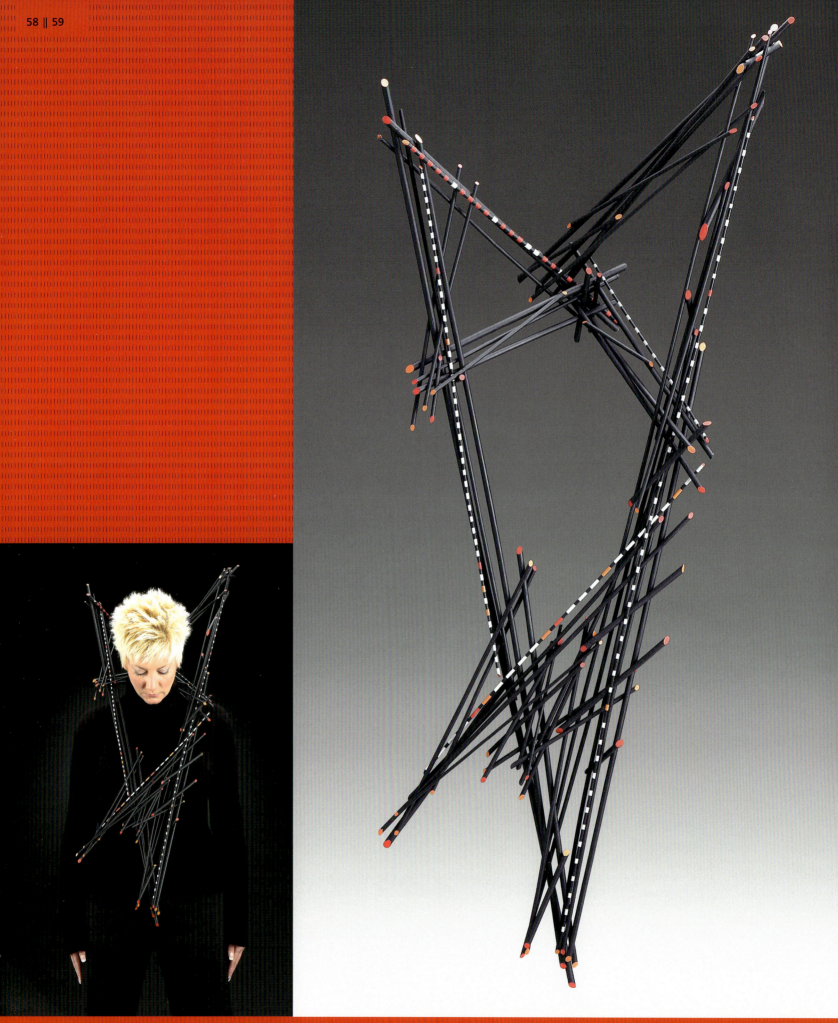

285 DIRECTIONAL FORCES, SCULPTURE FOR THE NECK, 1986, PAINTED WOOD, RIVETED AND PAINTED
H. 41" × W. 18 ½" × D. 7 ½"
PHOTOS: GARY POLLMILLER

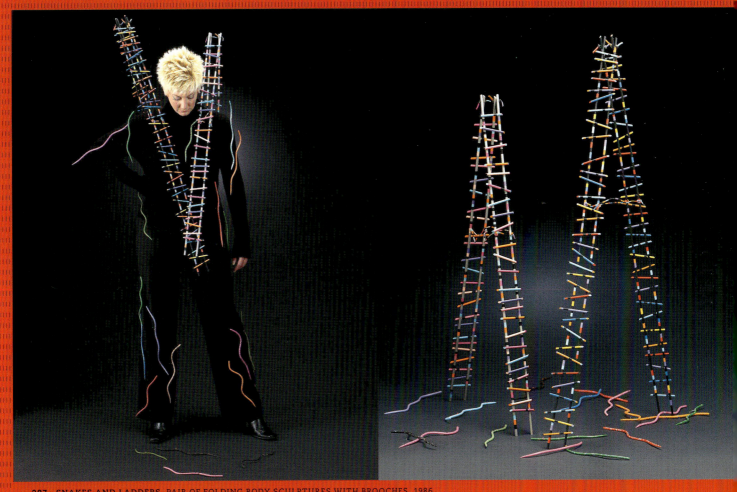

287 SNAKES AND LADDERS, PAIR OF FOLDING BODY SCULPTURES WITH BROOCHES, 1986,
LADDERS: PAINTED WOOD AND LEATHER, RIVETED AND PAINTED, BROOCHES: REED AND BROOCHES, FORMED AND PAINTED
LADDERS: H. 48 ½" × W. 3 ½" × D. 20 ½"
H. 41 ¾" × W. 3 ½" × D. 26 ¼"
SNAKE BROOCHES: AVERAGE, H. 13" × W. ¼" × D. ¼"
PHOTOS: GARY POLLMILLER

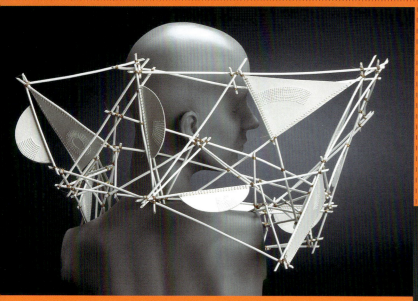

306 LIGHTER THAN AIR, NECKLACE, 1986,
PLASTIC RODS, PAPER, AND THREAD, TIED AND PIERCED
H. 11 ½" × W. 21" × D. 14 ⅛"
PHOTO: GARY POLLMILLER

296 NECKLACE FOR THE BACK, 1986,
PAINTED WOOD AND RUBBER, RIVETED AND PAINTED
H. 15 ½" × W. 22" × D. 9"
PHOTO: GARY POLLMILLER

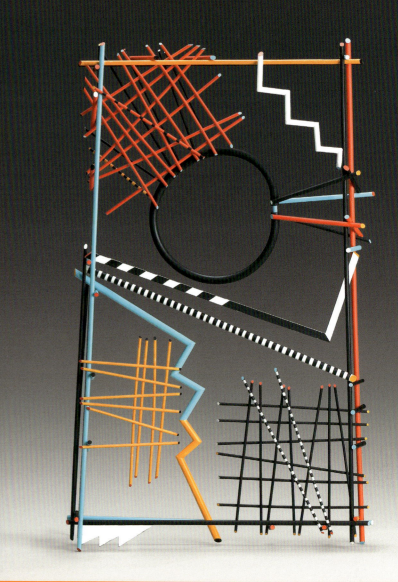

288 WITHIN A FRAME, SCULPTURE FOR THE NECK, 1986,
PAINTED WOOD AND RUBBER, RIVETED AND PAINTED
H. 36" × W. 22" × D. 2"
PHOTO: GARY POLLMILLER

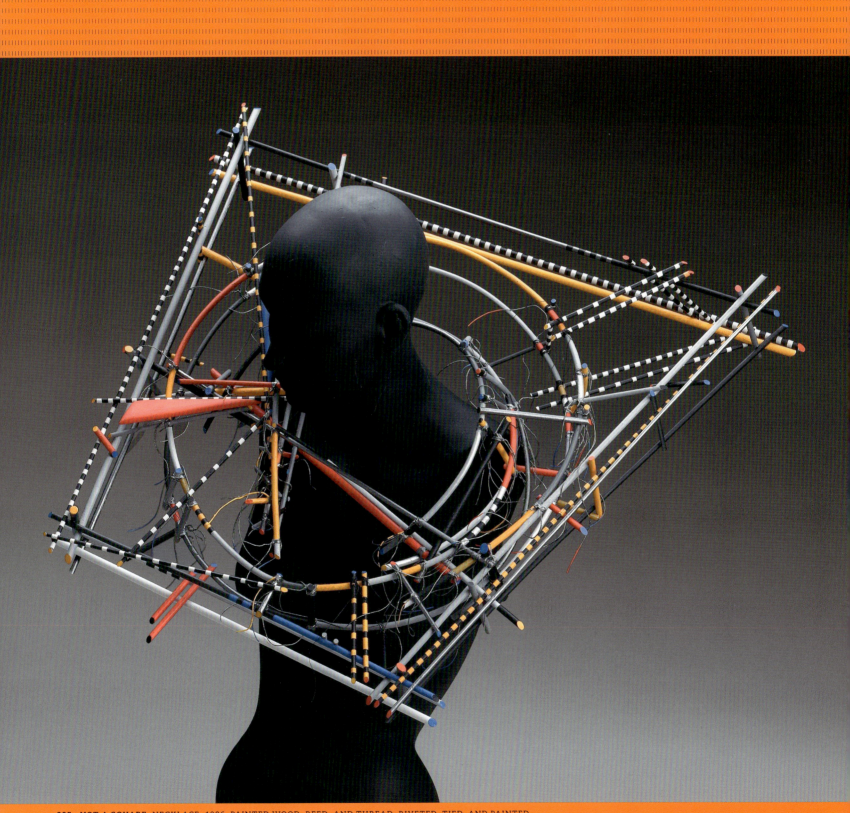

295 NOT A SQUARE, NECKLACE, 1986, PAINTED WOOD, REED, AND THREAD, RIVETED, TIED, AND PAINTED
H. 26" × W. 28 ½" × D. 5 ½"
PHOTO: GARY POLLMILLER

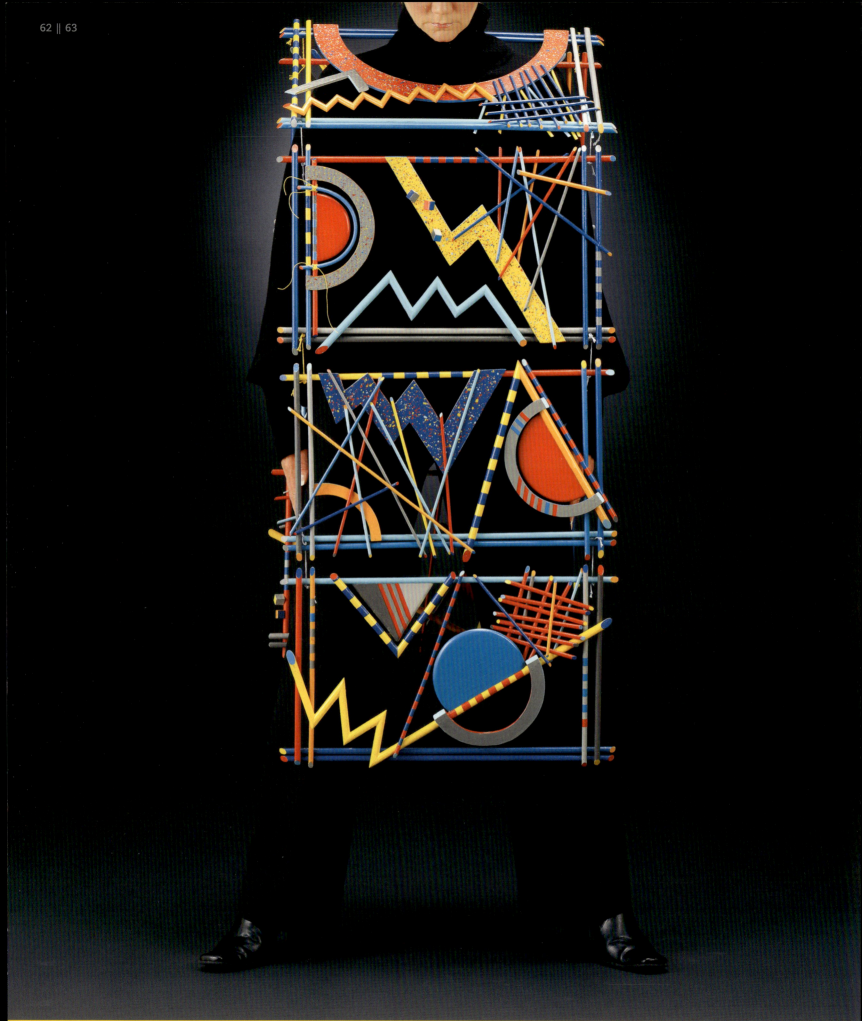

308 **IT FOLDS,** BODY SCULPTURE, 1987,
PAINTED WOOD, REED, AND CORD, RIVETED, PAINTED, AND TIED
FULL LENGTH: H. 96" × W. 22" × D. 1 ½"
PHOTO: GARY POLLMILLER

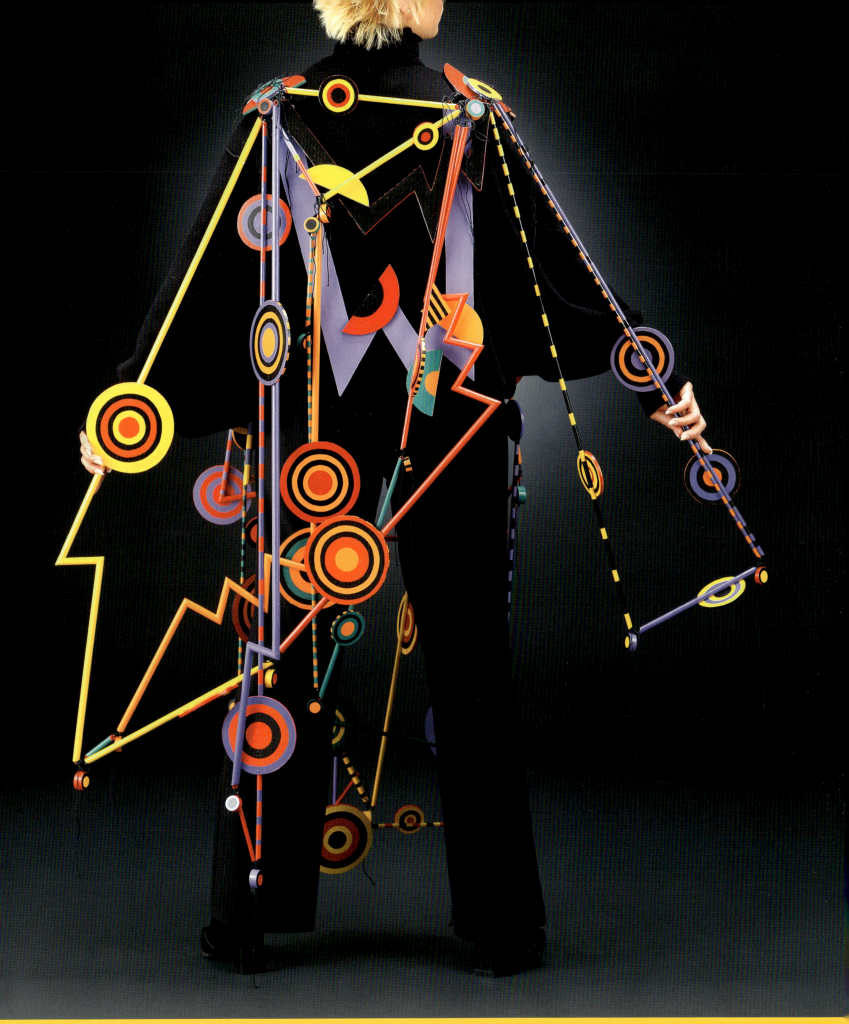

311 ANGLES AND CIRCLES, BODY SCULPTURE, 1987,
PAINTED WOOD, METAL EYELETS, AND CORD, RIVETED, PAINTED, AND TIED
SHOULDER TO BOTTOM: H. 55" × W. 26" × D. 6"
PHOTO: GARY POLLMILLER

317 PATTERNED NECKLACE, 1987, PAINTED WOOD, RIVETED AND PAINTED
H. 20" × W. 20 ½" × D. 4 ½"
COLLECTION: PAUL DERREZ AND WILLEM HOOGSTEDE, THE NETHERLANDS
PHOTO: GARY POLLMILLER

315 FETISH ARMLET, 1987, PAINTED WOOD, REED, AND THREAD,
PAINTED, RIVETED, AND TIED
H. 13" × W. 9" × D. 8 ½"
COLLECTION: SUZANNE ESSER, THE NETHERLANDS
PHOTO: GARY POLLMILLER

319 ODE TO DE KOONING, BACK SCULPTURE #2, 1987,
PAINTED WOOD AND NYLON STRAPS, RIVETED AND PAINTED
H. 27" × W. 19 ½" × D. 5 ½"
PHOTO: GARY POLLMILLER

318 BACK SCULPTURE #1, 1987, PAINTED WOOD
AND NYLON STRAPS, RIVETED AND PAINTED
H. 23" × W. 19 ½" × D. 6"
PHOTO: GARY POLLMILLER

320 BACK SCULPTURE WITH GRID, #3, 1988,
WOOD AND NYLON STRAPS, RIVETED AND PAINTED
H. 27 ¼" × W. 27" × D. 6 ⅜"
PHOTO: GARY POLLMILLER

ABSENCE AND SELF-AWARENESS: INVERTING THE SPACE OF SCULPTURE

Glen R. Brown

Like exoskeletons indicative of a separable, internal body, Marjorie Schick's wearable artworks invert an ancient paradigm. The classical sculpture, which persisted as a type in the West from antiquity through the early decades of the twentieth century, was invariably conceived as an independent body in space: an autonomous form that sought to duplicate the materiality of human beings partly by assuming the general condition of a mass suspended in infinite emptiness. Reinforcing the classical sculpture's sense of solidity and self-containment were the two methods of sculpting condoned by the academic tradition: carving, in which a block of dense matter was faceted for representational and expressive effects, and modeling, in which malleable materials such as clay, wax or plaster were worked into forms to be cast in the immobile medium of bronze. The products of both techniques can still conjure an uncanny sense of the body's physical presence. Schick's forms on the other hand – forms that exploit lessons about space laid down by the pioneers of modern *constructed* sculpture – serve more effectively as markers of the body's absence. The prominence of this absence imparts to Schick's works a perpetual sense of contingency, even when they are worn.

This contingency is not quite the same as the contingency of jewelry or costume, although these also tend, when not in use, to imply the absent body. Whereas jewelry and costume suggest absence as a mere consequence of temporary disuse, Schick's objects appear to indicate absence tendentiously, as if their aim were as much to call for the body as actually to receive it. The ability to be worn seems, in other words, to be employed by Schick as both a utilitarian trait and a rhetorical device. Her objects reflect an ongoing argument about ways in which sculpture can relate to the human body not as a mirror of the body's presence – a comparable independent mass that keeps the viewer at a perpetual remove – but rather as a set of parameters for a space that the viewer's body might conceivably occupy. In this respect Schick's works can be closely related to the general dematerialization of sculpture that took place in the 1960s and the subsequent relocation of the viewer that has characterized Western art in general since the 1970s.

Schick's challenge to the autonomous variety of sculpture that rests imperturbably on pedestals is paralleled by her obviously innovative attitude toward painting. (She is, after all, arguably every bit as much a painter as a sculptor, though clearly unconventional in both roles.) Decidedly not flat – despite the planes that often form part of the composition – Schick's works cannot be adequately described as panel paintings or even as painted reliefs. The fronts of her works are not privileged over the backs (in fact, the sense of front and back is only a consequence of the perceived relationship to the body when her works are worn). If one insists upon categorization, Schick's works could perhaps most accurately be described as paintings in the round. This invented term so manifestly describes a perfect cross between painting and sculpture however, that one naturally wonders whether the point is not precisely that Schick's works do not fit neatly within existing categories – at least not the categories of painting, sculpture and jewelry as they have long been defined in the discourse of Western art.

This point is important, since numerous parallels to Schick's wearable sculptures can be found in contexts outside that of fine art in the Western world. The Back Sculptures (cat. nos. 318–321), for example, a series of four pieces produced in the late 1980s, strongly suggest non-Western conceptions of sculptural form. As has often been the case with Schick's series, the Back Sculptures developed in response to guidelines set for an invitational exhibition: in that instance a late-1980s thematic show titled *East Meets West*. Charged with the task of producing work under demonstrable Asian influence, Schick eventually drew inspiration from the opulent costume of a Japanese *Hinamatsuri* doll that had been in her possession since childhood. Reminiscent of elaborately knotted obi, the Back Sculptures implicitly comment on the capacity to appreciate the formal properties of certain articles of attire with a sensitivity that exceeds mere fashion consciousness. Not exclusively analogous to Japanese costume, the Back Sculptures hint at a kind of three-dimensional aesthetic that has been only meagerly indulged in the modern West, and usually under the category of art jewelry.

Back Sculpture With Reeds (1988, cat. no. 321) – a work that through its parallels to utilitarian forms and its vibrant hard-edged geometric patterning evokes the impression of a Native American beaded cradleboard – raises awareness of three-dimensional form on a level beyond the visual and tactile. Whether or not the piece is actually worn, its fragility incites an intuitively empathic response: the frail "reeds," like an infant occupant, impose bodily restrictions and place limitations on the object's situation in space. Unlike a pedestal sculpture, *Back Sculpture With Reeds* forces reflection on movement *through* space, not mere suspension within it. Its wearable nature imparts to the striped reeds the character of slender prostheses; hence the absent body is evoked through an artificial extension of its physicality and vulnerability. Knowing that it is designed to be worn, one can only with difficulty separate *Back Sculpture With Reeds* from the kinesthetic self-awareness that preserves the body against inadvertent self-inflicted damage as it negotiates the often-dangerous spaces of the ordinary world.

The linking of this kind of self-awareness to the aesthetic experience accounts for much of both the strangeness and fascination of Schick's works. There is, no doubt, something clever about projecting painting into real three-dimensional space, as Schick has done in pieces such as the Kandinsky-esque *Angles and Circles, Body Sculpture* (1987, cat. no. 311), but artists such as Judy Pfaff, Matthew Ritchie, and Sarah Sze have done so on a far more imposing scale. What makes works like the *Angles and Circles, Body Sculpture* unique is the intimate way in which they actually or potentially envelop the body. Instead of exploding painting across a vast space through which one can wander, Schick's sculptures exploit spaces no larger than that occupied by the human form. Consequently, her works are perceived not only as hollows to be filled by the absent body but as structures to be carried by the body as material and aesthetic continuations of the physical self. *Angles and Circles, Body Sculpture*, whether or not it is actually worn, cannot be easily assigned to any traditional category of art because looming within it there is always the idea of the body in motion. Since this idea is sufficient to complete the piece, the body itself is ultimately dispensable, *Angles and Circles, Body Sculpture* cannot be classified as costume or jewelry any better than it can as painting or sculpture.

The vibrant colors, active lines, and forcefully intersecting planes of many of Schick's works dazzle the eye and in the process camouflage the profoundly metaphorical nature of her compositions. The figurative value of her forms is therefore most easily grasped in her quietest works, pieces such as *Yellow Ladderback Chair* (2001, cat. no. 434) which, like the inverse of a Claes Oldenburg painted-canvas sculpture, represents a soft piece of furniture in slightly smaller than life-sized scale. Implicitly to be draped over the body, either in front or from behind, the sculpture's "ladder back" becomes the stylized visual equivalent of a vertebral column and rib cage. External instead of internal and flexible rather than rigid, *Yellow Ladderback Chair* slips lithely into the intangible space between the real body and an actual piece of furniture and in the process becomes the metaphorical counterpart of each. The space it occupies, the conceptual space that envelops the body even when one is in direct contact with concrete objects in the world, is a space rarely explored by sculpture in the West. Schick's ongoing infiltration of this space with conceptual subtlety and visual intensity has simultaneously constructed an unusual body of sculptural work and established a unique and valuable paradigm for confronting the body through sculpture.

321 BACK SCULPTURE WITH REEDS, #4, 1988,
WOOD, REED, AND NYLON STRAPS, RIVETED AND PAINTED
H. 48" × W. 26" × D. 8"
PHOTO: GARY POLLMILLER

322 WALL RELIEF WITH BRACELET, 1988,
PAINTED WOOD WITH COLORED PENCIL AND MARKERS, RIVETED AND PAINTED
RELIEF: H. 19" × W. 20 ½" × D. 6"
BRACELET: H. 7" × W. 11 ¾" × D. 1 ¾"
PHOTO: GARY POLLMILLER

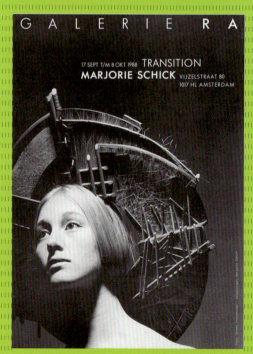

323 GALERIE RA POSTER, 1988
PHOTO: CARMEN FREUDENTHAL, COURTESY GALERIE
RA, AMSTERDAM

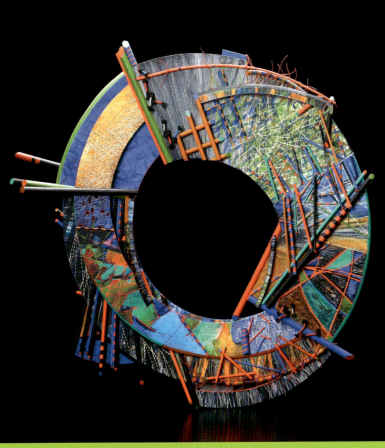

324 LETTING THE WOOD SHOW THROUGH, NECKLACE, 1988,
PAINTED WOOD, REED, AND CORD, RIVETED, CUT, WRAPPED, AND PAINTED
H. 21 ¾" × W. 23" × D. 2 ¼"
PHOTO: GARY POLLMILLER

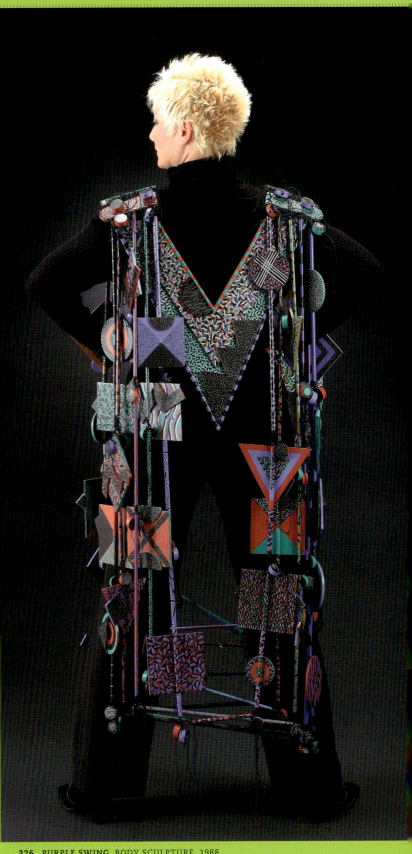

326 PURPLE SWING, BODY SCULPTURE, 1988,
PAINTED WOOD, SCREW EYES, AND CORD, RIVETED, PAINTED, AND TIED
SHOULDER TO BOTTOM: H. 52" × W. 23" × D. 16"
PHOTO: GARY POLLMILLER

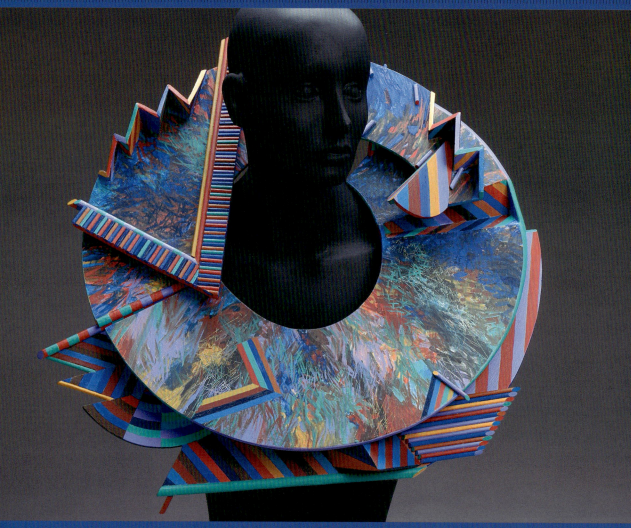

327 PURPLE RAYS, NECKLACE, 1988,
PAINTED WOOD, RIVETED AND PAINTED
H. 21 ½" × W. 23" × D. 5"
PHOTO: GARY POLLMILLER

328 COLLAR, 1988, PAINTED WOOD, RIVETED AND PAINTED
H. 25 ¾" × W. 31" × D. 6"
COLLECTION: MUSEUM OF ARTS & DESIGN, NEW YORK, GIFT OF
DR. JAMES B. M. SCHICK, ROBERT M. SCHICK, AND MRS. ELEANOR C. KRASK
PHOTO: GARY POLLMILLER

331 PAINTING WITH THREE NECKLACES, 1988,
PAINTED WOOD, RIVETED AND PAINTED
PAINTING: H. 33 ¾" × W. 22" × D. 2 ⅜"
EACH NECKLACE: H. 10" × W. 20" × D. ½"
PHOTOS: GARY POLLMILLER

332 CURVED HORIZON, HEAD SCULPTURE, 1989, PAINTED WOOD,
RUBBER, NYLON STRAPS, RIVETED AND PAINTED
H. 9" × W. 20 ½" × D. 14 ½"
WITH STRAPS EXTENDED: 67 ½" LONG
PHOTO: GARY POLLMILLER

333 NECKLACE, 1989, PAINTED WOOD AND REED, RIVETED AND PAINTED
H. 25" × W. 21" × D. 9 ¼"
COLLECTION: INDIANA UNIVERSITY ART MUSEUM, USA, 1990
PHOTO: GARY POLLMILLER

WE SPENT FOUR SABBATICALS ABROAD BOTH TRAVELING IN EUROPE AND LIVING IN LONDON. DURING OUR FIRST SABBATICAL IN 1976, WE MADE THE TRIP TO PFORZHEIM TO SEE THE SCHMUCKMUSEUM. WE WENT TWICE IN ONE DAY. WHEN WE RETURNED IN THE AFTERNOON, DR. FRITZ FALK WAS GIVING A TOUR IN ENGLISH TO A GROUP OF JEWELRY STUDENTS FROM MIDDLESEX POLYTECHNIC IN LONDON. I TRIED TO LISTEN TO EVERY WORD WITHOUT APPEARING TO BE EAVESDROPPING WHILE THINKING HOW FORTUNATE THE STUDENTS WERE TO HAVE SUCH AN INFORMATIVE TOUR FROM SUCH AN IMPORTANT PERSON.

WE RETURNED TO PFORZHEIM IN 1989 FOR THE "ORNAMENTA" EXHIBITION. WHILE THERE, WE SPOKE TO DR. FALK, WHO TURNED TO JIM AND ME AND ASKED IF WE WOULD LIKE TO HAVE A TOUR OF THE MUSEUM. WHAT A GLORIOUS MOMENT. THIRTEEN YEARS LATER WE WERE GIVEN OUR OWN SPECIAL TOUR. IT WAS AS IF A DREAM HAD COME TRUE AS WE WERE SHOWN THROUGH THE MUSEUM ON WHAT I CONSIDERED THE MOST MOMENTOUS TOUR OF MY LIFE.

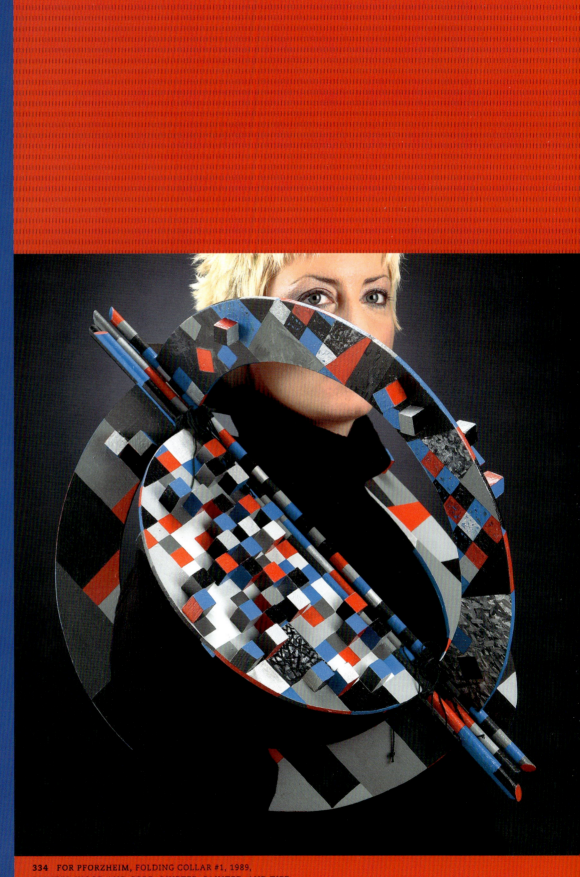

334 FOR PFORZHEIM, FOLDING COLLAR #1, 1989,
PAINTED WOOD AND CORD, RIVETED, PAINTED, AND TIED
H. 23" × W. 20 ½" × D. 1 ¾"
PHOTO: GARY POLLMILLER

335 FOR PFORZHEIM, FOLDING COLLAR #2, 1989,
PAINTED WOOD, RUBBER, AND CORD, RIVETED, PAINTED, AND TIED
H. 24″ × W. 21 ½″ × D. 1 ¾″
PHOTO: GARY POLLMILLER

336 FOR PFORZHEIM, FOLDING COLLAR #3, 1989,
PAINTED WOOD AND CORD, RIVETED, PAINTED, AND TIED
H. 24″ × W. 24″ × D. 1 ½″
PHOTO: GARY POLLMILLER

338 FOR PFORZHEIM, FOLDING COLLAR #5, 1989,
PAINTED WOOD AND CORD
H. 25 ½" × W. 23" × D. 3"
PHOTO: GARY POLLMILLER

337 FOR PFORZHEIM, FOLDING COLLAR #4, 1989,
PAINTED WOOD AND CORD, RIVETED AND PAINTED
H. 24 ½" × W. 22" × D. 2"
PHOTOS: GARY POLLMILLER

339 THREE-PART FOLDING SCREEN WITH TWO NECKLACES AND
FOUR BRACELETS, 1990, PAINTED WOOD, PEGGED, RIVETED, AND PAINTED
EACH SECTION OF SCREEN: H. 40" × W. 36" × D. 1 ³⁄₈"
LARGE COLLAR: H. 20" × W. 20" × D. ⁵⁄₈"
SMALL COLLAR: H. 9 ³⁄₄" × W. 9 ³⁄₄" × D. ⁵⁄₈"
BRACELET: H. 7" × W. 7" × D. ⁷⁄₈"
BRACELET: H. 7" × W. 7" × D. ⁷⁄₈"
BRACELET: H. 7" × W. 7" × D. 1"
BRACELET: H. 7" × W. 7" × D. ⁷⁄₈"
PRIVATE COLLECTION, THE NETHERLANDS
PHOTO OF SCREEN: ROD DUTTON
PHOTOS OF COLLAR AND BRACELET: MALCOLM TURNER

344 TRANSITION, WALL RELIEF WITH ARMLET, 1992, PAINTED PAPIER-MÂCHÉ,
WOOD, PLASTIC TUBING AND THREAD WRAPPED CORD, FORMED AND PAINTED
RELIEF: H. 17" × W. 25 ¼" × D. 4 ½"
ARMLET: H. 5 ½" × W. 8" × D. 8 ½"
COLLECTION: ARKANSAS ARTS CENTER FOUNDATION COLLECTION:
PURCHASE, RESTAURANT FUND, LITTLE ROCK, USA
PHOTO: GARY POLLMILLER

346 HEAD SCULPTURE AND COLLAR, 1992, PAINTED PAPIER-MÂCHÉ, FORMED AND PAINTED
HEAD SCULPTURE: H. 7 ¼" × W. 11 ½" × D. 11 ¼"
COLLAR: H. 17 ¾" × W. 20 ⅛" × D. 8"
COLLECTION: MUSEUM OF FINE ARTS, BOSTON, THE DAPHNE FARAGO COLLECTION
PHOTOS: GARY POLLMILLER

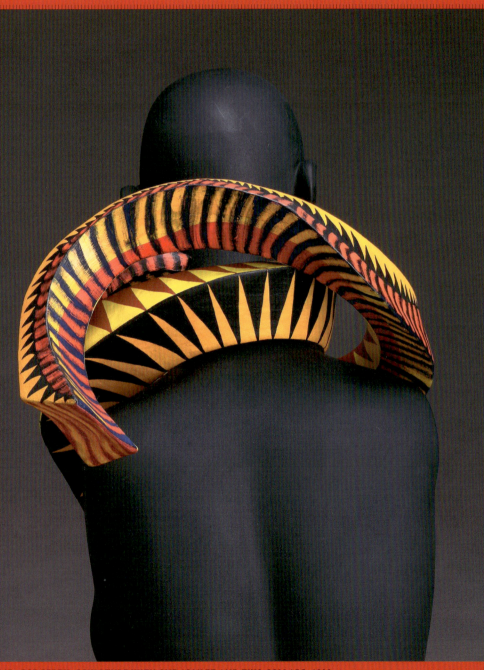

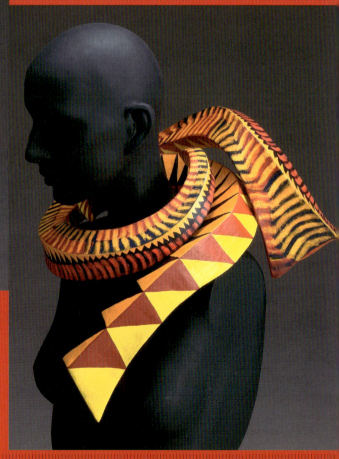

345 FOR PERTH, SCULPTURE WITH ONE ARMLET AND TWO COLLARS, 1992,
PAINTED PAPIER-MÂCHÉ, FORMED AND PAINTED
SCULPTURE: H. 12" × W. 16 ½" × D. 9 ¾"
ARMLET: H. 9" × W. 11 ⅜" × D. 10"
SMALL COLLAR: H. 4 ½" × W. 12 ¼" × D. 10 ¾"
LARGE COLLAR: H. 8" × W. 15 ¾" × D. 11 ¾"
PHOTOS: GARY POLLMILLER

"COMING FULL CIRCLE," IS WHAT JOEL DEGEN SAID WHEN I TOOK HIM PAPIER-MÂCHÉ PIECES TO PHOTOGRAPH IN 1990. "JUST LIKE DEXTER GORDON," HE ADDED, "RETURNING TO THE PLACE WHERE YOU STARTED." DURING A SABBATICAL LEAVE IN 1990, I WAS ARTIST-IN-RESIDENCE AT MIDDLESEX POLYTECHNIC, CREATING NEW OBJECTS OF WOOD, THE MATERIAL I HAD USED FOR NEARLY A DECADE. A HUGE SNOW AND SEVERAL BOMB THREATS MADE GETTING TO SCHOOL BY TUBE DIFFICULT, SO I RETURNED TO PAPIER-MÂCHÉ BECAUSE IT WAS QUIETER TO DO IN OUR FLAT ON KING'S ROAD.

IT FELT COMFORTABLE WORKING WITH PAPIER-MÂCHÉ AGAIN, BOTH IN LONDON AND IN KANSAS, RETURNING TO THE PROCESS THAT I FIND SO APPEALING. EACH PIECE IS A STUDY RELATING THE PAINTED SURFACE TO THE STRUCTURE. BECAUSE MY PAINTING HAD CHANGED DURING THE SIXTEEN YEARS SINCE I HAD LAST DONE PAPIER-MÂCHÉ, THE NEW PIECES WERE PAINTED WITH MORE LAYERS AND COMPLEXITY. THE PROCESS WAS THE SAME, BUT THE WORK WAS QUITE DIFFERENT.

350 HORN, COLLAR, 1992, PAINTED PAPIER-MÂCHÉ, FORMED AND PAINTED
H. 15 ½" × W. 16 ½" × D. 6"
PHOTO: GARY POLLMILLER

347 FOR THE KUNST RAI, COLLAR, 1992,
PAINTED PAPIER-MÂCHÉ, FORMED AND PAINTED
H. 20" × W. 23 ¾" × D. 9"
PHOTO: GARY POLLMILLER

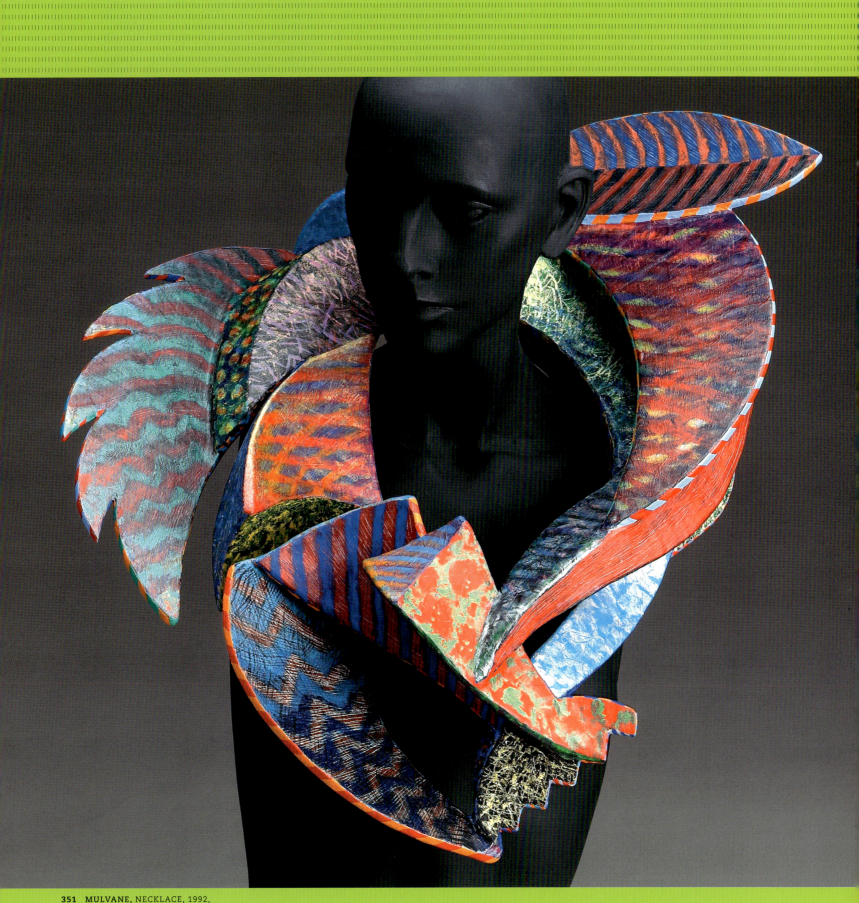

351 MULVANE, NECKLACE, 1992,
PAINTED PAPIER-MÂCHÉ, FORMED AND PAINTED
H. 19" × W. 22 ½" × D. 6"
PHOTO: GARY POLLMILLER

353 MY OWN PAISLEY, COLLAR AND BRACELET, 1993,
PAINTED PAPIER-MÂCHÉ, FORMED AND PAINTED
COLLAR: H. 11 ¾" × W. 15 ¾" × D. 7"
BRACELET: H. 6 ¾" × W. 6 ½" × D. 3"
PHOTOS: GARY POLLMILLER

354 FOR NORWAY, NECKLACE, 1993, PAINTED PAPIER-MÂCHÉ, FORMED AND PAINTED
H. 19" × W. 18 ½" × D. 5"
PHOTO: GARY POLLMILLER

357 FOR FINLAND, NECKLACE #1, 1993,
PAINTED PAPIER-MÂCHÉ, FORMED AND PAINTED
H. 18 ¾" × W. 20 ¼" × D. 4 ½"
PHOTO: GARY POLLMILLER

359 FOR FINLAND, NECKLACE #3, 1993,
PAINTED PAPIER-MÂCHÉ, FORMED AND PAINTED
H. 16 ½" × W. 18 ½" × D. 4 ½"
COURTESY GALERIE RA, AMSTERDAM
PHOTO: GARY POLLMILLER

358 FOR FINLAND, NECKLACE #2, 1993,
PAINTED PAPIER-MÂCHÉ, FORMED AND PAINTED
H. 15" × W. 19 ¾" × D. 3 ¾"
PHOTO: GARY POLLMILLER

356 WIND-BORNE, ARMLET, 1993, PAINTED PAPIER-MÂCHÉ, FORMED AND PAINTED
H. 8 ½" × W. 9" × D. 4 ½"
PHOTOS: GARY POLLMILLER

360 **SPRING GREEN**, NECKLACE, 1993, PAINTED PAPIER-MÂCHÉ, FORMED AND PAINTED
H. 23 ¾" × W. 23" × D. 6"
PHOTO: GARY POLLMILLER

364 DIPSY-DOODLE, NECKLACE, 1993, PAINTED PAPIER-MÂCHÉ, FORMED AND PAINTED
H. 10" × W. 13" × D. 5"
PHOTO: GARY POLLMILLER

363 DEFLECTION, NECKLACE, 1993, PAINTED PAPIER-MÂCHÉ, FORMED AND PAINTED
H. 19" × W. 18 ½" × D. 12"
PHOTO: GARY POLLMILLER

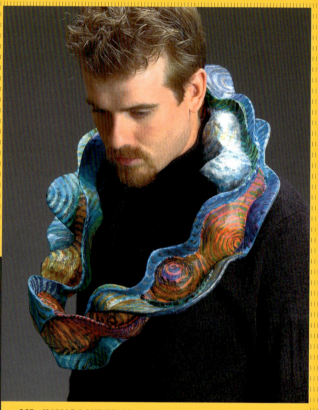

365 HAMAR LANDSCAPE, NECKLACE, 1993,
PAINTED PAPIER-MÂCHÉ, FORMED AND PAINTED
H. 19" × W. 18" × D. 5"
PHOTO: GARY POLLMILLER

367 THE SPIRAL, NECKLACE/HEAD SCULPTURE, 1994,
PAINTED PAPIER-MÂCHÉ, FORMED AND PAINTED
H. 10" × W. 7" × D. 11"
PHOTO: GARY POLLMILLER

375 ACRA GOLD, NECKLACE, 1995, PAINTED PAPIER-MÂCHÉ, FORMED AND PAINTED
H. 13 ¼" × W. 13 ¾" × D. 4 ½"
PHOTO: GARY POLLMILLER

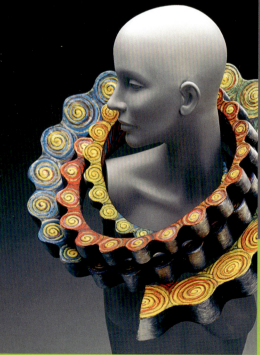

373 TRIBUTE TO PROFESSOR ALMA EIKERMAN, NECKLACE, 1995,
PAINTED PAPIER-MÂCHÉ, FORMED AND PAINTED
H. 18 ¼" × W. 19 ¾" × D. 4 ½"
PHOTOS: GARY POLLMILLER

"DO YOU EVER SEE ME GETTING LETTERS FROM MY PROFESSOR LIKE THAT?" JIM ASKED. EIKERMAN WROTE EIGHT-PAGE NEWSLETTERS ONCE OR TWICE EACH YEAR TO PAST STUDENTS. STARTING WITH HER OWN TRAVELS AND EXPERIENCES, SHE FOLLOWED WITH PAGES ON THE PROFESSIONAL ACCOMPLISHMENTS OF EVERYONE ELSE AND OFTEN ENDED WITH ADVICE: "SEEING ALL THE SLIDES AND AS MANY SHOWS AS POSSIBLE HELP[S] [TO] KEEP YOU IN THE KNOW BUT IT'S THE CONCENTRATED WORK THAT MANY OF YOU ARE DOING WORKING AS STEADILY AS POSSIBLE AT YOUR WORK BENCH THAT GIVES YOUR WORK DISTINCTION." (DECEMBER 1975) THIS SPECIAL BOND BRINGS US TOGETHER AT NATIONAL CONFERENCES. THE "TRIBUTE EIKERMAN KEPT HER GROUP CONNECTED. EVEN TODAY, THIS SPECIAL BOND BRINGS US TOGETHER AT NATIONAL CONFERENCES. THE "TRIBUTE TO PROFESSOR ALMA EIKERMAN" NECKLACE CONCERNS THE EXPERIENCES WE SHARED AND THE CONNECTIONS AMONG THOSE FORTUNATE ENOUGH TO HAVE STUDIED WITH HER.

376 RING OF FIRE, NECKLACE, 1995, PAINTED PAPIER-MÂCHÉ, FORMED AND PAINTED
H. 19" × W. 20" × D. 4"
COLLECTION: VICTORIA AND ALBERT MUSEUM, LONDON, UK
PHOTO: GARY POLLMILLER

378 EDGED WAVE, ARMLET, 1995, PAINTED PAPIER-MÂCHÉ,
FORMED AND PAINTED
H. 10 ⅛" × W. 7 ½" × D. 5"
COLLECTION: NATIONAL MUSEUMS
OF SCOTLAND, EDINBURGH, UK
PHOTO: GARY POLLMILLER

379 KATELLA, NECKLACE, 1995, PAINTED PAPIER-MÂCHÉ AND WOOD,
FORMED, RIVETED, AND PAINTED
H. 15 ½" × W. 17 ¼" × D. 4"
PHOTO: GARY POLLMILLER

380 GOLDEN FROST, NECKLACE, 1995, PAINTED PAPIER-MÂCHÉ,
FORMED AND PAINTED
H. 18" × W. 18 ½" × D. 7"
PHOTO: GARY POLLMILLER

385 ILLUSIONS, NECKLACE, 1996, PAINTED PAPIER-MÂCHÉ,
FORMED AND PAINTED
H. 16 ⅞" × W. 17" × D. 3 ¾"
PHOTO: GARY POLLMILLER

390 L.A./D.C. SUITE, ARMLET AND CONTAINER FOR ARMLET, 1996,
PAINTED PAPIER-MÂCHÉ, FORMED AND PAINTED
CONTAINER: H. 10 ½" × W. 12 ½" × D. 12 ⅝"
ARMLET: H. 6 ½" × W. 7 ⅛" × D. 3 ¼"
PHOTO: GARY POLLMILLER

391 L.A./D.C. SUITE, NECKLACE, 1996,
PAINTED PAPIER-MÂCHÉ, FORMED AND PAINTED
H. 13 ¾" × W. 13 ⅞" × D. 4 ½"
PHOTOS: GARY POLLMILLER

397 DE LA LUNA/DEL SOL, NECKLACE, 1998,
PAINTED CANVAS AND CORD, STITCHED, PAINTED, AND TIED
H. 34" × W. 27 ¼" × D. 3 ⅛"
PHOTOS: GARY POLLMILLER

MARJORIE SCHICK AND BRITAIN

Elizabeth Goring

Britain was an exhilarating place for jewelers in the early 1980s. The radical "movement" subsequently known as "The New Jewelry" was at its height, flourishing particularly in Amsterdam, Munich, and London, and some of the most exciting work to emerge from it was being made and exhibited in the UK.[1] Bold exploration of non-traditional materials coincided with, and was partly encouraged by, the explosion in the price of silver in the late 1970s.[2] This period of confident and vibrant experimentation around form, value and self-expression, the relationship between the work and the body, and interpretation through performance and photography had a profound influence on a generation of young British makers, for whom this new freedom of expression was an inspiration. There could have been no better moment for Marjorie Schick's work to arrive here.

Schick's close relationship with the British jewelry scene grew from the recognition by a number of key individuals of a convergence of interests. Her work had developed entirely independently, but it proved to have a strong resonance for those at the cutting edge in Europe. Schick was well aware of the new mood in Europe. In 1975, she had attended a lecture by Gijs Bakker and Emmy van Leersum at Kansas State University, and in 1976, during a period of sabbatical leave, she and her husband Jim had spent four months visiting exhibitions, museums, studios and jewelry schools in Scandinavia, Amsterdam, and Pforzheim. During this trip, which also included her first visit to London, she saw the exhibition "Jewellery in Europe" at the Victoria and Albert Museum,[3] and in 1980 she saw the pioneering "Susanna Heron: Bodywork" exhibition at the Crafts Council. In 1982, Schick was invited by Sharon Plant to send work to Aspects (cat. no. 178), the energetic London gallery with an explicit agenda to redefine contemporary jewelry.[4] Schick's first exposure in a public exhibition in Britain was also in 1982, in the provocative and influential exhibition "Jewellery Redefined," where her pieces sat easily within the context of work that often employed linear construction and brilliant color.[5] Although hers sprang from quite different roots, it exactly encapsulated the spirit of the moment. It is difficult today to recapture the impact that exhibition made, both positive and negative, but together with other simultaneous events in London it proved a revelation to many, engendering huge debate and influencing the creative direction of a significant number of current makers.[6]

In 1983, Schick and her husband were again on sabbatical leave and she returned to London, this time enrolling as a metalsmithing student for the spring term at the Sir John Cass School of Art where she created, somewhat surprisingly in retrospect, a silver decanter.[7] She came back the following summer as artist-in-residence intending to continue with metalworking, but Jim encouraged a re-think, pointing out the demand for her dowel pieces. A trip to a timber yard followed this perceptive steer. The family lived in a one-bedroom flat, their son sleeping in the living room, so Schick painted dowel pieces in the bathroom by night to avoid keeping everyone awake.

Schick's profile in Britain grew steadily. In 1985, she was invited to participate in Caroline Broad-head's insightful "New Tradition. The Evolution of Jewellery 1966–1985," an exhibition all the more valuable for being curated by one of this period's leading practitioners.[8] She was featured in Peter Dormer and Ralph Turner's *The New Jewelry*, an important published survey of the field, and a portrait of Schick wearing a painted dowel brooch illustrated a Dormer essay in *Aspects* magazine.[9] In October, Plant took Schick's work to the fifth Chelsea Crafts Fair alongside work by eleven other jewelers including Julia Manheim, Lam de Wolf, and Cathy Harris. By now, she was firmly positioned within the core group of pioneering artists.

Schick had been building a personal collection of jewelry, particularly by practitioners of the New Jewelry, and indeed had exhibited it at Pittsburg State University in 1982. It was through Aspects that she discovered the work of the young, talented Cathy Harris, which she started to collect.[10] The two first met in Amsterdam in 1986 at Galerie Ra's 10th anniversary show and became great friends, exchanging gifts by mail and exploring museums and galleries together when Schick was in London.[11] Harris's untimely death in 1994 sadly ended this close Anglo-American friendship, one which clearly enriched the lives of both.[12]

Schick and her work continued to be frequently visible in Britain during the 1990s. The Schicks were in London again in 1991. She was artist-in-residence first at Middlesex Polytechnic, then back at the Sir John Cass.[13] Her profile was particularly high in 1996. Two major early pieces, *Belt with Metal Pockets* (1967, cat. no. 45) and *Pectoral Body Piece* (1968–9, cat. no. 72), were shown in Turner's exhibition "New Times, New Thinking: Jewellery in Europe and America" at the Crafts Council.[14] Earlier that year, the Jewellers Exchange '96 international conference had been held in Newcastle, the first event of its kind in Britain.[15] Three venues hosted related exhibitions; Schick's work was well-represented, appearing in two of them.[16] Across the border in Scotland, her work was also in "Contemporary Jewelry from the USA," curated by Charon Kransen for Amanda Game at the Scottish Gallery, one of Britain's leading independent crafts galleries. The following year, she showed work in "USA Today" at the Lesley Craze Gallery, London. In 1998, Game and I invited her to participate in our millennial survey of international contemporary jewelry, "Jewellery Moves," at the National Museums of Scotland, where we installed her stunning neckpiece, *De La Luna/Del Sol* (cat. no. 397), prominently on open display on a podium at the exhibition's heart.[17] The Museum subsequently purchased *Edged Wave* Armlet (cat. no. 378) from the show for its collection.[18] Recently, *Ballycotton Bay* (cat. no. 431) ring was shown in "The Ring," an exhibition brought to Britain by Mobilia Gallery in 2002, and the masterly *Deception* chessboard (cat. no. 445) and gaming pieces in "Chess," toured here by Velvet da Vinci in 2003.[19]

There are limited opportunities to see American work in Britain, where its diversity and strengths remain largely unrecognized, and few American jewelry artists are household names. Marjorie Schick is certainly one of them. She has been prominent here for a quarter of a century, and her regular inclusion within the "canon," especially of the 1980s, might tempt some to consider her almost one of our own. However, this would be a misunderstanding. As David Watkins has perceptively pointed out, "Schick's earlier … body constructions were 'discovered' by Europe in the eighties, when they were found to be sympathetic with a non-precious jewellery avant-garde of the time. It was soon apparent that this was a chance meeting of interests, and that she pursued an independent agenda. Her work … is intrinsically 'American' in its outgoing, unfettered confidence."[20] In Britain, she is simultaneously familiar and exotic. Like other great artists she inhabits a place of her own making, one that is gloriously, exuberantly individual. With restless energy, she doggedly pursues her path, constantly devising and confronting new challenges, and invariably emerging triumphant. These are qualities much prized in Britain. We look forward to many repeat visits.

1   The movement had been gaining momentum in Britain during the 1970s, partly through shows like "Fourways," the touring exhibition featuring the work of Caroline Broadhead, Julia Manheim, Susanna Heron and Nuala Jamison. This traveled to 12 venues in England, Scotland and Wales during 1977 and 1978.

2   This resulted from the Hunt brothers' now notorious attempt to corner the worldwide market in the metal, an attempt which crashed spectacularly in 1980.

3   This Scottish Arts Council/Crafts Advisory Committee exhibition, curated by Ralph Turner, toured in 1975–6. Schick returned to Europe the following year, visiting Vienna and London, where she saw the third "Loot" exhibition at Goldsmiths Hall.

4   "Aspects has been at great pains to redefine modern jewellery," *Aspects* magazine/newsletter (January/March 1985), 7. The gallery, established by Plant in 1981, was an influential focus for those interested in pioneering contemporary jewelry and other craftforms.

5   This was a juried selection of 220 international works in non-precious materials, chosen from an entry of over 1,800. The exhibition was shown at the British Crafts Centre, London, from 1 October to 13 November 1982. The seven selectors were all key figures: Pierre Degen, Paul Derrez, Hermann Jünger, Julia Manheim, Jean Muir, Sarah Osborn and Ralph Turner. Schick exhibited three dowel brooches and three paper brooches (all 1982). Diana Hughes, *Jewellery Redefined* (London: British Crafts Centre, 1982), 52; exhibits 176–181. Schick attended the opening of the exhibition, as well as the associated symposium.

6   James Evans points to the compelling synchronicity of "Jewellery Redefined" with "Pierre Degen: New Work" (Crafts Council, 22 September to 24 October 1982), as well as "The Jewellery Project" (British Crafts Centre, 20 April to 26 June 1983) and other exhibitions, in *The New Jewellery: a documentational account*, an online survey at http://vads.ahds.ac.uk/learning/designingbritain/html/tnj.html. Schick saw the Pierre Degen show while she was in London for the opening of "Jewellery Redefined."

7   She explains this was because "I never made my teapot in graduate school so felt that was what I should do." (pers.comm.)

8   Schick showed *White Edges* (cat. no. 48) made in 1967 and re-painted in 1985. Schick and Arline Fisch were the only Americans included. Caroline Broadhead, *New Tradition. The Evolution of Jewellery 1966–1985* (London: British Crafts Council, 1985), 78.

9   Peter Dormer and Ralph Turner, *The New Jewelry. Trends and Traditions* (London: Thames and Hudson, 1985, revised 1994); Peter Dormer, "The Cultural Divide in new jewellery: Europe v America," in *Aspects* magazine/newsletter (January/March 1985), 6–7. Dormer wrote, "Schick … is now the most radical of American jewellers and in fact she has pushed her work to the point where it is more 'sculptural' than wearable ornament."

10 Long before they met, Schick described herself as "Cathy's American groupie" (pers.comm.).

11 Schick sent Harris "American trash" for her collages – at first, candy and gum wrappers, and canned food labels, later the candy bars themselves. Harris reciprocated with Sainsbury's Bourbon biscuits (pers.comm.).

12 Schick now holds "Cathy Harris days" for her students, celebrating her talent through showing slides and pieces from her collection (pers.comm.).

13 She also lectured at the Royal College of Art and West Surrey College of Art and Design, Farnham. She had lectured at both before, in 1985 and 1986 respectively.

14 Ralph Turner, *Jewelry in Europe and America. New Times, New Thinking* (London: Thames and Hudson, 1991), 38. Schick came to London to see the show, and to take a workshop with Geoff Roberts.

15 Based on the model of the Society of North American Goldsmiths' annual conferences, it led the following year to the establishment of the Association for Contemporary Jewellery. One of her dowel neckpieces was discussed by the keynote speaker, Helen W. Drutt English.

16 Exhibitions were held at the Shipley Museum and Art Gallery, Gateshead; the Cleveland Crafts Centre, Middlesbrough; and the Queens Hall Arts Centre, Hexham. Schick showed her *Katella* necklace and *Bodega Bay* armlet (both 1995, cat. nos. 379 and 374) in the Society of North American Goldsmiths' "American Revelations: new Jewellery" at the Shipley, while examples of her work from their important collection were shown in "Jewellery Innovations" at the Cleveland Crafts Centre.

17 We had seen Schick's work together at the extraordinary "Ornamenta 1" exhibition in Pforzheim in 1989, where her folding collars (cat. nos. 334–338) made a strong impression on us. Schick had also visited "Ornamenta 1" to attend the opening. The four other works in "Jewellery Moves" were *Edged Wave* Armlet (cat. no. 378); Necklace from *L.A./D.C. Suite* (cat. no. 391); and Container and Armlet also from *L.A./D.C. Suite* (cat. no. 390). Amanda Game and Elizabeth Goring, *Jewellery Moves. Ornament for the 21ˢᵗ century* (Edinburgh: NMS Publishing, 1998), 23.

18 Game and Goring (1998) fig. 23 illustrates *Edged Wave* Armlet (cat. no. 378). Other work in British public collections: *Ring of Fire* neckpiece (cat. no. 376) is in the Victoria and Albert Museum, London; Clare Phillips, *Jewels and Jewellery* (London: V & A Publications, 2000), 138; two of the three Cleveland Crafts Centre, Middlesbrough, pieces are illustrated in publications: an armpiece in *Jewellery Innovations* (exhibition catalogue, Cleveland Crafts Centre, 1996, 11 (pages unnumbered), and *Dowel Necklace #1* (cat. no. 163) in *International Contemporary Jewellery* (Middlesbrough: Cleveland Crafts Centre, undated but about 2000), loose card insert. This institution is now known as *mima*.

19 *The Ring. The art of the ring* (Cambridge, MA: Mobilia Gallery, 2001), introduction; *Chess* (San Francisco, CA: Velvet da Vinci, 2003), front cover and 8, no. 43.

20 David Watkins, *The Best in Contemporary Jewellery* (Mies, Switzerland: Rotovision, 1993), 146–7.

398 DE LA LUNA/DEL SOL, PINS, ONGOING SINCE 1998,
PAINTED CANVAS AND STAINLESS STEEL WIRE, STITCHED AND PAINTED
FROM H. 3 ½" × W. 1" × D. 1" TO H. 18" × W. 2" × D. 2"
COLLECTION: (ONE PIN) PORTER PRICE, USA
PHOTO: GARY POLLMILLER

394   GOLD AND SILVER TEAPOTS, BROOCHES AND TRAY, 1997, TRAY:
PAINTED WOOD, BROOCHES: PAINTED PAPIER-MÂCHÉ AND STAINLESS STEEL WIRE
TRAY: H. 1 ⅜" × W. 17" × D. 8 ¼"
EACH BROOCH: H. 5 ⅜" × W. 11 ¼" × D. 2"
PHOTOS: GARY POLLMILLER

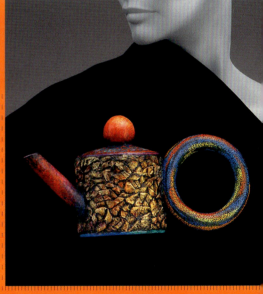

409 LA PALMA, NECKLACE, 1998,
PAINTED CANVAS AND METAL RODS, STITCHED AND PAINTED
H. 24" × W. 22 ¼" × D. 5"
PHOTO: GARY POLLMILLER

410 **PITTSBURG BRICK,** SHOULDER SCULPTURE ON WALL RELIEF, 1998,
SHOULDER SCULPTURE: PAINTED CANVAS, STITCHED AND PAINTED,
WALL RELIEF: PAINTED WOOD, CONSTRUCTED AND PAINTED
SHOULDER SCULPTURE: H. 13 ¾" × W. 46 ¾" × D. 1"
WALL RELIEF: H. 19" × W. 51 ⅞" × D. 3 ⅜"
PHOTOS: GARY POLLMILLER

411 QUETZALCOATL, NECKLACE AND WALL RELIEF, 1998,
NECKLACE: PAINTED CANVAS AND CORD, STITCHED, PAINTED, AND TIED,
WALL RELIEF: PAINTED WOOD, CONSTRUCTED AND PAINTED
NECKLACE: H. 16" × W. 16 ¾" × D. 1 ¾"
WALL RELIEF: H. 24" × W. 24 ⅛" × D. 1 ⅞"
PHOTOS: GARY POLLMILLER

THINKING ABOUT A THEME FOR A SABBATICAL LEAVE REQUEST, JIM SUGGESTED A SERIES OF PIECES RELATED TO PLACES LIVED IN OR VISITED. "QUETZALCOATL" AND "BOUND COLORS," NECKLACES ON WALL RELIEFS, BOTH REFERENCE ANCIENT CARVINGS IN MEXICO SEEN WHILE ON SABBATICAL. BECAUSE OF TRIPS TO AMSTERDAM, "DOUBLE DUTCH ARTISTS" HOLDS NECKLACES ABOUT TWO FAMOUS DUTCH ARTISTS, VAN GOGH AND MONDRIAN. A MAJOR STREET IN CALIFORNIA WHERE ROB LIVES AND DRAWINGS OF PALM FRONDS IN THE BACKYARD THERE INSPIRED "LA PALMA" NECKLACE. AT ONE TIME, DARK RED BRICKS WERE MANUFACTURED WHERE WE LIVE IN KANSAS RESULTING IN MANY OF OUR STREETS, SIDEWALKS, AND EVEN THE FIRE PLACE IN OUR KITCHEN BEING MADE OF THEM. A SHOULDER SCULPTURE, "PITTSBURG BRICK," CELEBRATES THIS HISTORY AND WHEN NOT WORN, RESTS ON A RELIEF PAINTED TO RESEMBLE DIRT AND GRASS.

412 BOUND COLORS, NECKLACE ON WALL RELIEF, 1998,
NECKLACE: PAINTED WOOD AND CANVAS, CONSTRUCTED,
STITCHED, PAINTED AND TIED, WALL RELIEF: PAINTED WOOD
NECKLACE: H. 21" × W. 21" × D. 1 ¼"
WALL RELIEF: H. 36 ¼" × W. 27 ⅜" × D. 1 ⅜"
PHOTOS: GARY POLLMILLER

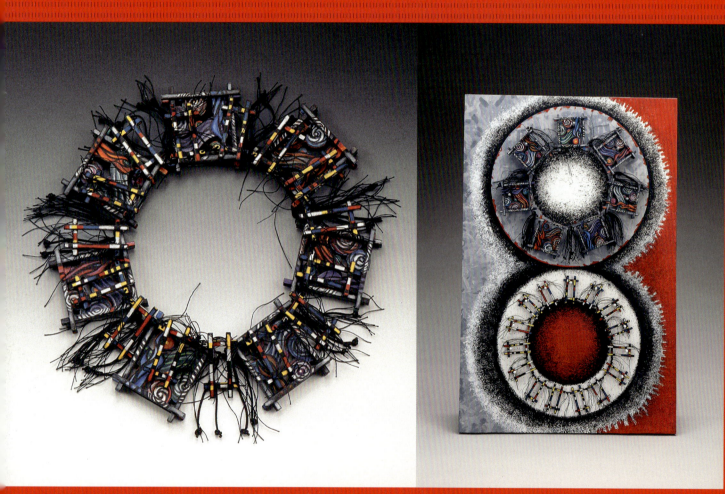

413 DOUBLE DUTCH ARTISTS, NECKLACES ON WALL RELIEF, 1998,
VAN GOGH NECKLACE: PAINTED WOOD AND CORD, CONSTRUCTED,
PAINTED AND TIED
MONDRIAN NECKLACE: PAINTED WOOD AND CORD, CONSTRUCTED, PAINTED, AND TIED
WALL RELIEF: PAINTED WOOD, CONSTRUCTED AND PAINTED
VAN GOGH NECKLACE: H. 15 ¼" × W. 15 ¼" × D. ¾"
MONDRIAN NECKLACE: H. 14" × W. 14" × D. ⅜"
WALL RELIEF: H. 33 ½" × W. 22 ¼" × D. 1 ⅝"
PHOTOS: GARY POLLMILLER

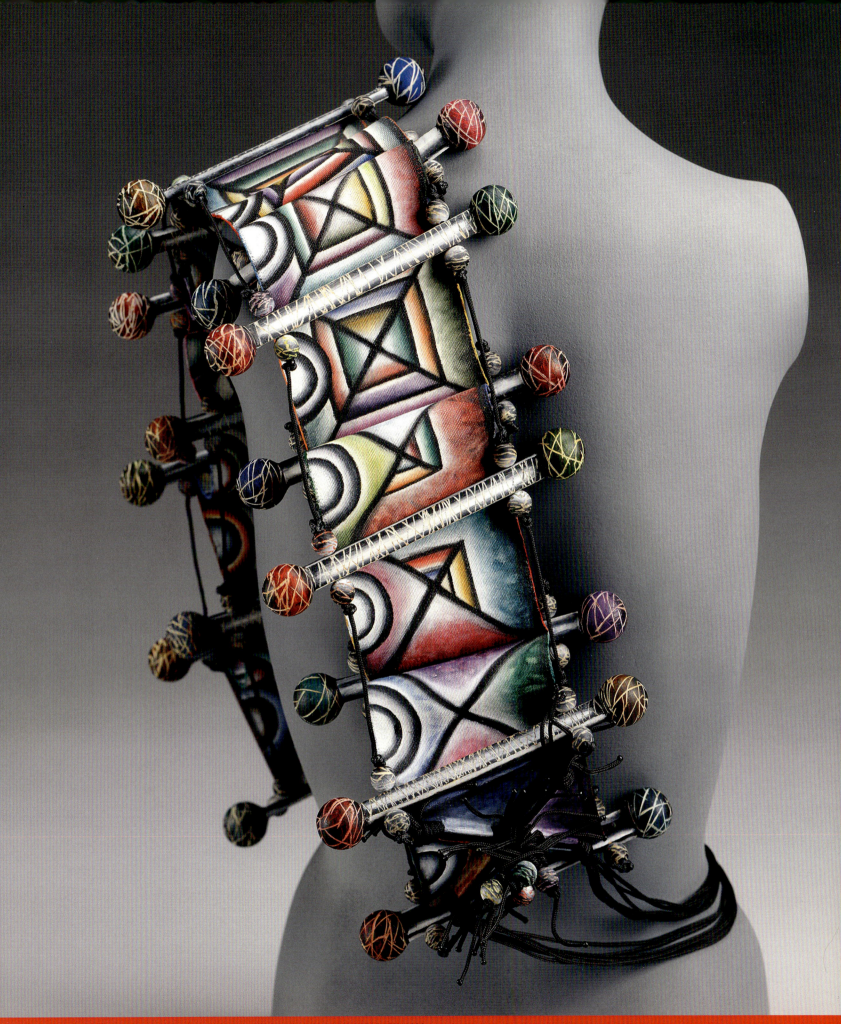

416 VARIATIONS ON A THEME, ACCORDION FOLDED BOOK/ NECKLACE/ SASH, 1999,
PAINTED CANVAS, WOOD, AND NYLON CORD, CONSTRUCTED, PAINTED, AND TIED
H. 36" × W. 7" × D. 4"
WITH CORDS EXTENDED, H. 82 ¾"
PHOTO: GARY POLLMILLER

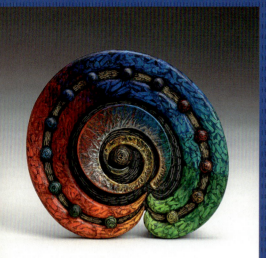

420 SPIRAL GALAXY, EARRING ON A STAND, 2000,
EARRING: PAINTED PAPIER-MÂCHÉ OVER WIRE WITH WOOD EARRING BACK,
STAND: PAINTED WOOD, FORMED, CONSTRUCTED, AND PAINTED
EARRING: H. 4 ¼" × W. 3 ⅝" × D. 1"
STAND: H. 7 ¾" × W. 8 ½" × D. 2 ½"
PHOTOS: GARY POLLMILLER

417 TEAPOT ARMLET, 1999, PAINTED PAPIER-MÂCHÉ AND WOOD, FORMED AND PAINTED
H. 5 ⅜" × W. 12 ½" × D. 6 ¼"
COLLECTION: SHARON M. CAMPBELL, USA
PHOTOS: GARY POLLMILLER

421 VIBRATIONS, PAIR OF COLLARS, 2000,
PAINTED CANVAS AND WOOD, CONSTRUCTED, STITCHED, AND PAINTED
H. 15 ⅞" × W. 15 ⅞" × D. 1 ¾"
H. 16" × W. 16" × D. 1 ½"
PHOTOS: GARY POLLMILLER

422 GAP OF DUNLOE, ARMLET WITH COMPANION SCULPTURE,
2000, PAINTED PAPIER-MÂCHÉ, FORMED AND PAINTED
SCULPTURE: H. 9" × W. 10" × D. 9½"
ARMLET: H. 4 ¼" × W. 8 ½" × D. 8 ⅛"
PHOTO: GARY POLLMILLER

423 FIFTY STATES, COMMEMORATIVE BODY SCULPTURE WITH EARRINGS,
2000, PAINTED CANVAS, WOOD, AND CORD, STITCHED, RIVETED, AND PAINTED
BODY SCULPTURE: SHOULDER TO BOTTOM, H. 54 ½" × W. 32" × D. ¾"
PAINTING FOR EARRINGS: H. 8 ⅞" × W. 7 ¼" × D. ⅞"
EARRINGS: ALASKA, H. 2" × W. 1 ½" × D. ¼"
HAWAII, H. 1 ½" × W. 2" × D. ¼"
PHOTOS: GARY POLLMILLER

425 YEMEN WINDOWS, BODY SCULPTURE, 2000,
PAINTED CANVAS, WOOD, AND CORD, STITCHED, PAINTED, AND TIED
TOTAL LENGTH: H. 100" × W. 15" × D. 1"
PHOTO: GARY POLLMILLER

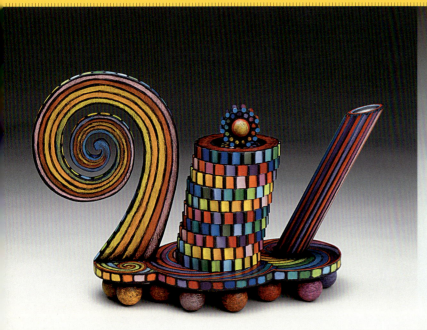

428 TEAPOT WITH TEN ARMLETS, 2001,
PAINTED WOOD, CONSTRUCTED AND PAINTED
TEAPOT: H. 13" × W. 20 ½" × D. 8 ¼"
EACH ARMLET: H. 5 ⅛" × W. 5 ⅛" × D. ⅝"
COLLECTION: DIANE AND SANDY BESSER, USA
PHOTOS: GARY POLLMILLER

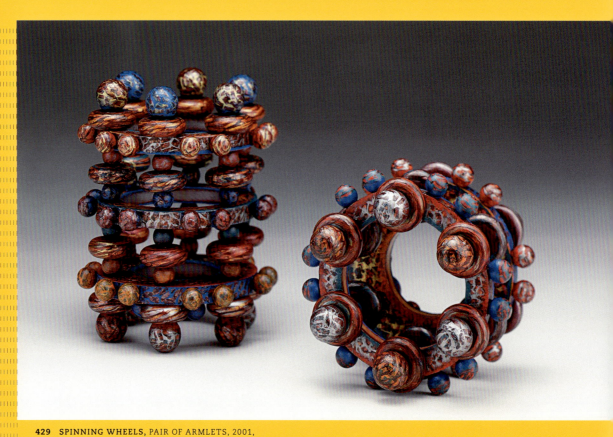

429 SPINNING WHEELS, PAIR OF ARMLETS, 2001,
PAINTED WOOD, CONSTRUCTED AND PAINTED
LARGE ARMLET: H. 7 ⅞" × W. 6 ½" × D. 6 ½"
SMALL ARMLET: H. 5 ½" × W. 6 ½" × D. 6 ½"
PHOTO: GARY POLLMILLER

433 SPEAK NO EVIL, MASK, 2001, PAINTED PAPIER-MÂCHÉ,
WOOD, AND CORD, FORMED, PAINTED, AND TIED
MASK: H. 16 ⅞" × W. 13 ¼" × D. 5 ¾"
WITH CORDS: H. 31" × W 13 ¼" × D. 5 ¾"
PHOTO: GARY POLLMILLER

431 BALLYCOTTON BAY, FINGER SCULPTURE WITH STAND, 2001,
PAINTED PAPIER-MÂCHÉ AND WOOD, FORMED AND PAINTED
FINGER SCULPTURE: H. 5" × W. 4" × D. 3 ¼"
STAND: H. 4" × W. 10" × D. 9"
ALICE AND LOUIS KOCH COLLECTION, SWITZERLAND
PHOTOS: GARY POLLMILLER

434 YELLOW LADDERBACK CHAIR, BODY SCULPTURE, 2001,
PAINTED CANVAS AND CORD, STITCHED, PAINTED, AND TIED
H. 55" × W. 13" × D. 2"
PHOTO: GARY POLLMILLER

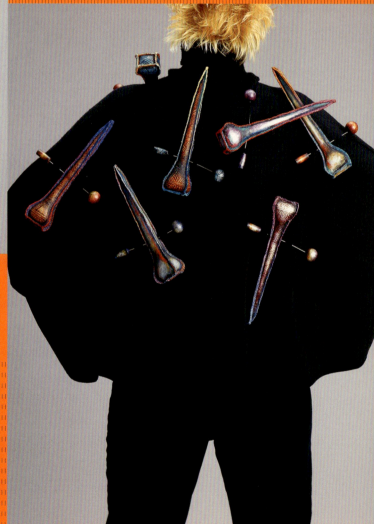

432 FOR WANT OF A NAIL, 19 HORSESHOE NAIL BROOCHES,
2001, PAINTED CANVAS, WOOD, AND STAINLESS STEEL WIRE,
STITCHED, CONSTRUCTED, AND PAINTED
CANVAS BROOCHES: H. 10" × W. 2 ¼" × D. 1 ½"
PINS: H. 6 ½" × W. 1" × D. 1"
PHOTO: GARY POLLMILLER

INSIDE OUT:
WEARING MARJORIE SCHICK'S SCULPTURE

Suzanne Ramljak

Any discussion of Marjorie Schick's wearable structures quickly leads to a consideration of their sculptural properties. Such a context is fitting given that Schick's creative project was spawned while she pondered how it might feel to be *inside* a sculpture by David Smith. Similar speculations have fueled Schick's work for the last forty years, as she has continued to explore the engaging potential of body sculpture.

Jewelry and sculpture are often compared, and it is common to claim that jewelry is small-scale or wearable sculpture. There are indeed similarities between the two formats, although there are also crucial differences. Schick's hybrid constructions draw on the best of both fields, and an assessment of her work in relation to sculpture and jewelry underlines the distinct, even radical, nature of her venture.

Sculpture is foremost an entity that occupies or displaces space. It exists in three dimensions. Whereas a piece of jewelry is also a dimensional object, volume and scale are constrained by ties to the human body. Schick's wearable forms eschew jewelry's traditional size, pushing scale and heft to the limit. "I like it to be dramatic, to take up a large area," she claims. "It takes nerve to wear objects of such large scale."[1] Accordingly her pieces, like *Yellow Ladderback Chair (Body Sculpture)* (2001, cat. no. 434), have been known to extend beyond four feet.

In addition to scale, sculpture and jewelry must both contend with the forces of gravity and weight. With sculpture these elements are experienced vicariously by the viewer, as implied properties. Jewelry, conversely, must deal with actual weight and the pull of gravity on object and wearer. Schick's commanding structures test the load bearing capacity of the body. While she opts for materials that are relatively light—like paper, dowels, and canvas—her works have still weighed in at over five pounds. As the artist states, "I am intrigued by the idea that the human body is capable of carrying large objects, both physically and visually."[2]

The expansive space and volume of most sculpture also involves an unyielding material presence. This is in contrast to much jewelry, which typically yields to the pressure and movement of the wearer. Jewelry shifts to accommodate the body, while sculpture demands that we adapt to it. Schick's wearable pieces reverse these priorities, with the human form becoming an accomplice to the jewelry, not vice versa. In effect, the sculpture wears the body, transforming it into a base to support the crafted object.

While reveling in sculpture's spatial command and materiality, Schick's work also partakes of jewelry's prime asset, namely touch. Although we may speak of tactility in relation to sculpture, the touch is usually vicarious. We almost invariably experience sculpture visually, not tactilely, especially within public settings. Touch is at the root of jewelry's ability to provide intimate involvement, and the potency of Schick's wearable sculptures is increased by this haptic quality.

Although Schick's elaborately painted pieces satisfy any visual appetite, they nonetheless subvert the hierarchy of senses, undermining vision in favor of varied sensory input. Vision has long ranked over the other senses in the Western tradition, with Aristotle placing it at the pinnacle of his sensory scale. Each sense involves a distinct way of relating to the world: sight is characteristically detached and analytic, whereas touch is more integrated and encompassing. Sight isolates, touch incorporates. Vision situates the observer outside the subject, at a distance, while touch puts us at the center of a tactile field. You can immerse yourself in touch but there is no way to similarly immerse yourself in sight.

By constructing her works so that we actually enter them, not just look at or hold them, Schick choreographs an enveloping sensory embrace. We typically remain outside of sculpture, gazing upon the various forms. When we wear Schick's works the sculpture is upon us: beholders become performers. In this regard her work shares traits with clothing, and several of her pieces actually assume the guise of garments, such as skirts or shawls.

So many aspects of contemporary culture conspire to distance us from our own bodily sensation. We amble about in a disconnected state, physically and psychically estranged. By re-embodying us within complex structures, Schick's works serve to counter such detachment. As in her *Cocoon for Spiral Necklace* (2003, cat. no. 444), we become enveloped in sensual richness. Instead of remaining outsiders looking in on life, her hybrid sculptures turn us inside out, situating us at the center of our own lived experience.

1   Cited in *Marjorie Schick, Body Works: Structure, Color, Space*, exhib. cat. (Little Rock, AR: Arkansas Arts Center, 2001).
2   Artist's Statement, early 1990s, published at http://www.pittstate.edu/art/marjo.html.

436 GOLDEN WEB, NECKLACE AND WALL RELIEF, 2001, WALL RELIEF:
PAINTED WOOD, CONSTRUCTED AND PAINTED, NECKLACE:
METAL, FABRIC, THREAD, AND WOOD, FORMED, WRAPPED, TIED, WOVEN, AND PAINTED
RELIEF: H. 32 ⅛" × W. 23 ⅝" × D. 5 ½"
NECKLACE: H. 13 ⅜" × W. 15 ¾" × D. 4 ⅝"
PHOTO: GARY POLLMILLER

438 AMENHOTEP I, PAIR OF COLLARS, 2002,
DOWEL COLLAR: PAINTED WOOD AND CORD, PAINTED, STRUNG AND TIED,
FEATHER COLLAR: PAINTED PAPIER-MÂCHÉ,
WOOD, PLASTIC, CORD, AND THREAD, PAINTED AND TIED
DOWEL COLLAR: H. 25 ¼" × W. 25 ¼" × D. 1"
FEATHER COLLAR: H. 27 ½" × 26 ¼" × D. ⅝"
PHOTO: GARY POLLMILLER

442 NIGHT BLOOM, EARRINGS ON RELIEF, 2003, RELIEF: PAINTED WOOD, EARRINGS: PAINTED WOOD, PLASTIC LAMINANT, AND STAINLESS STEEL WIRE, CONSTRUCTED, GLUED, AND PAINTED
RELIEF: H. 14 ¾" × W. 13 ¾" × D. 1 ⅞"
EARRINGS: H. 1 ¾" × W. 2" × D. ⅜"
PHOTO: GARY POLLMILLER

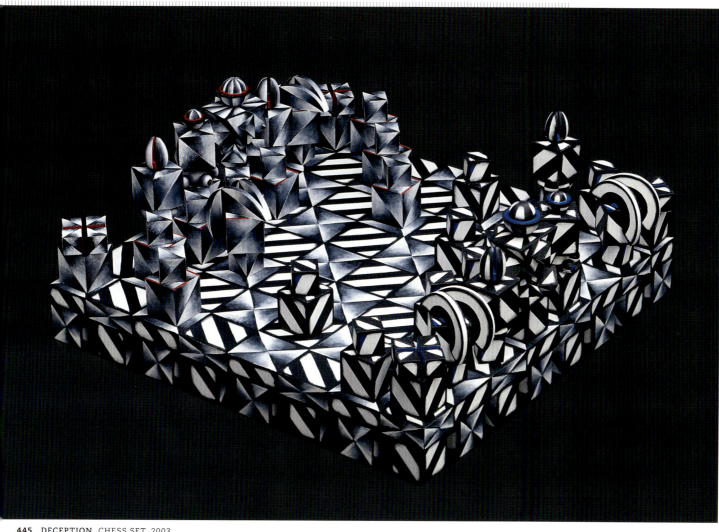

445 DECEPTION, CHESS SET, 2003,
CHESS BOARD: PAINTED WOOD, CONSTRUCTED AND PAINTED,
CHESS PIECES: PAINTED WOOD AND PLASTIC LAMINANT, PEGGED, GLUED, AND PAINTED
CHESS BOARD: H. 2 ½" × W. 18" × D. 18"
CHESS PIECES: FROM H. 2 ½" × W. 1 ½" × D. 1 ½" TO H. 5 ¼" × W. 3" × D. 2 ½"
PHOTO: GARY POLLMILLER

441 PROGRESSION, SUITE OF NECKLACES, ONGOING SINCE 2002,
PAINTED PAPER AND WOOD, PAPIER-MÂCHÉ PAPER ON WOOD
EACH: H. 14 ½" × W. 14 ½" × D. ¼"
PHOTO: GARY POLLMILLER

444 COCOON FOR SPIRAL NECKLACE, 2003,
SCULPTURE: PAINTED PAPIER-MÂCHÉ OVER STEEL RODS AND THREAD,
CONSTRUCTED, WRAPPED, AND PAINTED,
NECKLACE: PAINTED PAPIER-MÂCHÉ AND THREAD, FORMED, PAINTED, AND TIED
SCULPTURE: H. 31" × W. 24 ½" × D. 21"
NECKLACE: H. 26" × W. 14 ¼" × D. 4"
PHOTOS: GARY POLLMILLER

MARJORIE SCHICK: MAGIC AND SPIRIT

Paul Derrez

My first acquaintance with the work of Marjorie Schick was in 1982, during the selection for "Jewellery Redefined," an exhibition devoted to "multimedia, non-precious jewellery" organized by the British Crafts Centre in London. It represented the pinnacle of an alternative movement in jewelry which I, as the owner of the relatively new Gallery Ra, was enthusiastically promoting. The liberation of tradition and stereotype, which since the 1960s had brought about major changes in the political, social and cultural fields, also led to many new possibilities, to an explosion of energy and a sense of euphoria, in the world of jewelry design. While large costume-type jewelry had – occasionally – been made since the 1960s by, among others, Arline Fisch and Marjorie Schick in the US as well as Gijs Bakker and Emmy van Leersum in the Netherlands, the free and unlimited use of all kinds of materials created the real heyday of the "wearable object" in the early 1980s. These included the wallpaper brooches of Otto Künzli, the laminant necklaces of Gijs Bakker, the adornments of Lam de Wolf, the "hats" of Susanna Heron and the "frames" of Julia Manheim as well as the layered necklaces of David Watkins, the wearable collages of Pierre Degen and also my own pleated collar, inspired by the big lace collars in paintings by 17th-century Dutch masters. Whereas before these were often incidental pieces, possibly produced for theatrical purposes, in the first half of the 1980s wide-ranging thematic collections were designed. Photography became an important means to capture these jewelry designs on models or in special settings. The relocating of Gallery Ra in 1983 to a larger and more purpose-built space made it possible to present these developments to optimum effect.

The first solo exhibition of Marjorie Schick at Ra, in 1983, showed bracelets and necklaces made from wooden sticks, expressively and colorfully painted. Visitors to the gallery were overwhelmed by this explosion of form and color. Some responded skeptically to the work, others were wildly enthusiastic – and it was the latter group who also bought her pieces. The designs would hardly be worn, but were mainly given a place in the home as a visual statement.

Marjorie Schick became a regular exhibitor at Ra and her work continued to evolve and broaden. Over the years the open linear nature of her work shifted to become more compact and painterly. The use of thin wooden sticks made way for wooden surfaces, while papier-mâché led to organic, flowing forms. Later, works were created which consisted of a base for hanging them on a wall, which contained a piece of removable jewelry. All these developments could be followed at Ra in Marjorie's solo shows (1983, 1988, 1993, 1998) or in the gallery's five-yearly commemorative group shows (1986, 1991, 1996, 2001, 2006). It is exciting to see how Marjorie remains true to herself yet at the same time has a wonderful feel for specific themes. When I saw her chess game (cat. no. 445) in the Crafts Council Shop of London's Victoria and Albert Museum a few years ago, I was absolutely knocked out by it. The expressive power of the piece is staggering.

The fact that hardly any wearable objects are made by jewelry artists nowadays is further evidence of how independently Marjorie's body of work has evolved. And behind that spectacularly radical work is Marjorie the person – modest, friendly and amusing. A contrast that surprises all who get to know her. Often we try to plan our professional travels – for exhibitions or conferences – so that we're in a place at the same time. And when we do, it is always something special and good fun. Marjorie Schick is for me personally and professionally a warm-hearted and spiritual being.

447 TOOL BELT AND SCARF FOR SONIA DELAUNAY, 2003,
TOOL BELT: PAINTED WOOD, CORD, AND NICKEL SILVER,
CONSTRUCTED, PAINTED, AND TIED,
SCARF: PAINTED WOOD AND CORD, PAINTED AND TIED
TOOL BELT: H. 20" × W. 65" × 1 ¼"
SCARF: H. 45 ¾" × W. 5 ⅛" × D. ½"
PHOTOS: GARY POLLMILLER

446 POUR VOUS, TEAPOT WITH A BROOCH AS PART OF THE LID, 2003,
TEAPOT: PAINTED PAPIER-MÂCHÉ, WOOD, AND PLASTIC LAMINANT,
BROOCH: PAINTED WOOD, PLASTIC LAMINANT, AND STAINLESS STEEL WIRE,
TRAY: PAINTED WOOD AND PLASTIC LAMINANT,
THREE FORMS: CONSTRUCTED, GLUED, AND PAINTED
TEAPOT: H. 14" × W. 20 ½" × D. 6"
BROOCH: H. 4 ⅛" × W. 4 ⅛" × D. 2"
TRAY: H. 1 ½" × W. 18 ⅛" × D. 18 ⅛"
PHOTOS: GARY POLLMILLER

448 IN HENRI'S GARDEN, TWO NECKLACES AND WALL RELIEF, 2003,
WALL RELIEF: PAINTED PAPER ON WOOD, CONSTRUCTED AND PAPIER-MÂCHÉD WITH PAINTED PAPER,
FLOWER PETAL NECKLACE: PAINTED CANVAS, WOOD, PLASTIC LAMINANT, AND BRONZE RODS,
CONSTRUCTED, STITCHED, AND PAINTED,
SEED POD NECKLACE: PAINTED WOOD AND PLASTIC LAMINANT, CONSTRUCTED AND PAINTED
WALL RELIEF: H. 27 ¾" × W. 27 ½" × D. 9 ¼"
FLOWER PETAL NECKLACE: H. 31" × W. 30" × D. ⅝"
SEED POD NECKLACE: H. 15" × W. 15" × D. 2 ⅞"
PHOTOS: GARY POLLMILLER

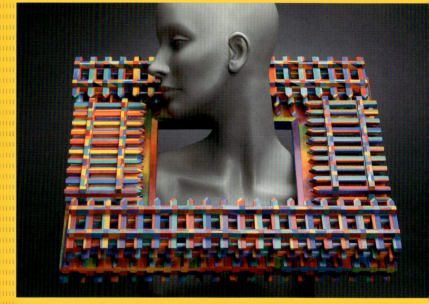

451 FENCES, NECKLACE, 2004,
PAINTED WOOD, CONSTRUCTED AND PAINTED
H. 18" × W. 18" × D. 3"
PHOTO: GARY POLLMILLER

452 RISER, ARMLET AND STAND, 2004,
PAINTED WOOD AND PLASTIC LAMINANT, CONSTRUCTED,
GLUED, AND PAINTED
ARMLET: H. 11 ¾" × W. 5 ⅞" × D. 4"
STAND: H. 4 ½" × W. 11 ¾" × D. 11 ¾"
PHOTOS: GARY POLLMILLER

450 CAROUSEL, NECKLACE, 2003,
PAINTED WOOD AND PLASTIC TOY ANIMALS,
CONSTRUCTED AND PAINTED
H. 5 ¾" × W. 22 ⅝" × D. 22 ⅝"
PHOTOS: GARY POLLMILLER

GROWING UP IS SOMETIMES DIFFICULT, ESPECIALLY WHEN, AS THE NEW KID IN THE SIXTH-GRADE CLASS, I WAS ESCORTED HOME AFTER SCHOOL BY THOSE "WISER AND BIGGER" WHO MEANT ONLY TO SCARE. MY FEAR WOULD CHANGE TO COMFORT WHEN I SAW THE PICKET FENCE AROUND OUR BACKYARD AND IS REPRESENTED BY THE "FENCES" NECKLACE. AS A YOUNGSTER OF SIX OR SEVEN, I MADE A DRAWING OF A FIGURE THAT I RECENTLY COPIED FOR THE "FROM CHILDHOOD" BROOCH ON A RELIEF. CITY LIGHTS, ESPECIALLY OF HIGH-RISE APARTMENT BUILDINGS, FASCINATED ME AS A TEENAGER AND INSPIRED "CHICAGO WINDOWS." WATCHING ROB GROW THROUGH A VARIETY OF CHILDHOOD EXPERIENCES IS CELEBRATED BY "CAROUSEL" NECKLACE.

454   THE PRAETORIAN GUARD, TEAPOTS WITH RINGS AND TRAY, 2004,
PAINTED WOOD AND PLASTIC LAMINANT, CONSTRUCTED, GLUED, AND PAINTED
TRAY: H. 2 ¾" × W. 19" × D. 19"
TEAPOTS: FROM H. 6" × W. 6 ½" × D. 3 ½" TO H. 6 ¼" × W. 7 ⅜" × D. 3 ⅞"
RINGS: FROM H. 3 ½" × W. 3 ½" × D. ⅝" TO H. 4" × W. 4" × D. ⅝"
PHOTOS: GARY POLLMILLER

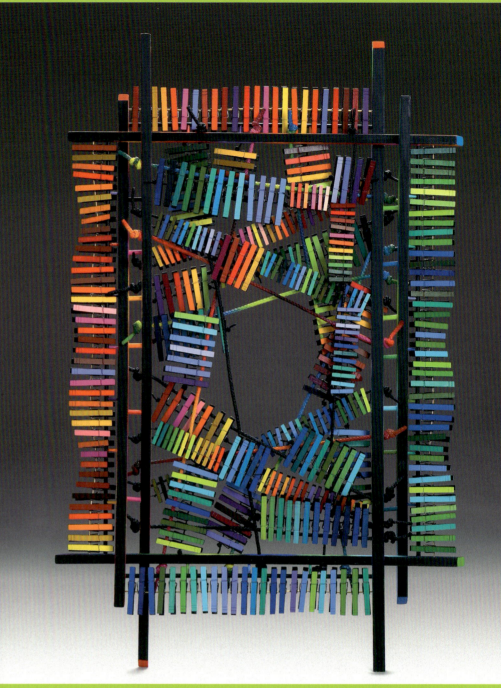

455 ODE TO CLOTHESPINS, SCULPTURE FOR THE NECK, 2004,
PAINTED WOOD, NYLON CORD, CLOTHESPINS, AND BRONZE RODS,
CONSTRUCTED, PAINTED, AND TIED
H. 44 ½" × W. 29 ⅜" × D. 4"
PHOTO: GARY POLLMILLER

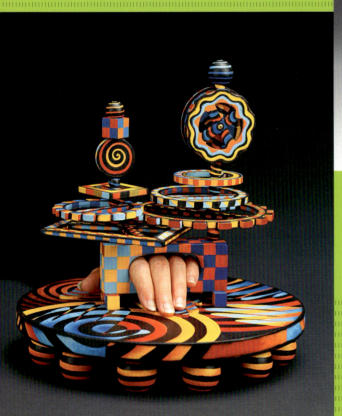

456 THE RING THAT GOT OUT OF HAND, HAND SCULPTURE AND
STAND, 2004,
HAND SCULPTURE: PAINTED WOOD, PLASTIC LAMINANT, AND
BRONZE RODS, STAND: PAINTED WOOD, CONSTRUCTED, GLUED,
PAINTED, AND RIVETED
HAND SCULPTURE: H. 9 ⅛" × W. 11 ¼" × D. 7 ½"
STAND: H. 2 ⅛" × W. 11 ⅝" × D. 11 ⅝"
PHOTO: GARY POLLMILLER

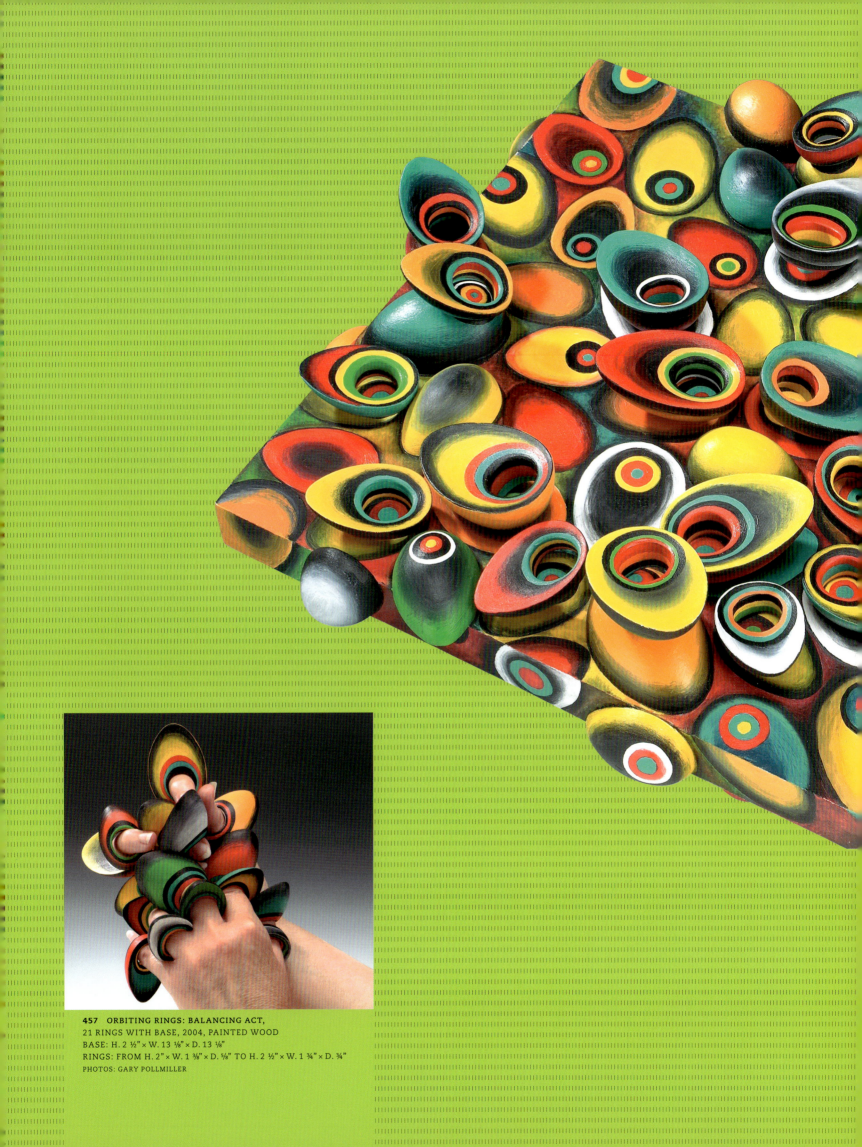

457 ORBITING RINGS: BALANCING ACT,
21 RINGS WITH BASE, 2004, PAINTED WOOD
BASE: H. 2 ½" × W. 13 ⅛" × D. 13 ⅛"
RINGS: FROM H. 2" × W. 1 ⅜" × D. ⅝" TO H. 2 ½" × W. 1 ¾" × D. ¾"
PHOTOS: GARY POLLMILLER

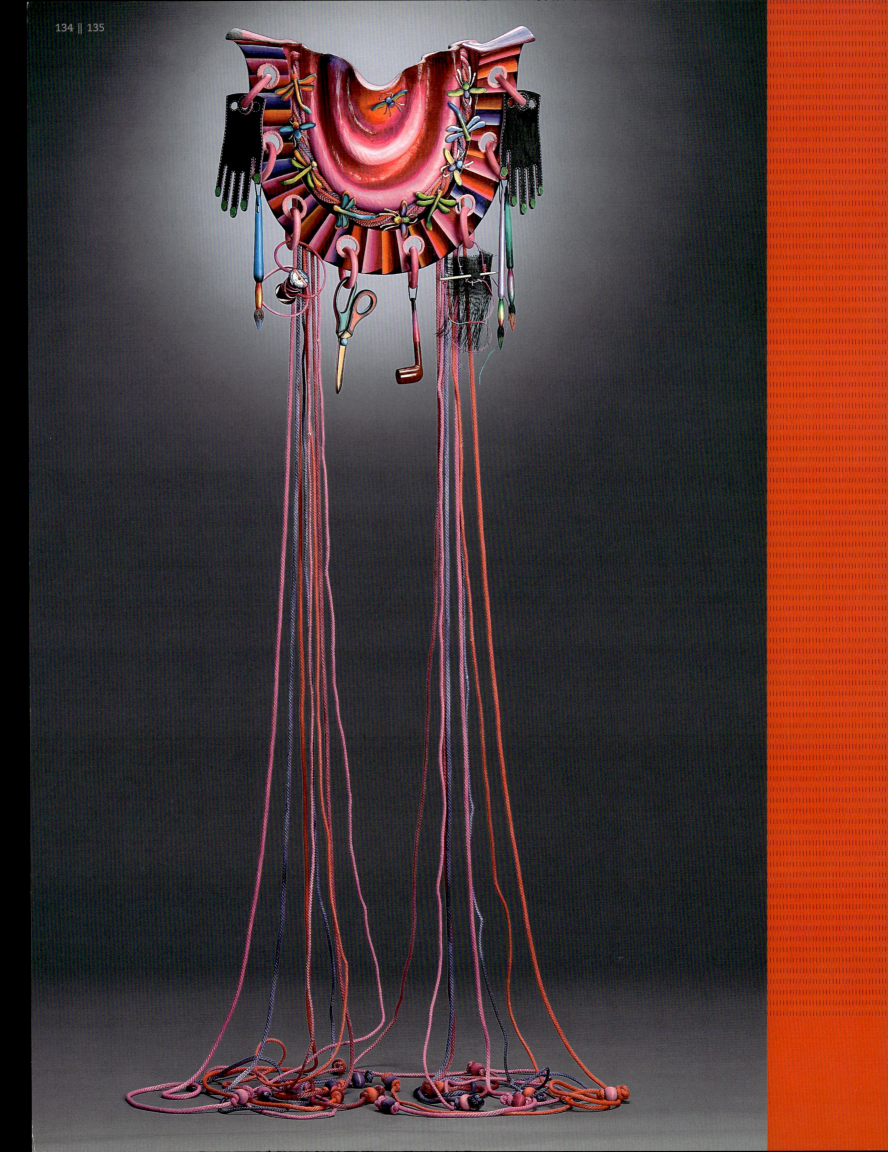

AN ADVENTUROUS SOUL

Helen Williams Drutt English

From Oskar Schlemmer's ballet costumes to the children's game of Pick Up Sticks, diverse images of colored rods of wood extend beyond the body. We witness curvatures of rubber counterpointed against the intricate constructions, and then a combustion of color that takes form in large, papier-mâché collars. All comprise images that bring one into the world of Marjorie Schick.

Can a series of intensely colored wood lines extend across the body or take off from the shoulder into the air and expand the concept of a brooch?

Can a hat constructed like a complex linear cage be worn at the Four Seasons or Brown's Hotel, in London, for tea? A chapeau as a rigid encasement of complex lines adorns the wearer, yet is ahead of its time.

Can a rubber hose encircle the neck and have its rigid semicircle bound together by the familiar miniature poles?

Can an adventurous soul hiding behind an aura of innocence find creative happiness in the Midwest? Can an intriguing mind surrounded by plains and wheat expand beyond its peer potential? Through the work, we know what lurks in the mind of Marjorie Schick.

What has happened to papier mâché is that the creative hand of Schick has expanded its potential into a form that embraces one, as if Elizabeth I reigns in the twenty-first century. The neck is hidden and one's head emerges from a well of color faceted into a volume that marks one's regal entrance into a new concept of adornment.

The *Liberty Torch* (cat. no. 395), of 1997, responded to the exhibition "Brooching It Diplomatically: A Tribute to Madeleine Albright," whose penchant for social jewelry symbols led her diplomatic pilgrimage throughout the world. Instead of the traditional American flag set with colored stones or the bold cast-gold eagle perched on a pearl, Marjorie designed a liberty torch for the late twentieth century; its robust form celebrates American history and, like the torches of cheerleaders, leads us toward an exuberant victory or lights the way to freedom.

A simple request was sent to artists: Create a commemorative medal that responds to an important historical event for the exhibition "Commemorative Medals: The Politics of History," 2000. No traditional tack or medallion from Marjorie! A trellis of states, one over another, designated with a shaped element that duplicates the configuration of a state and is strategically placed within the US continent, forms a double panel of attire entitled *Fifty States* (cat. no. 423). One wonders if this effort demanding meditative time would be possible in an East or West Coast studio, where the temptations of urban cultural seduction abound.

Drawn from a range of symbols and technical innovations that celebrate the work of Paris's former empress of fashion Elsa Schiaparelli, Schick compiled diverse elements with a shocking pink form for the exhibition "Challenging the Chatelaine!" (cat. no. 459). From every source that tantalized Elsa, Marjorie incorporated elements, including insects from the 1937–38 *Bug Necklace,* the pipe bottle from Shocking! perfume, as well as pleated edges reminiscent of her gown from 1936 and the 1950 costume for *Swan Lake* – a chatelaine! Multiple Schiaparelli objects – scissors, brushes, gloves stitched with attached fingernails—are applied to the elaborate shocking pink sash that is held up by long tendrils. They appear to be legs, but they are suspended like a reverse marionette.

Schick's research is exhaustive and detailed, a quality that is synonymous with her work. Within her cherubic countenance lives a labor-intensive creative soul whose contributions to the history of contemporary jewelry binds together America and Europe.

459 TRIBUTE TO ELSA SCHIAPARELLI, SASH-SHAPED CHÂTELAINE, 2005, PAINTED
PAPIER-MÂCHÉ, WOOD, FELT, LEATHER, NYLON CORD, PLASTIC, AND NICKEL WIRE,
FORMED, CONSTRUCTED, PAINTED, AND TIED
TOP PART OF CHÂTELAINE: H. 23" × W. 20 ½" × D. 4 ⅞"
WITH CORDS EXTENDED: 96" LONG
PHOTO: GARY POLLMILLER

458 **SELF-PORTRAIT,** BROOCH AND WALL RELIEF, BROOCH: 1996, RELIEF: 2004,
BROOCH: PAINTED PAPIER-MÂCHÉ, WOOD, AND STAINLESS STEEL WIRE,
FORMED, CONSTRUCTED, AND PAINTED,
RELIEF: PAINTED WOOD, CONSTRUCTED AND PAINTED
BROOCH: H. 6 ½" × W. 4 ¾" × D. 3 ¾"
RELIEF: H. 24" × W. 15 ⅝" × D. 3"
PHOTO: GARY POLLMILLER

460 GOLDEN DRAGON, ELBOW ARMLET AND STAND, 2005,
ARMLET: PAINTED PAPIER-MÂCHÉ,
STAND: PAINTED WOOD AND PLASTIC LAMINANT, CONSTRUCTED,
FORMED, GLUED, AND PAINTED
ARMLET: H. 5 ¼" × W. 9 ³⁄₁₆" × D. 8 ⅛"
STAND: H. 2" × W. 14 ⅛" × D. 12 ⅞"
PHOTO: GARY POLLMILLER

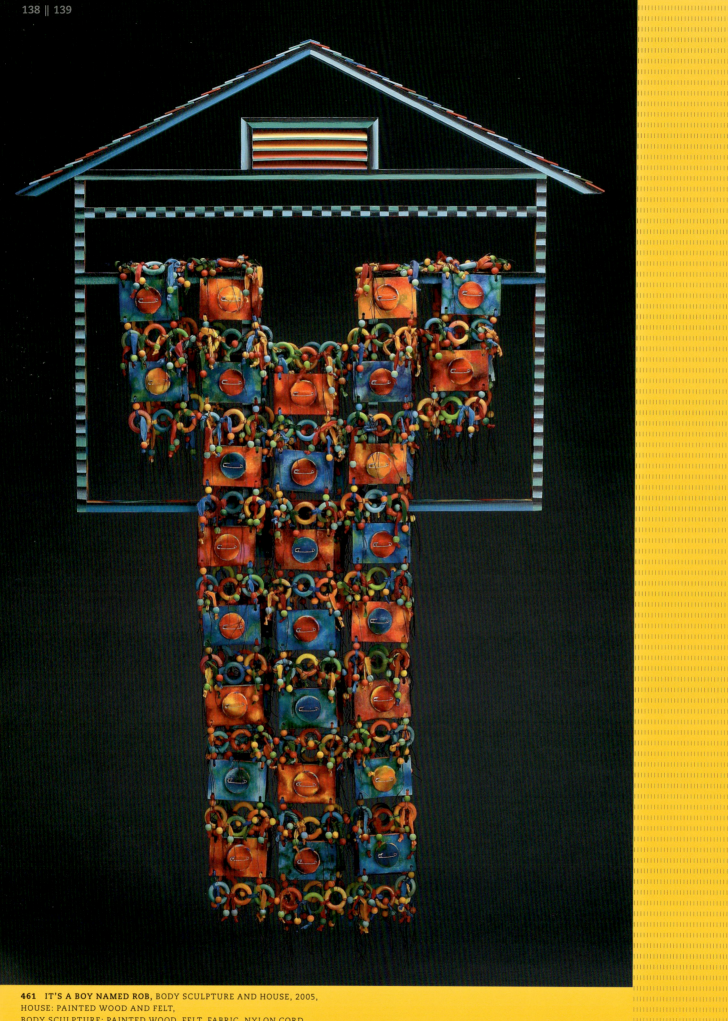

461 **IT'S A BOY NAMED ROB,** BODY SCULPTURE AND HOUSE, 2005,
HOUSE: PAINTED WOOD AND FELT,
BODY SCULPTURE: PAINTED WOOD, FELT, FABRIC, NYLON CORD,
AND SAFETY PINS, CONSTRUCTED, GLUED, PAINTED, AND TIED
HOUSE: H. 34 ⅞" × W. 45" × D. 1 ⅛"
BODY SCULPTURE: SHOULDERS TO BOTTOM, H. 49 ½" × W. 28 ½" × D. 1 ⅛"
PHOTO: GARY POLLMILLER

462 TEAPOT NECKLACE, 2005,
PAINTED WOOD, CONSTRUCTED AND PAINTED
H. 20 ⅝" × W. 23 ¾" × D. 6 ⅛"
PHOTO: GARY POLLMILLER

463 GRASS, NECKLACE, 2005,
PAINTED CANVAS AND WOOD, STITCHED, PAINTED, AND PEGGED
H. 22" × W. 22 ½" × D. 3 ¾"
PHOTOS: GARY POLLMILLER

464 SCHIAPARELLI'S CIRCLES, NECKLACE, 2005,
PAINTED WOOD, CANVAS, AND THREAD, STITCHED AND PAINTED
H. 30" × W. 30" × D. 1 ½"
WITH CORDS EXTENDED: 88" LONG
PHOTO: GARY POLLMILLER

467 SPIRALING DISCS, 32 NECK AND ARM RINGS, 2006,
PAINTED WOOD, CUT AND PAINTED
WHEN STACKED: H. 15 ½" × W. 12" × D. 12"
LARGEST RING: H. 12" × W. 12" × D. ½"
PHOTOS: GARY POLLMILLER

468 CONNECTIONS, BOOK NECKLACE (124 DOUBLE-SIDED PAGES) WITH STAND, NECKLACE STARTED IN 1999,
NECKLACE AND STAND: 2006, NECKLACE: PAINTED PAPIER-MÂCHÉ OVER SOLDERED RODS,
PAGES OF PAINTED AND STITCHED CANVAS AND OTHER FABRICS, VINYL, PLASTIC, ALUMINUM,
FOUND MATERIALS, AND THREAD, CONSTRUCTED, PAPIER-MÂCHÉD, STITCHED, AND PAINTED,
STAND: PAINTED WOOD, CONSTRUCTED AND PAINTED
NECKLACE: H. 20" × W. 20" × D. 10"
STAND: H. 10 ½" × W. 25" × D. 25"
PHOTO: GARY POLLMILLER

470 BANDS OF RINGS, 32 RINGS ON PEDESTALS, 2006,
RINGS: PAINTED WOOD,
PEDESTALS: PAINTED WOOD AND PLASTIC LAMINANT,
STANDS: PAINTED WOOD, CUT, CONSTRUCTED, GLUED, AND PAINTED
RINGS: FROM H. 1 ⅝" × W. 1 ⅝" × D. ¼" TO H. 3 ⅜" × W. 2 ⅛" × D. ¼"
RINGS ON PEDESTALS: FROM H. 3 ¾" × W. 2 ¼" × D. 1 ½" TO H. 8" × W. 2 ⅜" × D. 2 ⅜"
STANDS: H. 2 ⅜" × W. 26" × D. 26" AND H. 2 ¼" × W. 28" × D. 28"
PHOTOS: GARY POLLMILLER

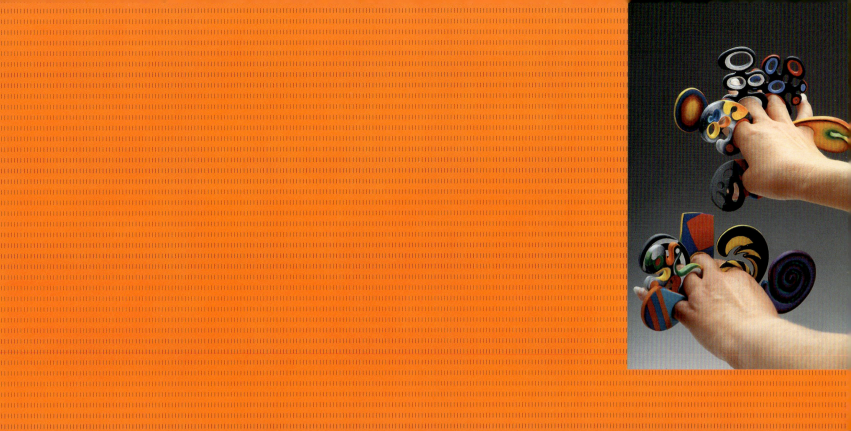

474 CHAGALL'S CIRCLES, NECKLACE, 2006,
PAINTED CANVAS, WOOD, AND THREAD, STITCHED, PAINTED, AND TIED
NECKLACE: H. 41" × W. 41" × D. 1"
WITH CORDS EXTENDED: 78" LONG
PHOTOS: GARY POLLMILLER

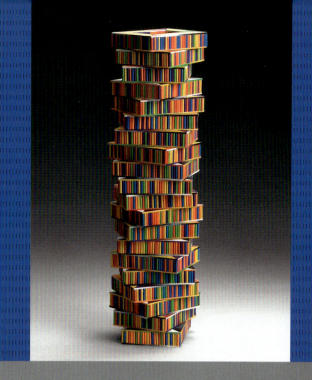

475 **MUCH ADO ABOUT TWENTY BRACELETS,** FOUR-PART FOLDING SCREEN WITH BRACELETS, 2006,
PAINTED WOOD, STEEL RODS, AND BRONZE RODS, CONSTRUCTED AND PAINTED
SCREEN WITH BRACELETS (TWO MIDDLE SECTIONS): H. 39 ⅝" × W. 49" × D. 1 ½"
SCREEN WITH BRACELETS (TWO END SECTIONS): H. 39 ⅝" × W. 46 ¼" × D. 1 ½"
WHEN EXTENDED, SCREEN IS 15 LINEAR FEET LONG
BRACELETS (EACH): H. 5" × W. 6" × D. 1 ⅜"
PHOTOS: GARY POLLMILLER

OEUVRE CATALOG

An asterisk after the title indicates that the
respective work is shown large-size in the
illustration section of the book, pages 20–145.
If no collection is listed, it means that the work
is in the possession of the artist.

001 BROOCH, 1961, STERLING SILVER,
PIERCED
H. 1 ⅜" × W. 1 ½" × D. ⅜"
PHOTO: GARY POLLMILLER

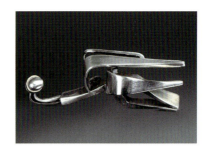

006 "BRAQUE" BIRD, BROOCH, 1963–4,
STERLING SILVER AND BRASS,
FORGED AND CONSTRUCTED
H. 1" × W. 2 ½" × D. ⅞"
PHOTO: GARY POLLMILLER

002 PENDANT, 1962, STERLING SILVER
WITH COLORED STONES IN RESIN,
CONSTRUCTED
H. 1 ⁵⁄₁₆" × W. 2 ⅛" × D. ¹⁄₁₆"
PHOTO: GARY POLLMILLER

007 RING, 1963, STERLING SILVER AND
COPPER, FORGED AND CONSTRUCTED
H. 1 ½" × W. ¹⁄₁₆" × D. ¾"
PHOTO: GARY POLLMILLER

003 RING WITH ALEXANDRITE, 1963,
STERLING SILVER WITH ALEXANDRITE,
FORGED AND CONSTRUCTED
H. 1 ½" × W. ⅞" × D. ⅝"
PHOTO: GARY POLLMILLER

008 COPPER PENDANT WITH CORALS,
1963, COPPER, STERLING SILVER, THREE
CORALS, AND CORD, CONSTRUCTED
PENDANT: H. 2 ½" × W. 1 ¾" × D. 1 ⅛"
PHOTO: GARY POLLMILLER

004 NECKLACE WITH BOX CLASP, 1963,
STERLING SILVER AND CORD,
CONSTRUCTED
H. 8 ¾" × W. 5" × D. ⅞"
PHOTO: GARY POLLMILLER

009 SMALL AND MIGHTY*, PIN, 1964,
BRASS, STERLING SILVER, AND IRON,
CONSTRUCTED
H. 2" × W. 2 ½" × D. 1 ½"
PHOTO: JOEL DEGEN

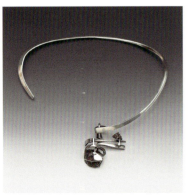

005 COLLAR, 1963, STERLING SILVER,
FORGED, CONSTRUCTED AND CAST
H. 5 ¾" × W. 6 ¾" × D. ⅝"
PHOTO: GARY POLLMILLER

010 FROM HOOK'S, NECKLACE, 1964,
BRASS AND IRON, CONSTRUCTED
H. 9" × W. 5 ⅛" × D. ⅞"
COLLECTION: BRENDA EUWER ADAMS, USA
PHOTO: GARY POLLMILLER

011 MANIPULATED SCREEN WIRE, NECKLACE, 1964, BRASS AND IRON, CONSTRUCTED
H. 8 ¾" × W. 6" × D. 1"
PHOTO: GARY POLLMILLER

016 IT MAKES SOUNDS, BROOCH WITH CLAPPER, 1965, STERLING SILVER, BRASS, AND BROWN STONE, FORGED AND CONSTRUCTED
H. 2 ½" × W. 1 ⅝" × D. 1 ½"
PHOTO: PETER R. LEIBERT

012 RING WITH CORAL, 1964, STERLING SILVER AND CORAL, CONSTRUCTED
H. 1 ⅝'' × W. 1 ⅛" × D. ⅞"
PHOTO: GARY POLLMILLER

017 REPOUSSED BROOCH WITH ALEXANDRITE, 1965, STERLING SILVER WITH ALEXANDRITE, REPOUSSED AND CONSTRUCTED
H. 2 ¾" × W. 1 ⅜" × D. 1 ⅛"
PHOTO: GARY POLLMILLER

013 FUSED AND TEXTURED, BROOCH, 1964, STERLING SILVER WITH SMOKEY TOPAZ
H. 2 ½" × W. 2" × D. ⅞"
PHOTO: GARY POLLMILLER

018 DRAWING IN METAL, ARMLET, 1965, BRASS AND STERLING SILVER, FORGED AND CONSTRUCTED
H. 3" × W. 3 ½" × D. 3"
PHOTO: GARY POLLMILLER

014 ALTERED COLOR, COLLAR WITH PENDANT, 1964, STERLING SILVER WITH TURQUOISE, FORGED AND CONSTRUCTED
H. 6 ¼" × W. 6 ⅜" × D. ⅞"
PHOTO: GARY POLLMILLER

019 BROOCH WITH OPEN BOX, 1965, STERLING SILVER AND COPPER, CONSTRUCTED AND FORGED
H. 2 ½" × W. 2 ¾" × D. 1 ⅛"
PHOTO: GARY POLLMILLER

015 FOR BETH, BROOCH, 1964, STERLING SILVER WITH "APACHE TEAR" STONE, FORGED AND CONSTRUCTED
H. 2 ⅜" × W. 1 ³⁄₁₆" × D. 1"
PHOTO: GARY POLLMILLER

020 PROTECTED AMETHYST, 1965, BRASS WITH AMETHYST, FORGED AND CONSTRUCTED
H. 4 ¼" × W. 3 ¾" × D. 2 ¹⁄₁₆"
PHOTO: GARY POLLMILLER

021 WITH TWO TOOTS, CONTAINER, 1964–5, COPPER, CONSTRUCTED AND FORGED
H. 5" × W. 3 ¾" × D. 3 ¾"
PHOTO: GARY POLLMILLER

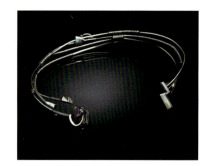

026 WRAPPED NECKLACE WITH A SLIDING ALEXANDRITE, 1966, STERLING SILVER WITH TWO ALEXANDRITES, WIRE WRAPPED AND CONSTRUCTED
H. 6 ⅛" × W. 7 ½" × D. ¾"
PHOTO: GARY POLLMILLER

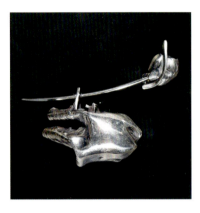

022 BROOCH WITH SEPARATE PIN, 1966, STERLING SILVER, REPOUSSED AND CONSTRUCTED
H. 3 ¾" × W. 1 ¾" × D. 1 ⅛"
COLLECTION: INDIANA UNIVERSITY ART MUSEUM, GIFT OF THE FINE ARTS JEWELRY DEPARTMENT, USA, 1986
PHOTO: PETER R. LEIBERT

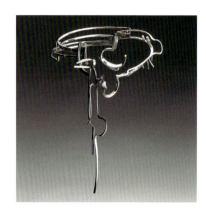

027 CONTINUOUS FORM, NECKLACE, 1966, STERLING SILVER, CONSTRUCTED AND FORGED
H. 11 ¼" × W. 7 ½" × D. 6 ½"
PHOTO: GARY POLLMILLER

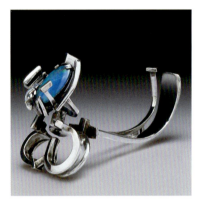

023 DOUBLE FINGER RING WITH BLACK OPAL*, 1966, STERLING SILVER WITH BLACK OPAL DOUBLET, CONSTRUCTED AND FORGED
H. 2 ½" × W. 4" × D. 2 ⅛"
PHOTO: JOEL DEGEN

028 FIRST FREE-FORM POT, 1966, BRASS, HAMMERED AND CONSTRUCTED
H. 10" × W. 7 ½" × D. 7 ⅞"
INCLUDED AS PART OF THE 1968 INDIANA UNIVERSITY EXPERIMENTAL METALSMITHING CARNEGIE GRANT PROJECT
PHOTO: GARY POLLMILLER

024 IT LOOKS LIKE A SCULPTURE, BROOCH, 1966, BRASS, FORGED AND CONSTRUCTED
H. 4 ⅜" × W. 1 ⅜" × D. 2 ⅛"
PHOTO: GARY POLLMILLER

029 FORGED SHOULDER SCULPTURE, 1966–7, STERLING SILVER, FORGED AND CONSTRUCTED
H. 6 ½" × W. 2 ⅞" × D. 3 ½"
PHOTO: GARY POLLMILLER

025 THREADS OF "SARAN" EXPERIMENT, NECKLACE, 1966, BRASS, IRON WIRE, AND SARAN THREADS, CONSTRUCTED, WRAPPED, AND KNOTTED
H. 11 ¼" × W. 5 ½" × D. 1 ¾"
PHOTO: GARY POLLMILLER

030 FOR ONE HAND, THREE FINGER SCULPTURES, 1967, BRASS, FORGED AND CONSTRUCTED
H. 4" × W. 3 ½" × D. 2 ¼"
H. 5" × W. 1 ⅝" × D. 2 ⅜"
H. 2 ½" × W. 1" × D. 1 ¾"
PHOTO: GARY POLLMILLER

031 PROJECTION, BROOCH, 1967,
BRASS, CONSTRUCTED
H. 2 ½" × W. 2 ½" × D. 2 ¼"
PHOTO: GARY POLLMILLER

036 ONE OF THE FIRST SIX, BRACELET,
1967, PAINTED PAPIER-MÂCHÉ, FORMED
AND PAINTED
H. 5 ¼" × W. 4 ½" × D. 2 ⅜"
PHOTO: GARY POLLMILLER

032 HAND SCULPTURE, 1967, STERLING
SILVER, REPOUSSED AND CONSTRUCTED
H. 5 ¼" × W. 3 ¼" × D. 1 ½"
PHOTO: GARY POLLMILLER

037 ONE OF THE FIRST SIX, BRACELET,
1967, PAINTED PAPIER-MÂCHÉ, FORMED
AND PAINTED
ESTIMATED: H. 4 ¼" × W. 5 ½" × D. 3"
COLLECTION: PAUL DERREZ AND
WILLEM HOOGSTEDE, THE NETHERLANDS
PHOTO: DR. JAMES B. M. SCHICK

033 FINGER SCULPTURE*, 1967,
STERLING SILVER, FORGED AND
CONSTRUCTED
H. 3 ⅝" × W. 4 ¼" × D. 1 ⅝"
PHOTO: JOEL DEGEN

038 ONE OF THE FIRST SIX, BRACELET,
1967, PAINTED PAPIER-MÂCHÉ, FORMED
AND PAINTED
H. 5 ½" × W. 5 ¼" × D. 2 ¾"
PHOTO: GARY POLLMILLER

034 TIGER PRINT EARRINGS*,
(FIRST PAPIER-MÂCHÉ JEWELRY), 1967,
PAINTED PAPIER-MÂCHÉ, FORMED
AND PAINTED
H. 3 ¾" × W. 1 ¾" × D. 1 ¾"
PHOTO: JOEL DEGEN

039 ONE OF THE FIRST SIX, BRACELET,
1967, PAINTED PAPIER-MÂCHÉ, FORMED
AND PAINTED
H. 3" × W. 7 ½" × D. 6 ½"
PHOTO: GARY POLLMILLER

**035 THE BEGINNING: THE FIRST
OF SIX,** BRACELET, 1967, PAINTED
PAPIER-MÂCHÉ (FIRST BRACELET),
FORMED AND PAINTED
H. 4 ¼" × W. 5 ¼" × D. 4 ½"
PHOTO: GARY POLLMILLER

040 ONE OF THE FIRST SIX, BRACELET,
1967, PAINTED PAPIER-MÂCHÉ, FORMED
AND PAINTED
H. 5" × W. 7" × D. 6 ⅜"
PHOTO: GARY POLLMILLER

041 RED AND GREEN PATTERNS,
NECK SCULPTURE, 1967, PAINTED
PAPIER-MÂCHÉ, FORMED AND PAINTED
H. 15" × W. 13" × D. 8 ¼"
PHOTO: GARY POLLMILLER

046 TEXTURED BRASS ARMLET*, 1967,
BRASS AND BRONZE, CONSTRUCTED
AND REPOUSSED
H. 5 ½" × W. 4 ½" × D. 4 ½"
INCLUDED AS PART OF THE 1968
INDIANA UNIVERSITY EXPERIMENTAL
METALSMITHING CARNEGIE GRANT
PROJECT
PHOTO: GARY POLLMILLER

042 PECTORAL, 1967, PAINTED PAPIER-
MÂCHÉ AND MONOFILAMENT, FORMED
AND PAINTED
H. 21" × W. 13" × D. 4 ¾"
PHOTO: GARY POLLMILLER

047 RING WITH AQUAMARINE, 1967,
STERLING SILVER WITH AQUAMARINE,
CONSTRUCTED
H. 2 ½" × W. 2 ½" × D. 1 ¾"
PHOTO: GARY POLLMILLER

043 OF THE TIMES, EARRINGS, 1967,
PAINTED PAPIER-MÂCHÉ, FORMED AND
PAINTED
H. 3 ½" × W. 2 ¼" × D. 1 ¼"
PHOTO: JOEL DEGEN

048 WHITE EDGES, ARMLET, 1967,
PAINTED PAPIER-MÂCHÉ, FORMED AND
PAINTED (RE-PAINTED IN 1985)
H. 7 ½" × W. 9 ½" × D. 6 ½"
PHOTO: GARY POLLMILLER

044 FOR JIM, NECKTIE (FIRST IN A
SERIES), 1967, PAINTED PAPIER-MÂCHÉ,
ELASTIC AND BRONZE, FORMED AND
PAINTED
H. 15" × W. 5" × D. 1 ¼"
COLLECTION: DR. JAMES B. M. SCHICK, USA
PHOTO: GARY POLLMILLER

049 TORSO SCULPTURE*, 1967,
PAINTED PAPIER-MÂCHÉ, FORMED AND
PAINTED
H. 20" × W. 14" × D. 11 ½"
PHOTO: GARY POLLMILLER

045 BELT WITH METAL POCKETS*,
1967, BRASS AND BRONZE, FORGED AND
CONSTRUCTED
H. 9 ½" × W. 17" × D. 14 ½"
LOST
PHOTO: GARY POLLMILLER

050 FIVE FINGERS ARMLET, 1967,
PAINTED PAPIER-MÂCHÉ, CONSTRUCTED
AND PAINTED
H. 7" × W. 15" × D. 9 ¾"
PHOTO: GARY POLLMILLER

051 STRIPED SHOULDER SCULPTURE*, 1967, PAINTED PAPIER-MÂCHÉ, FORMED AND PAINTED
H. 12 ½" × W. 24" × D. 20 ½"
PHOTO: GARY POLLMILLER

056 HELMET MASK*, 1968, PAINTED PAPIER-MÂCHÉ AND LEATHER, FORMED AND PAINTED
H. 26" × W. 16 ½" × D. 12 ½"
PHOTO: GARY POLLMILLER

052 BRACELET WITH THUMB PIECE, 1967–8, BRASS, FORGED AND CONSTRUCTED
H. 5" × W. 8" × D. 4 ¼"
PHOTO: GARY POLLMILLER

057 FOR THE FINGER OR THUMB, SCULPTURE, 1968, STERLING SILVER, FORGED AND CONSTRUCTED
ESTIMATED: H. 2 ½" × W. 2" × D. 2"
LOST
PHOTO: DR. JAMES B. M. SCHICK

053 RING WITH RUTILATED QUARTZ, 1968, STERLING SILVER WITH STONE CUT BY FRANCIS J. SPERISEN, CONSTRUCTED AND CAST
H. 1 ⅞" × W. 2 ½" × D. 1 ⅜"
PHOTO: GARY POLLMILLER

058 CHANGEABLE NECKTIE (METAL NECKTIE WITH PAPER INSERTS), 1968, BRONZE, ELASTIC, AND PAINTED PAPER, CONSTRUCTED AND PAINTED
H. 17 ½" × W. 4 ⅝" × D. 2 ½"
COLLECTION: DR. JAMES B. M. SCHICK, USA
PHOTO: GARY POLLMILLER

054 MODELED BEADS, 1968, PAINTED PAPIER-MÂCHÉ AND LEATHER, MODELED PAPIER-MÂCHÉ PULP
H. 4" × W. 21" × D. 1 ½"
PHOTO: GARY POLLMILLER

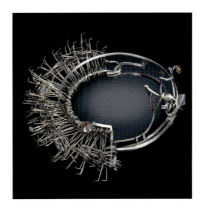

059 WHEATFIELDS*, NECKLACE, 1968, STERLING SILVER WITH TOPAZ STONES, CONSTRUCTED
H. 9 ½" × W. 9 ⅛" × D. 2 ¼"
(MADE IN A SIMILAR WAY TO ONE CREATED IN 1965 THAT IS IN THE COLLECTION OF THE INDIANA UNIVERSITY ART MUSEUM, GIFT OF THE FINE ARTS JEWELRY DEPARTMENT, USA, 1985)
PHOTO: GARY POLLMILLER

055 ANGULAR FINGER SCULPTURE, 1968, STERLING SILVER, CONSTRUCTED
H. 3" × W. 3 ⅝" × D. 1 ¾"
PHOTO: GARY POLLMILLER

060 ANGULAR SHOULDER SCULPTURE*, 1968, STERLING SILVER, CONSTRUCTED
BROOCH: H. 2 ½" × W. 6" × D. 4"
STICK PIN: H. 5" × W. 1 ½" × D. ¾"
PHOTO: GARY POLLMILLER

061   OPEN POT FORM*, 1968, STERLING SILVER, FORGED AND CONSTRUCTED ESTIMATED: H. 8 ½" × W. 8 ½" × D. 8" DONE AS PART OF THE 1968 INDIANA UNIVERSITY EXPERIMENTAL METAL-SMITHING CARNEGIE GRANT PROJECT COLLECTION: INDIANA UNIVERSITY ART MUSEUM, USA, 1969
PHOTO: LARRY LONG

066   LINEAR HELMET MASK, 1969, PAINTED PAPIER-MÂCHÉ OVER SOLDERED RODS, CONSTRUCTED AND PAINTED ESTIMATED: H. 18" × W. 16" × D. 16" PRIVATE COLLECTION
PHOTO: DR. JAMES B. M. SCHICK

062   FINGER SCULPTURE*, 1968, STERLING SILVER, CONSTRUCTED AND FORGED H. 2 ½" × W. 3 ⅝" × D. 1 ⅝"
PHOTO: GARY POLLMILLER

067   DRAWING TO WEAR: ORANGE, BLUE, AND GREEN*, 1969, PAINTED PAPIER-MÂCHÉ OVER SOLDERED RODS, CONSTRUCTED AND PAINTED H. 11 ½" × W. 26" × D. 23 ¼"
PHOTO: GARY POLLMILLER

063   RING WITH RUTILATED QUARTZ, 1968, STERLING SILVER WITH STONE CUT BY FRANCIS J. SPERISEN, CONSTRUCTED H. 2 ¾" × W. 3 ⅞" × D. 2"
PHOTO: GARY POLLMILLER

068   BLUE EYES*, HEAD SCULPTURE, 1969, BRASS, BRONZE, AND PLEXIGLAS, CONSTRUCTED AND FORGED H. 36 ¼" × W. 17 ¼" × D. 16"
PHOTO: GARY POLLMILLER

064   ORANGE, WHITE, AND BLUE ARMLET, 1968, PAINTED PAPIER-MÂCHÉ, FORMED AND PAINTED H. 14 ½" × W. 9 ½" × D. 8"
PHOTO: GARY POLLMILLER

069   ANGULAR NECKLACE, 1969, STERLING SILVER, CONSTRUCTED ESTIMATED: H. 11 ½" × W. 10" × D. 2 ½" PRIVATE COLLECTION
PHOTO: DR. JAMES B. M. SCHICK

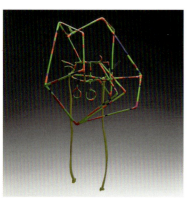

065   OPEN HEAD SCULPTURE*, 1968, PAINTED PAPIER-MÂCHÉ AND LEATHER, PAINTED PAPIER-MÂCHÉ OVER SOLDERED STEEL RODS H. 25" × W. 25 ½" × D. 16" WITH LEATHER STRAPS EXTENDED: 39 ½" LONG
PHOTO: GARY POLLMILLER

070   ARMLET: AFTER MY SCULPTURE, 1969, PAINTED PAPIER-MÂCHÉ, FORMED AND PAINTED ESTIMATED: H. 10" × W. 7 ⅞" × D. 8" COLLECTION: PAUL DERREZ AND WILLEM HOOGSTEDE, THE NETHERLANDS
PHOTO: DR. JAMES B. M. SCHICK

071 ARMLET WITH HOLE, 1969,
PAINTED PAPIER-MÂCHÉ, FORMED AND
PAINTED
H. 11" × W. 12" × D. 8"
PHOTO: GARY POLLMILLER

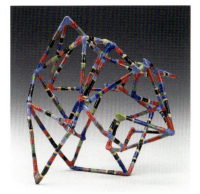

076 EIKERMAN'S ARMLET, 1970,
PAINTED PAPIER-MÂCHÉ OVER
SOLDERED STEEL RODS, CONSTRUCTED
AND PAINTED
H. 9" × W. 8 ¾" × D. 7 ½"
DONATED BY THE EIKERMAN FAMILY
IN HONOR OF ALMA EIKERMAN, USA
PHOTO: GARY POLLMILLER

072 PECTORAL*, 1968–9, BRASS
AND BRONZE, CONSTRUCTED
H. 25" × W. 17" × D. 17 ½"
LOST
PHOTO: GARY POLLMILLER

077 NECKTIE, 1970, PAINTED PAPIER-
MÂCHÉ, CONSTRUCTED AND PAINTED
ESTIMATED: H. 22" × W. 8" × D. 3"
PRIVATE COLLECTION, USA
PHOTO: DR. JAMES B. M. SCHICK

073 STRIPED RIBBON, ARMLET, 1970,
PAINTED PAPIER-MÂCHÉ, FORMED AND
PAINTED
H. 12" × W. 13" × D. 9 ½"
PHOTO: GARY POLLMILLER

078 LINEAR ARMLET, 1970, PAPIER-
MÂCHÉ OVER STEEL RODS, FORMED AND
PAINTED
H. 18" × W. 12" × D. 10"
PHOTO: GARY POLLMILLER

074 LAVENDER WATER, ARMLET, 1970,
PAINTED PAPIER-MÂCHÉ, FORMED AND
PAINTED
H. 11" × W. 14" × D. 9"
PHOTO: GARY POLLMILLER

079 IT BOUNCES, BROOCH, 1970,
BRASS WITH PAINTED RUBBER HOSE,
REPOUSSED, CONSTRUCTED, AND
PAINTED
H. 6" × W. 7" × D. 2 ⅝"
PHOTO: GARY POLLMILLER

075 FINGER SCULPTURE, 1970,
STERLING SILVER, CAST AND
CONSTRUCTED
H. 2 ¾" × W. 2 ⅛" × D. 1 ⅝"
PHOTO: GARY POLLMILLER

080 NECKLACE, 1970, PAINTED
PAPIER-MÂCHÉ AND LEATHER, FORMED,
PAINTED, AND TIED
H. 5 ¼" × W. 26" × D. 2 ¼"
PHOTO: GARY POLLMILLER

081 HELMET WITH PROPELLAR*, 1970, PAINTED PAPIER-MÂCHÉ AND WOOD, FORMED AND PAINTED
H. 14" × W. 14" × D. 7"
PHOTO: GARY POLLMILLER

086 FINGER SCULPTURE, 1971, STERLING SILVER, CONSTRUCTED
ESTIMATED: H. 3 ¼" × W. 2 ½" × D. 2"
LOST
PHOTO: MARJORIE SCHICK

082 DOTTED ARMLET, 1971, PAINTED PAPIER-MÂCHÉ, FORMED AND PAINTED
H. 9 ¼" × W. 8 ¾" × D. 5 ¾"
PHOTO: GARY POLLMILLER

087 COMPLIMENTARY CURVES, ARMLET, 1971, PAINTED PAPIER-MÂCHÉ, FORMED AND PAINTED
H. 11" × W. 10 ½" × D. 9 ¼"
PHOTO: GARY POLLMILLER

083 BRASS NECKTIE, 1971, BRASS, CONSTRUCTED
H. 20 ¾" × W. 8" × D. 3 ¾"
PHOTO: GARY POLLMILLER

088 PARALLEL MOVEMENT*, PAIR OF ARMLETS, 1971, PAINTED PAPIER-MÂCHÉ, FORMED AND PAINTED
H. 11 ½" × W. 12" × D. 10"
H. 11" × W. 11" × D. 9 ½"
PHOTO: GARY POLLMILLER

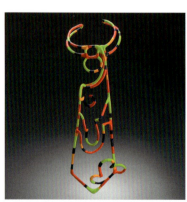

084 LINEAR NECKTIE WITH RED, 1971, PAINTED PAPIER-MÂCHÉ, PAINTED PAPIER-MÂCHÉ OVER SOLDERED STEEL RODS
H. 22 ¼" × W. 8 ½" × D. 6"
PHOTO: GARY POLLMILLER

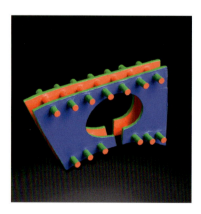

089 TWO LAYER BRACELET, 1972, PAINTED CARDBOARD AND WOOD DOWELS, CUT, DRILLED, AND PAINTED
H. 4" × W. 6 ½" × D. 2 ⅜"
PHOTO: GARY POLLMILLER

085 LINEAR NECKTIE WITH PURPLE, 1971, PAINTED PAPIER-MÂCHÉ, PAPIER-MÂCHÉ OVER SOLDERED STEEL RODS
H. 20 ½" × W. 8" × D. 5 ½"
PHOTO: GARY POLLMILLER

090 ORANGE AND BLUE SCULPTURE, 1972, PAINTED PAPIER-MÂCHÉ, FORMED AND PAINTED
H. 12 ¾" × 11 ½" × 18"
PHOTO: GARY POLLMILLER

091 FINGER SCULPTURE*, 1972,
STERLING SILVER, CONSTRUCTED
H. 6 ½" × W. 5" × D. ¼"
PHOTO: GARY POLLMILLER

096 EIKERMAN'S FIVE LAYER
BRACELET, 1973, PAINTED CARDBOARD
AND WOOD DOWELS, CUT, DRILLED,
AND PEGGED
H. 5" × W. 6 ½" × D. 3 ¾"
DONATED BY THE EIKERMAN FAMILY
IN HONOR OF ALMA EIKERMAN, USA
PHOTO: GARY POLLMILLER

092 CONTAINER FOR LONG PRETZELS,
1972, PAINTED PAPIER-MÂCIIÉ, FORMED
AND PAINTED
H. 9 ⅞" × W. 11" × D. 8 ¾"
PHOTO: GARY POLLMILLER

097 SUNRISE, NECKLACE, 1973,
PAINTED CARDBOARD AND LEATHER,
CUT, GLUED, PAINTED, AND TIED
H. 15" × W. 10 ½" × D. 2"
PHOTO: GARY POLLMILLER

093 THE CAGE*, BODY SCULPTURE,
1972, PAINTED PAPIER-MÂCHÉ, PAINTED
PAPIER-MÂCHÉ OVER SOLDERED STEEL
RODS
H. 46 ½" × W. 27" × D. 34"
PHOTO: GARY POLLMILLER

098 ARCHES, ARMLET, 1972–3, PAINTED
PAPIER-MÂCHÉ, FORMED AND PAINTED
H. 13" × W. 17" × D. 6"
PHOTO: GARY POLLMILLER

094 DOUBLE FINGER SCULPTURE, 1973,
STERLING SILVER, CONSTRUCTED
H. 2 ¼" × W. 5 ⅛" × D. 1 ½"
PHOTO: GARY POLLMILLER

099 YELLOW RAINBOW, ARMLET, 1973,
PAINTED PAPIER-MÂCHÉ, FORMED AND
PAINTED
H. 12" × W. 10 ½" × D. 11"
PHOTO: GARY POLLMILLER

095 2 AM NECKLACE, 1973, PAPER,
STRING, CRAYON, AND PAINT, DRAWN,
COLORED, PAINTED, AND KNOTTED
H. 30 ½" × W. 19 ½" × D. ¼"
PHOTO: GARY POLLMILLER

100 SHAVINGS, BUCKLE, 1973,
STERLING SILVER, CAST AND
CONSTRUCTED
H. 2 ½" × W. 3" × D. 1 ½"
PHOTO: GARY POLLMILLER

101 COPPER CONTAINER WITH RUBBER HOSES, 1973, COPPER AND RUBBER, CONSTRUCTED
H. 16" × W. 13" × D. 7 ½"
PHOTO: GARY POLLMILLER

106 GREEN DOT*, NECKTIE, 1974, CARDBOARD, WOOD DOWELS, AND LEATHER, CUT, PEGGED, AND TIED
H. 18" × W. 6 ½" × D. 2"
PHOTO: GARY POLLMILLER

102 BOWL FOR CHEESE PUFFS, 1973, PAINTED PAPIER-MÂCHÉ, FORMED AND PAINTED
H. 14" × W. 22" × D. 15"
PHOTO: GARY POLLMILLER

107 TUBES, BODY SCULPTURE, 1974, PAINTED NEWSPAPER, STEEL RODS, AND FELT, SCRUNCHED, STITCHED, SOLDERED, AND PAINTED
H. 60" × W. 25" × D. 21"
PHOTO: DR. JAMES B. M. SCHICK

103 TWO-FINGER RING WITH TOPAZ, 1974, STERLING SILVER WITH TOPAZ, CONSTRUCTED
H. 2 ¼" × W. 2 ½" × D. 2"
PRIVATE COLLECTION, USA
PHOTO: LARRY LONG

108 ROLL IT, NECKLACE, 1974, NEWSPAPER AND STRING, ROLLED, GLUED, WOVEN, AND TIED
H. 20" × W. 8" × D. ½"
PHOTO: GARY POLLMILLER

104 CLOUDS, NECKLACE, 1974, PAINTED CARDBOARD AND LEATHER, CUT, PAINTED, AND TIED
H. 17" × W. 14" × D. ½"
PHOTO: GARY POLLMILLER

109 FLEXIBLE BREAST PLATE, 1975, ROLLED PAPER, STRING AND PLASTIC COATED WIRE, WOVEN, ROLLED AND GLUED PAPER, KNOTTED
H. 33" × W. 17" × D. ½"
PHOTO: GARY POLLMILLER

105 STICKS AND BALLS, NECKLACE, 1974, PAINTED PING-PONG BALLS, WOOD, AND BRONZE, CONSTRUCTED AND PAINTED
H. 13 ½" × W. 14 ¾" × D. 2 ½"
PHOTO: GARY POLLMILLER

110 MOTHER'S ARMLET, 1975, NICKEL SILVER, PIERCED
H. 5 ½" × W. 2 ¼" × D. 2 ½"
PHOTO: GARY POLLMILLER

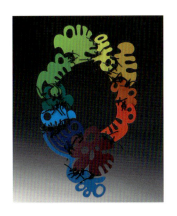

111 FULL OF HOLES, NECKLACE, 1975, PAINTED CARDBOARD AND LEATHER, CUT, PAINTED, AND TIED
H. 24" × W. 18" × D. ½"
PHOTO: GARY POLLMILLER

116 SLATS BODY SCULPTURE, 1975, PAINTED CARDBOARD, WOOD, AND PLASTIC COATED WIRE, CUT, PAINTED, AND ASSEMBLED
H. 36" × ESTIMATED: W. 24"
PHOTO: GARY POLLMILLER

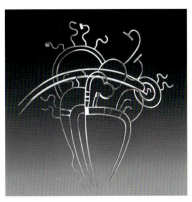

112 HAIR COMB*, 1975, STERLING SILVER, CONSTRUCTED
H. 10 ¾" × W. 6 ½" × D. 1"
PHOTO: GARY POLLMILLER

117 BRASS PECTORAL, 1975, BRASS AND FEATHERS, REPOUSSED, COILED, AND ASSEMBLED
H. 35" × W. 17" × D. 5"
PHOTO: GARY POLLMILLER

113 BRACELET, 1975, STERLING SILVER, CONSTRUCTED
H. 4 ⅜" × W. 5 ¼" × D. 4 ⅜"
PHOTO: GARY POLLMILLER

118 "BLACK, WHITE, AND READ ALL OVER,"* PONCHO, 1975, NEWSPAPER AND COTTON STRING, LOOM WOVEN AND TIED
ONE-HALF OF TOTAL LENGTH:
H. 62" × W. 27"
PHOTO: GARY POLLMILLER

114 FINGER SCULPTURE, 1975, STERLING SILVER, CONSTRUCTED
H. 4 ¾" × W. 4" × D. 2"
PHOTO: GARY POLLMILLER

119 BRASS NECKLACE*, 1976, BRASS, CONSTRUCTED
H. 16" × W. 11" × D. 2 ½"
PHOTO: GARY POLLMILLER

115 SLATS NECKLACE, 1975, CARDBOARD, WOOD DOWELS, AND COPPER, CUT AND ASSEMBLED
H. 17" × W. 17 ½" × D. 1 ⅝"
PHOTO: GARY POLLMILLER

120 SILVER RING WITH RESIN, 1976, STERLING SILVER AND RESIN, CONSTRUCTED
H. 2 ⅛" × W. 1 ⅞" × D. 1 ¾"
PHOTO: GARY POLLMILLER

121 FINGER SCULPTURE, 1976, STERLING SILVER, CONSTRUCTED
COLLECTION: MUSEUM OF FINE ARTS, BOSTON, THE DAPHNE FARAGO COLLECTION
H. 3 ½" × W. 2 ½" × D. 3"
PHOTO: GARY POLLMILLER

126 BRASS BOWL, 1978, BRASS, FORGED AND CONSTRUCTED
H. 7 ¾" × W. 4 ¼" × D. 2"
PHOTO: GARY POLLMILLER

122 FOR THE PAGEANT, MASK AND BODY PIECE, 1977, STRING AND ROLLED PAPER, WOVEN, TIED, AND PAINTED WITH ROLLED PAPER
BODY PIECE – SHOULDER TO BOTTOM:
H. 61" × W. 15" × D. 2"
MASK – TOP OF HEAD TO BOTTOM:
H. 57" × W. 14" × D. 2"
PHOTO: GARY POLLMILLER

127 FOR THE ASHTRAY SHOW, CONTAINER, 1978, BRASS, CONSTRUCTED
H. 5 ¼" × W. 8 ¾" × D. 8 ¼"
PHOTO: GARY POLLMILLER

123 PIERCED BUCKLE, 1977, BRASS, PIERCED AND CONSTRUCTED
H. 2 ½" × W. 4 ⁵⁄₁₆" × D. ½"
COLLECTION: DR. JAMES B. M. SCHICK, USA
PHOTO: GARY POLLMILLER

128 THE FORERUNNER, RING, 1978, PAINTED CARDBOARD AND WOOD DOWELS, CONSTRUCTED
ESTIMATED: H. 3" × W. 3" × D. 1 ½"
COLLECTION: THE SECOND NATIONAL RING SHOW, THE UNIVERSITY OF GEORGIA, ATHENS, USA
PHOTO: MARJORIE SCHICK

124 MOPPED: GREEN, BODY SCULPTURE, 1977, STRING AND RE-ASSEMBLED MOP, LOOM WOVEN, RYA KNOTTED
ESTIMATED: H. 60" × W. 26" × D. 21"
PHOTO: GARY POLLMILLER

129 THE CONCEALER*, MASK, 1978, STRING AND PAPER-COATED WIRE, LOOM WOVEN AND RYA KNOTTED
H. 16" × W. 14 ½" × D. 11"
PHOTO: GARY POLLMILLER

125 MOPPED: BEIGE*, BODY SCULPTURE, 1977, STRING AND REASSEMBLED MOP, LOOM WOVEN, RYA KNOTTED, AND DYED
ESTIMATED: H. 55" × W. 32" × D. 24"
PHOTO: GARY POLLMILLER

130 HOLES AND DOTS, NECKLACE, 1978, COPPER, CONSTRUCTED
H. 10" × W. 9 ¾" × D. 2"
PHOTO: GARY POLLMILLER

131 MORE HOLES, NECKLACE, 1978, PAINTED COPPER, STONEWARE, AND THREAD WRAPPED CORD, CONSTRUCTED AND PAINTED
H. 12 ½" × W. 9 ½" × D. 1"
PHOTO: GARY POLLMILLER

136 PAIR OF ARMLETS, 1979, BRASS, PIERCED
H. 5 ⅛" × W. 3 ⅝" × D. 3 ⅜"
H. 5 ⅛" × W. 3 ½" × D. 3"
PHOTO: GARY POLLMILLER

132 STRIPED BEADS, NECKLACE, 1978, PORCELAIN AND LEATHER, FORMED AND TIED
H. 14" × W. 13" × D. 1 ¼"
PHOTO: GARY POLLMILLER

137 PAIR OF ARMLETS, 1979, STERLING SILVER, PIERCED
H. 5" × W. 3 ½" × D. 2 ¾"
H. 5" × W. 3 ½" × D. 2 ¾"
PHOTO: GARY POLLMILLER

133 ALL TOGETHER NOW, NECKLACE, 1978, PORCELAIN, COPPER, THREAD, AND CORD, FORMED, WRAPPED, KNOTTED, AND ASSEMBLED
H. 11 ¼" × W. 9 ½" × D. 1 ½"
PHOTO: GARY POLLMILLER

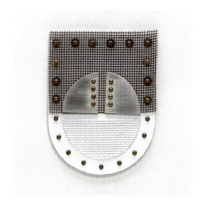

138 TRIPTYCH, 1979, PAPER, BRASS, AND NICKEL, EMBOSSED, PIERCED, CUT, AND BOLTED
EACH SECTION: H. 12 ¼" × W. 10 ½" × D. ⅞"
PHOTO: GARY POLLMILLER

134 WHAT I THREW AWAY MATTERS MOST, NECKLACE, 1978, STONEWARE, BRASS, THREAD, AND CORD, FORMED, WRAPPED, KNOTTED, AND ASSEMBLED
H. 13 ¾" × W. 10" × D. 1 ⅝"
PHOTO: GARY POLLMILLER

139 HAMMERED AND BURNISHED, NECKLACE, 1979, STONEWARE, COPPER, AND CORD, FORMED, BURNISHED, HAMMERED, DYED, AND TIED
H. 15 ¼" × W. 7" × D. 2 ⅝"
PHOTO: GARY POLLMILLER

135 ONE ANGLE BRACELET, 1979, BRASS, CONSTRUCTED
H. 2 ⅞" × W. 4" × D. 3 ½"
PHOTO: GARY POLLMILLER

140 CHECKED, NOT SQUARED, NECKLACE, 1979, STONEWARE, SHOELACES, AND COPPER, FORMED, STAMPED, AND TIED
H. 16 ¼" × W. 16 ½" × D. ½"
PHOTO: GARY POLLMILLER

141 UP AND AROUND, BRACELET, 1980,
COPPER AND NICKEL, CONSTRUCTED
H. 3 ¾" × W. 4 ¼" × D. 4 ½"
PHOTO: MALCOLM TURNER

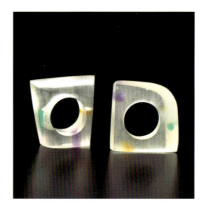

146 PAIR OF RINGS, 1980,
PLASTIC, CAST
H. 1 ¼" × W. 1 ¼" × D. ⁷⁄₁₆"
H. 1 ¼" × W. 1 ³⁄₁₆" × D. ⁵⁄₁₆"
PHOTO: GARY POLLMILLER

142 IT COILS, NECKLACE, 1980,
COPPER, CONSTRUCTED
H. 14 ¾" × W. 13" × D. 2 ¾"
PHOTO: GARY POLLMILLER

147 ARMLET/SCULPTURE, 1981, BRASS
AND COPPER, CONSTRUCTED
H. 7 ½" × W. 6 ½" × D. 2"
PHOTO: GARY POLLMILLER

143 THE COMBO, NECKLACE, 1980,
STONEWARE, THREAD, ROPE, AND
BRASS, FORMED, CONSTRUCTED,
WRAPPED, AND TIED
H. 17 ½" × W. 14 ½" × D. 2"
PHOTO: GARY POLLMILLER

148 STUDY IN VISUAL TENSIONS,
BROOCH #1, 1981, COPPER AND NICKEL,
ETCHED AND CONSTRUCTED
H. 2 ½" × W. 5 ¼" × D. 1 ¼"
PHOTO: GARY POLLMILLER

144 WITH A FOUND ETCHED PLATE,
ARMLET, 1980, COPPER, ETCHED AND
CONSTRUCTED
H. 3 ½" × W. 7" × D. 6 ⅞"
PHOTO: GARY POLLMILLER

149 STUDY IN VISUAL TENSIONS,
BROOCH #2, 1981, COPPER AND NICKEL,
ETCHED AND CONSTRUCTED
H. 3" × W. 3 ⅞" × D. 1"
PHOTO: GARY POLLMILLER

145 SUMMER EXPERIMENT*,
NECKLACE, 1980, PLASTIC, CAST AND
CONSTRUCTED
H. 15 ¼" × W. 18 ½" × D. 1 ¼"
COLLECTION: DR. JAMES B. M. SCHICK,
USA
PHOTO: GARY POLLMILLER

150 THE FAN BROOCH, 1981, STERLING
SILVER AND NICKEL, CONSTRUCTED
H. 5" × W. 5 ½" × D. ⅞"
PHOTO: GARY POLLMILLER

151 STANDING BROOCH, 1981,
STERLING SILVER, CONSTRUCTED
H. 2 ½" × W. 4 ⅝" × D. 1 ¼"
PHOTO: GARY POLLMILLER

156 PATTERNED METAL, BROOCH,
1982, NICKEL SILVER AND BRASS,
CONSTRUCTED
H. 6 ¾" × W. 4 ¾" × D. 1 ¼"
PHOTO: GARY POLLMILLER

152 FIBULA, 1981, COPPER, FORGED
H. 2 ½" × W. 4" × D. 1"
COLLECTION: DR. JAMES B. M. SCHICK,
USA
PHOTO: GARY POLLMILLER

157 TURNED ON BY FIBULAS, 1982,
COPPER AND BRASS, FORGED AND
CONSTRUCTED
LEFT TO RIGHT:
H. 4" × W. 3 ½" × D. 1"
H. 5" × W. 4" × D. 1 ½"
H. 4" × W. 4 ½" × D. 1 ½"
H. 3 ½" × W. 3 ½" × D. 1 ¼"
PHOTO: GARY POLLMILLER

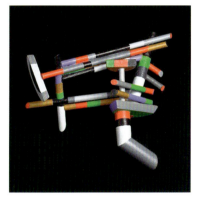

**153 BROOCH #1 (FIRST DOWEL
BROOCH),** 1981, PAINTED WOOD
DOWELS, PEGGED, RIVETED, AND
PAINTED
H. 5" × W. 4 ¾" × D. 1 ¾"
COLLECTION: DR. JAMES B. M. SCHICK,
USA
PHOTO: GARY POLLMILLER

158 PAPER AND WIRE BROOCH, 1982,
PAPER AND WIRE, PIERCED, THREADED,
GLUED
H. 2 ¾" × W. 1 ⅞" × D. ¼"
PHOTO: JAMES MUELLER

**154 SCULPTURAL CONTAINER
FOR SOAP,** 1982, COPPER AND NICKEL,
FORMED AND CONSTRUCTED
H. 8" × W. 7" × D. 4"
COLLECTION: KOHLER COMPANY
ARCHIVES COLLECTION, KOHLER,
WISCONSIN, USA
PHOTO: DR. JAMES B. M. SCHICK

159 ANGLED PLAY, BROOCH, 1982–83,
BRASS AND NICKEL SILVER,
CONSTRUCTED
H. 5 ¼" × W. 6 ⅜" × D. 1"
PHOTO: GARY POLLMILLER

155 HAVING TO DO WITH BONES,
NECKLACE, 1982, STERLING SILVER AND
BONE, CONSTRUCTED AND CAST
H. 8 ⅝" × W. 8 ⅞" × D. 2 ¼"
PHOTO: GARY POLLMILLER

160 THREE NECKLACES, 1982, PAPER,
STERLING SILVER, AND METALLIC
THREAD, CUT, PIERCED AND THREADED
EACH: H. 10 ½" × W. 5 ½"
PHOTO: GARY POLLMILLER

161 BROOCH, 1982, COPPER, NICKEL, CONSTRUCTED AND ETCHED
H. 4 ¼" × W. 5 ½" × D. 1"
PHOTO: GARY POLLMILLER

166 DOWEL NECKLACE #3, 1982, PAINTED WOOD, RIVETED AND PAINTED
ESTIMATED: H. 28" × W. 21" × D. 15"
COLLECTION: PAUL DERREZ AND WILLEM HOOGSTEDE, THE NETHERLANDS
PHOTO: DR. JAMES B. M. SCHICK

162 DOWEL BROOCH, 1982, PAINTED WOOD WITH NICKEL PIN STEM, RIVETED AND PAINTED
H. 5 ½" × W. 5 ¾" × D. 2"
PHOTO: GARY POLLMILLER

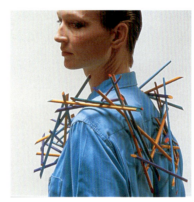

167 DOWEL NECKLACE # 4*, 1982, PAINTED WOOD, RIVETED AND PAINTED
ESTIMATED: H. 13" × W. 16" × D. 14"
PRIVATE COLLECTION, UK
PHOTO: HOGERS VERSLUYS, COURTESY GALERIE RA, AMSTERDAM

163 DOWEL NECKLACE #1*, 1982, PAINTED WOOD, RIVETED AND PAINTED
H. 19" × W. 19" × D. 9"
COLLECTION: MIDDLESBROUGH INSTITUTE OF MODERN ART, MIDDLESBROUGH, UK
PHOTO: HOGERS VERSLUYS, COURTESY GALERIE RA, AMSTERDAM

168 BROOCH*, 1982, PAINTED WOOD WITH NICKEL PIN STEM, RIVETED AND PAINTED
H. 5" × W. 5" × D. 1 ½"
PRIVATE COLLECTION
PHOTO: HOGERS VERSLUYS, COURTESY GALERIE RA, AMSTERDAM

164 DOWEL NECKLACE #2, 1982, PAINTED WOOD, RIVETED AND PAINTED
H. 30" × W. 17" × D. 11 ½"
PRIVATE COLLECTION, UK
PHOTO: DR. JAMES B. M. SCHICK

169 BROOCH, 1982, PAINTED WOOD WITH NICKEL PIN STEM, RIVETED AND PAINTED
H. 8 ½" × W. 6 ⅞" × D. 1 ⅛"
COLLECTION: MUSEUM OF FINE ARTS, HOUSTON, HELEN WILLIAMS DRUTT ENGLISH COLLECTION, GIFT OF THE MORGAN FOUNDATION IN HONOR OF CATHERINE ASHER MORGAN
PHOTO: TOM DUBROCK

165 GALERIE RA POSTER*, 1983
PHOTO: HOGERS VERSLUYS, COURTESY GALERIE RA, AMSTERDAM

170 BROOCH*, 1982, PAINTED WOOD WITH NICKEL PIN STEM, RIVETED AND PAINTED
H. 5" × W. 5" × D. 1 ½"
PRIVATE COLLECTION
PHOTO: HOGERS VERSLUYS, COURTESY GALERIE RA, AMSTERDAM

171 BRACELET, 1982, PAINTED WOOD,
RIVETED AND PAINTED
H. 8" × W. 7" × D. 1 ½"
PRIVATE COLLECTION
PHOTO: JOEL DEGEN

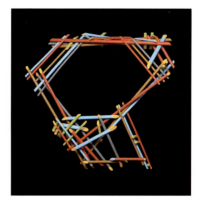

176 NECK PIECE, 1983, PAINTED WOOD,
RIVETED AND PAINTED
H. 14 ¾" × W. 15" × D. 4 ½"
COLLECTION: MUSEUM OF FINE ARTS,
HOUSTON, HELEN WILLIAMS DRUTT
ENGLISH COLLECTION, GIFT OF THE
MORGAN FOUNDATION IN HONOR OF
CATHERINE ASHER MORGAN
PHOTO: JOEL DEGEN

172 DECANTER, 1983, STERLING
SILVER, CONSTRUCTED
H. 9" × W. 4 ½" × D. 3 ¾"
PHOTO: GARY POLLMILLER

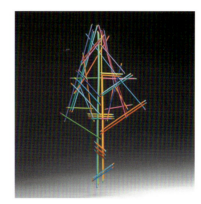

177 MASK, 1983, PAINTED WOOD,
RIVETED AND PAINTED
H. 30 ¼" × W. 17" × D. 12 ½"
PHOTO: GARY POLLMILLER

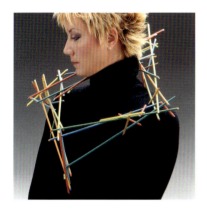

173 CELEBRATION*, NECKLACE, 1983,
PAINTED WOOD, RIVETED AND PAINTED
H. 23 ½" × W.19 ½" × D. 6"
PHOTO: GARY POLLMILLER

178 EXTENDED BROOCH*, 1983,
PAINTED WOOD AND NICKEL WIRE,
RIVETED AND PAINTED
H. 18" × W. 5 ¾" × D. 2"
PRIVATE COLLECTION, GERMANY
PHOTO: JOEL DEGEN

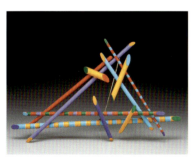

174 BROOCH, 1983, PAINTED WOOD
AND NICKEL, RIVETED AND PAINTED
ESTIMATED: H. 3 ½" × W. 7 ¾" × D. 1 ½"
PRIVATE COLLECTION
PHOTO: JOEL DEGEN

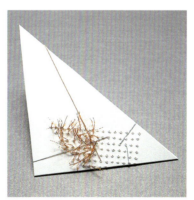

179 BROOCH, 1983, PAPER, THREAD,
AND PIN BACK, PIERCED, THREADED,
AND GLUED
H. 5 ⅝" × W. 2 ¾" × D. ⅜"
PRIVATE COLLECTION
PHOTO: JAMES MUELLER

175 BROOCH, 1983, PAINTED WOOD
AND NICKEL, RIVETED AND PAINTED
H. 14 ¼" × W. 7 ¼" × D. ⅞"
COLLECTION: MUSEUM OF FINE ARTS,
BOSTON, THE DAPHNE FARAGO
COLLECTION
PHOTO: JAMES MUELLER

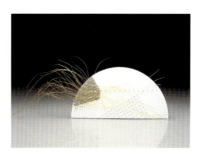

180 BROOCH, 1983, PAPER, THREAD,
SCREEN, AND PIN BACK, PIERCED,
THREADED AND GLUED
H. 2 ⅜" × W. 4 ¾" × D. ¼"
PRIVATE COLLECTION
PHOTO: JOEL DEGEN

181 BROOCH (ONE OF FOUR), 1983,
PAPER, THREAD, SCREEN, AND PIN
BACK, PIERCED, THREADED, AND GLUED
H. 4 ⅝" × W. 4 ⅝" D. ⅜"
PHOTO: JOEL DEGEN

186 BROOCH, 1983, PAINTED WOOD
AND NICKEL WIRE, RIVETED AND
PAINTED
H. 7" × W. 9" × D. 2 ½"
PRIVATE COLLECTION
PHOTO: JAMES MUELLER

182 BROOCH* (ONE OF FOUR), 1983,
PAPER, THREAD, SCREEN, AND PIN
BACK, PIERCED, THREADED, AND GLUED
H. 4 ⅝" W. 4 ⅝" × D. ⅜"
PHOTO: JOEL DEGEN

187 BRACELET, 1983, PAINTED WOOD,
RIVETED AND PAINTED
H. 9 ½" × W. 9 ½" × D. 5"
PRIVATE COLLECTION, USA
PHOTO: JAMES MUELLER

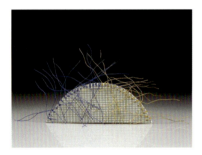

183 BROOCH, 1983, PAPER, SCREEN,
THREAD, AND PIN BACK, PIERCED,
THREADED, AND GLUED
H. 1 ½" × W. 4" × D. ⅜"
PRIVATE COLLECTION
PHOTO: JOEL DEGEN

188 BRACELET, 1983, PAINTED WOOD,
RIVETED AND PAINTED
H. 5 ½" × W. 6 ⅝" × D. 4 ⅜"
PHOTO: JOEL DEGEN

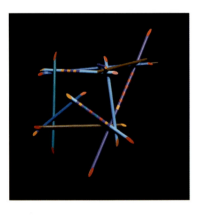

184 BROOCH, 1983, PAINTED WOOD
AND NICKEL WIRE, RIVETED AND
PAINTED
H. 10 ¼" × W. 7 ½" × D. 3"
PRIVATE COLLECTION, USA
PHOTO: JAMES MUELLER

189 BRACELET, 1983, PAINTED WOOD,
RIVETED AND PAINTED
H. 9 ¼" × W. 7 ¾" × D. 3 ½"
COLLECTION: MIDDLESBROUGH
INSTITUTE OF MODERN ART, MIDDLES-
BROUGH, UK
PHOTO: JOEL DEGEN

185 BROOCH WITH TWO STICK PINS,
1983, PAINTED WOOD, RIVETED AND
PAINTED
H. 9 ½" × W. 10 ½" × D. 2"
COLLECTION: MUSEUM OF ARTS &
DESIGN, NEW YORK, GIFT OF DONNA
SCHNEIER, 1997
PHOTO: MARTIN TUMA

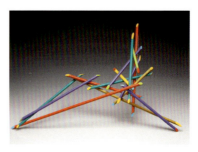

190 BROOCH, 1983, PAINTED WOOD
AND NICKEL WIRE, RIVETED AND
PAINTED
H. 8 ½" × W. 13" × D. 2 ¼"
PRIVATE COLLECTION
PHOTO: JOEL DEGEN

191 BRACELET, 1983, PAINTED WOOD,
RIVETED AND PAINTED
H. 5 ½" × W. 9 ½" × D. 1"
COLLECTION: MIDDLESBROUGH
INSTITUTE OF MODERN ART, MIDDLES-
BROUGH, UK
PHOTO: JOEL DEGEN

196 BROOCH, 1983, PAINTED WOOD
AND NICKEL WIRE, RIVETED AND
PAINTED
ESTIMATED: H. 4" × W. 4 ¾" × D. 2"
PRIVATE COLLECTION
PHOTO: JOEL DEGEN

192 BROOCH, 1983, PAINTED WOOD
AND NICKEL WIRE, RIVETED AND
PAINTED
H. 18" × W. 6 ½" × D. 2 ¼"
PRIVATE COLLECTION
PHOTO: JAMES MUELLER

197 EARRINGS, 1983, PAINTED WOOD
AND SILVER WIRE, RIVETED AND
PAINTED
H. 3 ¼" × W. 2 ½" × D. ⅞"
H. 3 ¼" × W. 3" × D. ¾"
PHOTO: JOEL DEGEN

193 BROOCH, 1983, PAINTED WOOD
AND NICKEL WIRE, RIVETED AND
PAINTED
H. 8" × W. 7 ½" × D. 1 ¼"
PRIVATE COLLECTION
PHOTO: JAMES MUELLER

198 LONG BROOCH, 1983, PAINTED
WOOD AND NICKEL WIRE, RIVETED AND
PAINTED
H. 17 ¾" × W. 2 ½" × D. 1"
PRIVATE COLLECTION, USA
PHOTO: JAMES MUELLER

194 BRACELET, 1983, PAINTED WOOD,
RIVETED AND PAINTED
H. 6" × W. 9 ¼" × D. 1 ⅜"
PRIVATE COLLECTION
PHOTO: JOEL DEGEN

199 BROOCH, 1983, PAINTED WOOD
AND NICKEL WIRE, RIVETED AND
PAINTED
H. 10 ¼" × W. 11 ¾" × D. 2 ½"
PRIVATE COLLECTION
PHOTO: JAMES MUELLER

195 BROOCH, 1983, PAINTED WOOD
AND NICKEL WIRE, RIVETED AND
PAINTED
H. 10 ½" × W. 7 ¼" × D. 1 ½"
PRIVATE COLLECTION, UK
PHOTO: JOEL DEGEN

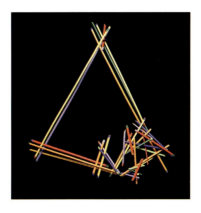

200 NECKLACE, 1983, PAINTED WOOD,
RIVETED AND PAINTED
H. 20" × W. 18 ½" × D. 2 ¾"
PRIVATE COLLECTION
PHOTO: JOEL DEGEN

201 BROOCH, 1983, PAINTED WOOD
AND NICKEL WIRE, RIVETED AND
PAINTED
H. 7 ¾" × W. 7 ⅜" × D. 1 ¼"
PRIVATE COLLECTION
PHOTO: JOEL DEGEN

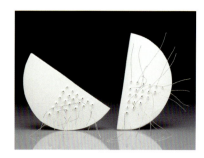

206 EARRINGS, 1984, PAPER, THREAD,
AND STERLING SILVER, CUT, PIERCED
AND GLUED
H. 1 ¼" × W. 2 ½"
PHOTO: JOEL DEGEN

202 BROOCH, 1983, PAINTED WOOD
AND NICKEL WIRE, RIVETED AND
PAINTED
H. 13" × W. 11 ½" × D. 3"
PRIVATE COLLECTION
PHOTO: JAMES MUELLER

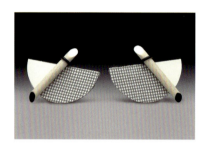

207 EARRINGS, 1984, PAPER, SCREEN,
PAINTED WOOD, RUBBER, AND
STERLING SILVER, CUT, GLUED, PAINTED
H. 1 ⅜" × W. 1 ¾" × D. ⅝"
PHOTO: JOEL DEGEN

203 BROOCH, 1983, PAINTED WOOD
AND NICKEL WIRE
H. 11" × W. 7 ¾" × D. 1 ½"
PRIVATE COLLECTION
PHOTO: JAMES MUELLER

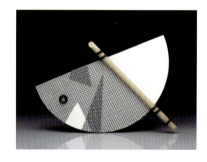

208 BROOCH, 1984, PAPER, SCREEN,
PAINTED WOOD, RUBBER, AND PIN
BACK, CUT, GLUED, AND STITCHED
H. 3" × W. 4 ½" × D. ¼"
PRIVATE COLLECTION
PHOTO: JOEL DEGEN

204 BROOCHES ON STANDS, 1983,
WOOD, PAPER, THREAD, AND NICKEL
WIRE, PIERCED, RIVETED, WRAPPED,
THREADED, TIED, AND GLUED BROOCH
WITH RED THREAD: H. 10 ¾" × W. 10" × D. ¾"
STAND FOR BROOCH: H. 7 ½" × W. 12" × D. 9"
BROOCH WITH BLUE THREAD:
H. 7 ½" × W. 7 ½" × D. ¾"
STAND FOR BROOCH: H. 8" × W. 9" × D. 6 ½"
BROOCH WITH GREEN THREAD:
H. 9" × W. 9" × D. ¾"
STAND FOR BROOCH: H. 8 ¾" × W. 13" × D. 9"
PHOTO: GARY POLLMILLER

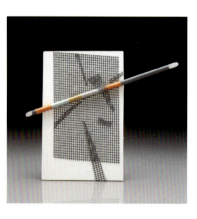

209 BROOCH, 1984, PAPER, SCREEN,
PAINTED WOOD, THREAD, AND PIN
BACK, CUT, GLUED, WRAPPED, AND
STITCHED
H. 2 ¾" × W. 4" × D. ¼"
PRIVATE COLLECTION
PHOTO: JOEL DEGEN

205 BRASS POT WITH RUBBER HOSE,
1983, BRASS AND RUBBER HOSE,
FORMED AND CONSTRUCTED
H. 8 ¾" × W. 8" × D. 8 ½"
PHOTO: GARY POLLMILLER

210 STICK PIN*, 1984, BRONZE, PAPER,
AND THREAD, CONSTRUCTED, PIECED,
GLUED, AND THREADED
H. 12 ¾" × W. 3 ⅛"
PHOTO: JOEL DEGEN

211 STICK PINS, 1984, BRONZE AND PAPER, CONSTRUCTED, PIERCED, GLUED, AND THREADED
TRIANGULAR PIN: H. 12 ½" × W. 5 ¾"
CURVED PIN: H. 12 ¾" × W. 4 ⅜"
RECTANGULAR PIN: H. 13 ⅞" × W. 3 ⅛"
SIMILAR TO ONES IN THE COLLECTION OF THE NATIONAL MUSEUM OF MODERN ART, KYOTO, JAPAN
PHOTO: GARY POLLMILLER

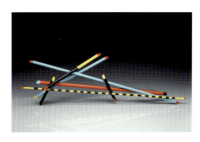

216 BROOCH, 1984, PAINTED WOOD AND NICKEL WIRE, RIVETED AND PAINTED
H. 6 ½" × W. 13" × D. 1 ¼"
PHOTO: JOEL DEGEN

212 NECKLACE, 1984, PAINTED WOOD AND RUBBER, RIVETED AND PAINTED
H. 15 ¾" × W. 13" × D. 3 ½"
COLLECTION: PHILADELPHIA MUSEUM OF ART, GIFT OF HELEN WILLIAMS DRUTT ENGLISH, PHILADELPHIA, AND THE ARTIST
PHOTO: JAMES MUELLER

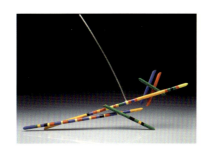

217 STICK PIN, 1984, PAINTED WOOD AND NICKEL WIRE, RIVETED AND PAINTED
H. 10 ½" × W. 11" × D. 1"
PRIVATE COLLECTION
PHOTO: JOEL DEGEN

213 NECKLACE, 1984, NATURAL AND PAINTED WOOD AND THREAD, RIVETED, PAINTED, AND TIED
H. 19 ¾" × W. 24" × D. 2"
PRIVATE COLLECTION
PHOTO: JAMES MUELLER

218 BROOCH, 1984, PAINTED WOOD AND NICKEL WIRE, RIVETED AND PAINTED
ESTIMATED: H. 9 ¾" × W. 13" × D. 1 ½"
COLLECTION: MUSEUM OF APPLIED ART, TRONDHEIM, NORWAY
PHOTO: JOEL DEGEN

214 BROOCH WITH STICK PIN*, 1984, PAINTED WOOD, RIVETED AND PAINTED
H. 11" × W. 9" × D. 2 ¾"
PRIVATE COLLECTION
PHOTO: JOEL DEGEN

219 BROOCH WITH DETACHABLE STICK PIN, 1984, PAINTED WOOD AND NICKEL WIRE, RIVETED AND PAINTED
H. 10 ¾" × W. 5 ½" × D. 1 ½"
PRIVATE COLLECTION
PHOTO: JOEL DEGEN

215 BROOCH WITH STICK PIN, 1984, PAINTED WOOD, RIVETED AND PAINTED
H. 10" × W. 10" × D. 2 ¼"
PHOTO: JOEL DEGEN

220 BROOCH WITH DETACHABLE STICK PIN, 1984, PAINTED WOOD AND NICKEL WIRE, RIVETED AND PAINTED
ESTIMATED: H. 6" × W. 10" × D. 4"
PRIVATE COLLECTION
PHOTO: JOEL DEGEN

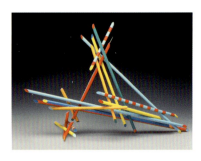

221 BROOCH WITH DETACHABLE STICK PIN*, 1984, PAINTED WOOD AND NICKEL WIRE, RIVETED AND PAINTED
H. 12 ¾" × W. 9" × D. 1 ¾"
PRIVATE COLLECTION, USA
PHOTO: JOEL DEGEN

226 NECKLACE, 1984, PAINTED WOOD, RIVETED AND PAINTED
H. 14" × W. 12 ½" × D. 1 ¼"
PRIVATE COLLECTION, UK
PHOTO: JOEL DEGEN

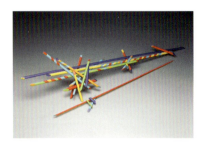

222 BROOCH WITH TWO STICK PINS*, 1984, PAINTED WOOD, RIVETED AND PAINTED
H. 14 ½" × W. 2" × D. 1"
COLLECTION: MUSEUM OF ARTS & DESIGN, NEW YORK, GIFT OF DONNA SCHNEIER, 1997
PHOTO: JOEL DEGEN

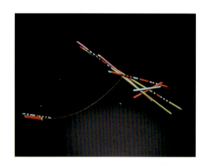

227 BROOCH, 1984, PAINTED WOOD AND NICKEL WIRE, RIVETED AND PAINTED
H. 15 ¾" × W. 14 ½" × D. 2"
PHOTO: GARY POLLMILLER

223 BROOCH WITH SEPARATE STICK PIN, 1984, PAINTED WOOD, RIVETED AND PAINTED
H. 14" × W. 7 ½" × D. 1"
PRIVATE COLLECTION
PHOTO: JOEL DEGEN

228 BROOCH, 1984, PAINTED WOOD AND NICKEL WIRE, RIVETED AND PAINTED
H. 15 ¾" × 12 ¾" × D. 2 ¼"
COLLECTION: THE WICHITA CENTER FOR THE ARTS, WICHITA, KANSAS, USA
PHOTO: JAMES MUELLER

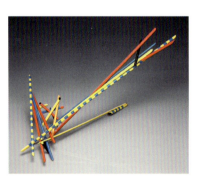

224 BROOCH WITH STICK PIN, 1984, PAINTED WOOD, RIVETED AND CONSTRUCTED
H. 17" × W. 7 ½" × D. 1 ½"
PRIVATE COLLECTION
PHOTO: JOEL DEGEN

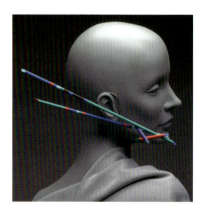

229 EAR SCULPTURE FOR THE RIGHT EAR, 1984, PAINTED WOOD AND NICKEL WIRE, RIVETED AND PAINTED
H. 2 ⅝" × W. 11 ¼" × D. ¾"
PHOTO: GARY POLLMILLER

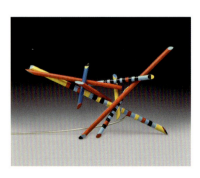

225 STICK PIN, 1984, PAINTED WOOD, NICKEL WIRE, AND RUBBER, RIVETED AND PAINTED
H. 11 ½" × W. 6" × D. 1 ⅜"
PRIVATE COLLECTION
PHOTO: JOEL DEGEN

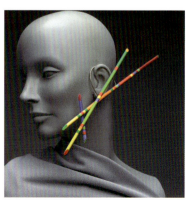

230 EAR SCULPTURE FOR THE LEFT EAR, 1984, PAINTED WOOD AND NICKEL WIRE, RIVETED AND PAINTED
H. 3" × W. 10 ½" × D. 1 ¼"
PHOTO: GARY POLLMILLER

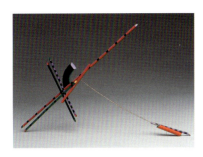

231 STICK PIN, 1984, PAINTED WOOD AND NICKEL WIRE, RIVETED AND CONSTRUCTED
H. 15 ½" × W. 13 ½" × D. 1 ⅛"
PHOTO: GARY POLLMILLER

236 BROOCH, 1984, PAINTED WOOD AND NICKEL WIRE, RIVETED AND PAINTED
H. 13 ½" × W. 7 ½" × D. 1 ½"
PHOTO: GARY POLLMILLER

232 BROOCH, 1984, PAINTED WOOD AND NICKEL WIRE, RIVETED AND PAINTED
H. 7 ¼" × W. 6 ⅞" × D. 1 ¾"
PRIVATE COLLECTION, UK
PHOTO: JOEL DEGEN

237 EARRINGS, 1984, PAINTED WOOD
H. 4 ½" × W. 3 ¾"
COLLECTION: MUSEUM OF ARTS & DESIGN, NEW YORK, GIFT OF DONNA SCHNEIER, 1997
PHOTO: MARTIN TUMA

233 BROOCH, 1984, PAINTED WOOD AND NICKEL WIRE, RIVETED AND PAINTED
H. 14 ½" × W. 11" × D. 2"
COLLECTION: NATIONAL MUSEUM OF ART, ARCHITECTURE AND DESIGN – MUSEUM OF DECORATIVE ARTS AND DESIGN, OSLO, NORWAY
PHOTO: MARJORIE SCHICK

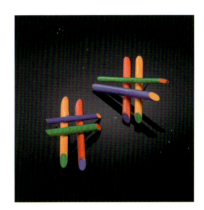

238 EARRINGS, 1984, PAINTED WOOD, CONSTRUCTED AND PAINTED
H. 2 ⅜" × W. 2 ¼" × D. ⅜"
PHOTO: GARY POLLMILLER

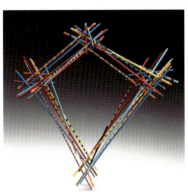

234 NECKLACE, 1984, PAINTED WOOD, RIVETED AND PAINTED
H. 22" × W. 22" × D. 3 ½"
PHOTO: GARY POLLMILLER

239 BRASS TABLE SCULPTURE, 1984, BRASS, CONSTRUCTED
H. 1 ½" × W. 9" × D. 3 ½"
PHOTO: GARY POLLMILLER

235 NECKLACE*, 1984, PAINTED WOOD AND RUBBER, RIVETED AND PAINTED
H. 21 ⅝" × W. 12" × D. 1 ¹⁵⁄₁₆"
COLLECTION: MUSEUM OF FINE ARTS, HOUSTON, HELEN WILLIAMS DRUTT ENGLISH COLLECTION, GIFT OF THE MORGAN FOUNDATION IN HONOR OF CATHERINE ASHER MORGAN
PHOTO: TOM DUBROCK

240 BROOCH, 1985, PAPER, PLASTIC ROD, THREAD, AND PIN BACK, PIERCED, GLUED AND THREADED
H. 2 ¾" × W. 6 ½" × D. ⅜"
PRIVATE COLLECTION
PHOTO: JOEL DEGEN

241 BROOCH, 1985, PAPER, PLASTIC ROD, PLASTIC ROD, AND THREAD, PIERCED, DRILLED, WRAPPED, AND TIED
H. 8" × W. 6" × D. ½"
PRIVATE COLLECTION
PHOTO: JOEL DEGEN

246 TRIANGULAR NECKLACE, 1985, PLASTIC ROD, STERLING SILVER, PAPER, AND THREAD, PIERCED, WRAPPED, TIED, AND GLUED
H. 14 ¼" × W. 15 ¼" × D. ⅜"
PHOTO: JOEL DEGEN

242 BROOCH, 1985, PLASTIC ROD, PAPER, THREAD, AND PIN BACK
H. 4 ¹³⁄₁₆" × W. 5" × D. ½"
PRIVATE COLLECTION
PHOTO: JOEL DEGEN

247 THREE BROOCHES, 1985, PAPER, PLASTIC ROD, THREAD, AND PIN BACKS, PIERCED, THREADED, WRAPPED, TIED, AND GLUED
EACH: H. 3 ¾" × W. 4 ½" × D. ⅜"
PRIVATE COLLECTION, USA
PHOTO: GARY POLLMILLER

243 PAIR OF BROOCHES, 1985, PAPER, PLASTIC ROD, THREAD, AND PIN BACKS, PIERCED, GLUED, WRAPPED, AND TIED
EACH: H. 4 ¼" × W. 4 ⅜" × D. ⅜"
PRIVATE COLLECTION
PHOTO: GARY POLLMILLER

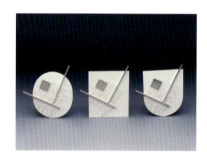

248 BROOCHES, 1985, PAPER, SILVER RODS, GOLD, THREAD, AND PIN BACKS, PIERCED, THREADED, AND TIED
EACH: H. 3 ⅜" × W. 3 ¾" × D. ⅜"
PRIVATE COLLECTIONS, USA
PHOTO: GARY POLLMILLER

244 SQUARE NECKLACE, 1985, PLASTIC ROD, STERLING SILVER, PAPER, AND THREAD, PIERCED, WRAPPED, TIED, GLUED
H. 15 ⅞" × W. 15 ³⁄₁₆" × D. ⅜"
COLLECTION: MUSEUM OF APPLIED ART, TRONDHEIM, NORWAY
PHOTO: JOEL DEGEN

249 BRACELET, 1985, NATURAL BIRCH STICKS, DOWELS, AND THREAD, RIVETED, PAINTED, AND TIED
ESTIMATED: H. 4 ¼" × W. 5 ½" × D. 2"
PRIVATE COLLECTION
PHOTO: JOEL DEGEN

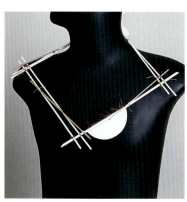

245 DIAMOND NECKLACE, 1985, PLASTIC ROD, COPPER, PAPER, AND THREAD, PIERCED, WRAPPED, TIED, AND GLUED
H. 13 ⁷⁄₁₆" × W. 12 ⅞" × D. ⅜"
PHOTO: JOEL DEGEN

250 BRACELET, 1985, DOWELS, PAINT, AND THREAD, RIVETED, PAINTED, AND TIED
H. 5 ¼" × W. 7 ¾" × D. 3"
PHOTO: GARY POLLMILLER

251 BROOCH WITH BARK*, 1985, BARK, AND PAINTED WOOD, RIVETED AND PAINTED
H. 6 ¾" × W. 8 ¼" × D. 1"
COLLECTION: GENE AND HIROKO-SATO PIJANOWSKI, USA
PHOTO: JOEL DEGEN

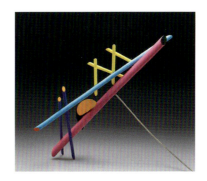

256 STICK PINS ON BASES*, 1985, STICK PINS: PAINTED WOOD, NICKEL WIRE, RUBBER, BASES: WOOD AND BRASS, RIVETED AND PAINTED
STICK PINS:
A. H. 7" × W. 7 ½" × D. 1 ⅜"
B. H. 8" × W. 6 ½" × D. 1 ¼"
C. H. 7 ½" × W. 6 ⅞" × D. ¾"
D. H. 7 ⅜" × W. 7 ¼" × D. 1 ¼"
E. H. 7 ⅜" × W. 8 ⅜" × D. ⅝"
F. H. 7" × W. 10 ⅛" × D. 1 ⅛"
PHOTO: JOEL DEGEN

252 BRACELET/BROOCH*, 1985, BIRCH WOOD, DOWELS, PAINT, AND THREAD, RIVETED AND TIED
H. 5 ⅝" × W. 8 ½" × D. 1"
PRIVATE COLLECTION
PHOTO: JOEL DEGEN

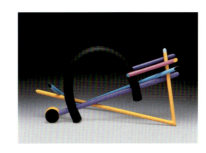

257 BRACELET, 1985, PAINTED WOOD AND RUBBER, RIVETED AND PAINTED
H. 4 ¾" × W. 5" × D. 3"
PHOTO: JOEL DEGEN

253 BROOCH, 1985, BIRCH WOOD, DOWELS, PAINT, AND THREAD, RIVETED, PAINTED, AND TIED
H. 11 ⅜" × W. 5 ¼" × D. 1 ¾"
PRIVATE COLLECTION
PHOTO: JOEL DEGEN

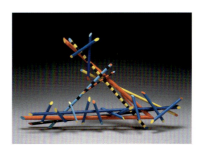

258 BROOCH, 1985, PAINTED WOOD AND NICKEL WIRE, RIVETED AND PAINTED
ESTIMATED: H. 12 ½" × W. 8 ½" × D. 2 ¼"
PRIVATE COLLECTION, USA
PHOTO: JOEL DEGEN

254 ALASKAN MEMORY, NECKLACE, 1985, BIRCH, DOWELS, PAINT, AND THREAD, RIVETED, PAINTED, AND TIED
H. 19 ¾" × W. 18" × D. 2"
PHOTO: GARY POLLMILLER

259 NECKLACE, 1985, PAINTED WOOD AND RUBBER, RIVETED AND PAINTED
H. 15 ½" × W. 14 ½" × D. 4 ¼"
COLLECTION: ROBERT M. SCHICK, USA
PHOTO: JOEL DEGEN

255 BROOCH, 1985, BIRCH, PAINTED DOWELS, AND THREAD, RIVETED, PAINTED, AND TIED
H. 6 ¾" × W. 4" × D. 1 ¾"
COLLECTION: JOHN PLOOF, USA
PHOTO: MARJORIE SCHICK

260 BRACELET, 1985, PAINTED WOOD AND RUBBER, RIVETED AND PAINTED
H. 8" × W. 4 ¾" × D. 4"
COLLECTION: MUSEUM OF ARTS & DESIGN, NEW YORK, GIFT OF DONNA SCHNEIER, 1997
PHOTO: EVA HEYD

261 **BROOCH ON A STAND,** 1985,
PAINTED WOOD AND NICKEL WIRE,
CONSTRUCTED AND PAINTED
H. 15" × W. 16" × D. 2"
COLLECTION: MUSEUM OF ARTS &
DESIGN, NEW YORK, GIFT OF DONNA
SCHNEIER, 1997
PHOTO: MARTIN TUMA

266 **BRACELET/BROOCH,** 1985,
PAINTED WOOD, RIVETED AND PAINTED
H. 6 ½" × W. 10 ¾" × D. 1 ¼"
PRIVATE COLLECTION
PHOTO: JOEL DEGEN

262 **HOW TO WEAR A BROOCH,** WALL
RELIEF MADE IN 2005 FOR BROOCH
NO. 261, PAINTED WOOD, STEEL RODS,
AND THREAD, CONSTRUCTED, PAINTED,
AND TIED
H. 9 ⅞" × W. 8 1/16" × D. 1"
PHOTO: GARY POLLMILLER

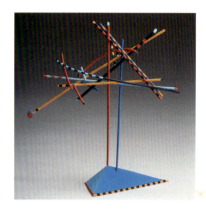

267 **HAIR COMB WITH BASE,** 1985,
HAIR COMB: PAINTED WOOD, BASE:
PAINTED WOOD AND BRASS, RIVETED
AND PAINTED
HAIR COMB: H. 10" × W. 10 ½" × D. 3 ½"
BASE: H. 1 ½" × W. 6 ⅞" × D. 3 ¼"
PHOTO: GARY POLLMILLER

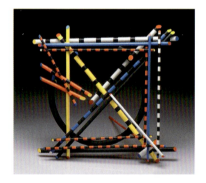

263 **BROOCH,** 1985, PAINTED WOOD
AND RUBBER, RIVETED AND PAINTED
H. 8 ½" × W. 7 ¾" × D. 1 ⅝"
PHOTO: JOEL DEGEN

268 **NECKLACE*,** 1985,
PAINTED WOOD, RIVETED
AND PAINTED
H. 31 ½" × W. 27" × D. 2"
PRIVATE COLLECTION, USA
PHOTO: GARY POLLMILLER

264 **NECKLACE,** 1985, PAINTED WOOD,
RIVETED AND PAINTED
H. 18" × W. 17 ½" × D. 1 ¾"
PHOTO: GARY POLLMILLER

269 **HEAD SCULPTURE*,** 1985,
PAINTED WOOD AND LEATHER,
RIVETED AND PAINTED
H. 11 ½" × W. 12 ¾" × D. 10"
WITH TIES: 33 ¾" LONG
PHOTO: GARY POLLMILLER

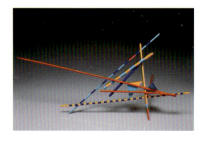

265 **STICK PIN,** 1985, PAINTED WOOD,
RIVETED AND PAINTED
H. 15 ½" × W. 8" × D. 2"
PRIVATE COLLECTION
PHOTO: JOEL DEGEN

270 **NECKLACE*,** 1985, PAINTED WOOD,
RIVETED AND PAINTED
H. 28 ¾" × W. 24 ½" × D. 7"
COLLECTION: INDIANA UNIVERSITY
ART MUSEUM PURCHASE IN HONOR OF
ALMA EIKERMAN, USA, 1989
PHOTO: GARY POLLMILLER

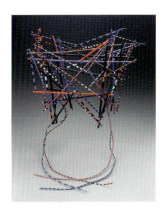

271 HEAD SCULPTURE, 1985, PAINTED WOOD AND LEATHER, RIVETED AND PAINTED
H. 17" × W. 17" × D. 12"
COLLECTION: MUSEUM OF FINE ARTS, HOUSTON, HELEN WILLIAMS DRUTT ENGLISH COLLECTION, GIFT OF THE MORGAN FOUNDATION IN HONOR OF CATHERINE ASHER MORGAN
PHOTO: JUD HAGGARD

276 BROOCH, 1985, PAINTED WOOD AND RUBBER, RIVETED AND PAINTED
H. 6" × W. 10 ½" × D. 2 ½"
PRIVATE COLLECTION, NORWAY
PHOTO: GARY POLLMILLER

272 BRACELET, 1985, PAINTED WOOD AND RUBBER, RIVETED AND PAINTED
H. 9 ½" × W. 7 ½" × D. 6 ¾"
COLLECTION: MUSEUM OF FINE ARTS, HOUSTON, HELEN WILLIAMS DRUTT ENGLISH COLLECTION, GIFT OF THE MORGAN FOUNDATION IN HONOR OF CATHERINE ASHER MORGAN
PHOTO: GARY POLLMILLER

277 BROOCH, 1985, PAINTED WOOD, RIVETED AND PAINTED
H. 11 ½" × W. 7 ¼" × D. 1 ½"
PRIVATE COLLECTION
PHOTO: JOEL DEGEN

273 EARRINGS, 1985, PAINTED WOOD, CONSTRUCTED AND PAINTED
LEFT: H. 2 ⅛" × W. 3 ⅛" × D. ¾"
RIGHT: H. 2 ⅛" × W. 2 ⅛" × D. ¾"
PHOTO: GARY POLLMILLER

278 BROOCH, 1985, PAINTED WOOD, RIVETED AND PAINTED
H. 11" × W. 6 ⅜" × D. 1 ⅜"
PRIVATE COLLECTION
PHOTO: JOEL DEGEN

274 EARRINGS, 1985, PAINTED WOOD, CONSTRUCTED AND PAINTED
LEFT: H. 2 ¼" × W. 1 ⅞" × D. ¾"
RIGHT: H. 2 ½" × W. 1 ⅝" × D. ½"
PHOTO: GARY POLLMILLER

279 BROOCH, 1985, PAINTED WOOD, RIVETED AND PAINTED
H. 8 ¼" × W. 11 ½" × D. 1 ½"
PHOTO: JOEL DEGEN

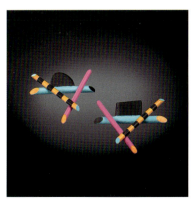

275 EARRINGS, 1985, PAINTED WOOD, CONSTRUCTED AND PAINTED
EACH: H. 2 ⅜" × W. 3" × D. ½"
PHOTO: GARY POLLMILLER

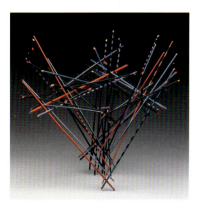

280 NECKLACE*, 1985, PAINTED WOOD, RIVETED AND PAINTED
H. 26" × W. 28" × D. 20"
COLLECTION: RENWICK GALLERY OF THE SMITHSONIAN AMERICAN ART MUSEUM, WASHINGTON, D.C.
PHOTO: GARY POLLMILLER

281 ARZO ORANGE*, NECKLACE, 1986,
PAINTED WOOD, RIVETED AND PAINTED
H. 20 ¾" × W. 23" × D. 10"
PHOTO: GARY POLLMILLER

286 RED ENDS, ARMLET, 1986, PAINTED
REED, WOOD, AND THREAD, RIVETED,
PAINTED, AND TIED
H. 9 ½" × W. 12 ½" × D. 7 ½"
PHOTO: GARY POLLMILLER

282 BROOCH WITH STICK PIN, 1986,
PAINTED WOOD AND NICKEL WIRE,
RIVETED AND PAINTED
H. 13" × W. 12 ½" × D. 2"
PHOTO: GARY POLLMILLER

287 SNAKES AND LADDERS*, PAIR OF
FOLDING BODY SCULPTURES WITH
BROOCHES, 1986, LADDERS: PAINTED
WOOD AND LEATHER, RIVETED AND
PAINTED, BROOCHES: REED AND PINS,
FORMED AND PAINTED
LADDERS: H. 48 ½" × W. 3 ½" × D. 20' ½"
H. 41 ¾" × W. 3 ½" × D. 26 ¼"
SNAKE BROOCHES:
AVERAGE, H. 13" × W. ¼" × D. ¼"
PHOTO: GARY POLLMILLER

283 ARMLET, 1986, PAINTED REED,
WOOD, AND THREAD, FORMED REED,
RIVETED, PAINTED, AND TIED
H. 9 ⅞" × W. 15 ½" × D. 13 ⅞"
PRIVATE COLLECTION
PHOTO: GAYDEN SHELL

288 WITHIN A FRAME*, SCULPTURE
FOR THE NECK, 1986, PAINTED WOOD
AND RUBBER, RIVETED AND PAINTED
H. 36" × W. 22" × D. 2"
PHOTO: GARY POLLMILLER

284 A PLANE OF STICKS*, SCULPTURE
FOR THE NECK, 1986, PAINTED WOOD,
RIVETED AND PAINTED
H. 27" × W. 36" × D. 6"
PHOTO: GARY POLLMILLER

289 BRACELET, 1986, PAINTED REED
AND WOOD, FORMED, RIVETED AND
TIED
H. 7" × W. 12" × D. 4 ¾"
COLLECTION: PAUL DERREZ AND
WILLEM HOOGSTEDE, THE NETHERLANDS
PHOTO: JOEL DEGEN

285 DIRECTIONAL FORCES*,
SCULPTURE FOR THE NECK, 1986,
PAINTED WOOD, RIVETED AND PAINTED
H. 41" × W. 18 ½" × D. 7 ½"
PHOTO: GARY POLLMILLER

290 ROUND FOLDING NECKLACE, 1986,
PAINTED REED, WOOD, AND THREAD,
FORMED, RIVETED, TIED, AND PAINTED
H. 17 ½" × W. 18" × D. 1"
PRIVATE COLLECTION, UK
PHOTO: JOEL DEGEN

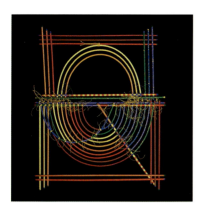

291 RECTANGULAR FOLDING NECKLACE, 1986, PAINTED REED, WOOD, AND THREAD, FORMED, RIVETED, TIED, AND PAINTED
H. 29" × W. 24" × D. 1 ½"
PRIVATE COLLECTION, THE NETHERLANDS
PHOTO: JOEL DEGEN

296 NECKLACE FOR THE BACK*, 1986, PAINTED WOOD AND RUBBER, RIVETED AND PAINTED
H. 15 ½" × W. 22" × D. 9"
PHOTO: GARY POLLMILLER

292 ONE OF A PAIR OF ARMLETS: BLUE, 1986, PAINTED REED, WOOD, AND THREAD, FORMED, RIVETED, TIED, AND PAINTED
H. 5" × W. 10 ¾" × D. 4 ¼"
PHOTO: GARY POLLMILLER

297 BROOCHES, 1986, PAPER, PAINTED WOOD, PLASTIC RODS, AND THREAD, PIERCED, RIVETED, AND TIED
EACH: H. 4" × W. 4" × D. ⅜"
PRIVATE COLLECTIONS
PHOTO: GARY POLLMILLER

293 ONE OF A PAIR OF ARMLETS: RED, 1986, PAINTED REED, WOOD, AND THREAD, FORMED, RIVETED, TIED, AND PAINTED
H. 4 ½" × W. 9 ¾" × D. 5"
PHOTO: GARY POLLMILLER

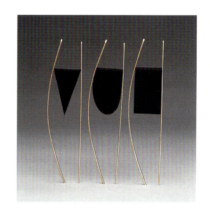

298 STICK PINS, 1986, PAPER AND BRONZE RODS, CONSTRUCTED, PIERCED, AND GLUED
EACH: H. 7 ¹¹/₁₆" × W. 1 ⅞" × D. ⅛"
PHOTO: GARY POLLMILLER

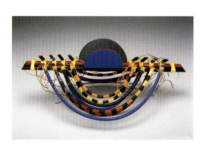

294 ARMLET, 1986, PAINTED REED, WOOD, AND THREAD, FORMED, RIVETED, TIED AND PAINTED
H. 5 ½" × W. 13 ½" × D. 6 ¼"
PHOTO: JOEL DEGEN

299 BRACELET, 1986, PLASTIC RODS, PAINTED WOOD, PAPER, AND THREAD, PIERCED, RIVETED, AND TIED
H. 4 ¼" × W. 5" × ¼"
PHOTO: GARY POLLMILLER

295 NOT A SQUARE*, NECKLACE, 1986, PAINTED WOOD, REED, AND THREAD, RIVETED, TIED, AND PAINTED
H. 26" × W. 28 ½" × D. 5 ½"
PHOTO: GARY POLLMILLER

300 BROOCH, 1986, PAPER, PLASTIC, THREAD, AND PIN BACK, STITCHED AND GLUED
H. 2 ⁹/₁₆" × W. 3 ½" × D. ⅛"
PHOTO: JOEL DEGEN

301 THREE STICK PINS, 1986, PAPER, PLASTIC RODS, THREAD, AND GLASS BEADS, PIERCED, THREADED, AND TIED EACH: H. 12 ½" × W. 2 ½" × D. ⅛"
PHOTO: GARY POLLMILLER

306 LIGHTER THAN AIR*, NECKLACE, 1986, PLASTIC RODS, PAPER, AND THREAD, TIED AND PIERCED H. 11 ½" × W. 21" × D. 14 ⅛"
PHOTO: GARY POLLMILLER

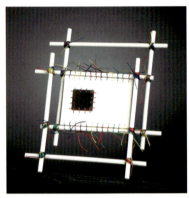

302 BROOCH, 1986, PAPER, PLASTIC RODS, GOLD, THREAD, AND PIN BACK, PIERCED AND TIED H. 4 ¼" × W. 3 ¾" × D. ¼"
PHOTO: GARY POLLMILLER

307 PAIR OF ARMLETS, 1986–7, WOOD AND RUBBER, RIVETED AND PAINTED PINK/ORANGE ARMLET: H. 6 ½" × W. 10 ⅛" × D. 3" BLUE/GREEN ARMLET: H. 6 ½" × W. 9 ½" × D. 3 ¼"
PHOTO: GARY POLLMILLER

303 BROOCH, 1986, PAPER, PLASTIC, BIRCH STICK, THREAD, AND PIN BACK, GLUED, PAINTED, AND STITCHED H. 2 ½" × W. 4" × D. ¼"
COLLECTION: DR. JAMES B. M. SCHICK, USA
PHOTO: GARY POLLMILLER

308 IT FOLDS*, BODY SCULPTURE, 1987, PAINTED WOOD, REED, AND CORD, RIVETED, PAINTED, AND TIED FULL LENGTH: H. 96" × W. 22" × D. 1 ½"
PHOTO: GARY POLLMILLER

304 TRIANGULAR NECKLACE, 1986, PLASTIC RODS, PAINTED WOOD, PAPER, AND THREAD, PAINTED, TIED, AND PIERCED H. 12 ⅜" × W. 13 ⅞" × D. ½"
PHOTO: GARY POLLMILLER

309 NECKLACE WITH ORANGE ZIG-ZAG, 1987, PAINTED WOOD AND RUBBER, RIVETED AND PAINTED H. 15 ½" × W. 18 ½" × D. 5"
COLLECTION: NATIONAL MUSEUM OF CONTEMPORARY ART, SEOUL, SOUTH KOREA
PHOTO: GARY POLLMILLER

305 RECTANGULAR NECKLACE, 1986, PLASTIC RODS, PAINTED WOOD, PAPER, AND THREAD, PAINTED, TIED, AND PIERCED H. 11 ⁵⁄₁₆" × W. 10 ⁵⁄₁₆" × D. ½"
PHOTO: GARY POLLMILLER

310 NECKLACE WITH ORANGE SPIRAL, 1987, PAINTED WOOD AND RUBBER, RIVETED AND PAINTED H. 14" × W. 22" × D. 2 ¾"
COLLECTION: NATIONAL MUSEUM OF CONTEMPORARY ART, SEOUL, SOUTH KOREA
PHOTO: GARY POLLMILLER

311 ANGLES AND CIRCLES*, BODY SCULPTURE, 1987, PAINTED WOOD, METAL EYELETS, AND CORD, RIVETED, PAINTED, AND TIED
SHOULDER TO BOTTOM:
H. 55" × W. 26" × D. 6"
PHOTO: GARY POLLMILLER

316 BROOCH, 1987, PAPER, SCREEN, WOOD, PAINT, AND THREAD, RIVETED, STITCHED, PAINTED AND TIED
H. 7 ½" × W. 8 ¼" × D. 1"
PHOTO: GARY POLLMILLER

312 BRACELET, 1987, PAINTED WOOD AND RUBBER, RIVETED AND PAINTED
H. 8" × W. 7 ⅞" × D. 2 ½"
PRIVATE COLLECTION
PHOTO: GARY POLLMILLER

317 PATTERNED NECKLACE (BACK VIEW)*, 1987, PAINTED WOOD, RIVETED AND PAINTED
H. 20" × W. 20 ½" × D. 4 ½"
COLLECTION: PAUL DERREZ AND WILLEM HOOGSTEDE, THE NETHERLANDS
PHOTO: GARY POLLMILLER

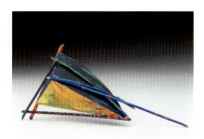

313 EDGE OF THE SHOULDER, BROOCH, 1987, PAINTED WOOD, RIVETED AND PAINTED
H. 13" × W. 6 ¾" × D. 2 ½"
PRIVATE COLLECTION, THE NETHERLANDS
PHOTO: GARY POLLMILLER

318 BACK SCULPTURE #1*, 1987, PAINTED WOOD AND NYLON STRAPS, RIVETED AND PAINTED
H. 23" × W. 19 ½" × D. 6"
PHOTO: GARY POLLMILLER

314 EDGE OF THE SHOULDER, BROOCH, 1987, PAINTED WOOD, RIVETED AND PAINTED
H. 9 ½" × W. 7" × D. 2 ¾"
PRIVATE COLLECTION, THE NETHERLANDS
PHOTO: GARY POLLMILLER

319 ODE TO DE KOONING, BACK SCULPTURE #2*, 1987, PAINTED WOOD AND NYLON STRAPS, RIVETED AND PAINTED
H. 27" × W. 19 ½" × D. 5 ½"
PHOTO: GARY POLLMILLER

315 FETISH ARMLET*, 1987, PAINTED WOOD, REED, AND THREAD, PAINTED, RIVETED, AND TIED
H. 13" × W. 9" × D. 8 ½"
COLLECTION: SUZANNE ESSER, THE NETHERLANDS
PHOTO: GARY POLLMILLER

320 BACK SCULPTURE WITH GRID, #3*, 1988, WOOD AND NYLON STRAPS, RIVETED AND PAINTED
H. 27 ¼" × W. 27" × D. 6 ¾"
PHOTO: GARY POLLMILLER

321 BACK SCULPTURE WITH REEDS, **#4***, 1988, WOOD, REED, AND NYLON STRAPS, RIVETED AND PAINTED
H. 48" × W. 26" × D. 8"
PHOTO: GARY POLLMILLER

326 PURPLE SWING*, BODY SCULPTURE, 1988, PAINTED WOOD, SCREW EYES, AND CORD, RIVETED, PAINTED, AND TIED
SHOULDER TO BOTTOM:
H. 52" × W. 23" × D. 16"
PHOTO: GARY POLLMILLER

322 WALL RELIEF WITH BRACELET*, 1988, PAINTED WOOD WITH COLORED PENCIL AND MARKERS, RIVETED AND PAINTED
RELIEF: H. 19" × W. 20 ½" × D. 6"
BRACELET: H. 7" × W. 11 ¾" × D. 1 ¾"
PHOTO: GARY POLLMILLER

327 PURPLE RAYS*, NECKLACE, 1988, PAINTED WOOD, RIVETED AND PAINTED
H. 21 ½" × W. 23" × D. 5"
PHOTO: GARY POLLMILLER

323 GALERIE RA POSTER*, 1988
PHOTO: CARMEN FREUDENTHAL, COURTESY GALERIE RA, AMSTERDAM

328 COLLAR*, 1988, PAINTED WOOD, RIVETED AND PAINTED
H. 25 ¾" × W. 31" × D. 6"
COLLECTION: MUSEUM OF ARTS & DESIGN, NEW YORK, GIFT OF DR. JAMES B. M. SCHICK, ROBERT M. SCHICK, AND MRS. ELEANOR C. KRASK
PHOTO: GARY POLLMILLER

324 LETTING THE WOOD SHOW THROUGH*, NECKLACE, 1988, PAINTED WOOD, REED, AND CORD, RIVETED, CUT, WRAPPED, AND PAINTED
H. 21 ¾" × W. 23" × D. 2 ¼"
PHOTO: GARY POLLMILLER

329 A PROTOTYPE, PAIR OF COLLARS, 1988, PAINTED WOOD, RIVETED AND PAINTED
H. 21" × W. 9 ¾" × D. ⅜"
H. 20 ½" × W. × 9 ½" × D. ⅜"
PHOTO: GARY POLLMILLER

325 ARMLET, 1988, PAINTED WOOD, RIVETED AND PAINTED
ESTIMATED: H. 6" × W. 7" × D. 3"
PRIVATE COLLECTION
PHOTO: GARY POLLMILLER

330 THREE INTO ONE, NECKLACES, 1988, PAINTED WOOD, RIVETED AND PAINTED
EACH: H. 9 ½" × W. 20 ½" × D. ⅜"
PRIVATE COLLECTION, THE NETHERLANDS
PHOTO: GARY POLLMILLER

331 PAINTING WITH THREE NECKLACES*, 1988, PAINTED WOOD, RIVETED AND PAINTED
PAINTING: H. 33 ¾" × W. 22" × D. 2 ¾"
EACH NECKLACE: H. 10" × W. 20" × D. ½"
PHOTO: GARY POLLMILLER

336 FOR PFORZHEIM*, FOLDING COLLAR #3, 1989, PAINTED WOOD AND CORD, RIVETED, PAINTED, AND TIED
H. 24" × W. 24" × D. 1 ½"
PHOTO: GARY POLLMILLER

332 CURVED HORIZON*, HEAD SCULPTURE, 1989, PAINTED WOOD, RUBBER, NYLON STRAPS, RIVETED AND PAINTED
H. 9" × W. 20 ½" × D. 14 ½"
WITH STRAPS EXTENDED: 67 ½" LONG
PHOTO: MALCOLM TURNER

337 FOR PFORZHEIM*, FOLDING COLLAR #4, 1989, PAINTED WOOD AND CORD, RIVETED AND PAINTED
H. 24 ½" × W. 22" × D. 2"
PHOTO: GARY POLLMILLER

333 NECKLACE (BACK VIEW)*, 1989, PAINTED WOOD AND REED, RIVETED AND PAINTED
H. 25" × W. 21" × D. 9 ¼"
COLLECTION: INDIANA UNIVERSITY ART MUSEUM, USA, 1990
PHOTO: GARY POLLMILLER

338 FOR PFORZHEIM*, FOLDING COLLAR #5, 1989, PAINTED WOOD AND CORD
H. 25 ½" × W. 23" × D. 3"
PHOTO: GARY POLLMILLER

334 FOR PFORZHEIM*, FOLDING COLLAR #1, 1989, PAINTED WOOD AND CORD, RIVETED, PAINTED, AND TIED
H. 23" × W. 20 ½" × D. 1 ¾"
PHOTO: GARY POLLMILLER

339 THREE-PART FOLDING SCREEN WITH TWO NECKLACES AND FOUR BRACELETS*, 1990, PAINTED WOOD, PEGGED, RIVETED, AND PAINTED
EACH SECTION OF SCREEN:
H. 40" × W. 36" × D. 1 ⅜"
LARGE COLLAR: H. 20" × W. 20" × D. ⅝"
SMALL COLLAR: H. 9 ¾" × W. 9 ¾" × D. ⅝"
BRACELET: H. 7" × W. 7" × D. ⅞"
BRACELET: H. 7" × W. 7" × D. ⅞"
BRACELET: H. 7" × W. 7" × D. 1"
BRACELET: H. 7" × W. 7" × D. ⅞"
PRIVATE COLLECTION, THE NETHERLANDS
PHOTO: ROD DUTTON

335 FOR PFORZHEIM*, FOLDING COLLAR #2, 1989, PAINTED WOOD, RUBBER, AND CORD, RIVETED, PAINTED, AND TIED
H. 24" × W. 21 ½" × D. 1 ¾"
PHOTO: GARY POLLMILLER

340 WALL RELIEF WITH BROOCH, 1991, PAINTED WOOD, RIVETED AND PAINTED
WALL RELIEF: H. 17 ½" × W. 13 ¾" × D. 3 ½"
BROOCH: H. 11 ¼" × W. 4 ½" × D. 3 ¾"
COLLECTION: DR. JAMES B. M. SCHICK, USA
PHOTO: GARY POLLMILLER

341 WALL RELIEF WITH BROOCH, 1991, PAINTED WOOD, RIVETED AND PAINTED
RELIEF: H. 16 ½" × W. 16 ½" × D. 3"
BROOCH: H. 5" × W. 5 ½" × D. 1 ½"
COLLECTION: ROBERT M. SCHICK, USA
PHOTO: JOEL DEGEN

346 HEAD SCULPTURE AND COLLAR*, 1992, PAINTED PAPIER-MÂCHÉ, FORMED AND PAINTED
HEAD SCULPTURE:
H. 7 ¼" × W. 11 ½" × D. 11 ¼"
COLLAR: H. 17 ¾" × W. 20 ⅛" × D. 8"
COLLECTION: MUSEUM OF FINE ARTS, BOSTON, THE DAPHNE FARAGO COLLECTION
PHOTO: GARY POLLMILLER

342 MIDNIGHT BLUE, SHOULDER SCULPTURE, 1991, PAINTED PAPIER-MÂCHÉ AND NICKEL WIRE, FORMED AND PAINTED
H. 7 ½" × W. 11 ½" × D. 8"
PHOTO: GARY POLLMILLER

347 FOR THE KUNST RAI*, COLLAR, 1992, PAINTED PAPIER-MÂCHÉ, FORMED AND PAINTED
H. 20" × W. 23 ¾" × D. 9"
PHOTO: GARY POLLMILLER

343 FEASTING ARMLETS, 1991, PAINTED PAPIER-MÂCHÉ, FORMED AND PAINTED
ARMLET: H. 8 ½" × W. 6" × D. 6 ½"
ARMLET: H. 6 ⅛" × W. 16 ¼" × D. 9 ⅛"
ARMLET: H. 6 ⅝" × W. 11 ¾" × D. 8 ⅝"
ARMLET: H. 13" × W. 11" × D. 8 ⅞"
PHOTO: JOEL DEGEN

348 FOR THE KUNST RAI, ARMLET, 1992, PAINTED PAPIER-MÂCHÉ, FORMED AND PAINTED
H. 9" × W. 9 ½" × D. 6 ¼"
PRIVATE COLLECTION, THE NETHERLANDS
PHOTO: GARY POLLMILLER

344 TRANSITION*, WALL RELIEF WITH ARMLET, 1992, PAINTED PAPIER-MÂCHÉ, WOOD, PLASTIC TUBING AND THREAD WRAPPED CORD, FORMED AND PAINTED
RELIEF: H. 17" × W. 25 ¼" × D. 4 ½"
ARMLET: 5 ½" × W. 8" × D. 8 ½"
COLLECTION: ARKANSAS ARTS CENTER FOUNDATION COLLECTION: PURCHASE, RESTAURANT FUND, LITTLE ROCK, USA
PHOTO: GARY POLLMILLER

349 MEMORIES OF NEW YORK, ARMLET, 1992, PAINTED PAPIER-MÂCHÉ, FORMED AND PAINTED
H. 10" × W. 10" × D. 4 ¾"
PHOTO: GARY POLLMILLER

345 FOR PERTH*, SCULPTURE WITH ONE ARMLET AND TWO COLLARS, 1992, PAINTED PAPIER-MÂCHÉ, FORMED AND PAINTED
SCULPTURE: H. 12" × W. 16 ½" × D. 9 ¾"
ARMLET: H. 9" × W. 11 ⅜" × D. 10"
SMALL COLLAR: H. 4 ½" × W. 12 ¼" × D. 10 ¾"
LARGE COLLAR: H. 8" × W. 15 ¾" × D. 11 ¾"
PHOTO: GARY POLLMILLER

350 HORN*, COLLAR, 1992, PAINTED PAPIER-MÂCHÉ, FORMED AND PAINTED
H. 15 ½" × W. 16 ½" × D. 6"
PHOTO: GARY POLLMILLER

351 MULVANE*, NECKLACE, 1992,
PAINTED PAPIER-MÂCHÉ, FORMED AND
PAINTED
H. 19" × W. 22 ½" × D. 6"
PHOTO: GARY POLLMILLER

356 WIND-BORNE*, ARMLET, 1993,
PAINTED PAPIER-MÂCHÉ, FORMED AND
PAINTED
H. 8 ½" × W. 9" × D. 4 ½"
PHOTO: GARY POLLMILLER

352 ARMLET, 1992, PAINTED
PAPIER-MÂCHÉ, FORMED AND PAINTED
H. 6 ½" × W. 7" × D. 1 ½"
PHOTO: GARY POLLMILLER

357 FOR FINLAND*, NECKLACE #1,
1993, PAINTED PAPIER-MÂCHÉ, FORMED
AND PAINTED
H. 18 ¾" × W. 20 ¼" × D. 4 ½"
PHOTO: GARY POLLMILLER

353 MY OWN PAISLEY*, COLLAR
AND BRACELET, 1993, PAINTED PAPIER-
MÂCHÉ, FORMED AND PAINTED
COLLAR: H. 11 ¾" × W. 15 ¾" × D. 7"
BRACELET: H. 6 ¾" × W. 6 ½" × D. 3"
PHOTO: GARY POLLMILLER

358 FOR FINLAND*, NECKLACE #2,
1993, PAINTED PAPIER-MÂCHÉ, FORMED
AND PAINTED
H. 15" × W. 19 ¾" × D. 3 ¾"
PHOTO: GARY POLLMILLER

354 FOR NORWAY*, NECKLACE, 1993,
PAINTED PAPIER-MÂCHÉ, FORMED AND
PAINTED
H. 19" × W. 18 ½" × D. 5"
PHOTO: GARY POLLMILLER

359 FOR FINLAND*, NECKLACE #3,
1993, PAINTED PAPIER-MÂCHÉ, FORMED
AND PAINTED
H. 16 ½" × W. 18 ½" × D. 4 ½"
COURTESY GALERIE RA, AMSTERDAM
PHOTO: GARY POLLMILLER

355 SHOULDER BROOCH, 1993, PAPIER-
MÂCHÉ WITH BRASS HOOK AND
STAINLESS STEEL PIN, FORMED AND
PAINTED
H. 4 ¾" × W. 10" × D. 3"
PRIVATE COLLECTION
PHOTO: GARY POLLMILLER

360 SPRING GREEN*, NECKLACE, 1993,
PAINTED PAPIER-MÂCHÉ, FORMED AND
PAINTED
H. 23 ¾" × W. 23" × D. 6"
PHOTO: GARY POLLMILLER

361 WHORLED, NECKLACE, 1993, PAINTED PAPIER-MÂCHÉ, FORMED AND PAINTED
H. 16 ¼" × W. 18 ½" × D. 4 ¼"
PHOTO: GARY POLLMILLER

366 RIDGED ARMLET, 1994, PAINTED PAPIER-MÂCHÉ, FORMED AND PAINTED
H. 5 ¾" × W. 7 ¼" × D. 4 ½"
PHOTO: GARY POLLMILLER

362 ZIGZAGS, COLLAR, 1993, PAINTED PAPIER-MÂCHÉ, FORMED AND PAINTED
H. 13" × W. 15 ¼" × D. 9 ½"
COLLECTION: MARION W. FULK, USA
PHOTO: GARY POLLMILLER

367 THE SPIRAL*, NECKLACE/HEAD SCULPTURE, 1994, PAINTED PAPIER-MÂCHÉ, FORMED AND PAINTED
H. 10" × W. 7" × D. 11"
PHOTO: GARY POLLMILLER

363 DEFLECTION*, NECKLACE, 1993, PAINTED PAPIER-MÂCHÉ, FORMED AND PAINTED
H. 19" × W. 18 ½" × D. 12"
PHOTO: GARY POLLMILLER

368 RED HELICON, NECKLACE, 1994, PAINTED PAPIER-MÂCHÉ AND RUBBER, FORMED AND PAINTED
H. 12 ¼" × W. 13 ¾" × D. 3 ¾"
PHOTO: GARY POLLMILLER

364 DIPSY-DOODLE*, NECKLACE, 1993, PAINTED PAPIER-MÂCHÉ, FORMED AND PAINTED
H. 10" × W. 13" × D. 5"
PHOTO: GARY POLLMILLER

369 MOON MIST, BROOCH, 1995, PAINTED PAPIER-MÂCHÉ AND STAINLESS STEEL WIRE, FORMED AND PAINTED
H. 4" × W. 7 ⅛" × D. 3 ½"
PHOTO: GARY POLLMILLER

365 HAMAR LANDSCAPE*, NECKLACE, 1993, PAINTED PAPIER-MÂCHÉ, FORMED AND PAINTED
H. 19" × W. 18" × D. 5"
PHOTO: GARY POLLMILLER

370 XCARET, BROOCH, 1995, PAINTED PAPIER-MÂCHÉ AND STAINLESS STEEL WIRE, FORMED AND PAINTED
H. 3 ¾" × W. 7 ⅝" × D. 1 ⅞"
PHOTO: GARY POLLMILLER

371 QUEEN ANNE, ARMLET, 1995, PAINTED PAPIER-MÂCHÉ, FORMED AND PAINTED
H. 5 ¼" × W. 10 ½" × D. 7 ¼"
PHOTO: GARY POLLMILLER

376 RING OF FIRE*, NECKLACE, 1995, PAINTED PAPIER-MÂCHÉ, FORMED AND PAINTED
H. 19" × W. 20" × D. 4"
COLLECTION: VICTORIA AND ALBERT MUSEUM, LONDON, UK
PHOTO: GARY POLLMILLER

372 RHYTHMS, NECKLACE, 1995, PAINTED PAPIER-MÂCHÉ AND RUBBER, FORMED AND PAINTED
H. 14 ½" × W. 8 ½" × D. 2 ½"
PHOTO: GARY POLLMILLER

377 SUMMER, 1995, PAINTED PAPIER-MÂCHÉ, FORMED AND PAINTED
H. 8 ½" × W. 8 ½" × D. 4 ½"
PHOTO: GARY POLLMILLER

373 TRIBUTE TO PROFESSOR ALMA EIKERMAN*, NECKLACE, 1995, PAINTED PAPIER-MÂCHÉ, FORMED AND PAINTED
H. 18 ¼" × W. 19 ¾" × D. 4 ½"
PHOTO: GARY POLLMILLER

378 EDGED WAVE*, ARMLET, 1995, PAINTED PAPIER-MÂCHÉ, FORMED AND PAINTED
H. 10 ⅛" × W. 7 ½" × D. 5"
COLLECTION: NATIONAL MUSEUMS OF SCOTLAND, EDINBURGH, UK
PHOTO: GARY POLLMILLER

374 BODEGA BAY, ARMLET, 1995, PAINTED PAPIER-MÂCHÉ, FORMED AND PAINTED
H. 7 ¾" × W. 8 ¾" × D. 4 ¾"
PHOTO: GARY POLLMILLER

379 KATELLA*, NECKLACE, 1995, PAINTED PAPIER-MÂCHÉ AND WOOD, FORMED, RIVETED, AND PAINTED
H. 15 ½" × W. 17 ¼" × D. 4"
PHOTO: GARY POLLMILLER

375 ACRA GOLD*, NECKLACE, 1995, PAINTED PAPIER-MÂCHÉ, FORMED AND PAINTED
H. 13 ¼" × W. 13 ¾" × D. 4 ½"
PHOTO: GARY POLLMILLER

380 GOLDEN FROST*, NECKLACE, 1995, PAINTED PAPIER-MÂCHÉ, FORMED AND PAINTED
H. 18" × W. 18 ½" × D. 7"
PHOTO: GARY POLLMILLER

381 BLUE MAGIC, ARMLET, 1996, PAINTED PAPIER-MÂCHÉ, FORMED AND PAINTED
H. 6" × W. 6 ¾" × D. 6 ¼"
PHOTO: GARY POLLMILLER

386 I TRUST, BROOCH, 1996, PAINTED PAPIER-MÂCHÉ AND STAINLESS STEEL PIN, FORMED AND PAINTED
H. 5" × W. 8 ¼" × D. 2 ⅛"
PHOTO: GARY POLLMILLER

382 ALPHABET SAMPLER, BROOCH, 1996, PAINTED PAPIER-MÂCHÉ AND NICKEL WIRE
H. 5 ¾" × W. 7" × D. 2 ¾"
PHOTO: GARY POLLMILLER

387 RIPPLING COLORS, TWO PAIRS OF EARRINGS ON A STAND, 1996, PAINTED WOOD AND STAINLESS STEEL WIRE, CONSTRUCTED AND PAINTED
STAND: H. 8 ½" × W. 8 ½" × D. 5 ⅛"
LARGE EARRINGS, EACH:
H. 2 ½" × W. 4 ⅛" × D. ⁹⁄₁₆"
SMALL EARRINGS, EACH:
H. 2" × W. 3" × D. ⁹⁄₁₆"
PHOTO: GARY POLLMILLER

383 STEPPING STONES, ARMLET, 1996, PAINTED PAPIER-MÂCHÉ, FORMED AND PAINTED
H. 8 ½" × W. 7 ½" × D. 7 ¾"
PHOTO: GARY POLLMILLER

388 RIBBED, EARRINGS ON A STAND, 1996, PAINTED WOOD AND STAINLESS STEEL WIRE, CONSTRUCTED AND PAINTED
ESTIMATED: STAND, H. 8" × W. 6 ¼" × D. 4 ¾"
ESTIMATED: EARRINGS,
H. 1 ½" × W. 2" × D. ¼"
PHOTO: GARY POLLMILLER

384 FLUTED HARMONIES, NECKLACE, 1996, PAINTED PAPIER-MÂCHÉ AND RUBBER, FORMED AND PAINTED
H. 29" × W. 9" × D. 2 ⅝"
PHOTO: GARY POLLMILLER

389 CRESCENTS, EARRINGS ON A STAND, 1996, PAINTED WOOD AND STAINLESS STEEL WIRE, CONSTRUCTED AND PAINTED
STAND: H. 9 ¼" × W. 9" × D. 2 ¾"
EACH EARRING: H. 4 ¼" × W. 3 ⅜" × D. ⅞"
PHOTO: GARY POLLMILLER

385 ILLUSIONS*, NECKLACE, 1996, PAINTED PAPIER-MÂCHÉ, FORMED AND PAINTED
H. 16 ⅞" × W. 17" × D. 3 ¾"
PHOTO: GARY POLLMILLER

390 L.A./D.C. SUITE*, ARMLET AND CONTAINER FOR ARMLET, 1996, PAINTED PAPIER-MÂCHÉ, FORMED AND PAINTED
CONTAINER: H. 10 ½" × W. 12 ½" × D. 12 ⅝"
ARMLET: H. 6 ½" × W. 7 ⅛" × D. 3 ¼"
PHOTO: GARY POLLMILLER

391 L.A./D.C. SUITE*, NECKLACE, 1996, PAINTED PAPIER-MÂCHÉ, FORMED AND PAINTED
H. 13 ¾" × W. 13 ⅞" × D. 4 ½"
PHOTO: GARY POLLMILLER

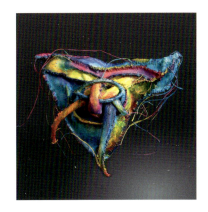

396 MEXICAN MARKET, BROOCH, 1998, PAINTED CANVAS, PAPIER-MÂCHÉ, AND THREAD, FORMED, STITCHED, AND PAINTED
H. 5 ½" × W. 7 ⅛" × D. 3"
PHOTO: GARY POLLMILLER

392 L.A./D.C. SUITE, BROOCH AND CONTAINER BOWL, 1996, PAINTED PAPIER-MÂCHÉ, FORMED AND PAINTED
BOWL: H. 6" × W. 8 ¾" × D. 9 ⅜"
BROOCH: H. 5 ⅛" × W. 4 ⅝" × D. 2 ⅜"
PHOTO: GARY POLLMILLER

397 DE LA LUNA/DEL SOL*, NECKLACE, 1998, PAINTED CANVAS AND CORD, STITCHED, PAINTED, AND TIED
H. 34" × W. 27 ¼" × D. 3 ⅛"
PHOTO: GARY POLLMILLER

393 WRAP AROUND TIME, BRACELET, 1997, STITCHED AND PAINTED CANVAS WITH WATCH, STITCHED AND PAINTED
H. 6" × W. 7" × D. 5 ½"
PHOTO: GARY POLLMILLER

398 DE LA LUNA/DEL SOL*, PINS, ONGOING SINCE 1998, PAINTED CANVAS AND STAINLESS STEEL WIRE, STITCHED AND PAINTED
FROM H. 3 ½" × W. 1" × D. 1" TO H. 18" × W. 2" × D. 2"
COLLECTION: (ONE PIN) PORTER PRICE, USA
PHOTO: GARY POLLMILLER

394 GOLD AND SILVER TEAPOTS*, BROOCHES AND TRAY, 1997, TRAY: PAINTED WOOD, BROOCHES: PAINTED PAPIER-MÂCHÉ AND STAINLESS STEEL WIRE
TRAY: H. 1 ⅜" × W. 17" × D. 8 ¼"
EACH BROOCH: H. 5 ⅜" × W. 11 ¼" × D. 2"
PHOTO: GARY POLLMILLER

399 CHICAGO WINDOWS, BODY SCULPTURE, 1998, PAINTED WOOD AND CORD, CONSTRUCTED, GLUED, PAINTED, AND TIED
TOTAL LENGTH: H. 96" × W. 15" × D. ⅜"
COLLECTION: MUSEUM OF FINE ARTS, BOSTON, GIFT OF ELEANOR KRASK AND MOBILIA GALLERY, CAMBRIDGE, MASSACHUSETTS, USA, ADDITIONAL PINS OF THIS TYPE, COURTESY GALERIE RA, AMSTERDAM
PHOTO: GARY POLLMILLER

395 LIBERTY TORCH, BROOCH, 1997, PAINTED PAPIER-MÂCHÉ WITH STAINLESS STEEL WIRE, FORMED AND PAINTED
H. 6" × W. 5 ⅛" × D. 1 ⅞"
COLLECTION: NATIONAL GALLERY OF VICTORIA, MELBOURNE, AUSTRALIA, PRESENTED BY HELEN WILLIAMS DRUTT ENGLISH, PHILADELPHIA, AND THE ARTIST
PHOTO: GARY POLLMILLER

400 QUE DUERMA CON LOS ANGELITOS [GO SLEEP WITH THE ANGELS], NECKLACE, 1998, PAINTED CANVAS, STITCHED AND PAINTED
H. 20" × W. 20" × D. 2"
PRIVATE COLLECTION
PHOTO: GARY POLLMILLER

401 AMSTERDAM WINDOWS: LACE CURTAINS, NECKLACE, 1998, PAINTED WOOD, LACE FABRIC, AND CORD, CONSTRUCTED, PAINTED AND TIED
H. 18" × W. 18" × D. ¾"
PRIVATE COLLECTION
PHOTO: JOEL DEGEN

406 THE COLORS OF LONDON: TUBE MAP, BROOCH, 1998, PAINTED PAPIER-MÂCHÉ, WOOD, AND STAINLESS STEEL WIRE, CONSTRUCTED, FORMED, AND PAINTED
H. 4 ½" × W. 5 ⅛" × D. 1"
COLLECTION: DR. JAMES B. M. SCHICK, USA
PHOTO: JOEL DEGEN

402 LA DEFENSE, ARMLETS, 1998, PAINTED CANVAS, STITCHED AND PAINTED
EACH: H. 6 ½" × W. 5" × D. 1 ⅜"
RED ARMLET: PRIVATE COLLECTION, THE NETHERLANDS
PHOTO: JOEL DEGEN

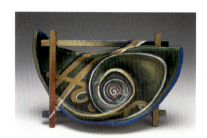

407 THE COLORS OF LONDON: SHOPPING HARRODS, BROOCH, 1998, PAINTED PAPIER-MÂCHÉ, WOOD, AND STAINLESS STEEL WIRE, CONSTRUCTED, FORMED, AND PAINTED
H. 3 ¾" × W. 5 ⅞" × D. 1"
PHOTO: JOEL DEGEN

403 THE COLORS OF LONDON: TAXI, BROOCH, 1998, PAINTED PAPIER-MÂCHÉ, WOOD, AND STAINLESS STEEL WIRE, CONSTRUCTED, FORMED, AND PAINTED
H. 4 ⅞" × W. 5 ½" × D. 1 ½"
COLLECTION: SUZANNE ESSER, THE NETHERLANDS
PHOTO: JOEL DEGEN

408 THE COLORS OF LONDON: A–Z GUIDE, BROOCH, 1998, PAINTED PAPIER-MÂCHÉ, WOOD, AND STAINLESS STEEL WIRE, CONSTRUCTED, FORMED, AND PAINTED
H. 6 ¼" × W. 7 ⅛" × D. 1 ⅞"
PHOTO: GARY POLLMILLER

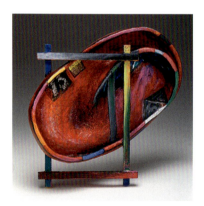

404 THE COLORS OF LONDON: BUS #73, BROOCH, 1998, PAINTED PAPIER-MÂCHÉ, WOOD, AND STAINLESS STEEL WIRE, CONSTRUCTED, FORMED, AND PAINTED
H. 6" × W. 6 ¼" × D. 1 ½"
PRIVATE COLLECTION, THE NETHERLANDS
PHOTO: JOEL DEGEN

409 LA PALMA*, NECKLACE, 1998, PAINTED CANVAS AND METAL RODS, STITCHED AND PAINTED
H. 24" × W. 22 ¼" × D. 5"
PHOTO: GARY POLLMILLER

405 THE COLORS OF LONDON: FOR PATCHY DRIZZLE, BROOCH, 1998, PAINTED PAPIER-MÂCHÉ, WOOD, AND STAINLESS STEEL WIRE, CONSTRUCTED, FORMED, AND PAINTED
H. 5 ½" × W. 7 ⅝" × D. 1 ¾"
PHOTO: JOEL DEGEN

410 PITTSBURG BRICK*, SHOULDER SCULPTURE ON WALL RELIEF, 1998, SHOULDER SCULPTURE: PAINTED CANVAS, STITCHED AND PAINTED, WALL RELIEF: PAINTED WOOD, CONSTRUCTED AND PAINTED
SHOULDER SCULPTURE: H. 13 ¾" × W. 46 ¾" × D. 1"
WALL RELIEF: H. 19" × W. 51 ⅞" × D. 3 ⅜"
PHOTO: GARY POLLMILLER

411 QUETZALCOATL*, NECKLACE AND WALL RELIEF, 1998, NECKLACE: PAINTED CANVAS AND CORD, STITCHED, PAINTED, AND TIED, WALL RELIEF: PAINTED WOOD, CONSTRUCTED AND PAINTED
NECKLACE: H. 16" × W. 16 ¾" × D. 1 ¾"
WALL RELIEF: H. 24" × W. 24 ⅛" × D. 1 ⅞"
PHOTO: GARY POLLMILLER

416 VARIATIONS ON A THEME*, ACCORDION FOLDED BOOK/ NECKLACE/ SASH, 1999, PAINTED CANVAS, WOOD, AND NYLON CORD, CONSTRUCTED, PAINTED, AND TIED
H. 36" × W. 7" × D. 4"
WITH CORDS EXTENDED, H. 82 ¾"
PHOTO: GARY POLLMILLER

412 BOUND COLORS*, NECKLACE ON WALL RELIEF, 1998, NECKLACE: PAINTED WOOD AND CANVAS, CONSTRUCTED, STITCHED, PAINTED AND TIED, WALL RELIEF: PAINTED WOOD
NECKLACE: H. 21" × W. 21" × D. 1 ¼"
WALL RELIEF: H. 36 ¼" × W. 27 ⅜" × D. 1 ⅜"
PHOTO: GARY POLLMILLER

417 TEAPOT ARMLET*, 1999, PAINTED PAPIER-MÂCHÉ AND WOOD, FORMED AND PAINTED
H. 5 ⅜" × W. 12 ½" × D. 6 ¼"
COLLECTION: SHARON M. CAMPBELL, USA
PHOTO

413 DOUBLE DUTCH ARTISTS*, NECKLACES ON WALL RELIEF, 1998, VAN GOGH NECKLACE: PAINTED WOOD AND CORD, CONSTRUCTED, PAINTED AND TIED, MONDRIAN NECKLACE: PAINTED WOOD AND CORD, CONSTRUCTED, PAINTED, AND TIED, WALL RELIEF: PAINTED WOOD, CONSTRUCTED AND PAINTED
VAN GOGH NECKLACE:
H. 15 ¼" × W. 15 ¼" × D. ¾"
MONDRIAN NECKLACE:
H. 14" × W. 14" × D. ⅜"
WALL RELIEF: H. 33 ½" × W. 22 ⅛" × D. 1 ⅝"
PHOTO: GARY POLLMILLER

418 PRIMARIES, ARMLETS, 2000, PAINTED CANVAS, STITCHED AND PAINTED
EACH: H. 6 ⅜" × W. 5" × D. 2 ⅜"
PHOTO: GARY POLLMILLER

414 SQUARES WITHIN SQUARES, NECKLACES, 1998, PAINTED WOOD, PEGGED AND PAINTED
H. 12 ¾" × W. 12 ¾" × D. ⁵⁄₁₆"
H. 11 ½" × W. 11 ½" × D. ⁵⁄₁₆"
H. 10 ¼" × W. 10 ¼" × D. ⁵⁄₁₆"
H. 9" × W. 9" × D. ⅜"
H. 7 ¾" × W. 7 ¾" × D. ⅜"
PHOTO: GARY POLLMILLER

419 CHECKERED, NECKLACE, BUILT IN 1991, REPAINTED IN 2000, PAINTED PAPIER-MÂCHÉ, FORMED AND PAINTED
H. 18 ½" × W. 22 ½" × D. 2 ¾"
PHOTO: GARY POLLMILLER

415 EARRINGS, 1998, PAINTED WOOD AND STAINLESS STEEL WIRE, CONSTRUCTED AND PAINTED
H. 2 ⅞" × W. 2 ⅞" × D. ⅜"
PHOTO: GARY POLLMILLER

420 SPIRAL GALAXY*, EARRING ON A STAND, 2000, EARRING: PAINTED PAPIER-MÂCHÉ OVER WIRE WITH WOOD EARRING BACK, STAND: PAINTED WOOD, FORMED, CONSTRUCTED, AND PAINTED
EARRING: H. 4 ¼" × W. 3 ⅝" × D. 1"
STAND: H. 7 ¾" × W. 8 ½" × D. 2 ½"
PHOTO: GARY POLLMILLER

421 VIBRATIONS*, PAIR OF COLLARS, 2000, PAINTED CANVAS AND WOOD, CONSTRUCTED, STITCHED, AND PAINTED
H. 15 ⁷/₈" × W. 15 ⁷/₈" × D. 1 ¾"
H. 16" × W. 16" × D. 1 ½"
PHOTO: GARY POLLMILLER

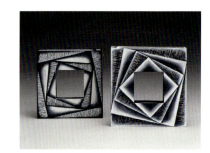

426 MOVING SQUARES, PAIR OF ARMLETS, 2000, PAINTED WOOD, CONSTRUCTED AND PAINTED
LARGE ARMLET: H. 6 ½" × W. 6 ½" × D. 1"
SMALL ARMLET: H. 6" × W. 6" × D. ¾"
PHOTO: GARY POLLMILLER

422 GAP OF DUNLOE*, ARMLET WITH COMPANION SCULPTURE, 2000, PAINTED PAPIER-MÂCHÉ, FORMED AND PAINTED
SCULPTURE: 9" × W. 10" × D. 9 ½"
ARMLET: 4 ¼" × W. 8 ½" × D. 8 ⅛"
PHOTO: GARY POLLMILLER

427 FRAMED, PAIR OF ARMLETS, 2000, PAINTED WOOD, CONSTRUCTED AND PAINTED
LARGE ARMLET: H. 7" × W. 7" × D. 1 ⅜"
SMALL ARMLET: H. 5 ½" × W. 5 ½" × D. ¾"
PHOTO: GARY POLLMILLER

423 FIFTY STATES*, COMMEMORATIVE BODY SCULPTURE WITH EARRINGS, 2000, PAINTED CANVAS, WOOD, AND CORD, STITCHED, RIVETED, AND PAINTED
BODY SCULPTURE: SHOULDER TO BOTTOM, H. 54 ½" × W. 32" × D. ¾"
PAINTING FOR EARRINGS:
H. 8 ⁷/₈" × W. 7 ¼" × D. ⁷/₈"
EARRINGS: ALASKA, H. 2" × W. 1 ½" × D. ¼"
HAWAII, H. 1 ½" × W. 2" × D. ¼"
PHOTO: GARY POLLMILLER

428 TEAPOT WITH TEN ARMLETS*, 2001, PAINTED WOOD, CONSTRUCTED AND PAINTED
TEAPOT: H. 13" × W. 20 ½" × D. 8 ¼"
EACH ARMLET: H. 5 ⅛" × W. 5 ⅛" × D. ⅝"
COLLECTION: DIANE AND SANDY BESSER, USA
PHOTO: GARY POLLMILLER

424 T-T-TEAPOT, NECKLACE, PAINTED WOOD AND CORD, CONSTRUCTED, PAINTED AND TIED
H. 25" × W. 11 ½" × D. 1"
INDIVIDUAL PARTS:
H. 2 ⁷/₈" × W. 2 ½" × D. ¾"
COLLECTION: GLORIA AND SONNY KAMM, USA
PHOTO: GARY POLLMILLER

429 SPINNING WHEELS*, PAIR OF ARMLETS, 2001, PAINTED WOOD, CONSTRUCTED AND PAINTED
LARGE ARMLET: H. 7 ⁷/₈" × W. 6 ½" × D. 6 ½"
SMALL ARMLET: H. 5 ½" × W. 6 ½" × D. 6 ½"
PHOTO: GARY POLLMILLER

425 YEMEN WINDOWS*, BODY SCULPTURE, 2000, PAINTED CANVAS, WOOD, AND CORD, STITCHED, PAINTED, AND TIED
TOTAL LENGTH: H. 100" × W. 15" × D. 1"
PHOTO: GARY POLLMILLER

430 ORBITAL SPHERES, ARMLET, 2001, PAINTED WOOD, CONSTRUCTED AND PAINTED
H. 5" × W. 6" × D. 6"
PRIVATE COLLECTION, SINGAPORE
PHOTO: GARY POLLMILLER

431 BALLYCOTTON BAY*, FINGER
SCULPTURE WITH STAND, 2001,
PAINTED PAPIER-MÂCHÉ AND WOOD,
FORMED AND PAINTED
FINGER SCULPTURE: H. 5" × W. 4" × D. 3 ¼"
STAND: H. 4" × W. 10" × D. 9"
ALICE AND LOUIS KOCH COLLECTION,
SWITZERLAND
PHOTO: GARY POLLMILLER

436 GOLDEN WEB*, NECKLACE AND
WALL RELIEF, 2001, WALL RELIEF:
PAINTED WOOD, CONSTRUCTED AND
PAINTED, NECKLACE: METAL, FABRIC,
THREAD, AND WOOD, FORMED,
WRAPPED, TIED, WOVEN, AND PAINTED
RELIEF: H. 32 ⅛" × W. 23 ⅝" × D. 5 ½"
NECKLACE: H. 13 ⅜" × W. 15 ¾" × D. 4 ⅝"
PHOTO: GARY POLLMILLER

432 FOR WANT OF A NAIL*,
19 HORSESHOE NAIL BROOCHES, 2001,
PAINTED CANVAS, WOOD, AND
STAINLESS STEEL WIRE, STITCHED,
CONSTRUCTED, AND PAINTED
CANVAS BROOCHES: H. 10" × W. 2 ¼" × D. 1 ½"
PINS: H. 6 ½" × W. 1" × D. 1"
PHOTO: GARY POLLMILLER

**437 SHADOWED BY THE LIGHT OF
A FULL MOON, A SCOOP FOR MOON
BEAMS,** SCOOP AND SHADOW, 2002,
SCOOP: PAINTED PAPIER-MÂCHÉ,
FORMED AND PAINTED, SHADOW:
PAINTED SCREEN WIRE, ALUMINUM
WIRE, AND THREAD, STITCHED AND
PAINTED
SCOOP: H. 16 ⅛" × W. 6" × D. 3"
SHADOW: H. 16 ⅛" × W. 7 ¼" × D. 2 ⅜"
PHOTO: GARY POLLMILLER

433 SPEAK NO EVIL*, MASK, 2001,
PAINTED PAPIER-MÂCHÉ, WOOD, AND
CORD, FORMED, PAINTED, AND TIED
MASK: H. 16 ⅞" × W. 13 ¼" × D. 5 ¾"
WITH CORDS: H. 31" × W 13 ¼" × D. 5 ¾"
PHOTO: GARY POLLMILLER

438 AMENHOTEP I*, PAIR OF COLLARS,
2002, DOWEL COLLAR: PAINTED WOOD
AND CORD, PAINTED, STRUNG AND
TIED, FEATHER COLLAR: PAINTED
PAPIER-MÂCHÉ, WOOD, PLASTIC, CORD,
AND THREAD, PAINTED AND TIED
DOWEL COLLAR: H. 25 ¼" × W. 25 ¼" × D. 1"
FEATHER COLLAR: H. 27 ½" × W. 26 ¼" × D. ⅝"
PHOTO: GARY POLLMILLER

434 YELLOW LADDERBACK CHAIR*,
BODY SCULPTURE, 2001, PAINTED
CANVAS AND CORD, STITCHED,
PAINTED, AND TIED
H. 55" × W. 13" × D. 2"
PHOTO: GARY POLLMILLER

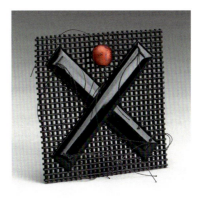

439 BROOCH, 2002, PLASTIC, PAINTED
WOOD, THREAD, STAINLESS STEEL
WIRE, PAINTED AND TIED
H. 4" × W. 4" × D. ¾"
32 BROOCHES MADE AS PINS TO TRADE
AT THE SOCIETY OF NORTH AMERICAN
GOLDSMITHS' PIN SWAP
COLLECTION: DR. JAMES B. M. SCHICK,
USA
PHOTO: GARY POLLMILLER

435 TAKE SIX, NECKLACE, 2001,
PAINTED PAPIER-MÂCHÉ AND CORD,
FORMED, PAINTED, AND TIED
H. 19" × W. 10" × D. 2"
PHOTO: GARY POLLMILLER

440 MOVING EYE, BROOCH, 2002,
PAINTED WOOD, CONSTRUCTED AND
PAINTED
H. 2 ⅞" × W. 4 ⅛" × D. 1 ¼"
COLLECTION: DR. JAMES B. M. SCHICK,
USA
PHOTO: GARY POLLMILLER

441 PROGRESSION*, SUITE OF NECKLACES, ONGOING SINCE 2002, PAINTED PAPER AND WOOD, PAPIER-MÂCHÉ PAPER ON WOOD
EACH: H. 14 ½" × W. 14 ½" × D. ¼"
PHOTO: GARY POLLMILLER

446 POUR VOUS*, TEAPOT WITH A BROOCH AS PART OF THE LID, 2003, TEAPOT: PAINTED PAPIER-MÂCHÉ, WOOD, AND PLASTIC LAMINANT, BROOCH: PAINTED WOOD, PLASTIC LAMINANT, AND STAINLESS STEEL WIRE, TRAY: PAINTED WOOD AND PLASTIC LAMINANT, THREE FORMS: CONSTRUCTED, GLUED, AND PAINTED
TEAPOT: H. 14" × W. 20 ½" × D. 6"
BROOCH: H. 4 ⅛" × W. 4 ⅛" × D. 2"
TRAY: H. 1 ½" × W. 18 ⅛" × D. 18 ⅛"
PHOTO: GARY POLLMILLER

442 NIGHT BLOOM*, EARRINGS ON RELIEF, 2003, RELIEF: PAINTED WOOD, EARRINGS: PAINTED WOOD, PLASTIC LAMINANT, AND STAINLESS STEEL WIRE, CONSTRUCTED, GLUED, AND PAINTED
RELIEF: H. 14 ¾" × W. 13 ¾" × D. 1 ⅞"
EARRINGS: H. 1 ¾" × W. 2" × D. ⅜"
PHOTO: GARY POLLMILLER

447 TOOL BELT AND SCARF FOR SONIA DELAUNAY*, 2003, TOOL BELT: PAINTED WOOD, CORD, AND NICKEL SILVER, CONSTRUCTED, PAINTED, AND TIED, SCARF: PAINTED WOOD AND CORD, PAINTED AND TIED
TOOL BELT: H. 20" × W. 65" × 1 ¼"
SCARF: H. 45 ¾" × W. 5 ⅛" × D. ½"
PHOTO: GARY POLLMILLER

443 AMOEBA, ARMLET WITH STAND, 2003, ARMLET: PAINTED WOOD, STAND: PAINTED WOOD AND PLASTIC LAMINANT
ARMLET: H. 7 ½" × W. 7 ¾" × D. 2 ½"
STAND: H. 5" × W. 2 ½" × D. 2 ⅛"
COURTESY GALERIE RA, AMSTERDAM
PHOTO: GARY POLLMILLER

448 IN HENRI'S GARDEN*, TWO NECKLACES AND WALL RELIEF, 2003, WALL RELIEF: PAINTED PAPER ON WOOD, CONSTRUCTED AND PAPIER-MÂCHÉD WITH PAINTED PAPER, FLOWER PETAL NECKLACE: PAINTED CANVAS, WOOD, PLASTIC LAMINANT, AND BRONZE RODS, CONSTRUCTED, STITCHED, AND PAINTED, SEED POD NECKLACE: PAINTED WOOD AND PLASTIC LAMINANT, CONSTRUCTED AND PAINTED
WALL RELIEF: H. 27 ¾" × W. 27 ½" × D. 9 ¼"
FLOWER PETAL NECKLACE:
H. 31" × W. 30" × D. ⅝"
SEED POD NECKLACE: H. 15" × W. 15" × D. 2 ⅞"
PHOTO: GARY POLLMILLER

444 COCOON FOR SPIRAL NECKLACE*, 2003, SCULPTURE: PAINTED PAPIER-MÂCHÉ OVER STEEL RODS AND THREAD, CONSTRUCTED, WRAPPED, AND PAINTED, NECKLACE: PAINTED PAPIER-MÂCHÉ AND THREAD, FORMED, PAINTED, AND TIED
SCULPTURE: H. 31" × W. 24 ½" × D. 21"
NECKLACE: H. 26" × W. 14 ¼" × D. 4"
PHOTO: GARY POLLMILLER

449 COLOR RHYTHMS, NECKLACE, BROOCH, AND STAND, 2003, NECKLACE: PAINTED PAPIER-MÂCHÉ, BROOCH: PAINTED WOOD, PLASTIC LAMINANT, AND STAINLESS STEEL WIRE, STAND: PAINTED WOOD, PLASTIC LAMINANT, AND STERLING SILVER WIRE, CONSTRUCTED AND PAINTED
NECKLACE: H. 11 ¹³⁄₁₆" × W. 11 ¹³⁄₁₆" × D. 1 ½"
BROOCH: H. 2 ⅞" × W. 2 ⅞" × D. ½"
STAND: H. 4 ⅞" × W. 8 ⅜" × D. 2 ½"
PRIVATE COLLECTION, USA
PHOTO: GARY POLLMILLER

445 DECEPTION*, CHESS SET, 2003, CHESS BOARD: PAINTED WOOD, CONSTRUCTED AND PAINTED, CHESS PIECES: PAINTED WOOD AND PLASTIC LAMINANT, PEGGED, GLUED, AND PAINTED
CHESS BOARD: H. 2 ½" × W. 18" × D. 18"
CHESS PIECES: FROM
H. 2 ½" × W. 1 ½" × D. 1 ½"
TO H. 5 ¼" × W. 3" × D. 2 ½"
PHOTO: GARY POLLMILLER

450 CAROUSEL*, NECKLACE, 2003, PAINTED WOOD AND PLASTIC TOY ANIMALS, CONSTRUCTED AND PAINTED
H. 5 ¾" × W. 22 ⅝" × D. 22 ⅝"
PHOTO: GARY POLLMILLER

451 FENCES*, NECKLACE, 2004, PAINTED WOOD, CONSTRUCTED AND PAINTED
H. 18" × W. 18" × D. 3"
PHOTO: GARY POLLMILLER

456 THE RING THAT GOT OUT OF HAND*, HAND SCULPTURE AND STAND, 2004, HAND SCULPTURE: PAINTED WOOD, PLASTIC LAMINANT, AND BRONZE RODS, STAND: PAINTED WOOD, CONSTRUCTED, GLUED, PAINTED, AND RIVETED
HAND SCULPTURE:
H. 9 ⅛" × W. 11 ¼" × D. 7 ½"
STAND: H. 2 ⅛" × W. 11 ⅝" × D. 11 ⅝"
PHOTO: GARY POLLMILLER

452 RISER*, ARMLET AND STAND, 2004, PAINTED WOOD AND PLASTIC LAMINANT, CONSTRUCTED, GLUED, AND PAINTED
ARMLET: H. 11 ¾" × W. 5 ⅞" × D. 4"
STAND: H. 4 ½" × W. 11 ¾" × D. 11 ¾"
PHOTO: GARY POLLMILLER

457 ORBITING RINGS: BALANCING ACT*, 21 RINGS WITH BASE, 2004, PAINTED WOOD
BASE: H. 2 ½" × W. 13 ⅛" × D. 13 ⅛"
RINGS: FROM H. 2" × W. 1 ⅜" × D. ⅝" TO H. 2 ½" × W. 1 ¾" × D. ¾"
PHOTO: GARY POLLMILLER

453 ECLIPSE OF THE MOON: EARTH'S SHADOW, VEILS, 2004, MOON VEIL: PAINTED AND GESSOED LINEN THREAD, EARTH'S SHADOW VEIL: PAINTED THREAD AND COPPER WIRE, TIED AND PAINTED
MOON VEIL: H. 84" × W. 84" × D. 2"
EARTH'S SHADOW VEIL:
H. 48" × W. 48" × D. 2"
PHOTO: GARY POLLMILLER

458 SELF-PORTRAIT*, BROOCH AND WALL RELIEF, BROOCH: 1996, RELIEF: 2004, BROOCH: PAINTED PAPIER-MÂCHÉ, WOOD, AND STAINLESS STEEL WIRE, FORMED, CONSTRUCTED, AND PAINTED, RELIEF: PAINTED WOOD, CONSTRUCTED AND PAINTED
BROOCH: H. 6 ½" × W. 4 ¾" × D. 3 ¾"
RELIEF: H. 24" × W. 15 ⅝" × D. 3"
PHOTO: GARY POLLMILLER

454 THE PRAETORIAN GUARD*, TEAPOTS WITH RINGS AND TRAY, 2004, PAINTED WOOD AND PLASTIC LAMINANT, CONSTRUCTED, GLUED, AND PAINTED
TRAY: H. 2 ¾" × W. 19" × D. 19"
TEAPOTS: FROM H. 6" × W. 6 ½" × D. 3 ½" TO H. 6 ¼" × W. 7 ⅜" × D. 3 ⅞"
RINGS: FROM H. 3 ½" × W. 3 ½" × D. ⅝" TO H. 4" × W. 4" × D. ⅝"
PHOTO: GARY POLLMILLER

459 TRIBUTE TO ELSA SCHIAPARELLI*, SASH-SHAPED CHÂTELAINE, 2005, PAINTED PAPIER-MÂCHÉ, WOOD, FELT, LEATHER, NYLON CORD, PLASTIC, AND NICKEL WIRE, FORMED, CONSTRUCTED, PAINTED, AND TIED
TOP PART OF CHÂTELAINE:
H. 23" × W. 20 ½" × D. 4 ⅞"
WITH CORDS EXTENDED: 96" LONG
PHOTO: GARY POLLMILLER

455 ODE TO CLOTHESPINS*, SCULPTURE FOR THE NECK, 2004, PAINTED WOOD, NYLON CORD, CLOTHESPINS, AND BRONZE RODS, CONSTRUCTED, PAINTED, AND TIED
H. 44 ½" × W. 29 ⅜" × D. 4"
PHOTO: GARY POLLMILLER

460 GOLDEN DRAGON*, ELBOW ARMLET AND STAND, 2005, ARMLET: PAINTED PAPIER-MÂCHÉ, STAND: PAINTED WOOD AND PLASTIC LAMINANT, CONSTRUCTED, FORMED, GLUED, AND PAINTED
ARMLET: H. 5 ¼" × W. 9 ³⁄₁₆" × D. 8 ⅛"
STAND: H. 2" × W. 14 ⅛" × D. 12 ⅞"
PHOTO: GARY POLLMILLER

461 IT'S A BOY NAMED ROB*, BODY SCULPTURE AND HOUSE, 2005, HOUSE: PAINTED WOOD AND FELT, BODY SCULPTURE: PAINTED WOOD, FELT, FABRIC, NYLON CORD, AND SAFETY PINS, CONSTRUCTED, GLUED, PAINTED, AND TIED
HOUSE: H. 34 ⅞" × W. 45" × D. 1 ⅛"
BODY SCULPTURE: SHOULDERS TO BOTTOM, H. 49 ½" × W. 28 ½" × D. 1 ⅛"
PHOTO: GARY POLLMILLER

466 COSECANT, NECKLACE, 2005, PAPER, WOOD, AND CORD, LAMINATED, GLUED, PAINTED, AND TIED
H. 14 ⅜" × W. 14 ⅜" × D. 1 ½"
PHOTO: GARY POLLMILLER

462 TEAPOT NECKLACE*, 2005, PAINTED WOOD, CONSTRUCTED AND PAINTED
H. 20 ⅝" × W. 23 ¾" × D. 6 ⅛"
PHOTO: GARY POLLMILLER

467 SPIRALING DISCS*, 32 NECK AND ARM RINGS, 2006, PAINTED WOOD, CUT AND PAINTED
WHEN STACKED: H. 15 ½" × W. 12" × D. 12"
LARGEST RING: H. 12" × W. 12" × D. ½"
PHOTO: GARY POLLMILLER

463 GRASS*, NECKLACE, 2005, PAINTED CANVAS AND WOOD, STITCHED, PAINTED, AND PEGGED
H. 22" × W. 22 ½" × D. 3 ¾"
PHOTO: GARY POLLMILLER

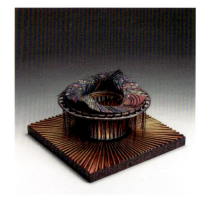

468 CONNECTIONS*, BOOK NECKLACE (124 PAGES) WITH STAND, NECKLACE STARTED IN 1999, NECKLACE AND STAND: 2006, NECKLACE: PAINTED PAPIER-MÂCHÉ OVER SOLDERED RODS, PAGES OF PAINTED AND STITCHED CANVAS AND OTHER FABRICS, VINYL, PLASTIC, ALUMINUM, FOUND MATERIALS, AND THREAD, CONSTRUCTED, PAPIER-MÂCHÉD, STITCHED, AND PAINTED, STAND: PAINTED WOOD, CONSTRUCTED AND PAINTED
NECKLACE: H. 20" × W. 20" × D. 10"
STAND: H. 10 ½" × W. 25" × D. 25"
PHOTO: GARY POLLMILLER

464 SCHIAPARELLI'S CIRCLES*, NECKLACE, 2005, PAINTED WOOD, CANVAS, AND THREAD, STITCHED AND PAINTED
H. 30" × W. 30" × D. 1 ½"
WITH CORDS EXTENDED: 88" LONG
PHOTO: GARY POLLMILLER

469 FROM CONNECTIONS, BROOCH, 2006, ANODIZED ALUMINUM, PAINTED WOOD, THREAD, AND STAINLESS STEEL WIRE, CONSTRUCTED, PAINTED AND TIED
H. 3 ¼" × W. 2 ¾" × D. ⅜"
COLLECTION: DR. JAMES B. M. SCHICK, USA
PHOTO: GARY POLLMILLER

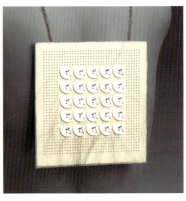

465 BUTTON, BUTTON, WHO HAS THE BUTTON? NECKLACE, 2005, PAPER, PLASTIC BUTTONS, PAINT, AND NYLON THREAD, LAMINATED, PIERCED, TIED, AND PAINTED
H. 7 ¼" × W. 6 ⅞" × D. ⅛"
PHOTO: GARY POLLMILLER

470 BANDS OF RINGS*, 32 RINGS ON PEDESTALS, 2006, RINGS: PAINTED WOOD, PEDESTALS: PAINTED WOOD AND PLASTIC LAMINANT, STANDS: PAINTED WOOD, CUT, CONSTRUCTED, GLUED, AND PAINTED
RINGS: FROM H. 1 ⅝" × W. 1 ⅝" × D. ¼"
TO H. 3 ⅝" × W. 2 ⅜" × D. ¼"
RINGS ON PEDESTALS: FROM
H. 3 ¾" × W. 2 ¾" × D. 1 ½"
TO H. 8" × W. 2 ⅜" × D. 2 ⅜"
STANDS: H. 2 ⅜" × W. 26" × D. 26"
AND H. 2 ¼" × W. 28" × D. 28"
PHOTO: GARY POLLMILLER

471 RADIANTS, PAIR OF NECKLACES,
2006, PAINTED PAPIER-MÂCHÉ AND
CORD, FORMED, PAINTED, AND TIED
LARGE: H. 31" × W. 28" × D. 3"
SMALL: H. 27" × W. 21" × D. 3"
PHOTO: GARY POLLMILLER

472 IT'S A COLOR RUN, NECKLACE,
2006, PAINTED PAPIER-MÂCHÉ AND
NYLON CORD, FORMED, PAINTED, AND
TIED
H. 37 ¼" × D. 2 ¾"
COURTESY MOBILIA GALLERY,
CAMBRIDGE, MASSACHUSETTS
PHOTO: GARY POLLMILLER

473 FROM CHILDHOOD, BROOCH AND
WALL RELIEF, 2006, BROOCH: PAINTED
WOOD AND STAINLESS STEEL WIRE,
RELIEF: PAINTED WOOD, CONSTRUCTED
AND PAINTED
BROOCH: H. 5 ⅜" × W. 5 3/16" × D. ⅝"
RELIEF: H. 11 ¾" × W. 11 ¾" × D. 1 ½"
PHOTO: GARY POLLMILLER

474 CHAGALL'S CIRCLES*, NECKLACE,
2006, PAINTED CANVAS, WOOD,
AND THREAD, STITCHED, PAINTED,
AND TIED
NECKLACE: H. 41" × W. 41" × D. 1"
WITH CORDS EXTENDED: 78" LONG
PHOTO: GARY POLLMILLER

**475 MUCH ADO ABOUT TWENTY
BRACELETS*,** FOUR-PART FOLDING
SCREEN WITH BRACELETS, 2006,
PAINTED WOOD, STEEL RODS, AND
BRONZE RODS, CONSTRUCTED AND
PAINTED
SCREEN WITH BRACELETS (TWO
SECTIONS): H. 39 ⅝" × W. 49" × D. 1 ½"
SCREEN WITH BRACELETS (TWO
SECTIONS): H. 39 ⅝" × W. 46 ¼" × D. 1 ½"
WHEN EXTENDED, SCREEN IS 15 LINEAR
FEET LONG
BRACELETS (EACH): H. 5" × W. 6" × D. 1 ⅜"
PHOTO: GARY POLLMILLER

EPILOGUE: A QUESTION OF DIMENSION AND DEFINITION

Fritz Falk

The question of what jewelry actually is has been addressed by sociologists, anthropologists, historians of culture and art, as well as ethnologists. Why do people adorn themselves? The answers offered are so manifold and diverse that they are both instructive and confusing, involving magical, material, or purely aesthetic reasons.

Jewelry must focus on human beings – members of early cultures, aristocrats and commoners, rural folk, urban punks, and wearers, male or female. But objects for adornment also display skills in craftsmanship and design, which may stem from venerable tradition, be conventionally derivative, or – liberated from all social and commercial constraints – may spring from entirely personal creativity.

Today there are traditional craftsmen in African tribal villages. There are goldsmiths and jewelers who prioritize the material value of their jewelry. Remarkably, since the mid-20th century, artists in jewelry, like sculptors and painters, and some architects, create objects to adorn the human body from an inner need to do so and with a decidedly individual take on design.

A one-off brooch, a bangle, a pendant, which document their creator's originality in modern modes of expression, may for all that remain a brooch, a bangle, or a pendant. However, some have overcome traditional forms of jewelry emphasizing and distinguishing parts of the body. This fascinating alternative is adorning the entire body with large objects, defying the usual categories of jewelry. This is body jewelry, which allows human beings in all their corporeality to become "total works of art jewelry."

While anthropologists might assign these works to phenomena familiar to them from faraway cultures, where they are embedded in magical and ritual contexts, in the present connection, by contrast, the focus is on the artistic, the aesthetic aspect.

Now Marjorie Schick's œuvre comes into our field of vision. Take, for example, a large, collar-like object of painted wood which, along with other Marjorie Schick body sculptures, was the cynosure of all eyes at the 1989 "Ornamenta 1" (cat. nos. 334–338). Although it is laid about the neck, it is not a piece of neck jewelry in the usual sense, certainly not a decorative accessory. This object by Marjorie Schick is, like all the artist's creations, a work of art as such, with which and through which the man or woman wearing it becomes a living work of art. How imaginatively Marjorie Schick creates associations with other artists when she expresses her reverence for a particular artist with a body sculpture such as Chagall's Circles (cat. no. 474)! In calling one of her works Tribute to Elsa Schiaparelli (cat. no. 459), she is wittily and perhaps with a pinch of irony paying tribute to fellow jewelry designers.

Marjorie Schick is certainly not the only artist to adorn the entire human body. Outstripping the field, however, she is an artist for whom the human being is not just a consumer but rather an integral constituent of her art. Thus, by so excitingly transposing adornment to a new intellectual and formal plane, Marjorie Schick challenges us to take up a stance. She is also challenging us to ask once again what jewelry actually is in order to find a definition appropriate to her work.

APPENDIX

SIGNIFIERS
Representative statements about my work at various times in my career

MARJORIE SCHICK, 2003, CELEBRATION NECKLACE
(SEE CAT. NO. 173)   PHOTO: GARY POLLMILLER

Looking back at my attempts to explain my artistic aspirations over the years, I am struck by how my concerns have elaborated a core interest in sculptural forms that involve the body, yet exist independently as works of art. This was my intention as I wrote the thesis statement for my Master of Fine Arts degree at Indiana University in 1966 and remains the essence of who I am as an artist as I explained in my artist statements in 1975, 1985, and 1999.

Taken together, these four statements explain what has been constant in my work and how my intentions have evolved over time. They, like the artwork documented in the pages of this book and the writings accompanying these pieces, reveal where I began and where I have come through a lifetime devoted to art. I could not have known in 1966 what I could achieve. It would have been surprising to me, I am sure, to know that what I saw in my work then would remain with me. Also surprising to me would have been the fact that this interest in sculpture for the human form would nurture such a varied body of work.

M.F.A. THESIS STATEMENT, 1966

Jewelry is an object of bodily adornment to enhance the wearer. Humans have exhibited a need or desire for decoration and ornamentation throughout their history, but this urge need not be satisfied with objects of ordinary importance. Instead, a piece of jewelry can perform its functions of adornment and give pleasure while existing as an art form in its own right.

The primary purpose of my jewelry is to stimulate and delight both the wearer and the viewer in a small scale world of imagination and fancy. I want the viewer to examine these sculptured forms, to see all the parts, and to somehow become involved in the object. My jewelry is an interpretation of my emotions and attitudes. That it is a reflection of my present environment is unavoidable. In this way my jewelry forms are a part of the contemporary world.

When I begin a piece of jewelry I have no preconceived image of what the end product will be. Preliminary ideas are derived mainly from drawings of natural objects and from experimental arrangements with pieces of metal, stone, and other materials. I feel that no material should arbitrarily be excluded from consideration. I build upon the initial idea, rework and refine it, and even cut the piece apart—until I arrive at a piece of jewelry which exhibits visual balance, harmonious negative and positive shapes, a strong silhouette shape, and unity between the whole and smaller parts. Although the techniques I use are not new, I try to create a three-dimensional form which is unique.

I derive inspiration for my pieces of jewelry from a variety of sources. The idea for the large silver necklace (*Continuous Form* [cat. no. 27]) evolved from a drawing. I began the object by repeating in metal one line in the drawing but then deviated from this, and I proceeded to build the object piece by piece, relating each new part to previously made lines, shapes, and spaces. The necklace was also inspired by the idea of making a contemporary breast plate. It was my intention to create a serious art object that would at the same time communicate a feeling of fantasy.

My last piece (*Wheatfields* [cat. no. 59] done prior to the thesis exhibition), the large necklace composed of many radiating lines and four brown stones, is the present development of experimentation with grouped linear forms which began with the small brass pin with extended iron lines (*Small and Mighty* [cat. no. 9].) The necklace was also inspired by Vincent van Gogh's *Wheat Field with Crows* (1890) in which one of the three horizontal bands making up the painting was composed of myriads of repeated long fine lines ending in short strokes moving at right angles from the shafts. The density and intensity of these massed lines which represented wheat in Van Gogh's painting motivated me to create a piece of jewelry that approximated the effect of those lines.

In these last two pieces I believe I have made the transition in my work from making objects which exist simply as articles of adornment to the making of objects which elicit from both the wearer and the viewer an emotional commitment. I do not want my jewelry to be a passive art form; instead, it must act upon the viewer and the wearer. My jewelry may surprise and if necessary disturb the viewer, but above all it must be aggressive—it must be notable.

In my work I have been concerned with exploring the relationships of lines, planes, and spaces in the construction of three-dimensional forms. I also consider color, texture, movement, sound, balance, weight, and, of course, how the object will fit the body. In my last pieces I have been more interested in the manipulation of forms in space and the projection of these forms into the immediate environment of the wearer. I intend my future pieces to continue these explorations into three-dimensional jewelry forms.

STATEMENT, 1975

I create body sculptures that are wearable, aiming for the intimacy that occurs when one places clothing or jewelry on the body. My pieces are large-scaled and require from the wearer a total commitment because they draw attention to the wearer in their theatrical appearance. The objects also require that the wearer be more conscious of his or her body such as how arms are placed against the body or how one moves through space.

In 1966, while preparing for my final graduate review at Indiana University, I looked at an issue of *Art in America* magazine that featured an article about the sculptor David Smith. Looking at his sculptures pictured in the fields at Bolton Landing, it occurred to me that one could experience the forms better if able to walk up to them and put an arm or a head through a hole in the form. In that way, the viewer of the sculpture could become a participant and actually become part of the sculpture. At that moment, I knew that what I wanted to do was to create sculptures to wear.

My metal jewelry at that time was sculptural but it was not until later that year, when in my first year of teaching, I started building with papier-mâché. The first six bracelets were not of an exceptional size, but as I made more pieces, I found the material was perfect for constructing large forms for the body because it was relatively light weight, and the fact that I could paint the pieces appealed to me a great deal. My goal was to create forms that were wearable but that existed as finished sculptures from all directions when not on the body.

The human body is large and capable of carrying great weight both visually and physically. In other cultures, large jewelry is worn and can cover a large portion of the body. Being aware of this made me unafraid to build body sculptures of any size even if wearable for only a short period of time. Some of my pieces enhance the body while others appear to engulf an arm or neck or even the entire body.

When wearing a flower corsage or ball gown, one must move through space more carefully, being more conscious of both large and small movements and how one walks through doorways and gets into and out of a car. Normally, wearing jewelry does not make people walk or move differently but why not? I am aiming for the experience of creating more awareness of one's physical presence. These objects create new experiences for the wearer, whether for a few minutes or for several hours. When the object is removed, there is the memory of how the piece felt while on the body as well as how the body felt in the object.

STATEMENT, 1985

Currently my work is a sculptural statement to wear made of painted wood and natural wood, rubber tubing, plastic rods and pierced paper. Technique does not interest me beyond the fact that it is a means of creating a form. My pieces should have a sense of presence about them no matter their size. Also, my works should have a timeless quality and be strong forms aesthetically now or in one-hundred years. My aim is to create visual tension between the directional forces and color relationships. I prefer that the viewer be shocked or even repelled than to remain passive.

The human figure is the reason for my work but the forms are complete in themselves when not being worn. These are not maquettes for larger works. They are conceived and created in relationship to the scale of the human figure. While they are meant to be worn, they are also meant to be finished sculptures when not on a person.

The closest I am to pure joy is to be in the studio, started on a new piece, the radio turned up loud, and the challenges still ahead of me to be met, yet imagining a suite of works building upon these ideas. At the moment, my aim is combining straight lines with curves and emphasizing the contrasts between them using straight dowels with natural birch sticks. It is also occurring in the pieces made of straight plastic rods with curved shapes of pierced paper.

As a teacher, I try to instill in my students a sense of excitement and involvement in what they are doing in addition to an appreciation for self-discipline.

STATEMENT, 1999

In creating jewelry and body sculptures, I make objects that are finished sculptures when not on the body. The large scale and sculptural qualities make the wearer extremely conscious of the body as well as of the space around the object, thus a moving sculpture. When the piece is removed and viewed as a sculpture, either on the wall, on a painting, or on a pedestal, the wearer holds memories of how the object felt and affected mobility, how it heightened awareness of the body, and how it caused those who encountered it to react.

Aesthetics and wearability are my prime considerations. Three-dimensional structure and painted color are of equal importance in my work. Created of non-traditional materials, these objects are personal studies in shape, color, space, pattern, and rhythm. The materials, such as stitched and stuffed canvas or plywood, are a means to an end. Canvas is often chosen because it is the material painters use and my work is as much about the painted surfaces as the three-dimensional structure. Wood is another choice of materials selected for its weight and its rigidity. It works well for the building or constructing of the forms and is also easily painted.

Innovation in my work results from a consistently experimental approach to form and materials. Size and three-dimensionality intentionally push the boundaries of wearability. Ultimately, I approach aesthetic problems in the same way any fine artist would.

TIMELINE

1941   Born August 29, Taylorville, Illinois.

1957–9 Classes for high school students at the School of the Chicago Art Institute.

1959   Graduated from Evanston Township High School, Evanston, Illinois (studied fashion design with Frank Tresise).

        Started undergraduate program at the University of Wisconsin, Madison.

1963   Completed Bachelors of Science degree (with Honors) in Art Education, University of Wisconsin (studied jewelry with Arthur Vierthaler).

        Married James B. M. Schick.

        Started graduate program at Indiana University, Bloomington.

1966   Completed Masters of Fine Arts degree (with Distinction) in Jewelry Design and Metalsmithing, Indiana University (studied with Professor Alma Eikerman).

1966–7 Taught Jewelry Design at the University of Kansas, Lawrence, with Professor Carlyle H. Smith. Started the first papier-mâché pieces.

        Trip to Bloomington to see Professor Eikerman and to New York to meet with Paul J. Smith at the American Craft Museum (now the Museum of Arts & Design) to show him her new papier-mâché bracelets.

1967–present   Began a teaching career at Pittsburg State University, Kansas. Subjects taught include Jewelry, Crafts, Weaving, Visual Explorations, Design, Art Education, Senior and Graduate Exhibition, Senior and Graduate Seminars, and a Special Topics class in Body Coverings.

1970   Birth of son Robert M. Schick.

1975   Lectured at the Philadelphia College of Art, an early off-campus presentation.

1976   Sabbatical leave that included four months of travel in Europe looking at museums, jewelry studios, and jewelry schools.

1978   Audited a Ceramics class and created ceramic jewelry.

        Created a ring of thick-ply cardboard and dowels.

1979   Enrolled in a Plastics class at Pittsburg State University and made jewelry of plastic.

1981   Created her first dowel stick brooch.

        Created the first thread "drawings" that inspired jewelry of paper-and-wire and paper-and-thread.

1982   A solo show at a Coffeyville Community College forced the creation of two new series of works, six brooches of painted dowels and six brooches of paper-and-wire. Having no showcases and only a brick wall, the situation demanded a solution of hanging the brooches on covered plywood mountings. This show supplied the six pieces that were entered in the "Jewellery Redefined" exhibition.

        Attended the opening of "Jewellery Redefined: First International Exhibition of Multi-Media Non-Precious Jewellery" at the British Crafts Centre and related symposium in London.

        Installed the Schick jewelry collection exhibition at Pittsburg State University.

        Invitations to exhibit at Galerie Ra in Amsterdam and Aspects Gallery in London.

1983   Sabbatical leave to study metalsmithing (for one term) at the Sir John Cass, City of London Polytechnic (now the Department of Art, Media and Design, London Metropolitan University).

        Attended the opening of the new Galerie Ra in Amsterdam.

        Returned to Amsterdam for first solo exhibition at Galerie Ra (with mother).

MARJORIE SCHICK AS THE "QUEEN OF
TOMORROW" ON A HOMECOMING FLOAT
AT EASTERN ILLINOIS UNIVERSITY,
CHARLESTON, 1947

DR. JAMES B. M. SCHICK,
2005, YELLOWSTONE
NATIONAL PARK, WYOMING
PHOTO: MARJORIE SCHICK

ROBERT SCHICK, 1971, 15 MONTHS, HOLDING "EIKERMAN'S ARMLET"
(CAT. NO. 76)   PHOTO: DR. JAMES B. M. SCHICK

MARJORIE, JAMES, AND ROBERT SCHICK IN SAN FRANCISCO,
2001

MARJORIE SCHICK, 1996, ARROWMONT SCHOOL OF
ARTS AND CRAFTS, GATLINBURG, TENNESSEE
PHOTO: ELLEN CHEEK

HARRIETE ESTEL BERMAN
AND MARJORIE SCHICK, 1993,
SOCIETY OF NORTH
AMERICAN GOLDSMITHS,
CINCINNATI (MARJORIE
SCHICK WEARING A BROOCH
BY CATHY HARRIS)
PHOTO: MARCIA LEWIS

BREITENHOLZ, GERMANY,
FROM WHICH JIM'S GREAT-
GRANDFATHER LEFT IN 1854
FOR AMERICA
PHOTO: DR. JAMES B. M. SCHICK

MARJORIE SCHICK, 1996, ARROWMONT SCHOOL OF
ARTS AND CRAFTS, GATLINBURG, TENNESSEE
PHOTO: ELLEN CHEEK

PROFESSOR ALMA EIKERMAN, 1990, AT THE
CONTEMPORARY KOREAN METALSMITHING
EXHIBITION, ST. LOUIS, MISSOURI
PHOTO: MARJORIE SCHICK

MARJORIE SCHICK AND
HELEN W. DRUTT ENGLISH,
1986

HELEN W. DRUTT ENGLISH AND
DIRK ALLGAIER, MUNICH, 2007

PERFORMANCE OF "CHOREOGRAPHING THE OBJECT:
AN EVENING OF VISUAL ART AND DANCE" AT
PITTSBURG STATE UNIVERSITY, PITTSBURG, KANSAS,
1977   PHOTO: DR. JAMES B. M. SCHICK

1984   Artist-in-Residence (summer) at the Sir John Cass.

1985   Curated the "Body Works and Wearable Sculpture" international invitational exhibition for the Visual Arts Center of Alaska, Anchorage.

In Alaska, was presented a gift of striped birch sticks that inspired a series of brooches, bracelets, and a necklace as well as pieces made with black and unpainted dowels.

1986   Introduced plywood into her work after discovering a need to create planes in the pieces in addition to lines of dowels.

Began to concentrate on larger forms for the body.

Solo exhibitions at VO Galerie in Washington, D.C. and at the Helen Drutt Gallery in Philadelphia.

1987   Explored a variety of brush strokes, the layering of paint, and painted textures.

Started the first in a series of back sculptures.

A solo show of painted dowel pieces titled "Jewelry: Marjorie Schick" at the Alexander Hogue Gallery at the University of Tulsa caused a re-evaluation of what to call the work. As soon as the show was installed, a person walked through the exhibition, carefully looked at each object, and turned and asked "Where's the jewelry?"

1988   Constructed her first wall relief to hold a bracelet.

Made her first "painting" to hold three necklaces.

"Transition" solo exhibition, Galerie Ra, Amsterdam.

Trip to South Korea with American metalsmiths organized by Komelia Okim.

1989   Attended the opening of "Ornamenta I" in Pforzheim, Germany.

Solo exhibition at the Nordenfjeldske Kunstindustrimuseum, Trondheim, Norway.

1990   Retrospective at Indiana University as the recipient of the 1990 School of Fine Arts Distinguished Alumni Award.

Commission for a folding screen in Utrecht, the Netherlands.

1991   Sabbatical leave to be Artist-in-Residence at Middlesex Polytechnic and at the Sir John Cass, London.

Faculty exchange through Pittsburg State University to lecture at Silapakorn University in Bangkok, Thailand.

1992   Attended the opening of "Design Visions Triennial" in Perth, Australia, and lectured for the Jewellers and Metalsmiths Group of Australia National Conference.

1993   Åkersvika-Addenda, ten-day workshop in Hamar, Norway, sponsored by the Cultural Section of the 1994 Lillehammer Olympic Organizing Committee.

1994   Invited to exhibit at Mobilia Gallery in Cambridge, Massachusetts, where Libby and JoAnne Cooper curate numerous theme shows inspiring pieces such as *Yellow Ladderback Chair* for a chair exhibition, *Variations on a Theme* Folding Book Necklace/Sash for a book show, *Spiraling Discs* (that create a vessel form) for "Basket (R)evolution" and numerous wearable teapots for teapot exhibitions.

1996   Introduced canvas, the material of painters, into the work.

Created three sets of earrings mounted on reliefs for "Earrings: Classic and Wild" at Electrum Gallery, London.

1998   Sabbatical leave – trip to Mexico to visit eight historical sites to research color for exhibitions.

Lived and worked in London for six weeks.

"Sense of Place" solo exhibition at Galerie Ra, Amsterdam.

"Time, Color, Place" exhibition at Mobilia Gallery, Cambridge, Massachusetts.

2000   Was made a Fellow of the American Craft Council.

2002   Started the *Progression* suite of necklaces that inspired the beginning of a series of autobiographical works including *It's a Boy Named Rob, Fences, From Childhood, Carousel,* and *Ode to Clothespins.*

2004   Interviewed (by Tacey Rosolowski) for the Archives of American Art Oral History Program, Smithsonian Institution, as part of the Nanette L. Laitman Documentation Project for Craft and Decorative Arts in America.

2007   The beginning of the retrospective "Sculpture Transformed: the Work of Marjorie Schick" curated by Tacey Rosolowski and organized by International Arts and Artists of Washington, D.C. The venues selected for the retrospective included:

    San Francisco Museum of Craft + Design, San Francisco, California, June–September, 2007

    Indiana University Art Museum, Bloomington, Indiana, October–December, 2007

    Marianna Kistler Beach Museum of Art, Kansas State University, Manhattan, Kansas, January–March, 2008

    Fuller Craft Museum, Brockton, Massachusetts, May–September, 2008

    Muskegon Museum of Art, Muskegon, Michigan, December, 2008–February, 2009.

PROFESSIONAL BACKGROUND

1983
Extended Study Program, Sir John Cass School of Art, City of London Polytechnic (now the Department of Art, Media and Design, London Metropolitan University), UK

1967–present
Professor of Art, Pittsburg State University, Pittsburg, Kansas

1966
Instructor, University of Kansas, Lawrence

1966
Master of Fine Arts (with Distinction) Jewelry-Metalsmithing, Indiana University, Bloomington

1963
Bachelor of Science (with Honors) Art Education, University of Wisconsin, Madison

WORKS IN PUBLIC COLLECTIONS

Arkansas Arts Center, Little Rock, Arkansas, USA
Gemeentelijk Van Reekummuseum, Apeldoorn, the Netherlands
Indiana University Fine Arts Museum, Bloomington, Indiana, USA
Kohler Company Art Collection, Kohler, Wisconsin, USA
Middlesbrough Institute of Modern Art, Middlesbrough, UK
Museum of Applied Art, Trondheim, Norway
Museum of Arts & Design, formerly the American Craft Museum, New York, USA
Museum of Fine Arts, Boston, Massachusetts, USA
Museum of Fine Arts, Houston, Texas, USA
National Gallery of Victoria, Melbourne, Australia
National Museum of Art, Architecture, and Design, Museum of Decorative Arts and Design, Oslo, Norway
National Museum of Contemporary Art, Seoul, South Korea
National Museum of Modern Art, Kyoto, Japan
National Museums of Scotland, Edinburgh, UK
Philadelphia Museum of Art, Pennsylvania, USA
Renwick Gallery of the Smithsonian American Art Museum, Washington, D.C., USA
Victoria and Albert Museum, London, UK
Wichita Center for the Arts, Wichita, Kansas, USA

PROFESSIONAL AWARDS AND DISTINCTIONS (SELECTED)

2005
University Professor (honorary rank), Pittsburg State University (renewal)

2004
Interviewed by Tacey Rosolowski for the Archives of American Art Oral History Program, Smithsonian Institution, as part of the Nanette L. Laitman Documentation Project for Craft and Decorative Arts in America
Kansas Artist Fellowship Award, Crafts

2002
Governor's Artist of the Year Award

2000
Fellow of the American Craft Council
University Professor (honorary rank), Pittsburg State University

1997
Outstanding Faculty Award, Pittsburg State University

1990
Distinguished Alumni Award, School of Fine Arts, Indiana University

1985
Mid-America Arts Alliance/National Endowment for the Arts, Fellowship Award in Crafts

1983
"International Jewellery Art Exhibition", the 5th Tokyo Triennial, Isetan Art Museum, Tokyo, Japan, Award

EXHIBITIONS

SOLO EXHIBITIONS

2003
A RETROSPECTIVE, Alice C. Sabatini Gallery, Topeka and Shawnee County Public Library, Topeka, Kansas

2001
BODY WORKS: STRUCTURE, COLOR, SPACE, Decorative Arts Museum, Arkansas Arts Center, Little Rock, Arkansas

1998
A SENSE OF PLACE, Galerie Ra, Amsterdam, the Netherlands
TIME, COLOR, PLACE, Mobilia Gallery, Cambridge, Massachusetts

1991
BODY SCULPTURE, Solo Exhibition, Boger Gallery, College of the Ozarks, Branson, Missouri

1990
A RETROSPECTIVE, Indiana University Fine Arts Gallery, Indiana University, Bloomington, Indiana, as part of the 1990 School of Fine Arts Distinguished Alumni Award

1989
Museum of Applied Art, Trondheim, Norway

1988
TRANSITION, Galerie Ra, Amsterdam, the Netherlands
BODY CONSTRUCTIONS, Hiestand Galleries, Miami University, Oxford, Ohio
University of Missouri Fine Arts Gallery, the University of Missouri, Columbia

1987
JEWELRY, Alexander Hogue Gallery, the University of Tulsa, Oklahoma
BODYWORKS, Fred Jones Junior Memorial Art Center, University of Oklahoma, Norman

1986
Helen Drutt Gallery, Philadelphia, Pennsylvania
DIFFERENT DIRECTIONS IN PAPER, VO Galerie, Washington, D.C.

1985
JEWELRY AND DRAWINGS, Kansas State University Union Gallery, Manhattan, Kansas

1983
Galerie Ra, Amsterdam, the Netherlands

1982
Friends University Library Gallery, Wichita, Kansas
Coffeyville Community College, Coffeyville, Kansas

1981
Muchnic Gallery, Atchison, Kansas
JEWELRY AND DRAWINGS, Davis Gallery, Idaho State University, Pocatello, Idaho

1975
Art Department Gallery, University of Delaware, Newark, Delaware
The Stone House Gallery, Fredonia, Kansas

GROUP EXHIBITIONS (SELECTED)

2007
JEWELRY BY ARTISTS: THE DAPHNE FARAGO COLLECTION, the Lee Gallery, Museum of Fine Arts, Boston, Massachusetts
SIGNS OF LIFE, Facèré Jewelry Art Gallery, Seattle, Washington
TOPEKA COMPETITION 28, Alice C. Sabatini Gallery, Topeka and Shawnee County Public Library, Kansas, juried (award)

2006
RADIANT: 30 Years Ra, Galerie Ra, Amsterdam, the Netherlands
LUCCA PREZIOSA 2006: NO BODY DECORATION, RESEARCH JEWELLERY AS REDEFINITION OF THE HUMAN BODY, Villa Bottini, Lucca, Italy
CHALLENGING THE CHÂTELAINE!, co-organized by Helen Drutt: Philadelphia, and the Designmuseo, Helsinki
THE EDGES OF GRACE: PROVOCATIVE, UNCOMMON CRAFT, curated by Gail M. Brown, Fuller Craft Museum, Brockton, Massachusetts

BASKET (R)EVOLUTION, curated by Mobilia Gallery, Fuller Craft Museum, Brockton, Massachusetts
MIDWEST METAL ARTISTS INVITATIONAL, Fine Arts Center Gallery, Northeastern Illinois University
LIFE INSIGHT: THE HUMAN EXPERIENCE, curated by Gail M. Brown, Kentucky Museum of Art and Craft, Louisville, Kentucky
PARAMETERS OF PRECIOUSNESS, Gahlberg Gallery, College of DuPage, Glen Ellyn, Illinois
METALISMS: SIGNATURE WORKS IN JEWELRY AND METALSMITHING, Center for Visual Arts, Metropolitan State College of Denver, Colorado
THE NECKLACE SHOW, Velvet da Vinci Gallery, San Francisco, California
CELEBRATION OF THE NECKLACE, Mobilia Gallery at SOFA (Sculpture Objects and Functional Art) Chicago
TOYS DESIGNED BY ARTISTS EXHIBITION, Arkansas Arts Center, Little Rock, Arkansas

2005
SCHMUCK 2005, Sonderschau der 57. Internationalen Handwerksmesse, Munich, Germany
100 BROOCHES: Celebrating 500 Brooches by Lark Books, Velvet da Vinci Gallery, San Francisco and traveled
CRAFTS, ETC.: CONTEMPORARY JEWELRY DESIGN AND METALSMITHING BY MASTER ARTIST CRAFTSMEN, curated by Robly A. Glover, Buddy Holly Center, Lubbock, Texas
MAGNIFICENT EXTRAVAGANCE: ARTISTS AND OPULENCE, Charles A. Wustum Museum of Fine Arts, Racine, Wisconsin
THE TEAPOT REDEFINED IV, Mobilia Gallery at SOFA, Chicago
CELEBRATING THE NECKLACE, Mobilia Gallery, Cambridge, Massachusetts
KANSAS ARTIST CRAFTSMAN ASSOCIATION MEMBERS' EXHIBITION, Alice C. Sabatini Gallery, Topeka and Shawnee County Public Library, Topeka, Kansas

2004
A VIEW FROM AMERICA: CONTEMPORARY JEWELRY (1974–2003), organized by Helen W. Drutt English, Gold Treasury at the Royal Institute, Melbourne Institute of Technology, Australia
HOUDT van SIERADEN, Lous Martin Galerie, Delft, the Netherlands
TREASURES FROM THE VAULT: JEWELRY FROM THE PERMANENT COLLECTION, Museum of Arts & Design (formerly the American Craft Museum) New York
RINGS, curated by Robert Ebendorf, Cannon Gallery of the Gallery of Art and Design, North Carolina State University, Raleigh, and traveled in the US

SCULPTURAL JEWELRY, Mobilia Gallery at SOFA, New York
KANSAS ARTIST CRAFTSMAN ASSOCIATION MEMBERS' EXHIBITION, Manhattan Arts Center, Manhattan, Kansas

2003
CHESS: CHESSMEN BY INTERNATIONAL ARTISTS, Velvet da Vinci Gallery, San Francisco, California; Vennel Gallery, Irvine, Scotland; The Gallery, Ruthin Craft Centre, Denbighshire, Wales; Crafts Council Shop at the Victoria and Albert Museum, London, England; the John Michael Kohler Arts Center, Sheboygan, Wisconsin; Thomas Mann I/O Gallery, New Orleans, Louisiana
JEWELS AND GEMS, Renwick Gallery of the Smithsonian American Art Museum, Washington, D.C.
JEWELRY BEYOND JEWELRY, Hunterdon Museum of Art, Clinton, New Jersey
ART FOR THE EAR, Mobilia Gallery at SOFA, New York
TEAPOTS, Mobilia Gallery at SOFA, Chicago
PLANTING, POTTING AND PRUNING: ARTISTS AND THE CULTIVATED LANDSCAPE, Charles A. Wustum Museum of Fine Arts, Racine, Wisconsin
TOPEKA COMPETITION 25, Alice C. Sabatini Gallery, Topeka and Shawnee County Public Library, Topeka, Kansas, juried
KANSAS ARTIST CRAFTSMAN ASSOCIATION JURIED MEMBERS' EXHIBITION, Lawrence Arts Center, Lawrence, Kansas
TWO MUCH: Kathlene Allie and Marjorie Schick Exhibition of Paintings and Wearable Sculptures, Carnegie Art Center, Parsons, Kansas

2002
ZERO KARAT: THE DONNA SCHNEIER GIFT TO THE AMERICAN CRAFT MUSEUM, the Museum of Arts & Design, New York
CHRISTMAS EXHIBITION 2002, Electrum Gallery, London, England
MATERIAL EXPLORATIONS: WEARABLE OBJECTS OF NON-TRADITIONAL MATERIALS, Munson-Williams-Proctor Arts Institute, Utica, New York, juried
A MODERN BESTIARY: ARTISTS VIEW THE ANIMAL KINGDOM, Charles A. Wustum Museum of Fine Arts, Racine, Wisconsin
STEEL CITY: CONTEMPORARY AMERICA IN METAL, White Gallery, Sangre de Cristo Arts and Conference Center, Pueblo, Colorado
JUST BRACELETS, J. Cotter Gallery, Beaver Creek, Avon, Colorado
SCULPTURAL JEWELRY, Mobilia Gallery at SOFA, Chicago
TOPEKA COMPETITION 24, Alice C. Sabatini Gallery, Topeka and Shawnee County Public Library, Topeka, Kansas, juried (award)

WOVEN IN HARMONY, (with Rebecca Bluestone and Soon-Cho) Spiva Center for the Arts, Joplin, Missouri

2001
MASKERADE: CONTEMPORARY MASKS BY FIFTY ARTISTS, Galerie Ra, Amsterdam, and traveled to the Ruthin Crafts Centre, Wales; Cleveland Craft Centre (now the Middlesbrough Institute of Modern Art), Middlesbrough, England
CHRISTMAS EXHIBITION 2001, Electrum Gallery, London, England
THE RING, Mobilia Gallery, Cambridge, Massachusetts and traveled in the US and to the Ruthin Crafts Centre, Wales
SITTING PRETTY: A GROUP EXHIBITION EXPLORING THE CHAIR FORM, Mobilia Gallery, Cambridge, Massachusetts, and SOFA, New York
THE TEAPOT REDEFINED, Mobilia Gallery at SOFA, Chicago
ONCE UPON A TIME: ARTISTS EXAMINE FAIRYTALES, MYTHS AND LEGENDS, Charles A. Wustum Museum of Fine Arts, Racine, Wisconsin
JUST BRACELETS, J. Cotter Gallery, Vail, Colorado
CRAFTS AT THE TURN OF THE MILLENNIUM, SELECTIONS FROM HELEN DRUTT: PHILADELPHIA, the Monmouth Museum, Lincroft, New Jersey
OPEN LINKS: A JEWELRY AND METALS EXHIBITION, Willard Wankelman Gallery, Bowling Green State University, Bowling Green, Ohio
TOPEKA COMPETITION 23, Mulvane Art Museum, Washburn University, Topeka, Kansas, juried

2000
ZIERAT: INTERNATIONAL CONTEMPORARY JEWELRY INVITATIONAL, Russell Hill Rogers Gallery, Southwest School of Art and Craft, San Antonio, Texas; Hand Workshop Art Center, Richmond, Virginia; Kestner Museum, Hannover, Germany; Galerie CEBRA, Düsseldorf, Germany; Galerie Beeld and Aambeeld, Enschede, the Netherlands; and the Nederlands Textielmuseum, Tilburg, the Netherlands
VIRTUAL GALLERY OF CONTEMPORARY JEWELLERY, organized by the Birmingham Institute of Art and Design, University of Central England, Birmingham, England
THE ANATOMY OF LOVE: VALENTINE'S DAY JEWELRY INVITATIONAL EXHIBITION, Objects of Desire Gallery, Louisville, Kentucky
BOSTON TEA: A PARTY, Mobilia Gallery, Cambridge, Massachusetts
STRUCTURE, SYMBOL AND SUBSTANCE: THE POWER OF JEWELRY, Mobilia Gallery, Cambridge, Massachusetts
COMMEMORATIVE MEDALS/TROPHIES: THE

POLITICS OF HISTORY, Helen Drutt: Philadelphia Gallery, Philadelphia, Pennsylvania
SCULPTURAL JEWELRY, Mobilia Gallery at SOFA, New York
THE TEAPOT REDEFINED, Mobilia Gallery at SOFA, Chicago
FOUR MEDIA, FOUR WOMEN, Swogger Gallery, the Columbian, Wamego, Kansas
EXHIBITION OF THE WORK OF AMERICAN CRAFT COUNCIL FELLOWS, Blue Alcove Room, Museum of Fine Arts, Santa Fe, New Mexico
EXHIBITION IN MOTION, part of the SNAG (Society of North American Goldsmiths) Conference, Cambridge Multicultural Arts Center, Cambridge, Massachusetts
KANSAS ARTIST CRAFTSMAN ASSOCIATION MEMBERS' EXHIBITION, Marianna Kestler Beach Museum of Art, Kansas State University, Manhattan, Kansas

1999
BOOK ART, Mobilia Gallery at SOFA, New York
MATERIALS HARD AND SOFT, Center for the Visual Arts, Denton, Texas, juried
CONTAINMENT, Morris University Center Art Gallery, Southern Illinois University at Edwardsville and I Space Gallery, Chicago
2ND SPIVA CONTEMPORARY CRAFTS BIENNIAL, Spiva Center for the Arts, Joplin, Missouri
JEWELRY/CERAMICS INVITATIONAL, Art Gallery, Southwest Missouri State University (now Missouri State University), Springfield, Missouri
THE TEAPOT REDEFINED II, Mobilia Gallery at SOFA, Chicago

1998
JEWELLERY MOVES, Royal Museum, the National Museums of Scotland, Edinburgh
BROOCHING IT DIPLOMATICALLY: A TRIBUTE TO MADELEINE K. ALBRIGHT, Helen Drutt: Philadelphia Gallery; Het Kruithuis Municipal Museum of Contemporary Art, 's-Hertogenbosch, the Netherlands; Museum of Art and Design, Helsinki, Finland; the Tarbekunstimuuseum, Estonia; and the Museum of Contemporary Crafts, New York
KUNST RAI, International Art Fair for Galerie Ra, Amsterdam, the Netherlands,
CRAFT AS A VERB, Mississippi Museum of Art, Jackson
SCULPTURAL JEWELRY, Mobilia Gallery at SOFA, Chicago
TOPEKA COMPETITION 22, Mulvane Art Museum, Washburn University, Topeka, Kansas, juried

1997
NEW JEWELLERY FROM THE U.S.A., curated by Charon Kransen, Galería Hipòtesi at the Escola Massana, Barcelona, Spain

U.S.A. TODAY, the Lesley Craze Gallery, London
NIEUWE HEDENDAAGSE AMERIKAANSE JUWELEN, Artbox, Waregem, Belgium
CELEBRATING AMERICAN CRAFT: AMERICAN CRAFT 1975–1995, the Danish Museum of Decorative Art, Copenhagen, Denmark
CHRISTMAS EXHIBITION 1997, Electrum Gallery, London
CENTENNIAL METALS EXHIBITION: JEWELRY, HOLLOWARE, IRONWORK, the Society of Arts and Crafts, Boston
THE TEAPOT REDEFINED, Mobilia Gallery, Cambridge, Massachusetts
WATCHING AND WAITING, Mobilia Gallery, Cambridge, Massachusetts
SCULPTURAL JEWELRY, Mobilia Gallery at SOFA, Chicago
FORMULATIONS: METALS INVITATIONAL, Carroll Reece Museum, East Tennessee State University, Johnson City, Tennessee
METALS, ETC., NATIONAL JEWELRY AND METALS COMPETITION, Lubbock Fine Arts Center, Lubbock, Texas
3 GENERATIONS: MENTORS, TEACHERS, AND STUDENTS, MODERN JEWELRY FROM THE 1940's TO THE PRESENT, Mobilia Gallery, Cambridge, Massachusetts
TOPEKA COMPETITION 21, Gallery of Fine Arts, Topeka and Shawnee County Public Library, Topeka, Kansas, juried (honorable mention)
KANSAS ARTIST CRAFTSMAN ASSOCIATION MEMBERS' EXHIBITION, Marianna Kistler Beach Museum of Art, Kansas State University, Manhattan

1996
SUBJECTS 96, Retretti Art Centre, Punkaharju, Finland
JEWELLERY IN EUROPE AND AMERICA: NEW TIMES, NEW THINKING, Crafts Council Gallery, London and the National Museum and Gallery at Cardiff, Wales
CONTEMPORARY JEWELLERY FROM U.S.A., curated by Charon Kransen, the Scottish Gallery, Edinburgh, Scotland
EARRINGS: CLASSIC AND WILD, Electrum Gallery, London
SCHMUCKSZENE '96, 47. Internationale Handwerksmesse, Munich, Germany
REVELATIONS: NEW JEWELRY BY MEMBERS OF THE SOCIETY OF NORTH AMERICAN GOLDSMITHS, Shipley Art Gallery, Newcastle, England, and traveled in the UK and US
JEWELLERY PAST, PRESENT AND FUTURE (20 Years Ra), Galerie Ra, Amsterdam, the Netherlands and traveled to the Crafts Victoria Gallery in Melbourne, Australia
CHRISTMAS EXHIBITION 1996, Electrum Gallery, London
NATIONAL HERITAGE AND DIVERSITY:

NATIONAL INVITATIONAL METAL ARTS EXHIBITION, Montgomery College Art Gallery, Rockville, Maryland
METALPLUS, Art Gallery, Weber State University, Ogden, Utah
OLD MEETS NEW: SAMPLER ART AT SOFA – CONTEMPORARY INTERPRETATIONS, Mobilia Gallery at SOFA, Chicago
NATIONAL SUMMER FACULTY INVITATIONAL, Sandra J. Blain Galleries, Arrowmont School of Art and Crafts, Gatlinburg, Tennessee
MOBILIA GALLERY SPECIAL EXHIBITION Highlighting the Best of the "Studio Movement" for the Collectors Circle from the American Craft Museum, Mobilia Gallery, Cambridge, Massachusetts
BEYOND BOUNDS III: A FRAME OF MIND, Johnson County Community College, Overland Park, Kansas
ALUMNI SELF-PORTRAIT EXHIBITION, Fine Arts Gallery, Indiana University, Bloomington
MATERIALS: HARD AND SOFT, 10th Annual National Contemporary Crafts Competition, Meadows Gallery, Center for the Visual Arts, Denton, Texas, juried
TOPEKA COMPETITION 20, Gallery of Fine Arts, Topeka and Shawnee County Public Library, Topeka, Kansas, juried
CERAMICS AND JEWELRY/METALS EXHIBITION: Student and Faculty Work from Regional Universities, Students' Gallery, Southwest Missouri State University, Springfield, Missouri

1995
A MOVEABLE FEAST: HELEN WILLIAMS DRUTT COLLECTION 1964–1994, Museum Bellerive, Zurich, Switzerland; Museum Voor Moderne Kunst, Ostend, Belgium; Stedelijk Museum, Amsterdam, the Netherlands
CHRISTMAS EXHIBITION 1995, Electrum Gallery, London
JEWELRY FROM THE PERMANENT COLLECTION, American Craft Museum, New York
JEWELRY: VARIED VISIONS, Artables Gallery, Houston, Texas
50TH ANNIVERSARY: FACULTY INVITATIONAL, Sandra J. Blain Galleries, Arrowmont School of Art and Crafts, Gatlinburg, Tennessee
EXHIBITION IN PRINT: 1994, SOFA, Chicago
ART JEWELRY: AN HISTORICAL VIEW – A SURVEY OF CONTEMPORARY WORK FROM THE 1940's TO THE PRESENT, Mobilia Gallery, Cambridge, Massachusetts

1994
ÅKERSVIKA-ADDENDA 1994, Galerie Puntgaaf, Groningen, the Netherlands
CHRISTMAS EXHIBITION 1994, Electrum Gallery, London
HOLIDAY SHOW, Sybaris Gallery, Detroit, Michigan

KPMG PEAT MARWICK COLLECTION OF AMERICAN CRAFT: A GIFT TO THE RENWICK, Renwick Gallery of the Smithsonian American Art Museum, Washington, D.C.
INDIVIDUAL OBJECTS: THE WORK OF SEVEN NATIONALLY KNOWN METALSMITHS, Haynes Fine Arts Gallery, Montana State University, Bozeman, Montana
INVITATIONAL JEWELRY EXHIBITION, Mobilia Gallery, Cambridge, Massachusetts
ONE OF A KIND: AMERICAN ART JEWELRY TODAY, Mobilia Gallery, Cambridge, Massachusetts
HAYSTACK SUMMER FACULTY, Blue Heron Gallery of Contemporary American Crafts, Deer Island, Maine
BEYOND BOUNDS II: A BARELY CONTAINED AFFAIR, Gallery of Art, Johnson County Community College, Overland Park, Kansas
TOPEKA COMPETITION 18, Gallery of Fine Arts, Topeka and Shawnee County Public Library, juried (award)
THE FUNCTIONAL OBJECT REDEFINED, A MIXED MEDIA EXHIBIT FEATURING WORK BY REGIONAL ARTISTS, Boger Gallery, College of the Ozarks, Branson, Missouri
KANSAS METALSMITHING: THE HISTORY AND INFLUENCE, Art and Design Gallery, University of Kansas, Lawrence, Kansas

1993
KUNST RAI '93, Galerie Ra, Amsterdam, the Netherlands, International Art Fair (featured)
ÅKERSVIKA-ADDENDA EXHIBITION, Norges Bank Gallery, Hamar, Norway
THE ART OF JEWELLERY, Setagaya Museum, Tokyo, Japan, and the Itami City Craft Center, Itami, Japan
SUBJECTS: INTERNATIONAL JEWELRY EXHIBITION, Design Forum, Helsinki, Finland
AHEAD OF FASHION: HATS OF THE 20TH CENTURY, Philadelphia Museum of Art
CONTEMPORARY METAL: FORM AND NARRATIVE, Krannert Art Museum, University of Illinois at Urbana-Champaign and I Space Gallery, Chicago
A KANSAS CONTRIBUTION: AN EXHIBITION CELEBRATING THE YEAR OF AMERICAN CRAFT, Johnson County Community College Art Gallery, Overland Park, Kansas
NEW ACQUISITIONS: CRAFT TODAY U.S.A., American Craft Museum, New York
PATTERN: NEW FORM/NEW FUNCTION, Sandra J. Blain Art Galleries, Arrowmont School of Arts and Crafts, Gatlinburg, Tennessee, juried
CONTEMPORARY JEWELRY 1964–1993, SELECTED WORKS FROM THE HELEN WILLIAMS DRUTT COLLECTION, the Arkansas Arts Center Decorative Arts Museum, Little Rock, Arkansas

ARROWMONT FACULTY: MIXED MEDIA, Sandra J. Blain Galleries, Arrowmont School of Arts and Crafts, Gatlinburg, Tennessee
THE BODY ADORNED: AN EXHIBITION OF JEWELRY, curated by Rachelle Thiewes, Main Gallery, Fox Fine Arts Center, University of Texas at El Paso
KANSAS CHOOSES KANSAS II, Mulvane Art Museum, Washburn University, Topeka, Kansas, nominated by Robert Russell

1992
DESIGN VISIONS, Triennial Exhibition, the Art Gallery of Western Australia, Perth, Australia
MODERN JEWELRY: 1964 TO PRESENT, HELEN WILLIAMS DRUTT COLLECTION, Museum of Applied Arts, Helsinki, Finland
SOUVENIRS OF NEW YORK: JEWELRY AND OBJECTS INSPIRED BY THE CITY, Aaron Faber Gallery, New York, New York
FIBER AND METAL INVITATIONAL U.S.A. – 1992, Craft Alliance Gallery, St. Louis, Missouri
ARROWMONT FACULTY: MIXED MEDIA, Sandra J. Blain Galleries, Arrowmont School of Arts and Crafts, Gatlinburg, Tennessee
OFF THE WALL (benefit/auction), American Craft Museum, New York
TOPEKA COMPETITION 16, Fine Arts Gallery, Topeka and Shawnee County Public Library, Topeka, Kansas

1991
THE BANQUETING TABLE (15 years Ra), Galerie Ra, Amsterdam, the Netherlands
ARROWMONT FACULTY, MIXED MEDIA EXHIBITION, Art Gallery, Arrowmont School of Arts and Crafts, Gatlinburg, Tennessee

1990
BODY ART: SELECTED INVITATIONAL INTERNATIONAL EXHIBITION, Security Pacific Galleries, Costa Mesa, California
BUILDING A PERMANENT COLLECTION; A PERSPECTIVE ON THE 1980's, American Craft Museum, New York
JEWELRY: MEANS + MEANINGS, Ornamental Metals Museum, Memphis, Tennessee; the American Craft Museum, New York, and traveled
ARROWMONT SUMMER FACULTY EXHIBITION, Art Gallery, Arrowmont School of Arts and Crafts, Gatlinburg, Tennessee
TEACHING ART: MAKING ART, Spiva Art Gallery, Missouri Southern State College (now Missouri Southern State University), Joplin, Missouri
PITTSBURG STATE UNIVERSITY ART FACULTY EXHIBITION, Cottey College, Nevada, Missouri

1989
ORNAMENTA I, International Invitational Exhibition of Contemporary Jewelry, Schmuckmuseum, Pforzheim, Germany
INVITATIONAL METALS EXHIBITION, John B. Davis Gallery, Idaho State University, Pocatello, Idaho
HATS, HELMETS, AND OTHER HEADGEAR, Faith Nightingale Gallery, San Diego, California
CRAFT TODAY: U.S.A., American Craft Museum, and traveled to twelve countries in Europe for a two-year period
LUBBOCK ARTS FESTIVAL, Lubbock, Texas
ARCHAEOLOGY OF THE PRESENT: EAST MEETS WEST IN DESIGN, Crystal Palace, Jacob K. Javits Convention Center, New York City, and traveled in the US and Europe
KANSAS ARTIST CRAFTSMAN ASSOCIATION 1989 MEMBERS' JURIED EXHIBITION, Norman R. Eppink Art Gallery, Emporia State University, Emporia, Kansas

1988
MARILYN GRISHAM/MARJORIE SCHICK, Kurdian Gallery, Wichita Art Museum, Wichita, Kansas
DREAMWORLDS: EIGHT ARTISTS FROM AUSTRALIA AND THE UNITED STATES, San Diego State University Art Gallery, San Diego, California
THE CLEVELAND CONTEMPORARY JEWELLERY COLLECTION, curated by Ralph Turner, the Cleveland Crafts Centre, Middlesbrough, England
GALERIE RA SELECTS, Gemeentelijk Van Reekummuseum, Apeldoorn, the Netherlands
CONTEMPORARY METALCRAFT EXHIBITION, Korean/American Show, Walker Hill Art Center Museum, Seoul, South Korea
MASTER JEWELERS, Susan Cummins Gallery, Mill Valley, California
SELECTED WORKS: 1987–88 FROM THE HELEN DRUTT GALLERY/PHILADELPHIA, the Clark Gallery, Lincoln, Massachusetts
THE 12TH BIENNIAL NATIONAL INVITATIONAL EXHIBITION, University Art Galleries, Illinois State University, Normal
BEWITCHED BY CRAFT, a benefit auction at the American Craft Museum, New York
SCULPTURE TO WEAR, the Society for Art in Crafts, Pittsburgh, Pennsylvania

1987
SCHMUCKSZENE '87, Internationale Handwerksmesse, Munich, Germany
UNA BRILLANTE IDEA, Positvra Gallery, Barcelona, Spain
THE WICHITA NATIONAL 1987, the Wichita Art Association (now the Wichita Center for the Arts), Wichita, Kansas, juried

RITUAL AND MAGIC, Alexander Hogue Gallery, University of Tulsa, Oklahoma
THE ELOQUENT OBJECT, Philbrook Museum of Art, Tulsa, Oklahoma, and traveled in the US and Japan
PRIMARY OBJECTIVE: COLOR, Group Show, Quadrum Gallery, Chestnut Hill, Massachusetts
ART: ON THE MOVE, Chattahoochee Valley Art Association, LaGrange, Georgia
50TH ANNIVERSARY METALS EXHIBITION, Contemporary Crafts Gallery, Portland, Oregon

1986
INTERNATIONAL JEWELLERY ART EXHIBITION OF THE 6TH TOKYO TRIENNIAL, Yurakucho Art Forum, Tokyo, Japan; Tsukashin Hall, Osaka, Japan
JEWELRY: FORM AND IDEA, Gemeentelijk Van Reekummuseum, Apeldoorn, the Netherlands
10 YEARS RA, Galerie Ra, Amsterdam, the Netherlands
CRAFT TODAY: POETRY OF THE PHYSICAL, inaugural exhibition, American Craft Museum, New York, and traveled
PAPER, WOOD, METAL, CLAY, FILM, Boca Raton Museum of Art, Boca Raton, Florida
MODERN JEWELRY 1964–1986: the Helen Williams Drutt Collection, the Cleveland Art Institute, Cleveland, Ohio; the Philadelphia Museum of Art, Philadelphia, Pennsylvania
CONTEMPORARY ARTS: AN EXPANDED VIEW, curated by Helen Williams Drutt English, the Monmouth Museum, Lincroft, New Jersey, and the Squibb Gallery, Princeton, New Jersey
CONTEMPORARY CRAFTS: A CONCEPT IN FLUX, National Craft Showroom, New York
CONTEMPORARY ARTS: AN EXPANDING VIEW, Wellesley College Museum, Jewett Arts Center, Wellesley, Massachusetts
REFLECTIONS: THE INNER IMAGE, Reflections Gallery, La Mesa, California
SMALL SCULPTURE INVITATIONAL, University of Texas at Arlington, Texas
BLOSSOM FESTIVAL ART EXHIBITION, Kent State University, Kent, Ohio
TEACHING ART/MAKING ART, Spiva Art Gallery, Missouri Southern State College, Joplin, Missouri
A KANSAS BESTIARY, Kurdian Gallery, Wichita Art Museum, Wichita, Kansas
CRAFTS EXHIBITION, the Salina Arts Center, Kansas Wesleyan University, Salina, Kansas

1985
NYA SMYCKEN, Kulturhuset, Stockholm, Sweden
FORM, FORMEL, FORMALISMUS, Internationale Schmuckschau, 1985, Sonderschau der Internationalen Handwerksmesse, Munich, Germany

NEW TRADITION: THE EVOLUTION OF JEWELLERY 1966–1985, the British Crafts Centre, London, England, and traveled in England
CRAFTS FAIR CHELSEA, 1985, Chelsea Old Town Hall, London, England
BODY WORKS AND WEARABLE SCULPTURE, Visual Arts Center of Alaska, Anchorage, Alaska
AMERICAN JEWELRY NOW, sponsored by the US Information Agency, curated by the American Craft Museum, toured in Asia and New Zealand
REFLECTIONS: A TRIBUTE TO ALMA EIKERMAN, MASTER CRAFTSMAN: Works by Eikerman and 41 of her Former Students, Indiana University Art Museum, Bloomington, Indiana
THE WICHITA NATIONAL DECORATIVE ARTS EXHIBITION, Wichita Art Association, Wichita, Kansas, juried (purchase award)
CONTEMPORARY JEWELRY REDEFINED: ALTERNATIVE MATERIALS, Pittsburgh Center for the Arts, Pittsburgh, Pennsylvania
WEARABLE ART, Cortland Arts Council Gallery, Cortland, New York
THE BODY ADORNED: EXPRESSIONS OF DRESS AND DECORATION, International Gallery, San Diego, California
CONTEMPORARY JEWELRY, Artifacts Gallery, Indianapolis, Indiana
CONTEMPORARY ARTISTS JEWELRY/SALE EXHIBIT, Philbrook Museum of Art, Tulsa, Oklahoma

1984
SCHMUCK UND GERÄT, 1959–1984, Sonderschau der Internationalen Handwerksmesse, Munich, Germany
CONTEMPORARY JEWELLERY – THE AMERICAS, AUSTRALIA, EUROPE, AND JAPAN, the National Museum of Modern Art, Kyoto, Japan, and the National Museum of Modern Art, Tokyo, Japan
CELEBRATION '84: A SENSE OF OCCASION, Contemporary Art Gallery at Harbourfront Centre, Toronto, Ontario, Canada, and traveled in Canada
21 GOLDSMITHS, A SPECIAL EXHIBITION OF WORK BY 21 INTERNATIONAL CONTEMPORARY JEWELERS WORKING IN DIVERSE MEDIA, Helen Drutt Gallery, Philadelphia, Pennsylvania
EXHIBITION '84, City of London Polytechnic (now London Metropolitan University), Sir John Cass Faculty of Arts Department of Fine and Applied Art Show, Department of Silversmithing and Jewellery, London (as Artist-in-Residence)
MODERN JEWELRY: 1966–1984 from the Collection of Helen Williams Drutt, Château Dufresne, Musée des Arts Décoratifs, Montreal, Canada
JEWELRY: U.S.A., American Craft Museum, New York, and traveled in the US for two years

JEWELRY AND BEYOND: Recent Metalwork by Distinguished Members of the Society of North American Goldsmiths, Mitchell Museum of Art, Mount Vernon, Illinois, and the Fashion Institute of Technology, New York
METALS INVITATIONAL, McFall Gallery, Bowling Green State University, Ohio
KANSAS ARTIST CRAFTSMAN ASSOCIATION EXHIBITION, Garvey Art Center and the Whittier Fine Art Gallery, Friends University, Wichita, Kansas

1983
ROBERT RUSSELL/MARJORIE SCHICK SABBATICAL EXHIBITION, Whitesitt Hall Art Gallery, Pittsburg State University, Kansas
INTERNATIONAL JEWELLERY ART EXHIBITION, the 5th Tokyo Triennial, Isetan Art Museum, Tokyo, Japan, juried (Fine Works Award)
10 JEWELERS, Gemeentelijk Van Reekummuseum, Apeldoorn, the Netherlands
KANSAS ARTIST CRAFTSMAN ASSOCIATION "THREE-PLUS" EXCHANGE EXHIBITION, Paraguay/American Cultural Centre, Asunción, Paraguay
INTERNATIONAL JEWELLERY, Aspects Gallery, London

1982
ROBERT A. NELSON/MARJORIE SCHICK, Norman R. Eppink Art Gallery, Emporia State University, Kansas
JEWELLERY REDEFINED: FIRST INTERNATIONAL EXHIBITION OF MULTI-MEDIA NON-PRECIOUS JEWELLERY, British Crafts Centre, London, and traveled, juried
28TH ANNUAL SMALL SCULPTURE AND DRAWING SHOW, Art Gallery, Ball State University, Muncie, Indiana, juried
ART OF THE BATH, Craft Alliance Gallery, St. Louis, Missouri, juried (award)
THE SEQUOYAH SHOW: ANNUAL REGIONAL ART SHOW, Fine Arts Center, University of Arkansas, Fayetteville, juried
KANSAS ARTIST CRAFTSMAN ASSOCIATION MEMBERS' EXHIBITION, Hays Arts Council, Hays, Kansas
SMOKEY HILL ART EXHIBITION, Hays Public Library, Hays, Kansas, juried
TOPEKA CRAFTS EXHIBITION VI, Gallery of Fine Arts, Topeka and Shawnee County Public Library, Topeka, Kansas, juried
7TH COFFEYVILLE COMMUNITY COLLEGE SPRING ART EXHIBITION, Coffeyville Community College, Coffeyville, Kansas

1981
GOOD AS GOLD: ALTERNATIVE MATERIALS IN AMERICAN JEWELRY, Renwick Gallery of the Smithsonian American Art Museum, Washington, D.C., and traveling for two years

METALSMITH '81, A NATIONAL EXHIBITION OF JURIED AND INVITATIONAL WORK BY THE MEMBERSHIP OF THE SOCIETY OF NORTH AMERICAN GOLDSMITHS, Art and Design Gallery, University of Kansas, Lawrence, Kansas

OBJECTS '81, Western Colorado Center for the Arts, Grand Junction, Colorado, juried

TOPEKA CRAFTS EXHIBITION V, Gallery of Fine Arts, Topeka and Shawnee County Public Library, Topeka, Kansas, juried

26TH ANNUAL DESIGNER-CRAFTSMEN EXHIBITION, Union Gallery, University of Kansas, Lawrence, Kansas, juried

KANSAS ARTIST CRAFTSMAN ASSOCIATION FALL EXHIBIT, Wichita Art Association, Wichita, Kansas, juried

1980

CREATIVE CLOTHING: BODY SCULPTURE EXHIBITION AND PAGEANT, Gallery, University of Waterloo Arts Centre, University of Waterloo, Waterloo, Ontario, Canada, juried

ART AS BODY ADORNMENT, NATIONAL EXHIBITION AND PERFORMANCE, University of Delaware, Newark, Delaware

COPPER 2: the Second Copper/Brass/Bronze Exhibition, Museum of Art, University of Arizona, juried

PACKAGES, Edna Carlsten Gallery, University of Wisconsin-Stevens Point, Wisconsin

TOPEKA CRAFTS EXHIBITION IV, Gallery of Fine Arts, Topeka and Shawnee County Public Library, Topeka, Kansas, juried

KANSAS ARTIST CRAFTSMAN ASSOCIATION EXHIBITION, Wichita Art Association, Wichita, Kansas

ARTISTS FROM SOUTHEAST KANSAS, Cedar Crest, Governor's Mansion, Topeka, Kansas

GROUP SHOW, Coffeyville Community College, Coffeyville, Kansas

1979

25TH ANNUAL DRAWING AND SMALL SCULPTURE SHOW, Art Gallery, Ball State University, Muncie, Indiana, juried

3RD NATIONAL RING SHOW, Visual Arts Gallery, University of Georgia, Athens, and traveling

NEW ARTISTS, Aaron Faber Gallery, New York

3RD NATIONAL EXHIBITION OF PACKAGES, Edna Carlsten Gallery, University of Wisconsin-Stevens Point, Wisconsin

TOPEKA CRAFTS EXHIBITION III, Gallery of Fine Arts, Topeka and Shawnee County Public Library, Topeka, Kansas, juried

9 WOMEN ARTISTS '79, Spiva Art Gallery, Missouri Southern State College, Joplin, Missouri

GROUP SHOW OF 5 ARTISTS, Park Central Gallery, Springfield, Missouri

PITTSBURG STATE UNIVERSITY FACULTY SHOW, Artworks Gallery, Joplin, Missouri

1978

ROBERT BLUNK/MARJORIE SCHICK EXHIBITION, Barton County Community College, Great Bend, Kansas

CHOREOGRAPHING THE OBJECT, Dance Performance with Jewelry and Body Sculptures, Bronx Museum of Art, New York City, sponsored by the Women's Caucus for the National College Art Association; the Kansas City Art Institute, Kansas City, Missouri; the Albrecht Art Gallery, St. Joseph, Missouri; the University of Missouri, Columbia, Missouri; Lindenwood College, St. Charles, Missouri; Loretto Academy, Kansas City; and Pittsburg State University, Pittsburg, Kansas

ARTISTS' MASKS, Art Gallery, Fontbonne College, St. Louis, Missouri

ONE-PLUS-ONE, Invitational Multi-Media Exhibition, Lee Hall Gallery, Northern Michigan University, Marquette, Michigan

1ST NATIONAL SPOON AND ASHTRAY SHOW, the Sangre de Christo Arts Center, Pueblo, Colorado

2ND NATIONAL RING SHOW, Visual Arts Gallery, University of Georgia, and traveling

PACKAGES, Edna Carlsten Gallery, University of Wisconsin-Stevens Point, Wisconsin

TOPEKA CRAFTS EXHIBITION II, Gallery of Fine Arts, Topeka and Shawnee County Public Library, Topeka, Kansas, juried

24TH ANNUAL DESIGNER-CRAFTSMEN EXHIBITION, Union Gallery, University of Kansas, Lawrence, Kansas, juried

WOMEN IN THE ARTS INVITATIONAL, Lee Hall Gallery, Northern Michigan University, Marquette, Michigan

1977

10TH BIENNIAL NATIONAL ART SHOW, 2nd Crossing Gallery, Valley City State College (now Valley City State University), Valley City, North Dakota, juried

PACKAGES, Edna Carlsten Gallery, University of Wisconsin-Stevens Point, Wisconsin

TOPEKA CRAFTS EXHIBITION I, Gallery of Fine Arts, Topeka and Shawnee County Public Library, Topeka, Kansas, juried

11TH ANNUAL KANSAS ARTIST CRAFTSMAN EXHIBITION, Mulvane Art Museum, Washburn University, Topeka, Kansas

FACULTY WOMEN'S SHOW, Kiva Center, Wichita, Kansas

MAM '77 METALCRAFTS, Kansas City Public Library, Kansas City, Missouri

SELECTED KANSAS ARTISTS EXHIBITION, Rotunda of the State Capitol, Topeka, Kansas

23RD ANNUAL KANSAS DESIGNER-CRAFTSMEN EXHIBITION, Union Gallery, University of Kansas, Lawrence, Kansas

1976

CONTEMPORARY CRAFTS EXHIBITION, 1976, Delaware Art Museum, Wilmington, Delaware, juried

PROFESSIONAL INVITATIONAL JEWELRY EXHIBITION, Fine Arts Gallery, University of Missouri, Columbia, Missouri

FIBER AND METALS, AN INVITATIONAL EXHIBITION, Davis Gallery, Fine Arts Building, Idaho State University, Pocatello, Idaho

ART PROFESSORS' INVITATIONAL EXHIBIT, Spiva Art Gallery, Missouri Southern State College, Joplin, Missouri

1975

CONTEMPORARY CRAFTS EXHIBITION, 1975, Delaware Art Museum, Wilmington, juried

ONE-PLUS-ONE, KANSAS DESIGNER CRAFTSMAN ASSOCIATION EXHIBITION, Mulvane Art Museum, Washburn University, Topeka, Kansas

1974

ONE-PLUS-ONE, KANSAS DESIGNER CRAFTSMAN ASSOCIATION EXHIBITION, Mulvane Art Museum, Washburn University, Topeka, Kansas

KANSAS METALSMITHS EXHIBITION, Wichita Art Association, Wichita, Kansas

1973

HARRY KRUG, PRINTS: MARJORIE SCHICK, JEWELRY, Birger Sandzen Memorial Gallery, Lindsborg, Kansas

JUDY ABRAHAM – MARJORIE SCHICK: EXHIBIT OF PAINTINGS AND BODY SCULPTURES, Whitesitt Hall Art Gallery, Kansas State College of Pittsburg (now Pittsburg State University), Pittsburg, Kansas

4TH INTERNATIONAL INVITATIONAL EXPOSITION OF CONTEMPORARY JEWELRY, AT HOME Gallery of Art, Toulouse, France

NATIONAL JEWELRY INVITATIONAL, Art Gallery, Virginia Commonwealth University, Richmond, Virginia

JULIE: ARTISANS GALLERY, New York, New York

MADE WITH METAL, NATIONAL INVITATIONAL SHOW, Eastern Washington State College, Cheney, Washington

INVITATIONAL CRAFT EXHIBIT, Rich's Department Store, Atlanta, Georgia

ONE-PLUS-ONE, KANSAS DESIGNER CRAFTSMAN ASSOCIATION EXHIBITION, Mulvane Art Museum, Washburn University, Topeka, Kansas

THE NEW PIONEER WOMAN, FORGING FRONTIERS ON THE PLAINS OF KANSAS IN METAL, FIBERS, AND CLAY, Century II Hall, Wichita, Kansas, and traveled in Kansas

1972
JEWELRY AND HOLLOWARE INVITATIONAL '72, Design Center Gallery, Iowa State University, Ames, Iowa
22ND ANNUAL MAY COMPETITIVE, Spiva Art Gallery, Missouri Southern State College, Joplin, Missouri
KANSAS ARTIST CRAFTSMAN ASSOCIATION EXHIBITION, Mulvane Art Museum, Washburn University, Topeka, Kansas

1971
FOR MEN ONLY, Lee Nordness Galleries, New York, New York
OBJECTS: FIFTH ANNUAL EXHIBITION, Western Colorado Center for the Arts, Grand Junction, Colorado, juried
INTER-D2, AN EXHIBITION OF CONTEMPORARY CRAFTS, McAllen International Museum, McAllen, Texas, juried
WOMEN '71, University Center Galleries, Northern Illinois University, DeKalb, Illinois, juried
8TH ANNUAL SOUTHERN TIER ARTS AND CRAFTS SHOW, Corning Glass Center, Corning, New York, juried
7TH NATIONAL ARTS AND CRAFTS EXHIBITION, Jackson, Mississippi, juried (honorable mention)
DESIGNER/CRAFTSMAN '71, Richmond Art Center, Civic Center Plaza, Richmond, California, juried (award)
2ND INVITATIONAL CONTEMPORARY CRAFTS SHOW, Hathorn Gallery, Skidmore College, Saratoga Springs, New York
41ST ANNUAL EXHIBITION, Springfield Art Museum, Springfield, Missouri, juried
17TH ANNUAL DESIGNER-CRAFTSMEN EXHIBITION, Union Gallery, University of Kansas, Lawrence, Kansas, juried (honorable mention)
KANSAS ARTIST CRAFTSMAN ASSOCIATION 1971 SHOW, Mulvane Art Museum, Washburn University, Topeka, Kansas

1970
FACE COVERINGS: PRIMITIVE MASKS TO SPACE HELMETS, Museum of Contemporary Crafts, New York, New York
GOLDSMITH '70, St. Paul Art Center, St. Paul Minnesota, and traveled to the American Craft Museum, New York, and other venues
1970 WICHITA NATIONAL INVITATIONAL BIENNIAL EXHIBITION, Wichita Art Association, Wichita, Kansas
FASHION SHOW, Wilmington Society of the Fine Arts, Wilmington, Delaware
6TH NATIONAL ARTS AND CRAFTS EXHIBITION, Jackson, Mississippi, juried
40TH ANNUAL EXHIBITION, Springfield Art Museum, Springfield, Missouri, juried

NORTHERN MICHIGAN UNIVERSITY'S 1ST ANNUAL INVITATIONAL SHOW, Marquette, Michigan
KANSAS ARTIST CRAFTSMAN ASSOCIATION SHOW, Mulvane Art Museum, Washburn University, Topeka, Kansas, and traveled
ALEX BARDE – MARJORIE SCHICK EXHIBIT, Central State College (now University of Central Oklahoma), Edmond, Oklahoma
"8" GROUP SHOW OF THE FACULTY OF THE DEPARTMENT OF ART, Kansas State College of Pittsburg (now Pittsburg State University), Jewish Community Center Gallery, Kansas City, Missouri

1969
FASCINATING PAPER, Museum of Applied Arts of Zurich, Switzerland
1ST ICASALS COMPETITION, West Texas Museum, Texas Technological College, Lubbock, juried
5TH NATIONAL ARTS AND CRAFTS EXHIBITION, Jackson, Mississippi, juried
AMERICAN CRAFTSMEN'S COUNCIL SOUTH CENTRAL CRAFTSMEN 1969 EXHIBITION, Gilpin County Arts Association Gallery, Central City, Colorado, juried (award)
MADE WITH PAPER, Civic Fine Arts Association, Sioux Falls, South Dakota
INVITATIONAL CONTEMPORARY JEWELRY EXHIBIT BY FIFTY OUTSTANDING CRAFTSMEN, Lawrence University, Appleton, Wisconsin
CONTEMPORARY CRAFTS EXHIBITION, 1969, Delaware Arts Center, Wilmington, Delaware, juried
39TH ANNUAL EXHIBITION, Springfield Art Museum, Springfield, Missouri, juried
16TH ANNUAL DESIGNER-CRAFTSMEN EXHIBITION, Union Gallery, University of Kansas, Lawrence, Kansas, juried (award)

1968
MADE WITH PAPER, American Craft Museum, New York, New York; the Museum of Contemporary Art, Chicago; Hemisfair, San Antonio; City Art Museum, St. Louis; West Coast Museums, and Mexico City, Mexico
1968 NATIONAL INVITATIONAL DECORATIVE ARTS AND CERAMIC EXHIBITION, Wichita Art Association, Wichita, Kansas
PAPER IS, Monmouth Museum, Red Bank, New Jersey
SOUTHWEST CRAFTSMEN 1968, Dallas Museum of Fine Arts, Dallas, Texas, juried
38TH ANNUAL EXHIBITION, Springfield Art Museum, Springfield, Missouri, juried
EXPERIMENTAL METALSMITHING CARNEGIE GRANT PROJECT EXHIBITION, Indiana University, Bloomington, Indiana
WALKER/SCHICK, Kansas State Teachers

College (now Emporia State University), Emporia, Kansas

1967
AMERICAN JEWELRY TODAY, Everhart Museum, Scranton, Pennsylvania, juried
14TH ANNUAL DESIGNER-CRAFTSMEN EXHIBITION, Union Gallery, University of Kansas, Lawrence, Kansas, juried

1966
19TH NATIONAL DECORATIVE ARTS AND CERAMICS EXHIBITION, Wichita Art Association, Wichita, Kansas, juried
MID-STATES CRAFTS EXHIBITION, Evansville Museum of Arts and Sciences, Evansville, Indiana, juried

1965
AMERICAN JEWELRY TODAY EXHIBITION, Everhart Museum, Scranton, Pennsylvania
GREATER FALL RIVER ART ASSOCIATION 9TH ANNUAL NATIONAL SHOW, Greater Fall River, Massachusetts, juried (award)
INDIANA CRAFTS '65, John Herron Museum of Art, Indianapolis, Indiana, juried
1965 ART CENTER ASSOCIATION ANNUAL EXHIBITION, J.B. Speed Art Museum, Louisville, Kentucky, juried

1964
JEWELRY '64, State University College, Plattsburgh, New York, juried
18TH NATIONAL DECORATIVE ARTS AND CERAMICS EXHIBITION, Wichita Art Association, Wichita, Kansas, juried (award)

BIBLIOGRAPHY

BOOKS (SELECTED) IN WHICH WORK IS PICTURED

"ARTISTS IN THE WORLD." NO: *Nouvel Objet*. Seoul, South Korea: Design House Publications, 1996.
ASTFALCK, Jivan, Caroline Broadhead, and Paul Derrez. *New Directions in Jewellery*. London, England: Black Dog Publishing, 2005.
BELL, Robert. *Design Visions*. Perth, Australia: Art Gallery of Western Australia, 1992.
DORMER, Peter, and Ralph Turner. *The New Jewelry: Trends + Traditions*. London, England: Thames and Hudson, 1985.
DRUTT ENGLISH, Helen Williams, and Peter Dormer. *Jewelry of Our Time: Art, Ornament and Obsession*. New York: Rizzoli, 1995.
ERLHOFF, Michael, Fritz Falk, Jens-Rüdiger Lorenzen, Wilhelm Mattar, and Sabine Strobel. *Ornamenta I: Internationale Schmuckkunst*.

Munich, Germany: Prestel-Verlag, Schmuck-museum Pforzheim, 1989.

EVANS, Chuck. *Jewelry, Contemporary Design and Technique.* Worcester, Massachusetts: Davis, 1983.

FALINO, Jeannine. "Women Metalsmiths" in *Women Designers in the USA 1900–2000: Diversity and Difference,* Pat Kirkham, ed. New Haven, Connecticut: Yale University Press, 2000.

GAME, Amanda, and Elizabeth Goring. *Jewellery Moves: Ornament for the 21st Century.* Edinburgh, Scotland: National Museums of Scotland, 1998.

HOWELL-KOEHLER, Nancy. *Soft Jewelry: Design, Techniques, and Materials.* Englewood Cliffs, New Jersey: Prentice Hall, 1976.

LAPLANTZ, David and Shereen, eds. *Jewelry/ Metalwork Survey #2: A Way of Communicating.* Bayside, California: Shereen LaPlantz, 1992.

LAPLANTZ, David, ed. *Jewelry/Metalwork Survey #3: Ideas, Images, Imagemakers 1993.* Bayside, California: Shereen LaPlantz, 1993.

LE VAN, Marthe, Introduction by juror Robert W. Ebendorf. *1000 Rings: Inspiring Adornments for the Hand.* Asheville, North Carolina: Lark Books, 2004.

LE VAN, Marthe, Introduction by juror Charon Kransen. *500 Bracelets: An Inspiring Collection of Extraordinary Designs.* Asheville, North Carolina: Lark Books, 2005.

LE VAN, Marthe, Introduction by juror Marjorie Simon. *500 Brooches: Inspiring Adornments for the Body.* Asheville, North Carolina: Lark Books, 2005.

LE VAN, Marthe. *The Art of Paper Jewelry.* Asheville, North Carolina: Lark Books, 2006.

LE VAN, Marthe, Introduction by juror Marjorie Schick. *500 Necklaces: Contemporary Interpretations of a Timeless Form.* Asheville, North Carolina: Lark Books, 2006.

LE VAN, Marthe, Introduction by juror Alan Revere. *500 Earrings: New Directions in Contemporary Jewelry.* Asheville, North Carolina: Lark Books, 2007.

LEWIN, Susan Grant. *One of a Kind: American Art Jewelry Today.* New York: Abrams, 1994.

MANHART, Marcia, and Tom Manhart, eds. *The Eloquent Object.* Tulsa, Oklahoma: The Philbrook Museum of Art, 1987.

MARGETTS, Martina. *International Crafts.* London, England: Thames and Hudson, 1991.

MAYER, Barbara. *Contemporary American Craft Art: A Collector's Guide.* Salt Lake, Utah: Gibbs M. Smith, 1988.

MEILACH, Dona Z. *Art Jewelry Today.* Atglen, Pennsylvania: Schiffer Publishing, 2003.

MEILACH, Dona Z. *Teapots: Makers and Collectors,* Atglen, Pennsylvania: Schiffer Publishing, 2005.

MORTON, Phillip. *Contemporary Jewelry.* New York: Holt, Rinehart and Winston, 1976.

PHILLIPS, Clare. *Jewels and Jewellery.* London, England: Victoria and Albert Publications, 2000.

TURNER, Ralph. *Jewelry in Europe and America: New Times, New Thinking.* London, England: Thames and Hudson, 1996.

WATKINS, David. *The Best in Contemporary Jewelry.* London, England: B.T. Batsford, 1993.

WICKS, Silvia. *Jewellery Making Manual.* London, England: MacDonald, 1985.

PERIODICALS (SELECTED) **IN WHICH WORK IS PICTURED**

"1983 INTERNATIONAL JEWELLERY ART EXHIBITION." *Four Seasons of Jewelry* (February 1983): 30–39.

"'93 THE ART OF JEWELLERY." *JJDA News* (No. 25, 1993): 4–12.

"AMERICAN CRAFT COUNCIL AWARDS 2000." *American Craft* (October/November 2000): 90–101.

"ART OF ADORNMENT: JEWELLERY." *Holland Herald: Magazine of the Netherlands* (June 1988): 25.

BELL, Robert. "Design Visions." *Craft Arts International* (No. 25, 1992): 32–38.

BENESH, Carolyn L. E. "Brooching It Diplomatically." *Ornament* (Summer 1999): 62–63.

"BODY ART." *Metalsmith* (Winter 1991): 44–45.

BROCK, Judith, ed. "Marjorie Schick: New Dimensions in Jewelry." *In . . . Joplin!* (February 1987): 31–32.

BROWN, Glen R. "Marjorie Schick: Engaging Memory." *Ornament* (Spring 1999): 30–33.

"CONTEMPORARY METALCRAFT IN AMERICA; 24 ARTISTS." *Monthly Crafts* (June 1988): 28–75.

CROMMELIN, Liesbeth. "The Breakthrough: 10 Years Galerie Ra." *Art Aurea* (4/1986): 26–39.

DERREZ, Paul. "The New Jewellery: Death of a Movement." *Crafts* (May/June 1987): 16–21.

DERREZ, Paul. "20 Years of Galerie Ra." *Object Magazine* (December 1997): 62–64.

DINSMORE, John N. "Conceptual Crafts." *Craft Range, the Mountain-Plains Crafts Journal* (July/ August 1979): 30–31.

DORMER, Peter. "The Cultural Divide in New Jewellery: Europe v America." *Aspects* (January– March 1985): unpaginated.

DUNAS, Michael. "Marjorie's Schticks." *Metalsmith* (Summer 1987): 24–31 and front cover.

FARIELLO, Mary Ann. "Jewelry Now." *New Art Examiner* (February 1987): 52–53.

FARRIS-LARSON, Gail. "Reflections: A Tribute to Alma Eikerman." *Metalsmith* (Winter 1986): 46–47.

FINKELSTEIN, Lydia Brown. "Marjorie Schick: A Retrospective." *Metalsmith* (Summer 1990): 42.

FISCH, Arline M. "Forms for the Head: Hats to Helmets." *Ornament* (Spring 1989): 17–21.

FRIEDLICH, Donald, Martha Glowacki, Susan Kingsley, Bruce Metcalf, and Kate Wagle. "1994 Exhibition in Print." *Metalsmith* (1994 Exhibition in Print): 33.

"GALLERY." *American Craft* (October/November 1985): 80.

"GALLERY." *American Craft* (June/July 2003): 76.

"GALLERY." *Art Jewelry* (July 2006): 51.

"GALLERY." *Art Jewelry* (November 2006): 50–51.

"GALLERY: MIXED MEDIA." *American Craft* (February/March 1988): 82.

HIRAMATSU, Yasuki. "The 5th Tokyo Triennial: International Jewellery Art Exhibition." *European Jeweler* (April 1984): 104–9.

"INTERNATIONALE SCHMUCKSCHAU MÜNCHEN." *Gold und Silber* (April 1984): 61–64.

JOHNSON, Mark M. "Craft Today." *Arts and Activities* (January 1987): 5–7.

KIEFER, Geraldine Wojno. "Metal Mastered: Alma Eikerman." *American Craft* (December/ January 1986): 16–23 and back cover.

KUHN, Roger. "The VO Galerie: A European Jewelry Showcase in the American Capitol." *Metalsmith* (Fall 1985): 16–19.

LEWIS, Frank C. "The Pleasures of Excess." *Metalsmith* (Summer 1997): 16.

"MARJORIE SCHICK." *Four Seasons of Jewelry* (October 1988): unpaginated.

METCALF, Bruce. "Zero Karat: The Donna Schneier Gift to the American Craft Museum." *Metalsmith* (Winter 2003): 53.

NEWS. *Ornament* (Spring 1986): 19.

NEWS. "Reflections: A Tribute to Alma Eikerman, Master Craftsman." *Ornament* (May 1985): 59.

ORNAMENT I JOURNAL (September 1989): front cover.

PIJANOWSKI, Hiroko and Gene. "Marjorie Schick: Drawings to Wear/Sculpture to Wear." *Four Seasons of Jewelry* (June 1986): 56–63.

RACKOW, Paula S. "All That Glitters." *MD Magazine: New Horizons for the Physician* (February 1985): 289–92.

ROSOLOWSKI, Tacey A. "Marjorie Schick." *American Craft* (October/November 2002): 66–69 and front cover.

ROSOLOWSKI, Tacey A. "Marjorie Schick: Objects of Self-Consciousness." *Metalsmith* (Winter 2004): 24–33 and front cover.

"SCHICK CHIC-IN PAPIER-MÂCHÉ." *IN-VIEW: News and Events at the Victoria and Albert Museum* (September–December 1997): 7.

SCHICK, Marjorie. "Body Sculpture." *The Little Balkans Review: A Southeast Kansas Literary and Graphics Quarterly* (Winter 1988–89): 32–37.

SIMON, Marjorie. "Jewelry Beyond Jewelry." *Metalsmith* (Summer 2004): 46.

TURNER, Ralph. "USA Today." *Crafts* (July/August 1997): 57.

"WEAR IT, OR HANG IT ON THE WALL – WORK CHALLENGES 'WEARABILITY.'" *Arkansas Arts Center Works* (May/June 2001): 10.

WIEDERSPOHN, Anja. "Marjorie Schick: Frauen der Erinnerung." *Schmuck* (November 1999): 71.
WOLF, Toni Lesser. "The Intimate Art." *ARTnews* (November 1989): 122–29.

EXHIBITION CATALOGS (SELECTED) **IN WHICH WORK IS PICTURED**

AAV, Marianne, Helen Williams Drutt English, and Kimmo Sarje. *Challenging the Châtelaine!* Helsinki, Finland: Designmuseo, 2006.
ADAMSON, Jeremy, Jon C. Madonna, and Michael W. Monroe. *KPMG Peat Marwick Collection of American Art: A Gift to the Renwick Gallery.* Washington, D.C.: Renwick Gallery of the Smithsonian American Art Museum, 1994.
BENNETT, Jamie, Connie Gibbons, Robly Glover, and Nancy Slagle. *Metals, Etc.* Lubbock, Texas: Fine Arts Center, 1997.
BROWN, Gail M., and Gretchen Keyworth. *The Edges of Grace: Provocative, Uncommon Craft.* Brockton, Massachusetts: Fuller Craft Museum, 2006.
CROMMELIN, Liesbeth, and Paul Derrez. *10 Years Ra.* Amsterdam, the Netherlands: Galerie Ra, 1986.
DEN BESTEN, Liesbeth. *Sieraden: Vorm en Idee.* Apeldoorn, the Netherlands: Gemeentelijk Van Reekummuseum, 1986.
DERREZ, Paul, Liesbeth den Besten, Marjan Unger, Herman Hoeneveld, and Gert Staal. *Passion and Profession: Jewellery in Past, Present and Future.* Amsterdam, the Netherlands: Galerie Ra, 1996.
DERREZ, Paul, Agaath Witteman, Theo Fransen, and Ronald Ockhuysen. *Maskerade: Contemporary Masks by Fifty Artists.* Amsterdam, the Netherlands: Galerie Ra, 2001.
DERREZ, Paul, Ralph Turner, Liesbeth den Besten, and Marjan Boot. *Radiant: 30 Years Ra.* Amsterdam, the Netherlands: Galerie Ra, 2006.
DOE, Donald Bartlett. *Kansas Chooses Kansas II.* Topeka, Kansas: Mulvane Art Museum, Washburn University, 1993.
DOUGAN, David. *Crafts Fair Chelsea 1985.* London, England: Chelsea Old Town Hall, 1985.
DRUTT ENGLISH, Helen Williams, and Wayne Higby. *Contemporary Arts: An Expanding View.* Lincroft, New Jersey: The Monmouth Museum, 1986.
DRUTT ENGLISH, Helen Williams, and Wendy Steiner. *Brooching It Diplomatically.* Philadelphia, Pennsylvania: Helen Drutt: Philadelphia, 1998.
ENGLANDER, Lisa, and Bruce W. Pepich. *A Modern Bestiary: Artists View the Animal Kingdom and Going to the Dogs: Man's Best Friend as Seen by Artists.* Racine, Wisconsin: Charles A. Wustum Museum of Fine Arts, 2002.
FAZZI, Maria Pacini, ed. *Lucca Preziosa 2006, No Body Decoration: Research Jewellery as Redefinition of the Human Body.* Florence, Italy: Villa Botini, 2006.
FISCH, Arline M. *Jewelry and Beyond: Recent Metalwork by Distinguished Members of the Society of North American Goldsmiths.* Mount Vernon, Illinois: Mitchell Museum, 1984.
FOSTER, Joan E., Vincent Tovell, Marie Shaw-Rimmington, Paul J. Smith, Kathleen Nugent Mangan and Anita Aarons. *Celebration '84: A Sense of Occasion.* Toronto, Ontario, Canada: the Art Gallery at Harbourfront, 1984.
GLOVER, Robly A., and Catherine Prose. *Crafts, Etc.: Contemporary Jewelry Design and Metalsmithing by Master Artist Craftsmen.* Lubbock, Texas: Buddy Holly Center, 2005.
HEIKKILÄ, Juhani, and Petteri Ikonen. *Subjects: International Jewellery Art Exhibition.* Helsinki, Finland: Design Forum, 1993.
HEIKKILÄ, Juhani, and Petteri Ikonen. *Subjects 96: International Jewellery Art Exhibition.* Punkaharju, Finland: Retretti Art Centre, 1996.
HIRAMATSU, Yasuki, Kenji Adachi, Shu Eguchi, Fritz Falk, Masayoshi Homma, and Kiyoshi Seike. *1983 International Jewellery Art Exhibition: The 5th Tokyo Triennial.* Tokyo, Japan: Isetan Art Museum, 1983.
ILSE-NEUMAN, Ursula, and David Revere McFadden. *Zero Karat: The Donna Schneier Gift to the American Craft Museum.* New York: the American Craft Museum, 2002.
JOHNSTONE, Mark, and Wendy Mickell. *Body Art.* Costa Mesa, California: Security Pacific Gallery, 1990.
KAWAKITA, Michiaki, and Kenji Adachi. *Contemporary Jewellery: the Americas, Australia, Europe and Japan.* Tokyo, Japan: The National Museum of Modern Art, 1984.
LANDY, Audrey, and Lora Childs. *Art: On the Move.* LaGrange, Georgia: Chattahoochee Valley Art Association, 1987.
LÖSCHE, Wolfgang, and Dorothea Prühl. *Schmuck 2005: Sonderschau der 57. Internationalen Handwerksmesse.* Munich, Germany: Bayerischer Handwerkstag, 2005.
LORENE, Karen, ed. *Signs of Life.* Seattle, Washington: Facèré Jewelry Art Gallery, 2007.
MAWDSLEY, Richard. *American Revelations: New Jewellery by Members of the Society of North American Goldsmiths.* Newcastle, England: Shipley Gallery, 1996.
MEYER, James C., Paula Hovde, and Paul N. Perrot. *Jewelry Now.* Richmond, Virginia: The Hand Workshop, 1986.
MOSNES, Jostein, and Esther Helen Slagsvold Hekne. *Åkersvika-Addenda.* Hamar, Norway: Old Norges Bank Gallery, 1993.
NICKL, Peter. *Schmuck und Gerät: 1959–1984. Sonderschau der Internationalen Handwerksmesse.* Munich, Germany: Bayerischer Handwerkstag, 1984.
NICKL, Peter. *Form, Formel, Formalismus: Schmuck 1985. Sonderschau der Internationalen Handwerksmesse.* Munich, Germany: Bayerischer Handwerkstag, 1985.
NICKL, Peter. *Schmuckszene '87. Internationale Handwerksmesse.* Munich, Germany: Bayerischer Handwerkstag, 1987.
NICKL, Peter. *Schmuck '96: Sonderschau der 48. Internationalen Handwerksmesse.* Munich, Germany: Bayerischer Handwerkstag, 1996.
OSBORN, Sarah, Lindsay Wilcox, and Diana Hughes, *Jewellery Redefined: the 1st International Exhibition of Multi-Media Non-Precious Jewellery 1982.* London, England: British Crafts Centre, 1982.
OWEN, Paula, and Barbel Helmert. *Zierat Zierat.* San Antonio, Texas: Russell Hill Rogers Gallery, 2001
PEPICH, Bruce W., and Libby and JoAnne Cooper. *The Ring: The Art of the Ring.* Cambridge, Massachusetts: Mobilia Gallery, 2001.
SCHEPERS, Wolfgang, Paula Owen, Barbel Helmert, and Martha J. Havemann. *Zierat: International Contemporary Jewelry Invitational.* Hannover, Germany: Kestner-Museum, 2001.
SCHICK, Marjorie. *Body Works and Wearable Sculpture Exhibition.* Anchorage, Alaska: Visual Arts Center of Alaska, 1985.
SHIMBUN, Nihon Keizai, and others. *1986 International Jewellery Art Exhibition.* Tokyo, Japan: Yurakucho Art Forum, 1986.
SMITH, Paul J., Richard Mawdsley, Arline M. Fisch, Sharon Church, Helen Drutt, and John Paul Miller. *Jewelry USA.* New York: American Craft Museum II, 1984.
SMITH, Paul J., and Arline M. Fisch. *American Jewelry Now.* New York: American Craft Museum, 1985.
SMITH, Paul J., and Edward Lucie-Smith. *Craft Today: Poetry of the Physical.* New York: American Craft Museum, 1986.
SMITH, Paul J. *Craft Today: USA.* Paris, France: Musée des Arts Décoratifs, 1989.
TOMLINSON, Michael. *Jewelry: Means: Meaning.* Knoxville, Tennessee: Ewing Gallery of Art and Architecture, the University of Tennessee, 1989.
VAN OOSTSTROOM, Martijn, Adelei van der Velden, and Paul Derrez. *The Banqueting Table: Designed by Thirty-nine Artists.* Amsterdam, the Netherlands: Galerie Ra, 1991.
VELVET DA VINCI GALLERY. *Chess: Chessmen by International Artists.* San Francisco, California: Velvet Da Vinci, 2003.
VOLLMER, Stephen, and Rachelle Thiewes. *The Body Adorned: An Exhibition of Jewelry.* El Paso, Texas: Main Gallery, Fox Fine Arts Center, University of Texas at El Paso, 1993.

MARJORIE SCHICK WITH HER MOTHER, ELEANOR KRASK, ARROWMONT SCHOOL OF ARTS AND CRAFTS, GATLINBURG, TENNESSEE, 1990
PHOTO: CYNTHIA GARRISON

AUTHORS' BIOGRAPHIES

TACEY A. ROSOLOWSKI, Ph.D., is a freelance writer who has published numerous articles and catalogue essays on contemporary jewelry, and lectures widely in the field. She is curator of the touring retrospective, "Sculpture Transformed: The Work of Marjorie Schick" (2007–09). In 2003 she was the James Renwick Fellow in American Craft at the Smithsonian Institution's Renwick Gallery in Washington, D.C., a fellowship awarded in support of her research on the aesthetics of jewelry. She has a Ph.D. in Comparative Literature from the State University of New York at Buffalo and an M.S. in Design and Environmental Analysis from Cornell University. She resides in Buffalo, New York.

GLEN R. BROWN, Ph.D., is a Professor of 20th-Century and Contemporary Art History at Kansas State University and has authored numerous essays on contemporary jewelry for *Metalsmith* and *Ornament* magazines. He is an elected member of the International Academy of Ceramics, Geneva, Switzerland, and an Associate Fellow of the International Quilt Study Center, Lincoln, NE.

PAUL DERREZ, world-renowned jeweler and owner of the avant-garde Galerie Ra in Amsterdam, is a sought-after visiting lecturer, writer, and juror for international art councils and awards. He trained as a goldsmith at the Vakschool in Schoonhoven and then moved to Amsterdam where he established Galerie Ra in 1976. His works are in public collections including the Stedelijk Museum in Amsterdam, Die Neue Sammlung in Munich, and the Powerhouse Museum in Sydney, Australia.

HELEN WILLIAMS DRUTT ENGLISH is the founder of the Helen Drutt Gallery in Philadelphia. She has lectured internationally and is the recipient of several honors and awards. Her work in the field continues as she organizes seminal exhibitions for museums internationally and contributes to numerous monographs. Most recently, she was appointed curatorial consultant to the Museum of Fine Arts, Houston, in support of their acquisition of her jewelry collection, and she serves as a consultant to the Designmuseo, Helsinki, Finland. In 1979 *American Craft Magazine* stated that her gallery was to crafts, what Alfred Stieglitz's Gallery 291 was to photography early in the twentieth century.

FRITZ FALK who holds a doctorate in art history and is also a master goldsmith, was the director of the Schmuckmuseum Pforzheim from 1971 to 2003. Playing a paramount role in shaping the museum collection, he presided during his tenure over more than a hundred exhibitions with a wide-ranging thematic focus on the international art of jewelry.

ELIZABETH GORING, Ph.D., is a curator, writer and jewelry historian. She is a Principal Curator at the National Museums of Scotland, Edinburgh, where she created and developed the Modern Jewelry Collection from 1983 to 2004. She is an Honorary Research Fellow in the Institute for Art History, University of Glasgow, and Edinburgh College of Art.

SUZANNE RAMLJAK, a writer, art historian, and curator, is currently editor of *Metalsmith* magazine. She was formerly editor of *Sculpture* and *Glass Quarterly*, as well as associate editor of *American Ceramics*. Ramljak has contributed to several books and catalogues, and has lectured widely on twentieth-century art.

HELEN SHIRK (M.F.A. Indiana University, 1969) is Professor of Art Emerita at San Diego State University. Her metalwork is included in many public collections, including the Victoria and Albert Museum, Schmuckmuseum Pforzheim, National Gallery of Australia, Houston Museum of Fine Arts, Mint Museum of Craft and Design, and Cooper-Hewitt National Design Museum.

PAUL J. SMITH, Director Emeritus of the American Craft Museum (now the Museum of Arts & Design) New York, is widely recognized for his imaginative programming and international activities that have expanded public appreciation of crafts and design. Having joined the staff of the American Craftmen's Council in 1957, he served as Director of the Museum from 1963 to 1987. Currently he is an independent curator and consultant.

TRAGBARE SKULPTUREN
DER SCHMUCK VON MARJORIE SCHICK

Deutsche Übersetzung von Uta Hasekamp

S. 7ff.

DANKSAGUNG

Bevor es Mobiltelefone gab und bevor ich in meinem Büro an der Universität ein Telefon hatte, sagte Jim manchmal: „Du hast die Prüfung bestanden, Marj. Miss Eikerman hat gestern Abend zu Hause angerufen und du warst noch in der Uni und hast im Atelier gearbeitet." Meine Mentorin, Professor Alma Eikerman, und ich sind die ganzen Jahre nach dem Abschluss meines Schmuckstudiums an der Indiana University in Kontakt geblieben. Eikerman schrieb mir oft und rief manchmal auch an. Wenn ich ihre Anrufe auch nicht gerne verpasste, war es doch gut, dass ich in diesen Momenten arbeitete. Über künstlerische Gestaltung, Zeichnen, Techniken und Schmuckgeschichte hinaus lehrte sie uns Selbstdisziplin und die Wichtigkeit harter Arbeit. Als fortgeschrittene Studenten vermerkten wir auf Stundenzetteln, wann wir im Atelier waren, und sie hat das oft überprüft. In einem Rundbrief schrieb sie 1975: „Der Hauptzweck Eurer Existenz als Kunsthandwerker ist es, jedes Jahr, jeden Monat so viel zu produzieren, wie es Euch möglich ist." Wenn ich ihren Anruf verpasste, weil ich im Atelier arbeitete, war dies ein wichtiger Hinweis darauf, dass ich mein Leben richtig gestaltete.

Viele Jahre lang nahm Jim, wenn er zu Hause am Telefon vorbeiging, den Hörer ab, obwohl das Telefon nicht geklingelt hatte, und sagte: „Ja, Miss Eikerman, sie hat hart gearbeitet", oder er erzählte einem imaginären Anrufer, dass ich das nicht getan hatte.

Eikerman lehrte ihre Schüler auch, gut zu leben. Als Belohnung für ihre Mühen lud sie ihre Erstsemester, wenn sie die Böden an ihre Silberschalen gelötet hatten, regelmäßig auf eine Süßspeise zu sich nach Hause ein. Das von ihr selbst entworfene hypermoderne Haus hatte sie mit zeitgenössischer Kunst aller Art angefüllt, mit Gegenständen, die sie auf ihren Reisen erworben hatte, wunderschönen Büchern und kleinen Dingen wie Besteck aus Skandinavien, wo sie Metallbearbeitung studiert hatte. Sie war elegant, hatte Stil, Energie, liebte das Abenteuer und Herausforderungen, und sie riet uns, Geld für Reisen zu sparen, da diese „eine Investition in die Forschung – und für ein besseres Leben" seien.

Mit seinem hervorragenden Verstand und seinem großen Herzen hat mich Jim, Professor für amerikanische Geschichte an der Pittsburg State University, entschlossen und in aller Hinsicht unterstützt. Er hat mir die Ideen für Arbeiten wie *Liberty Torch* (Fackel der Freiheit) und die Körperskulptur *50 States* gegeben. Außerdem hat er Fotos gemacht, mich umhergefahren, für mich geschrieben, meine Texte redigiert, er hat mir beigebracht, einen Computer zu benutzen, und mir für dieses Buch einen neuen gekauft, und er hat die Ferien um meine Museumsbesuche herum geplant. Wie glücklich ich bin, einen Ehemann zu haben, der mich gelenkt und meine Arbeit, was immer auch geschah, unterstützt und ermutigt hat, wie auch eine Mentorin, für die ich noch immer arbeite. Dieses Buch ist Dr. James B. M. Schick und Professor Alma Eikerman gewidmet, denn ich glaube, dass es ohne sie mein Werk nicht gäbe.

Ein besonderer Dank gilt auch meiner Mutter, Eleanor Curtin Krask, die das Vorbild einer hart arbeitenden, hingebungsvollen Kunstlehrerin ist. Sie hat alles für mich getan und gegeben, darunter auch dieses Buch, ihr außergewöhnliches letztes Geschenk.

Dirk Allgaier von Arnoldsche Art Publishers hat die lange Reise von Stuttgart nach Kansas, in das abgelegene Pittsburg, unternommen, um mich bei der Auswahl der Bilder zu beraten und mich durch dieses Buch zu führen. Indem sie Hunderte von Entscheidungen traf, hat die preisgekrönte Grafikerin Silke Nalbach atemberaubend schöne Seiten geschaffen, die dem Leser Lust darauf machen, nachzusehen, was als Nächstes kommt. Die Lektorin Julia Vogt hat alle Texte mit ihrem scharfen Auge geprüft, um sicherzugehen, dass alles perfekt ist. Helen Williams Drutt English hat das Projekt mit Arnoldsche Art Publishers von Anfang an unterstützt. Die Arnoldsche steht für ausgezeichnete Qualität und Kreativität und hat eine Vielzahl hervorragender Bücher herausgebracht. Deshalb ich bin dankbar, dass sie und der Verleger, Dieter Zühlsdorff, sich zu diesem Buchprojekt bereit erklärt haben.

Die Autorin des umfassendsten Beitrags, Dr. Tacey Rosolowski, und auch alle anderen Autoren, Dr. Glen Brown, Paul Derrez, Helen Williams Drutt English, Dr. Fritz Falk, Dr. Elizabeth Goring, Suzanne Ramljak, Helen Shirk und Paul J. Smith, haben großzügig mit ihren Erkenntnissen und ihrem Urteil zu diesem Buch beigetragen.

Durch die Objektive ihrer Kameras haben die Fotografen Joel Degen, Tom DuBrock, Rod Dutton, Carmen Freudenthal, Jud Haggard, Eva Heyd, Peter R. Leibert, Larry Long, James Mueller, Gary Pollmiller, James B. M. Schick, Martin Tuma, Malcolm Turner und Hogers Versluys mein Werk professionell und klar präsentiert.

Stil, Anmut, Schneid und Geduld ist der Beitrag all derer, die meine Arbeiten als Models vorgeführt haben: Kathlene Allie, Petra Blaisse, Elizabeth Hake, Cora Hardy, Beth Neubert, Annie Pennington Parthasaraty und Jared Webb. Die von Ted Monsour geschenkten Schaufensterpuppen sind für die Präsentation der Arbeiten ebenfalls von Bedeutung gewesen.

Ende der 1980er Jahre, als ich meine rechte Hand zum ersten Mal überanstrengte, stellte ich einen Studenten als Hilfe ein. Meine Hand musste heilen, doch ich hatte weiterhin Arbeiten fertigzustellen. Seitdem habe ich viele – derzeitige oder ehemalige – Studenten der Pittsburg State University engagiert. Diese unersetzlichen Assistenten haben mich beim Entstehen der Stücke unterstützt, mich beraten und mir geholfen, Termine einzuhalten. Unter anderem haben sie geschnitten, genäht, geschmirgelt, grundiert, gesägt, gedübelt, gemalt und Transportkästen gebaut. Ich habe von ihnen gelernt und das Zusammensein mit ihnen, ihre Ideen und ihre Hilfe sehr genossen. Ich danke jedem Einzelnen von ihnen: Keegan Adams, Linda Allee Maggio, Kathlene Allie, Carl Barnett, Melanie Buckler, John Cohorst, Walter Delp, Jana Dunn, Randy French, Anna Friederich-Maggard, Matt Frost, Kristan Hammond, Ukiko Honda, Cherlyn Ingram, David Ingram, Hong Kim, Craig Krug, Janet Lewis, Kelley Losher, Jillian Palone, Annie Pennington Parthasarathy, Connie Rogers, Curtis Wakeman und Jared Webb. Falls ich versehentlich jemanden vergessen habe, möchte ich mich entschuldigen.

Ich habe mir zu Hause nie ein Atelier eingerichtet, sondern habe nachts und an Wochenenden immer mein Klassenzimmer als solches genutzt. Ich weiß die Geduld und die Toleranz meiner Studenten zu schätzen, welche die Arbeiten niemals angerührt haben – nicht einmal, als ich 32 bemalte Ringe auf Sockeln (für Bands of Rings [Ringbänder]) mehr als ein Jahr lang auf einem Regal im Klassenzimmer stehen ließ. Sie haben mich gefordert und angespornt, härter zu arbeiten.

Meine Lehrtätigkeit an der Pittburg State University hat mein Leben bereichert, und die Universität hat mich auf vielfältige Weise unterstützt. Unter anderem gewährte sie Jim und mir vier Forschungsurlaube und auch freie Zeit, um während des Semesters zu reisen, wenn es notwendig war. Meine Vorgesetzten und meine Kollegen, die ich bewundere, sind loyale Freunde gewesen und haben mir mit Rat und sogar mit künstlerischer Hilfe beiseite gestanden, wenn ich sie darum bat.

Was den Bundesstaat Kansas betrifft, schätze ich die Unterstützung und die Anerkennung vonseiten der Kansas Art Commission sehr, die mir den Governor's Arts Award und den Artist Fellowship Award in Crafts verlieh. Die KAC und auch die Kansas Artist Craftsman Association lassen uns Kunsthandwerker in diesem Staat fühlen, dass wir Teil einer größeren Gemeinschaft und in unseren Bemühungen nicht allein sind.

Tacey Rosolowski kontaktierte die International Arts and Artists in Washington, D. C. und überzeugte sie, eine Retrospektive meiner Werke als Wanderausstellung zu organisieren und zu fördern, eine Schau, die sich sehr von ihrer sonstigen Tätigkeit unterscheidet. Diese Ausstellung war der Ansporn für die Entstehung dieses Buches.

Wenn ich mir Jims hundertprozentigen Einsatz als Lehrer an der Universität ansehe und weil ich Alma Eikermans Hingabe für ihre Schüler miterleben konnte, bin ich mir der Wichtigkeit und des Wertes einer erfolgreichen Lehrtätigkeit bewusst. In meinem Leben hat es viele inspirierende und erstaunliche Lehrer gegeben, sowohl an der Evanston Township High School als auch an der University of Wisconsin, der Indiana University und der Sir John Cass School of Art in London. Noch heute profitiere ich vom Unterricht dieser Lehrer und bin für ihre Unterstützung dankbar. Insbesondere die Indiana University hat meine Arbeit großzügig unterstützt, indem sie mir zwei Ausstellungen ermöglichte, die über den Bereich der im Klassenzimmer gesammelten Erfahrungen weit hinausgehen.

Die Körperskulptur It's A Boy Named Rob (Es ist ein Junge, und er heißt Rob) erinnert an die Geburt unseres Sohnes. Sie ist mit Sicherheitsnadeln bedeckt, die durch farbige Kreise gesteckt wurden, und bezieht sich auf die Geburtsanzeigen, die ich für Freunde machte. Dieses Gebilde hängt von dem Bild eines blauen Hauses herab, denn in dieser Arbeit geht es um die Familie und das Zuhause. Rob ermöglichte es Jim und mir, das Leben durch seine Augen zu erfahren, und er inspiriert mich noch heute. Das Foto von Rob als Baby, auf dem er einen neuen, als Geschenk für Eikerman gedachten Armschmuck hält (s. S. 202), zeigt seine Ehrfurcht und sein Staunen über alles in der Welt.

In einem Rundbrief an ihre Schüler schrieb die unglaubliche (das ist das Wort, das sie selbst oft verwendete) Alma Eikerman: „Ich sende Euch meine besten Wünsche. Ich hoffe, dass Ihr mit Gesundheit und Glück und mit Zeit für Eure schöpferischen Unternehmungen gesegnet sein werdet." Wie glücklich ich bin, mich guter „Gesundheit" und einer Überfülle von „Glück" zu erfreuen, und dank der erstaunlichen und nicht nachlassenden Unterstützung durch Jim bin ich auch mit dem Geschenk von viel „Zeit" für meine „schöpferischen Unternehmungen" gesegnet. Dies war eine ungeheuerliche gemeinsame Leistung. Ich danke Euch allen.
Marjorie Schick

S. 11ff.

MARJORIE SCHICK: GRENZÜBERSCHREITUNGEN, FORMERWEITERUNGEN

Tacey A. Rosolowski

Wenn Marjorie Schick im Ausland ist, hört sie: „Ihre Werke sind so amerikanisch". In den Vereinigten Staaten stimmt die Schmuck- und Kunsthandwerkszene darin überein, dass ihre Arbeiten etwas eindeutig Europäisches haben.[1] Beide Betrachtungsweisen sind natürlich zutreffend. Im Laufe der Jahre hat sich Schick mühelos zwischen den Kontinenten hin und her bewegt, sie hat gelehrt, Vorträge gehalten, an Kursen teilgenommen, ihren Beitrag zu einer weit verzweigten Gemeinschaft von Schmuckkünstlern geleistet und Kraft aus dieser geschöpft. Schick ist durch und durch Amerikanerin, sie wurde in Illinois geboren und hat die meiste Zeit ihres Lebens in Pittsburg im Bundesstaat Kansas gelebt. Sie ist ein Kind des Mittleren Westens, und eine Art Pioniergeist kennzeichnet ihre künstlerischen Unternehmungen. Schick wurde zu einer Metallschmiedin und Schmuckdesignerin ausgebildet, doch bekannt wurde sie durch ihre großen und farbenfrohen Körperskulpturen aus unterschiedlichen Materialien. Die europäische Note in Schicks Werk resultiert aus ihren klaren Überzeugungen, dass Schmuck eine Kunstgattung und der menschliche Körper für die Vervollständigung eines plastischen Gegenstandes wesentlich ist. Mehr als vier Jahrzehnte lang ist es ihr Ziel gewesen, das Verständnis von Skulptur zu verändern, indem sie den menschlichen Körper, durch direkte Berührung oder kinästhetische Wahrnehmung, in Kontakt mit der künstlerischen Form bringt. Ihre Arbeiten entziehen sich der Klassifizierung. Sie erweitern das Ausdrucksspektrum der Skulptur und setzen die künstlerischen Möglichkeiten des menschlichen Körpers selbst frei.

Schicks berufliche Laufbahn begann in den 1960er Jahren. Zuvor hatte ihr ein eingehendes Studium der keltischen und afrikanischen Ornamentik und der Ornamente der Wikingerzeit wie auch des Werks von Schmuckkünstlerinnen wie Alma Eikerman und Margaret De Patta wichtige Erkenntnisse vermittelt. Doch für konzeptuelle Anregungen hatte sie sich stets Bildhauern zugewandt, wie David Smith, Alexander Calder, Julio González, Barbara Hepworth und dem Keramikkünstler Hans Coper. Aufgrund ihres vielseitigen künstlerischen Ansatzes war Schick in einer guten Position, in die lebhafte Diskussion über das Wesen der Kunst einzusteigen, in die Künstler auf beiden Seiten des Atlantiks involviert waren. Die traditionellen Gattungsgrenzen verschwommen, als sich neue Formen des künstlerischen Ausdrucks entwickelten. Schicks Zeitgenossen in der Welt des Schmucks waren wichtige Künstler wie Emmy van Leersum, Gijs Bakker, Caroline Broadhead, Wendy Ramshaw und David Watkins – eine lockere Gemeinschaft von „New Jewelers" (neuen Schmuckkünstlern), die mit der Größe von Schmuckstücken und dem Körperteil, an dem diese getragen wurden, experimentierten, kostbare Materialien ablehnten und zugunsten einer größeren Materialvielfalt innovative Techniken und Formen entwickelten.

In den 1970er Jahren schuf sich Schick innerhalb der europäischen und amerikanischen Avantgarde ihre eigene Nische. Sie war Gastkünstlerin der Ausstellung „Choreographing the Object: An Evening of Visual Art and Dance" (Die Choreografie des Gegenstandes: Ein Abend mit Bildender Kunst und Tanz), welche von Mary Ann Bransby kuratiert worden war und Schicks experimentellem Ansatz eine einzigartige Bühne verschaffte. An jedem der fünf Aufführungsorte betraten die Besucher einen leeren, einer Galerie benachbarten Raum und ließen sich auf dem Boden nieder. Nacheinander erschienen Tänzerinnen und Tänzer und interpretierten Arbeiten von Bransby, Schick und anderen: Eckige Bewegungen flößten Schicks geometrischen Schmuckstücken und Körperskulpturen Leben ein; sich wiegende Hüften verwandelten ihren breiten Metallgürtel in ein Musikinstrument. Danach stellte jeder Tänzer das getragene Schmuckstück in der Galerie auf, wo es nach der Performance betrachtet werden konnte. Skulptur wurde zum „Happening" – zum Ereignis sinnlicher Wahrnehmung –, was Schick mit allen ihren Arbeiten beabsichtigt. Das Verständnis einer vom menschlichen Körper unabhängig präsentierten Skulptur wird durch die unmittelbare körperliche Erfahrung der Skulptur verwandelt (Abb. 1). Schick erinnert sich auch daran, wie eine andere Tänzerin umherrannte und sich schnell drehte und dabei die schweren Fasern einer langen Körperskulptur in Bewegung versetzte. Fasziniert schaute sie zu, wie Staubpartikel nach oben schwebten, als ob die Skulptur – und die Bewegungen des Tänzers – den gesamten Raum buchstäblich ausfüllten.

Das erstaunlich weite Spektrum von Schicks Arbeiten nährt sich aus der Feinsinnigkeit ihrer künstlerischen Sensibilität. Schick macht Skulpturen, will damit aber den Raum jenseits einer lokalisierbaren Masse oder Linie aktivieren. Sie malt, um der Form die expressive Gestik von Bewegung und Stimmung zu verleihen. Sie schafft Ornamente, doch geht sie dabei über alles gemeinhin als dekorativ Geltende hinaus. Sie fertigt ihre Objekte in langen Arbeitsstunden, doch möchte sie nicht, dass ihre Mühe sichtbar wird oder von der ästhetischen Wirkung der Werke ablenkt. Selbst wenn ihre Arbeit unabhängig vom menschlichen Körper präsentiert wird, setzt sie eine Vielzahl von Reaktionen frei: das empirische Verständnis der Form, das Bewusstsein komplexer räumlicher Beziehungen, die verstärkte sinnliche Wahrnehmung eines künstlerisch gestalteten Umfelds.

Schicks künstlerische Laufbahn lässt sich in zwei Hauptphasen einteilen. Die erste umfasst ihr weiterführendes Studium an der Indiana University und dauerte bis in die 1980er Jahre an. Während dieser Zeit schuf Schick ihr bildliches Vokabular und gab den aus der modernen Abstraktion bezogenen Erkenntnissen ihre eigene Prägung. Zunächst erkundete sie die Grundlagen des Volumens, der Linie, des Raumes und der Masse. Außerdem schuf sich Schick eine solide Basis, von der aus sie sich voller Selbstvertrauen über ihre Ausbildung hinaus entwickeln konnte. So verschrieb sie sich in der zweiten Phase ihrer Laufbahn ganz und gar künstlerischen Interessen, die schon viele Jahre latent vorhanden gewesen waren.

Schick wurde 1941 in Taylorville im US-Bundesstaat Illinois geboren. Ihrer Mutter Eleanor Krask war ihre eigene berufliche Laufbahn sehr wichtig, so dass sie, als Schick noch ein Kind war, auf die Universität zurückkehrte, um ihren Bachelor und ihren Magister zu machen. Als alleinerziehende Mutter war Krask im traditionellen Amerika der Nachkriegsjahre ein überaus wichtiges Vorbild für die kleine Marjorie. Als Kunstlehrerin füllte sie das Haus mit künstlerischen Materialien und auch mit Büchern und Zeitschriften, so dass ihre Tochter Künstler und Schmuckkünstler der Vergangenheit und Gegenwart kennenlernte. Krask brachte ihrer Tochter das Nähen, das Herstellen von Collagen und das Malen bei. Schon früh verbesserte Marjorie ihre handwerklichen Fähigkeiten und machte sich mit einer großen Anzahl künstlerischer Mittel vertraut. Als ihre Mutter eine Stelle in Evanston, Illinois, nur wenig nördlich von Chicago, antrat, kam Marjorie in den Genuss des reichen künstlerischen Lehrangebots der Evanston Township High School und belegte Kurse in Kunstgeschichte, Emaillieren und Modedesign. Sie träumte davon, Modeschöpferin zu werden. Samstags fuhr sie nach Chicago, wo sie an der School of Art am Art Institute of Chicago Kurse in Aquarellmalerei, Modedesign und Illustrieren besuchte.[2]

Später machte Schick ihren Bachelor of Science in Kunsterziehung an der University of Wisconsin-Madison. Kurz nachdem sie James B. M. Schick, einen Geschichtsdoktoranden, geheiratet hatte, entschied sie sich, den Master of Fine Arts anzustreben. Es ist nicht weiter überraschend, dass es Schick mit ihren umfangreichen Kenntnissen und Fähigkeiten schwerfiel, sich für einen Schwerpunkt innerhalb der Angewandten Künste zu entscheiden. Doch der glückliche Zufall spielt im Leben eines Künstlers häufig eine Rolle, und Schick gibt zu, dass sie sich auf Jims Rat hin entschloss, sich auf Schmuck zu konzentrieren. (Heute ist Jim Schick, wie auch Marjorie, Professor an der Pittsburg State University; er hat seine Frau stets mit Zeit, Energie, Ideen und auch dem gelegentlichen Schuss Kritik, den ein jeder Künstler benötigt, unterstützt.) Schmuck sollte sich als das ideale Gebiet erweisen, in dem sie ihr Interesse für Form, Materialien und die zeremoniellen Aspekte weiterentwickeln konnte, die das Erleben und die Präsentation eines Gegenstandes mit sich bringen.

Während ihres weiterführenden Studiums an der Indiana University wurde Schick von Alma Eikerman betreut, die sie anspornte, Schmuckformen und konzeptuelle Inhalte zu erkunden. *Textured Brass Armlet* (Strukturierter Messing-Armschmuck; 1967, Abb. 2) untersucht die Beziehung der Materialstruktur zur Masse, während der Halsschmuck *Wheatfields* (Weizenfelder; 1968, Kat.-Nr. 59) Linien dicht zu einer Masse zusammendrängt (eine Hommage an die Pinselstriche Van Goghs in einem Gemälde von Weizenfeldern). Diese Interessen sollten in Schicks gesamter Laufbahn Bestand haben. *Shoulder Sculpture* (Schulterskulptur; 1968, Kat.-Nr. 60) erkundet die Beziehung einer Form zur Anatomie des Körpers: Ein Gefüge von Ebenen ist im Schlüsselbein verankert; es antwortet auf sich verändernde Winkel, indem es nach oben kippt, von der Brust und Schulter zum Ansatz des Nackens. Ein anderes Gefühl vermitteln *Bracelet* (Armschmuck; 1975, Kat.-Nr. 113), *Finger Sculptures* (Fingerskulpturen; 1967, 1968, 1972, Kat.-Nrn. 33, 62, 91) und *Hair Sculpture* (Haarskulptur; 1975, Kat.-Nr. 112). In diesen abstrakten Studien befreien sich die Linien von der Masse, doch kommt man nicht umhin, ihren überschwänglichen Kurven eine eigene Persönlichkeit und Emotionen zuzuschreiben. Sie erinnern an Alexander Calders Karikaturen aus Draht und an die ausdrucksstarken Skulpturen von Julio González.

Während ihres weiterführenden Studiums widersetzte sich Schicks Sinn für Form den im Schmuck üblichen Konventionen. 1966 las sie einen Artikel über den Bildhauer David Smith und stellte sich vor, wie es sich anfühlen würde, ihre Hand oder ihren Kopf durch eine Öffnung in seinen Skulpturen zu stecken. Zuvor hatte sie eine kleine Brosche mit hervorstehenden schwarzen Drähten geschaffen (Abb. 3), die Schick in ihren eigenen Worten „das Selbstvertrauen gab, Formen aus dem Körper in den Raum hinauszuführen". Diese beiden künstlerischen Entdeckungen sollten sich als wesentlich erweisen. Doch damit sich ihre experimentellen Arbeiten zu Rauminhalt, Linie und Maßstab wirklich befreien konnten, musste sie auf Einflüsse zurückgreifen, die mit ihrer Ausbildung als Metallschmiedin nichts gemein hatten.

„Meine eigentliche Liebe", bestätigt Schick, „waren von jeher außergewöhnliche Materialien." Direkt nach dem Abschluss ihres weiterführenden Studiums brachte sie sich selbst das Arbeiten mit Papiermaché bei und fand in ihren Experimenten mit der Masse, der Form und – nicht weniger wichtig – der Farbe eine neue plastische Freiheit. Das Ergebnis war eine Reihe von Armreifen aus Papiermaché (die auch zu ihrer ersten Begegnung mit Paul Smith, dem Direktor des American Craft Museum, führte). Während der gesamten 1970er Jahre schuf Schick Arbeiten sowohl aus Metall als auch aus Papiermaché oder anderen unüblichen Materialien und stellte sie aus, doch schätzte sie ihre unkonventionelleren Arbeiten immer als „weniger wichtig" ein. (Der Begriff „closet art" – private oder sogar heimliche Kunst – beschreibt das komplexe Verhältnis der Künstler gegenüber diesen zweitrangigen oder heimlichen Werkgruppen.) In den 1960er Jahren ermöglichten es Schick leichte und formbare Materialien, ihr künstlerisches Spektrum auszuweiten. In *Blue Eyes* (Blaue Augen; 1969, Kat.-Nr. 68), *Linear Shoulder Sculpture* (Lineare Schulterskulptur; 1969, Kat.-Nr. 67) und *The Cage* (Der Käfig; 1972, Abb. 4) fangen schwebende Linien den Raum ein und umgeben menschliche Formen. Schick hüllte den Draht vieler dieser Gebilde in Papiermaché ein und bemalte sie farbig – während ihrer Arbeit an den experimentellen Armreifen war sie „süchtig" nach Farbe geworden.

Schicks Experimente mit der Linie erreichten mit der *Dowel-Stick*-(Rundholzstab-) Werkgruppe der 1980er Jahre ihren Höhepunkt. Diese Arbeiten erregten internationale Aufmerksamkeit und veranlassten Hiroko Sato zu dem Kommentar, dass Schick den wichtigsten amerikanischen Einfluss auf europäische Schmuckkünstler ausübe.[3] Sie zeigten auch deutlich die konzeptuelle Verwandtschaft der Künstlerin mit Zeitgenossen wie Pierre Degen (Großbritannien) und Noam Ben Jacov (Niederlande), die ebenfalls ihr eigenes, eindrucksvolles künstlerisches Umfeld schufen. Schicks *Directional Forces* (Richtungskräfte; 1986, Kat.-Nr. 285) ist ein meisterhaftes Beispiel für eine konstruktivistische Form, die sie in ihre eigene Sprache umgesetzt hat. Das abstrakte Werk wird durch seine Bindungen an den Körper lebendig. Zu einem künstlerischen Ganzen wird es durch die in skulpturaler Hinsicht bedeutsame Verwendung der Farbe, die das Auge durch die Komposition leitet und ihr eine kraftvolle Bewegtheit verleiht. Das Stück hat eine bezwingende Präsenz. Wie Michael Dunas bemerkt, „erweitern" alle Arbeiten dieser Werkgruppe „den Raum des Körpers und bilden ein Energiefeld, in dem der Schmuck und sein Träger interagieren".[4]

Schick hat angemerkt, dass es Schmuck für dreißig Jahre und für drei Stunden gibt. Und dann schafft sie noch Schmuckstücke für dreißig Sekunden. Der flüchtigste Kontakt mit einer Form schafft ein umfassendes Bewusstsein: von dem Wechsel der Lage in der Bewegung, vom Spiel der Formen und Räume im nun veränderten Umkreis des Körpers und von dem Gefühl für Selbstdarstellung des Trägers im sozialen Raum. In *Arzo Orange* (1986, Abb. 5) scheint eine Struktur, die im Begriff ist, zusammenzufallen oder sich wieder aufzurichten, innezuhalten. Wenn diese Arbeit getragen wird, rahmt sie das Gesicht und füllt den Bereich um den Hals aus, dessen Intimsphäre wir als selbstverständlich ansehen. Vielleicht steht die Skulptur für die sich verändernden Stimmungen ihres Trägers, wenn dessen Bewegungen förmlicher oder bewusster werden. Vielleicht stellt jede orangefarbene Linie einen Kommentar zu diesen Gefühlen dar, markieren die blauen Spitzen eines jeden Stiftes die Anfänge und Enden der vom Träger formulierten Sätze.

Die *Dowel-Stick*-Werkgruppe verlieh Schicks konzeptuellen Überlegungen zur Abstraktion als Form deutlichen Ausdruck. Nichtsdestoweniger repräsentierte diese Gruppe nur einen kleinen Teil ihrer Sichtweise. Rudolf Arnheim hat angemerkt, dass „es keine direkte Umwandlung von Erfahrung in Form gibt, sondern vielmehr eine Suche nach etwas Äquivalentem".[5] Schicks Bewusstsein ist für Eindrücke empfänglich, die sie aus von Fasern aufsteigenden Staubpartikeln, aus Landschaften und Sprache, aus der Architektur und selbst aus kosmologischen Ereignissen bezieht. Seit den 1980er Jahren, der zweiten Phase ihres Werks, hat sie ihre konzeptuellen Interessen durch solche Anregungen mit Leben erfüllt. Teekannen wurden Broschen, zerlegten sich in eine Reihe von Armreifen oder dehnten sich aus, um Schulter und Hals zu rahmen. Ein Gebäude von Mies van der Rohe wurde in eine dem Körper angeglichene Skulptur verwandelt. Sich verändernde und durchsichtige Farbwolken verfestigten sich in einen Kokon für einen spiralförmigen Hals-schmuck. Schick hielt sich bei ihrer Erkundung leuchtender Farben nicht zurück. Sie schuf Formen, die durch Atmosphäre, Humor und spielerisches Nebeneinandersetzen oder Verschieben stark beein-flusst sind.

Bei *Wall Relief with Bracelet* (Wandrelief mit Armschmuck; 1988, Abb. 6) und *Painting with Three Necklaces* (Gemälde mit drei Hals-schmuckstücken; 1998, Kat.-Nr. 331) handelt es sich um Schicks erste Wandinstallationen. Während der sechs Wochen Arbeit an dem Halsschmuck-Gemälde, bei dem sie sich gezwungen sah, auch die Rückseite zu bemalen, erlebte sie einen jener Momente, in de-nen sich der Künstler oder die Künstlerin mit einer neuen Idee selbst in Erstaunen versetzt. Sie erinnert sich daran, dass sie dach-te, „Ach, was mache ich denn eigentlich? Ich bin keine Malerin." Seit Jahren schon hatte sie Gegenstände bemalt, doch passte sie mit diesem neuen Schritt Maltechniken direkter an ihr künstleri-sches Vorhaben an. Sie fing an, „Rundgemälde", wie sie Glen Brown nennt, zu schaffen, bei denen sie die Farbe auftrug, um die Vorstel-lung, dass ein flaches Kunstwerk nur von einer Seite betrachtet werden sollte, außer Kraft zu setzen.[6] Solche Installationen verlei-hen Schmuckobjekten ästhetische Parallelleben: Wenn ein Arm- oder Halsschmuck getragen wird, wird er mit dem Körper eins; wenn er auf dem zugehörigen Relief befestigt wird, integriert er sich darin völlig. Die Farbe verstärkt diese körperliche Verschmelzung und bestimmt auch die einzigartige Ganzheit eines jeden Elements. Im Wandrelief *Transition* (1992, Kat.-Nr. 344) verlaufen Ranken von links oben hinab und schlängeln sich elegant oberhalb der rechten oberen Ecke. Sie scheinen den Armreifen in Bewegung zu verset-zen, der sich in die entgegengesetzte Richtung wendet. Wenn der Armreif entfernt wird, haben beide Stücke eine voneinander unab-hängige Ausdruckskraft – der Armreif setzt seine farbigen Kreise in Bewegung, und das Relief verlockt den Betrachter, näher zu kom-men und die gemalte Vertiefung in seiner Mitte zu untersuchen.

Bei diesen „Rundgemälden" verschwimmen die Grenzen zwi-schen Handwerk, Ornament, Malerei und Skulptur. (Schick hat ex-plizite Hommagen an Maler geschaffen, beispielsweise *In Henri's Garden* [In Henris Garten; 2003, Kat.-Nr. 448] an Henri Rousseau und *Double Dutch Artists* [ein Wortspiel, das sowohl mit „Hollän-disches Künstlerdoppel" als auch mit „Kauderwelschkünstler" über-setzt werden könnte; 1998, Kat.-Nr. 413] an Mondrian und Van Gogh.) Diese Hybridformen resultieren nicht aus einem theoreti-schen Programm, sondern gehen aus Schicks Arbeitsprozess her-vor. Sie macht nur selten Skizzen ihrer Ideen und zieht es stattdes-sen vor, mit dem Material in ihren Händen zu beginnen, wobei sie die plastische Form und die sich entwickelnden Farbkombinationen direkt und in einem arbeitsintensiven Prozess entwickelt. Für die Bemalung des frei stehenden Armschmucks *Edged Wave* (Kantige Welle; 1995, Kat.-Nr. 378) benötigte sie beispielsweise mehr als 60 Stunden, was nicht allein auf die vielen aufgetragenen Farbschich-ten zurückzuführen ist. „Dieses Stück besteht hauptsächlich aus Kanten", erläutert Schick (ein Interesse, das sie aus ihrer Ausbil-dung zur Schmuckkünstlerin beibehalten hat, in der sie lernte, sich Stärke und Anordnung von Kanten für ästhetische und technische

Erfordernisse zunutze zu machen).[7] Sie bemühte sich sehr, ein Sys-tem von farbigen Mustern zu erarbeiten, das eine sich wellende Kante mit der anderen und der organisch wirkenden mittleren Öff-nung verbindet. Die Farbe stellt für sie stets die größte Herausfor-derung dar, die sie als „ein Ungeheuer" beschreibt. *For the Kunst Rai* (1992, Abb. 7) zeigt ein moiréartiges Muster, das die flachen und gewölbten Kanten zweier Skulpturen verbindet. Das Ergebnis prä-sentiert sich visuell und formal dynamisch: Der eckige skulptur-hafte Halsschmuck bringt sich vorsichtig ins Gleichgewicht, wäh-rend der Armreif zu rollen und sich krampfartig zusammenzuzie-hen scheint.

Wie die Arm- und Halsschmuckstücke auf Reliefs erweitern die-se Paarformen das Terrain für das Studium der Beziehungen im Raum. Schick bewundert die Untersuchungen der Bildhauerin Bar-bara Hepworth zu skulpturalen Beziehungen zwischen Gruppen plastischer Objekte. Ihre eigenen Paare beschreibt Schick als „Skulptur und ein Freund", wobei sie eine Atmosphäre von Affini-tät und Gespräch hervorruft. Dies ist nur angemessen, da dieser aufgeladene ästhetische Raum seine Grenzen auch dem Träger ge-genüber öffnen wird. *For Perth, Sculpture with Two Collars and One Armlet* (Skulptur mit zwei Kragen und einem Armschmuck; 1992, Kat.-Nr. 345) und *LA:DC Suite* (1996; Kat.-Nr. 391) und sogar die *Spiraling Discs* (Sich in die Höhe schraubende Scheiben; 2006, Kat.-Nr. 467), eine Folge von 32 Hals- und Armschmuckstücken, verviel-fältigen das ästhetische Spiel mit positiven und negativen Bezie-hungen zwischen Objekten, deren Anordnung immer wieder ver-ändert werden kann. Es ist deshalb nicht überraschend, dass Schick Richard Serra beipflichtet, dem zufolge das Verständnis von Skulp-tur ein kinästhetisches ist, das nicht allein „auf dem Bild oder An-blick oder dem optischen Bewusstsein, sondern auf einem körper-lichen Bewusstsein im Bezug auf Raum, Zeit und Bewegung" be-ruht.[8] Schick versetzt den Betrachter (und definiert ihn neu), so dass er durch den direkten Körperkontakt und aus der plastischen Form selbst heraus dieses Fließen des Raumes erfährt.

Ein kleiner, aber wesentlicher Paradigmenwechsel ermöglichte es Schick, ihre Skulpturgemeinschaften zu vergrößern. 1998 be-gann sie, Multiples aus modularen Einheiten herzustellen. Der Be-trachter fragt sich, wie es wäre, mit *Deception* (Täuschung; 2003, Kat.-Nr. 445) Schach zu spielen, dessen Spielsteine einen Raum markieren, der einem an Escher erinnernden Trugbild zu entstam-men scheint. *Bands of Rings* (Ringbänder; 2006, Kat.-Nr. 470) und *Orbiting Rings: Balancing Act* (Kreisende Ringe: Balanceakt; 2004, Kat.-Nr. 457) fordern den Betrachter auf, seine Hände in sinnlich gekurvte Formen zu tauchen – und davon gibt es viele, mehr als genug, um ein Verlangen nach Entzücken zu stillen. Die wachsen-de Größe der Werke zieht ein weiteres Spektrum von Gefühlsreak-tionen nach sich. *For Pforzheim* (1989, Kat.-Nr. 334–338), eine Reihe von fünf faltbaren Kragen, die jeweils fast 60 Zentimeter Durch-messer haben, kann flach liegend präsentiert werden, wobei die Einzelteile wie die Seiten eines Buches geöffnet und geschlossen sind (Abb. 8). Nur teilweise geöffnet legen sie sich um einen Hals. Ganz geöffnet können sie zu Präsentations- und Ansichtszwecken als Gruppe von Gyroskopen – Kreisel, die sich in einem beweglichen

Lager drehen – aufgehängt werden. *Progression* (Fortschreiten; 2007, Kat.-Nr. 441), eine Folge aus 66 quadratischen Halsschmuckstücken, die jeweils für ein Jahr im Leben der Künstlerin stehen, veranschaulicht durch ein Entlangschlängeln auf dem Boden das Vergehen der Zeit. *Much Ado About Twenty Bracelets* (Viel Lärm um 20 Armschmuckstücke; 2006, Kat.-Nr. 475) konfrontiert den Betrachter mit Winkeln. Abschnitte des riesigen faltbaren Schirms verlaufen in Winkelformationen über eine Strecke von fast fünf Metern. Seine eindrucksvolle Form und die Armschmuckstücke, die er hält, ziehen den Betrachter in die Binnenwelten von Winkelbeziehungen hinein, die auf jede Oberfläche gemalt sind.

Im Kontext solcher Werke könnte die Installation *Eclipse of the Moon: Earth's Shadow* (Mondfinsternis: Erdschatten; 2004, Abb. 9) eigentlich seltsam fehl am Platz erscheinen. Diese großen Schleier ineinander verschlungener Fasern, ein dunkler und ein heller, werden als sich überschneidende Zonen an der Wand angebracht, um das helle, reflektierte Mondlicht und den Erdschatten zu repräsentieren. Sie werfen auch Falten, während sich Licht und Schatten ohne Widerstände über einen Körper ergießen. Die Mehrzahl von Schicks Arbeiten besteht aus starren Materialien und zeigt ihr Interesse an der Masse und begrenzten Rauminhalten. *Eclipse* zeigt jedoch deutlich ihr andauerndes Interesse an den plastischen und kinetischen Möglichkeiten von Fasern. In den 1970er Jahren formte Schick aus Schnüren und Seilen Körperskulpturen und Masken. Sie schuf Zeichnungen aus Papier und Faden, die in den 1980er Jahren zu einer Serie von Schmuckstücken aus diesen Materialien führten. Sie hat mit Kleidungsstücken gearbeitet: mit zwei ägyptisierenden Kragen für *Amenhotep I* (2002, Kat.-Nr. 438), dem halbbeweglichen Schal und Gürtel *For Sonia Delaunay* (2003, Kat.-Nr. 447) und zwei großen tragbaren Formen zu Ehren von Elsa Schiaparelli, in dem für die Modedesignerin typischen grellen Rosa. In *Purple Swing* (Lila Schaukel; 1988, Kat.-Nr. 326) sind an langen Fasern geometrische Gebilde aufgehängt, die bei der geringsten Bewegung zittern und schwingen, und ein „schwarzer Regen" (der Begriff stammt von Schick) erweitert das künstlerisch gestaltete Umfeld des Buch-Halsschmucks *Connections* (Verbindungen; 2006, Abb. 10).

Etwas derart Fließendes und eine solche Empfänglichkeit für den Körper erinnern an Sartres Beobachtung, dass die Wahrnehmung selbst eines weit entfernten Gegenstandes so unmittelbar empfunden werden kann wie eine zärtliche Berührung. „Die Wärme der Luft, der Atem des Windes, die Strahlen der Sonne", sagt Sartre, „sind mir alle gegenwärtig [...] und legen mein Fleisch durch das ihre frei."[9] Ob sie nun starr oder fließend sind, Schicks Arbeiten laden ihre Betrachter wie ihre Träger ein, ein Objekt ganz und gar anzunehmen, indem sie die Skulptur und die menschliche Gestalt verwandeln: Beide werden durch die Stimmung, die Atmosphäre und das Spielerische der Arbeit lebendig. Über diese Konzentration auf die ästhetische Wahrnehmung hinaus verlangt jedes Stück nach einer Auseinandersetzung mit Vorstellungen über Größe, die Grenzen des Schmucks und des Ornaments, und mit der Frage, was es heißt, plastisch zu arbeiten.

Schicks Werk hat schon immer Anlass zur Kontroverse gegeben. Ihr Beitrag zum Schmuck der Gegenwart und zum Kunsthandwerk entsteht aus ihrer Fähigkeit, die Grenzen von Gattungen und Materialien zu überschreiten, den Körper mit der Form zu verbinden, Befindlichkeiten über Kontinente hinweg zu vermitteln. Schick beschreibt sich selbst als „leise Rebellin". Als Person, mit der Sanftheit ihrer Stimme und ihrer ganzen Art, scheint sie überraschend anders zu sein als ihr Werk. Ihre Hartnäckigkeit hat es ihr zudem ermöglicht, fünf Jahrzehnte lang „ihren eigenen Weg zu gehen". Angetrieben wird sie von ihrer Berufung, „aus Schmuck eine bildende Kunst zu machen". 1966, als junge Frau, bekräftigte Marjorie Schick: „Mein Schmuck mag den Betrachter überraschen und, falls nötig, auch verstören, doch vor allem muss er aggressiv sein – er muss auffallen."[10] 2002 hat die reife Künstlerin diese Verpflichtung noch einmal bestätigt: „Ich möchte, dass meine Werke furchtlos sind." Sie waren und sind es immer noch, in ihrem Maßstab, ihrer Farbe und ihrem unnachgiebigen Drang nach außen, in den Raum. Schicks Werk schließt den Träger ein, übernimmt die Kontrolle, definiert den menschlichen Körper und Wahrnehmungen in räumlicher und ästhetischer Hinsicht neu. Wenn ein Werk eine solche Durchsetzungskraft erlangt hat, ist dies allerdings nur auf die Furchtlosigkeit der Künstlerin selbst zurückzuführen.

1 Eine von Marjorie Schick erzählte Anekdote. Wenn nicht anderweitig vermerkt, stammen die Zitate aus Interviews, die ich von 1999 bis 2006 mit der Künstlerin geführt habe.
2 Marjorie Schick im Interview mit Tacey A. Rosolowski, 4.–6. April 2004, Nanette L. Laitman Documentation Project for Craft and Decorative Arts in America. Archives of American Art, Smithsonian Institution. Im Internet: www.aaa.si.edu/collections/oralhistories/transcripts/schick04.htm: see 12–15 (Zugriffsdatum: 12/7/06).
3 Hiroko Sato und Gene Pijanowksi, „Marjorie Schick: Drawing to Wear/Sculpture to Wear", in: *Four Seasons of Jewelry* (Japan), Bd. 67, Juni 1986, S. 56–63, hier S. 59.
4 Michael Dunas, „Marjorie's Schtick", in: *Metalsmith*, Bd. 5, Nr. 3, Sommer 1986, S. 24–31, hier S. 28.
5 Rudolf Arnheim, *Towards a Psychology of Art*, Berkeley: University of California Press 1966, S. 266.
6 Siehe Glen R. Brown, „Abwesenheit und Eigenwahrnehmung: Die Umkehrung des Skulpturraums", S. 226–227 in diesem Band.
7 Mitteilung der Künstlerin an Elizabeth Goring, November 1999.
8 Siehe Lynne Cook, „Richard Serra: *Torqued Ellipses*". Im Internet: http://www.diacenter.org/exhibs/serra/ellipses/essay.html.
9 Jean-Paul Sartre, *Being and Nothingness*, übersetzt von Hazel Barnes, New York: Pocket Books 1956, S. 506.
10 Marjorie Schick, „Thesis Statement" im Rahmen der Ausstellung anlässlich der Erlangung des Master of Fine Arts, Fachbereich Schmuck und Metallbearbeitung, Indiana University, 12.–20. Mai 1966.

S. 21 *Marjorie Schick*

„Mutter, ich habe da diesen jungen Mann getroffen, Jim Schick. Er will Geschichtsprofessor werden." Im Herbst nach unserer Heirat 1963 sollte er mit seiner Dissertation beginnen, und so strebte auch ich einen weiterführenden Abschluss an.

Die Fragen auf dem Bewerbungsformular für mein Aufbaustudium erwiesen sich als schwierig. Für welchen Abschluss sollte ich mich bewerben? Ich entschied mich für den M. F. A. (Master of Fine Arts), da er aus drei Buchstaben bestand und die anderen Abschlüsse nur zwei hatten. Dann musste ich einen Schwerpunkt wählen.

Da ich nicht wusste, welches künstlerische Fach mir während meines bisherigen Studiums am besten gefallen hatte, fragte ich Jim – die Person, die mich durch mein Leben geleitet hat. Er hatte mich vier Jahre lang auf dem College beobachtet und war der Meinung, dass ich Schmuck am liebsten mochte. So wählte ich Schmuckdesign und Metallbearbeitung. So einfach hat er meine Zukunft entschieden. Dafür bin ich ihm für immer dankbar.

Als ich frisch verheiratet an der Indiana University angekommen war, schrieb ich meiner Mutter: „Ich habe solche Angst. Was mache ich hier nur?" Und als ich zum ersten Mal Alma Eikerman, Professorin für Schmuckdesign und Metallbearbeitung, begegnete, hatte ich vor Angst weiche Knie. Mit der Zeit habe ich an Selbstvertrauen gewonnen, doch noch immer gehört es zu meinem Leben, sie zufriedenzustellen.

S. 22   *Marjorie Schick*

Ein fantastisches Kleid mit einem Tigerfellmuster, das ich 1967 von dem Geld kaufte, welches ich an meiner neuen Arbeitsstelle an der University of Kansas verdient hatte, brachte mich auf die Idee, große, dazu passende Ohrringe zu machen. Sie waren so schwer, dass ich sie mit einem Nylonfaden über meinem Kopf befestigte. Ich entschied mich, mit Papiermaché zu arbeiten, experimentierte und fragte andere, wie man damit umgehe. Die aufwendige Arbeit gefiel mir. Und noch besser war es, dass ich alle möglichen zusammengehefteten, geklebten, verdrahteten oder gelöteten Metall- oder Pappstücke im Unterbau mit Papierstreifen und Klebstoff bedecken konnte. Und das Allerbeste war, dass ich diese Formen bemalen konnte.

Darauf folgten sechs Armreifen. Acrylfarbe war etwas Neues, und ich fing mit einem Farbkasten für Anfänger aus dem Uni-Buchladen an, nachdem ich eine lavendelblau angemalte Pillendose im Werkzeugkasten eines Studenten gesehen hatte. Das Malen war eine Herausforderung und fühlte sich richtig an. Ganz offensichtlich hatte sich mein Interesse für Farbe durchgesetzt, auch wenn ich zunächst nur mit schwarzer Farbe auf braunem Papier arbeitete.

S. 25

INITIATION
Helen Shirk

1966 schloss Marjorie Schick ihr Studium an der Indiana University mit dem Master of Fine Arts ab. Als ich dort mein weiterführendes Studium aufnahm, war ihre Anwesenheit im Atelier für Schmuck und Metallbearbeitung noch deutlich zu spüren. Ich erinnere mich, dass ich im Erdgeschoss aus dem Aufzug stieg und diese wilde Anhäufung von Metalldraht und gehämmerten Formen im Schmuckschaukasten sah. Das Werk strömte eine für seine Größe unverhältnismäßige Kühnheit und Energie aus, es faszinierte mich und zog mich an. Wer hatte das gemacht? Später fand ich heraus, dass es Schmuck von Marjorie Schick war – eine gewagte Verbindung des Körpers mit der plastischen Form, die sich künftig als ihr eigentliches Gebiet erweisen sollte.

Auf dem Programm von Professor Alma Eikerman an der Indiana University standen die Ausbildung in den üblichen Metallbearbeitungstechniken, Materialexperimente und die Formbearbeitung in Verbindung mit dem Studium historischer Gegenstände und der Kunst der Gegenwart. Dieser strenge Lehrplan lässt sofort und in vielerlei Hinsicht an Marjorie denken. So bestätigt sie selbst, dass die Ausbildung unter Professor Eikerman grundlegenden Einfluss auf ihre schmuckkünstlerischen Leistungen hatte. Beide kamen aus dem Mittleren Westen, Marjorie aus Illinois und Alma aus Kansas, und beide blieben während ihrer langen Laufbahn als Lehrerinnen in dieser Region. Ihre Visionen umfassten jedoch die ganze Welt, mit all der Inspirationskraft und dem ganzen Potential, die dort zu finden sind. Eikerman hatte Ende der 1930er Jahre an der Columbia University in New York Malerei, Design, Kunstgeschichte und Metallbearbeitung studiert und war später nach Dänemark und Schweden gereist, um weitere technische Fähigkeiten in der Herstellung von Hohlkörpern zu erlangen. In ihrem ganzen Leben zogen sie Museumssammlungen und Meister des Kunsthandwerks zu Studienzwecken und zur Inspiration ins Ausland. Die Früchte dieser Reisen teilte sie großzügig mit ihren Schülern. Eikerman war beispielhaft in ihrer völligen Hingabe an ihre Kunst sowie in ihrer Leidenschaft für das Lernen, das Schaffen und das Lehren; in ihrer Arbeit war sie ganz der Gegenwart verpflichtet. In den 1960er und 1970er Jahren sahen ihre Schülerinnen, zu denen auch Marjorie zählte, in ihr ein Modell für die berufstätige Frau, die viel erreichen konnte, und eine der nur sehr wenigen Professorinnen, die in der fast ausschließlich männlichen Domäne der Metallbearbeitung lehrten. Nicht zuletzt durch Eikerman sieht die Situation heute ganz anders aus.

1967 war Schicks Werk eindeutig von Eikermans Bekenntnis zur Dreidimensionalität beeinflusst. Der geschmiedete und zusammengesetzte Armschmuck (Kat.-Nr. 46), das Schulterstück und die Ringe, die sie in dieser frühen Phase schuf, zeigen eine ungezügelte Energie und Kühnheit in Materialbehandlung und Formaufbau. Jedes Stück machte sich das gesamte jeweilige Körperteil, einschließlich des umgebenden Raumes, zunutze, ob es sich nun um einen Finger, eine Schulter oder einen Arm handelte. Beim Entwurf einer Arbeit war die Form Schicks vordringliches Anliegen, und alle Aspekte wurden hinsichtlich ihrer Fähigkeit, mit dem menschlichen Körper zusammenzuwirken, untersucht. Die Struktur des Materials, die Farbschichten und -muster und die Veränderungen im Material wurden dazu genutzt, das Potential der Grundform zu steigern. Diese Konzentration auf die gesamte dreidimensionale Form ist bis heute eine Konstante in Schicks Werk geblieben.

Kurz nach dem Abschluss ihres Studiums wurde Schick von Professor Eikerman gebeten, an einem Projekt teilzunehmen, in dem es um die Entwicklung experimenteller Metallformen ging und das durch ein Stipendium der Carnegie Foundation finanziert wurde. Jeder der neun Teilnehmer sollte drei Hohlformen entwickeln, jeweils eine aus Kupfer, Messing und Silber (Kat.-Nr. 61). Ich war auch an diesem Projekt beteiligt und erinnere mich an die lebhaften Diskussionen, die ausgelöst wurden, als Schick 1967 ihre Arbeiten einreichte. Ihre ersten beiden Formen zeichneten sich durch eine unmittelbare und spontane Herangehensweise an das Metall aus, die eine Antithese zur damals vorherrschenden skandinavischen Kühle und Präzision darstellte. Bei ihrer dritten Arbeit, derjenigen aus Silber, handelte es sich scheinbar um einen Behälter, doch hatte sie keinen Boden – was für Kommentare das nach sich zog! War das erlaubt? Alle ihre für dieses Stipendium geschaffenen Stücke spiegelten das Selbstvertrauen und die Bereitschaft wider, die Möglichkeiten des Materials auszuschöpfen und die Grenzen des Hohlkörpers in Frage zu stellen. Seitdem hat Schicks einzigartige Arbeit mit plastischen Formen für den menschlichen Körper in einer großen Bandbreite von Materialien internationale Anerkennung erlangt. Eikermans Mentorschaft der jungen Marjorie Schick während der ersten Jahre ihrer künstlerischen Entwicklung hat auf grundlegende Weise zur Entstehung dieses außerordentlichen Werks beigetragen, das die Schmuckkonventionen und -materialien immer wieder in Frage stellt.

S. 26 *Marjorie Schick*

Glücklicherweise gefielen die neuen Armreifen aus Papiermaché Eikerman, die ja auf Metall spezialisiert war, so gut, dass sie vorschlug, sie auf unserer Reise an die Ostküste Paul Smith im American Craft Museum in New York zu zeigen. Ich saß ihm nervös an seinem Tisch gegenüber und zog die sechs Papiermaché-Armreifen aus einer Tasche. Er nahm sich sofort einige und ging mit ihnen aus dem Zimmer. Als er zurückkam, sagte er, dass sie im Museum eine Ausstellung „Made With Paper" (Aus Papier) planten und für diese gerne drei davon hätten. Zu meiner Überraschung schlug er außerdem vor, dass ich ihn über weitere Papiermachéarbeiten auf dem Laufenden halten sollte.

Nach unserem Aufenthalt in New York reisten Jim und ich nach Virginia weiter, für ihn ein Forschungsaufenthalt. Bei unserer Ankunft brachte er mich sofort in eine Eisenwarenhandlung, um Metallscheren, Maschendraht und Tapetenkleister zu kaufen. Während er in den Bibliotheken arbeitete, blieb ich in unseren Motelzimmern, konstruierte Formen und produzierte Papiermaché.

S. 32 *Marjorie Schick*

Nachdem ich einige Stücke aus Papiermaché gemacht hatte, die nur aus Flächen bestanden, fragte Jim: „Gibt es auch eine Möglichkeit, Linien aus Papiermaché zu machen?" Bei der Heilsarmee kaufte ich eine Menge alter Bügel, die ich auf dem Amboss auseinanderbog, zurechtschnitt, zu neuen Formen bog und mit Silberlot zusammenlötete. Als das lineare Gebilde fertig war, wickelte ich die Stangen mit Papiermaché-Streifen ein und bemalte dann die entstandenen Formen. Die *Dowel-Stick* (Rundholzstab)-Arbeiten aus den 1980ern beziehen sich auf die früheren linearen Formen aus Papiermaché, doch ist ihre Konstruktionsart weniger kompliziert.

S. 42

EINE WÜRDIGUNG
Paul J. Smith

Mit ihren einzigartigen Körperskulpturen, die alle traditionellen Kategorien überschreiten, leistete Marjorie Schick Pionierarbeit. In ihrer gesamten glanzvollen Karriere hat Marjorie seit den späten 1960er Jahren ein eindrucksvolles Werk geschaffen, das nicht nur in den Vereinigten Staaten ohnegleichen ist, sondern auch in der internationalen Schmuckkunst einen bedeutenden Platz einnimmt.

Mit dem menschlichen Körper als zentralem Thema hat sie eine große Vielfalt dramatischer, theatralischer Formen erkundet und geschaffen, in denen sich grafische Bildlichkeit und komplexe Konstruktionen vereinen. Ein wichtiger Aspekt ihrer Arbeit ist die innovative Verwendung unedler Materialien in einer reichen Farbenpalette, woraus konzeptionelle Aussagen entstehen, die am Körper getragen oder als unabhängige Objekte präsentiert werden können.

Ich habe sie in mehreren wichtigen Ausstellungen präsentiert und betrachte sie als außergewöhnliche Künstlerin, die den am Körper getragen Schmuck und die Skulptur auf eine neue Ebene erhoben hat. Über ihre eindrucksvollen Referenzen in Form von Auszeichnungen, Ausstellungen und der Präsenz in Museumssammlungen hinaus hat sie ihre Begabung großzügig durch ihre Lehrtätigkeit und in Workshops geteilt. Diese Untersuchung von Marjorie Schicks Werk kommt genau zur rechten Zeit und ist eine angemessene Würdigung ihres wichtigen Beitrags zu den Künsten in Amerika.

S. 47 *Marjorie Schick*

Ich ging nervös auf und ab und wartete bange darauf, dass mir Jim die Post aus den Niederlanden brachte. Das Überraschungspaket war von Paul Derrez, einem der Juroren der Londoner Ausstellung „Jewellery Redefined" (Schmuck, eine Neudefinition), für die ich Arbeiten eingereicht hatte, die aber noch nicht eröffnet worden war. Er schrieb: „Ihre Arbeiten haben mir sehr gut gefallen!", und fügte hinzu, dass er gerne mehr sehen würde. Zu diesem Zeitpunkt hatte ich nur sechs Rundholzstabbroschen und sechs aus Papier und Draht gemacht. Er hatte die beiden neuen Werkgruppen gesehen und davon die Hälfte für die Ausstellung angenommen.

Pauls Brief war zu schön, um wahr zu sein. Ich antwortete ihm, dass ich keine Dias von neuen Arbeiten hätte, aber ihm in sechs Wochen Bilder schicken würde. Als er diese sah, forderte mich Paul auf, Arbeiten an die Galerie Ra zu senden. Zwei Wochen später schrieb mir Sharon Plant von der Galerie Aspects in London mit einer ähnlichen Anfrage. Mein Leben sollte sich für immer ändern. Obwohl ich eine Vollzeitstelle als Lehrbeauftragte hatte, schuf ich pausenlos weitere Werke, und von nun an reisten wir häufig nach Amsterdam und London.

S. 51 *Marjorie Schick*

„Mama, ist dir klar, dass Du auf jedem Familienfoto aus diesem Sommer einen Pinsel in der Hand hast?" Das war Robs Kommentar, nachdem wir 1984 den Sommer in London verbracht hatten. Was für ein Luxus: so viele Stunden für die Arbeit, für Museumsbesuche und um Leute zu treffen.

Als Artist in Residence am Sir John Cass hatte ich in diesem Sommer an einer Serie von Broschen gearbeitet, die zu Studien über Methoden der Befestigung wurden. Ein scharfsinniger Tutor hatte mich auf etwas aufmerksam gemacht, das sich für meine Arbeiten als wichtig herausstellen sollte: Es ist besser, wenn der Betrachter die Brosche erst als Objekt wahrnimmt und erst dann erkennt, dass sie auch getragen werden kann. Wenn man aber das Objekt erst als Brosche wahrnimmt, rückt der Gedanke, wie sie getragen werden soll, in den Vordergrund. Wenn diese Beobachtung auch unbedeutend erscheint, ist sie doch von immenser Wichtigkeit und zwang mich dazu, über bessere und manchmal weniger offensichtliche Arten der Befestigung einer Brosche nachzudenken.

S. 67f.

ABWESENHEIT UND EIGENWAHRNEHMUNG: DIE UMKEHRUNG DES SKULPTURRAUMS
Glen R. Brown

Wie Außenskelette, die auf einen ablösbaren inneren Körper hindeuten, kehren Marjorie Schicks tragbare Kunstwerke ein uraltes Muster um. Die klassische Skulptur, die in der abendländischen Kunst von der Antike bis in die ersten Jahrzehnte des 20. Jahrhunderts Bestand hatte, wurde stets als unabhängiger Körper im Raum aufgefasst: eine autonome Form, welche die Stofflichkeit menschlicher Wesen zu reproduzieren suchte und als deren Voraussetzung in manchen Fällen der Grundzustand einer in einer unendlichen Leere einfach vorhandenen Masse angenommen wurde. Die Festigkeit und die Autarkie der klassischen Skulptur wurde durch die beiden von der akademischen Lehre akzeptierten Arten der Bildhauerei bekräftigt: das Schnitzen oder Meißeln, bei dem ein Block dichter Masse mit zahlreichen Oberflächen versehen wurde, die etwas darstellen und ausdrücken sollten, und das Modellieren, bei dem formbare Materialien wie Lehm, Wachs oder Gips in Formen gearbeitet wurden, die dann in starre Bronze gegossen wurden. Das mit Hilfe beider Techniken Entstandene kann das ein wenig unheimliche Gefühl der physischen Anwesenheit eines Körpers evozieren. Schicks Formen jedoch – Formen, welche die von den Wegbereitern der *zusammengesetzten* Skulptur der Moderne niedergelegten Erkenntnisse über den Raum nutzen – dienen im Grunde eher als Hinweise auf die Abwesenheit des Körpers. Das Hervortreten dieser Abwesenheit verleiht Schicks Werken, selbst wenn sie getragen werden, eine anhaltende Kontingenz, sie vermitteln das Gefühl, dass etwas geschehen könnte, aber nicht zwangsläufig muss.

Diese Kontingenz ist mit der Kontingenz, die Schmuck oder Bekleidung eigen ist, nicht ganz identisch, wenn auch diese – wenn sie nicht getragen werden – den abwesenden Körper tendenziell voraussetzen. Während Schmuck und Bekleidung nahe legen, dass Abwesenheit lediglich aus einem zeitweisen Nichtgebrauch resultiert, scheinen Schicks Objekte auf eine zielgerichtete Abwesenheit hinzudeuten, als ob es ebenso sehr ihr Sinn und Zweck wäre, den Körper herbeizurufen, wie der, ihn tatsächlich aufzunehmen. Anders ausgedrückt scheint die Fähigkeit, getragen zu werden, von Schick sowohl auf die Nützlichkeit gerichtet zu sein als auch als rhetorisches Mittel eingesetzt zu werden. Ihre Objekte reflektieren die noch nicht abgeschlossene Diskussion, auf welche Art und Weise sich die Skulptur auf den menschlichen Körper beziehen kann, und zwar nicht als Spiegel der Anwesenheit des Körpers – als vergleichsweise unabhängige Masse, die den Betrachter stets auf Distanz hält –, sondern vielmehr als Reihe von Rahmenbedingungen für einen Raum, den der Körper des Betrachters denkbarerweise einnehmen könnte. In dieser Hinsicht können Schicks Arbeiten eng mit der allgemeinen Entmaterialisierung der Skulptur in den 1960er Jahren in Beziehung gebracht werden wie auch mit dem darauf folgenden Standortwechsel des Betrachters, der die abendländische Kunst seit den 1970er Jahren kennzeichnet.

Schicks Herausforderung der autonomen Ausprägung der Skulptur, die unerschütterlich auf Sockeln ruht, geht mit ihrer offensichtlich innovativen Einstellung zur Malerei einher. (Sie ist im Grunde genommen wohl ebenso sehr Malerin wie Bildhauerin, wenn auch auf beiden Gebieten offensichtlich unkonventionell.) Obwohl Ebenen häufig einen Teil der Komposition von Schicks Arbeiten bilden, sind diese Arbeiten nicht flach und können folgerichtig nicht als Tafelbilder, ja nicht einmal als bemalte Reliefs bezeichnet werden. Ihre Vorderseiten haben keinen Vorrang vor den Rückseiten (und tatsächlich ist die Vorstellung von Vorder- und Rückseite nur eine Konsequenz aus der Beziehung der Arbeiten zum Körper, wie sie wahrgenommen werden kann, wenn diese Arbeiten getragen werden). Wenn man auf eine Kategorisierung nicht verzichten möchte, könnten Schicks Werke vielleicht am treffendsten als Rundgemälde bezeichnet werden. Dieser erfundene Begriff beschreibt jedoch so offensichtlich eine ideale Schnittstelle zwischen der Malerei und der Skulptur, dass man sich natürlich fragt, ob es nicht vielmehr gerade darum geht, dass Schicks Arbeiten sich nicht so ohne weiteres in bereits vorhandene Kategorien einordnen lassen – zumindest nicht in die Kategorien der Malerei, der Skulptur und des Schmucks, die seit langem im Diskurs über die abendländische Kunst festgelegt worden sind.

Dieser Punkt ist wichtig, weil sich zahlreiche Parallelen zu Schicks tragbaren Skulpturen außerhalb der bildenden Künste des Abendlandes finden. Die *Back Sculptures* (Rückenskulpuren; Kat.-Nr. 318–321) beispielsweise, eine Ende der 1980er Jahre entstandene, vierteilige Werkreihe, lassen eindeutig an nicht-abendländische Vorstellungen von der plastischen Form denken. Wie es bei Schicks Werkgruppen häufig der Fall ist, entwickelten sich die *Back Sculptures* als Antwort auf die Leitlinien einer Ausstellung, zu der Schick eingeladen wurde, in diesem Fall einer thematisch ausgerichteten Schau der späten 1980er Jahre mit dem Titel „East Meets West" (Osten trifft auf Westen). Die Aufgabe lautete, etwas deutlich von Asien Beeinflusstes zu schaffen, und so ließ sich Schick schließlich von dem prächtigen Kostüm einer japanischen Hina-Matsuri-Puppe inspirieren, die sie seit ihrer Kindheit besaß. Die an einen kompliziert gebundenen Obi, einen japanischen Gürtel, erinnernden *Back Sculptures* kommentieren implizit das Vermögen, das für bestimmte Kleidungsstücke Übliche mit einer Einfühlsamkeit zu würdigen, die über bloßes Modebewusstsein hinausgeht. Doch über japanische Kleidung hinaus weisen die *Back Sculptures* auf eine Art dreidimensionale Formensprache hin, der man in der modernen Kunst des Westens nur selten zugesprochen hat; wenn überhaupt, geschah dies üblicherweise in der Schmuckkunst.

Back Sculpture With Reeds (Rückenskulptur mit Schilfrohren; 1988, Kat.-Nr. 321) – ein Werk, das durch seine formtechnischen Parallelen mit nützlichen Dingen und seine lebhafte, hartkantige geometrische Musterung den Eindruck eines mit Perlen besetzten indianischen Wiegenbrettes vermittelt – hebt das Bewusstsein für die dreidimensionale Form auf ein Niveau, das über das Visuelle und Taktile hinausgeht. Ob die Arbeit nun getragen wird oder nicht – ihre Zerbrechlichkeit ruft intuitives Mitgefühl hervor: Die schwachen „Schilfrohre" erzwingen, wie ein darin sitzendes Kind, körperliche Einschränkungen und beschränken die Position des Objekts im Raum. Anders als eine Skulptur auf einem Sockel erzwingt *Back Sculpture With Reeds* das Nachdenken über die Bewegung *durch* den Raum, es geht nicht allein um das bloße Vorhandensein darin. Ihre Tragbarkeit verleiht den gestreiften Schilfrohren den Anschein schlanker Prothesen; auf diese Weise wird der abwesende Körper durch eine künstliche Erweiterung seiner Körperlichkeit und Verwundbarkeit evoziert. Mit dem Wissen, dass die Arbeit entwickelt wurde, um getragen zu werden, kann man *Back Sculpture With Reeds* nur schwer von der kinästhetischen Eigenwahrnehmung trennen, die den Körper vor ungewolltem, selbst herbeigeführtem Schaden beim Durchschreiten der häufig gefährlichen Räume des Alltags bewahrt.

Das Verknüpfen dieser Art von Eigenwahrnehmung mit dem ästhetischen Erleben trägt wesentlich zu der Eigentümlichkeit und Faszination bei, die von Schicks Arbeiten ausgehen. Die Projizierung der Malerei in den realen, dreidimensionalen Raum, wie es Schick mit Arbeiten wie der kandinskyartigen *Body Sculpture* (Körperskulptur; 1987, Kat.-Nr. 311) getan hat, hat zweifelsohne etwa Cleveres, aber Künstler wie Judy Pfaff, Matthew Richie und Sarah Sze haben Entsprechendes in einem viel eindrucksvolleren Maßstab gemacht. Was Arbeiten wie *Body Sculpture* so einzigartig macht, ist die Vertraulichkeit, mit der sie tatsächlich oder potenziell den Körper einhüllen. Statt die Malerei über einen riesigen Raum hinaus auszudehnen, durch den man sich bewegen kann, erschließen die Skulpturen Schicks Räume, die nicht größer sind als die, welche der menschliche Körper beschreibt. Folglich werden ihre Werke nicht allein als Hohlräume wahrgenommen, die es mit dem abwesenden Körper zu füllen gilt, sondern als Strukturen, die als materielle und künstlerisch gestaltete Fortsetzungen des physischen Ichs vom Körper getragen werden. *Body Sculpture*, ob getragen oder nicht, kann nicht ohne weiteres einer traditionellen Kunstgattung

zugeordnet werden, da sich in ihr stets die Vorstellung des in Bewegung befindlichen Körpers abzeichnet. Da diese Vorstellung genügt, das Werk zu vollenden, ist der Körper selbst letztendlich entbehrlich, und *Body Sculpture* kann genauso wenig als Kleidungsstück oder Schmuckstück klassifiziert werden wie als Gemälde oder Skulptur.

Die kräftigen Farben, die dynamischen Linien und die sich wirkungsvoll durchschneidenden Ebenen vieler Arbeiten Schicks verwirren das Auge und lenken auf diese Weise von dem tiefen symbolischen Gehalt ihrer Kompositionen ab. Der übertragene Sinn ihrer Formen wird deshalb besser in ihren leisesten Arbeiten verständlich, wie in *Yellow Ladderback Chair* (Gelber Stuhl mit Sprossenlehne; 2001, Kat.-Nr. 434), welcher, wie die Umkehrung einer Skulptur aus bemalter Leinwand von Claes Oldenburg, ein weiches Möbelstück darstellt, das etwas kleiner ist als der wirkliche Gegenstand. Stillschweigend verlangt diese Skulptur danach, entweder von vorne oder von hinten über den Körper gelegt zu werden, und ihre „Sprossenlehne" wird zum stilisierten bildlichen Äquivalent einer Wirbelsäule und eines Brustkorbes. Äußerlich statt innerlich und eher beweglich als steif gleitet *Yellow Ladderback Chair* geschmeidig in den nicht fassbaren Raum zwischen dem realen Körper und einem tatsächlichen Möbelstück und wird dabei zum symbolischen Gegenstück für beide. Der Raum, den er einnimmt, der Raum der Vorstellung, der den Körper selbst im unmittelbaren Kontakt mit konkreten Gegenständen einhüllt, ist ein Raum, der von der Skulptur des Abendlandes nur selten erkundet wird. Durch Schicks von konzeptueller Raffinesse und visueller Intensität gekennzeichnetes, anhaltendes Eindringen in diesen Raum ist ein ungewöhnliches plastisches Werk und zugleich ein einzigartiges und wertvolles Beispiel für die Thematisierung des Körpers mittels der Skulptur entstanden.

S. 75 *Marjorie Schick*

Wir verbrachten vier Forschungsurlaube im Ausland, während derer wir in Europa umherreisten und in London lebten. 1976, während unseres ersten Forschungsurlaubs, fuhren wir nach Pforzheim, um das Schmuckmuseum zu sehen. Wir besuchten es zweimal an einem Tag. Als wir am Nachmittag zurückkehrten, gab Dr. Fritz Falk einer Gruppe von Schmuckdesign-Studenten vom Middlesex Polytechnic in London eine englischsprachige Führung. Ich versuchte, jedes Wort zu verstehen, ohne den Anschein zu vermitteln, dass ich lauschte, und dachte, wie glücklich diese Studenten doch waren, dass sie eine so lehrreiche Führung von einer so wichtigen Person erhielten.

1989 kehrten wir anlässlich der Ausstellung „Ornamenta 1" nach Pforzheim zurück. Dort sprachen wir mit Dr. Falk, der sich an Jim und mich wandte und fragte, ob wir Interesse an einer Führung durch das Museum hätten. Was für ein wunderbarer Augenblick! 13 Jahre später bekamen wir unsere eigene Sonderführung. Als uns auf der meiner Ansicht nach wichtigsten Führung meines Lebens das Museum gezeigt wurde, schien es mir, als ob ein Traum in Erfüllung gegangen war.

S. 83 *Marjorie Schick*

„Nun hat sich der Kreis geschlossen", sagte Joel Degen, als ich ihm 1990 einige Papiermaché-Arbeiten zum Fotografieren brachte. „Genau wie Dexter Gordon", fügte er hinzu, „bist Du an deinen Ausgangspunkt zurückgekehrt." Während eines Forschungsurlaubs im Jahr 1990 war ich Artist in Residence am Middlesex Polytechnic und machte neue Objekte aus Holz, dem Material, das ich fast ein Jahrzehnt lang verwendet hatte. Starker Schneefall und einige Bombendrohungen machten es schwierig, mit der U-Bahn zur Uni zu fahren, und so kehrte ich zur Papiermaché zurück, weil das in unserer Wohnung in der King's Road nicht so viel Lärm verursachte.

Bei der erneuten Arbeit mit Papiermaché, in London und auch in Kansas, fühlte ich mich wohl, denn ich kehrte zu dem Arbeitsprozess zurück, der mir so gut gefällt. Jedes Stück ist eine Studie, die die bemalte Oberfläche mit der Struktur der Arbeit in Beziehung setzt. Da sich meine Malweise in den 16 Jahren seit der letzten Papiermachéarbeit verändert hatte, wurden diese neuen Stücke in mehr Schichten und komplizierter bemalt. Der Prozess war der gleiche, doch das entstandene Werk war etwas ganz anderes.

S. 95 *Marjorie Schick*

„Hast Du jemals gesehen, dass ich solche Briefe von meinem Professor bekommen habe?", fragte Jim. Ein- oder zweimal im Jahr schrieb Eikerman achtseitige Rundbriefe an ihre ehemaligen Schüler. Sie begann mit ihren eigenen Reisen und Erlebnissen, darauf folgten die beruflichen Leistungen von allen anderen, und häufig schloss sie mit Ratschlägen: „Alle Dias und so viele Ausstellungen wie möglich zu sehen, ist hilfreich, damit Ihr auch weiterhin im Bilde seid, aber es ist die konzentrierte, kontinuierliche Arbeit, die viele von Euch an der Werkbank leisten, die Eure Arbeiten auszeichnet." (Dezember 1975)

Eikerman hielt ihre Gruppe zusammen. Noch heute führt uns diese besondere Bindung auf Konferenzen in den USA zusammen. Der Halsschmuck Tribute to Professor Alma Eikerman (Hommage an Professor Alma Eikerman) ist unseren gemeinsamen Erlebnissen und der Verbindung derjenigen gewidmet, die so glücklich waren, bei ihr zu studieren.

S. 101ff.

MARJORIE SCHICK UND GROSSBRITANNIEN
Elizabeth Goring

Anfang der 1980er Jahre war Großbritannien für Schmuckkünstler ein aufregendes Land. Die radikale „Bewegung", die später als „The New Jewelry" (Neuer Schmuck) bekannt wurde, war auf ihrem Höhepunkt angelangt, wobei sie besonders stark in Amsterdam, München und London vertreten war. In Großbritannien wurden damals einige der aufregendsten Arbeiten geschaffen und ausgestellt.[1] Das kühne Erkunden unkonventioneller Materialien fiel zeitlich und zum Teil auch ursächlich mit der Explosion des Silberpreises Ende der 1970er Jahre zusammen.[2] Diese Phase des selbstbewussten und lebhaften Experimentierens mit Form, Wert und Selbstdarstellung sowie die Beziehung zwischen dem Werk und dem Körper und die Interpretation dieser Phänomene durch künstlerische Aktionen und die Fotografie übten einen beträchtlichen Einfluss auf eine Generation junger britischer Kunstschaffender aus, für welche diese neue Ausdrucksfreiheit eine Inspiration darstellte. Es hätte gar keinen besseren Zeitpunkt für Majorie Schicks Arbeiten in Großbritannien geben können.

Die enge Beziehung Schicks zur britischen Schmuckszene begründete sich darin, dass einige entscheidende Künstler erkannten, dass Schick und sie gleichartige Interessen hatten. Ihre Arbeit hatte sich völlig unabhängig entwickelt, fand aber bei den innovativsten Künstlern Europas starke Resonanz. Schick war sich dieser neuen Stimmung in Europa wohl bewusst. 1975 hatte sie einen Vortrag von Gijs Bakker und Emmy van Leersum an der Kansas State University gehört, und 1976 hatten sie und ihr Mann Jim während eines Forschungsurlaubs vier Monate damit verbracht, Ausstellungen, Museen, Ateliers und Schmuckschulen in Skandinavien, Amsterdam und Pforzheim zu besuchen. Während dieser Reise, auf der sie auch London zum ersten Mal besuchte, sah sie die Ausstellung „Jewellery in Europe" (Schmuck in Europa) im Victoria and Albert Museum in London[3], und 1980 sah sie dort im Crafts Council die wegweisende Ausstellung „Susanna Heron: Bodywork" (Susanna Heron: Körperarbeit). 1982 forderte Sharon Plant Schick auf, Aspects, der tatkräftigen Londoner Galerie, die sich die Neudefinition des zeitgenössischen Schmucks auf die Fahnen geschrieben hatte, einige ihrer Arbeiten (Kat.-Nr. 178) zukommen zu lassen.[4] Öffentlich stellte Schick in Großbritannien erstmals 1982 aus und das im Rahmen der provokanten und einflussreichen Ausstellung „Jewellery Redefined" (Schmuck, eine Neudefinition), wo ihre Stücke sich gut in die häufig durch einen linearen Aufbau und starke Farben gekennzeichneten weiteren Exponate einfügten.[5] Wenn sie auch andere Wurzeln hatten, verkörperten ihre Werke doch ganz den Geist der Zeit. Heute kann man kaum noch die positive und negative Wirkung, die diese Ausstellung hatte, begreiflich machen, doch zusammen mit weiteren, zur gleichen Zeit in London stattfindenden Ereignissen war sie für viele eine Offenbarung. Sie löste eine weitreichende Debatte aus und beeinflusste die gestalterische Richtung vieler Kunstschaffender von Heute.[6]

1983 nahmen Schick und ihr Mann erneut Forschungsurlaub, und Schick kehrte nach London zurück. Dieses Mal schrieb sie sich im Fachbereich Metallbearbeitung für das Frühjahrstrimester an der Sir John Cass School of Art ein, wo sie, was im Rückblick etwas überraschend scheint, eine silberne Karaffe schuf.[7] Im folgenden Sommer kam sie als Artist in Residence ein weiteres Mal zurück mit der Absicht, weiter in Metall arbeiten. Jim ermunterte sie jedoch, sich das noch einmal zu überlegen, und wies darauf hin, dass ihre *Dowel Pieces* (Rundholzstab-Arbeiten) sehr gefragt seien. Ein Besuch in einer Holzhandlung war die Folge dieses klugen Hinweises. Die Familie lebte in einer Wohnung mit nur einem Schlafzimmer, und ihr Sohn schlief im Wohnzimmer. So bemalte Schick ihre *Dowel Pieces* nachts im Badezimmer, damit niemand wach wurde.

Schick wurde in Großbritannien immer bekannter. 1985 wurde sie eingeladen, an Caroline Broadheads erkenntnisreicher Ausstellung „New Tradition. The Evolution of Jewellery 1966–1985" (Neue Tradition. Schmuckentwicklung 1966–1985) teilzunehmen. Diese Schau war umso wichtiger, als sie von einer der führenden Künstlerinnen der Zeit kuratiert worden war.[8] Schick wurde in *The New Jewelry*, der wichtigen Überblickspublikation von Peter Dormer und Ralph Turner, ausführlich vorgestellt, und ihr Porträt, auf dem sie eine bemalte Rundholzstab-Brosche trägt, bebilderte einen Beitrag von Dormer in der Zeitschrift *Aspects*.[9] Im Oktober präsentierte Plant Schicks Arbeiten auf der fünften Chelsea Crafts Fair zusammen mit Werken von elf anderen Schmuckkünstlern, darunter Julia Manheim, Lam de Wolf und Cathy Harris. Inzwischen hatte Schick in der Kerngruppe wegbereitender Künstler ihren festen Platz.

Schick hatte sich zudem ihre eigene Sammlung von Schmuck, insbesondere von Künstlern der New Jewelry-Bewegung, aufgebaut und diese 1982 an der Pittburg State University auch ausgestellt. Durch Aspects entdeckte sie die Arbeiten der jungen, talentierten Cathy Harris, die sie zu sammeln anfing.[10] Die beiden Künstlerinnen trafen sich erstmals 1986 in Amsterdam, in der Ausstellung anlässlich des zehnjährigen Bestehens der Galerie Ra, und wurden enge Freundinnen. Per Post tauschten sie Geschenke aus, und wenn Schick in London war, erkundeten sie gemeinsam Museen und Galerien.[11] Leider setzte Harris' viel zu früher Tod im Jahr 1994 dieser engen angloamerikanischen Freundschaft, die das Leben beider Frauen bereichert hatte, ein Ende.[12]

Schick und ihr Werk waren auch in den 1990er Jahren häufig in London zu sehen. 1991 waren die Schicks wieder in London. Marjorie Schick war zunächst Artist in Residence am Middelsex Polytechnic, dann erneut am Sir John Cass.[13] Insbesondere 1996 stand sie sehr in der Öffentlichkeit. Zwei der wichtigsten frühen Werke, *Belt with Metal Pockets* (Gürtel mit Metalltaschen; 1967, Kat.-Nr. 45) und *Pectoral Body* (Brustkörper; 1968/69, Kat.-Nr. 72), wurden in der von Turner kuratierten Ausstellung „New Times, New Thinking: Jewellery in Europe and America" (Neue Zeiten, neues Denken: Schmuck in Europa und Amerika) im Crafts Council gezeigt.[14] Zuvor im selben Jahr hatte in Newcastle die internationale Konferenz „Jewellers Exchange '96" stattgefunden, die erste ihrer Art in Großbritannien.[15] An drei Orten gab es mit der Konferenz verbundene Ausstellungen, Schicks Werke waren in zweien von ihnen zu sehen und somit gut repräsentiert.[16] In Schottland wurden ihre Arbeiten in „Contemporary Jewelry from the USA" (Zeitgenössischer Schmuck aus den USA) ausgestellt. Die Ausstellung war von Charon Kransen für Amanda Game in der Scottish Gallery in Edinburgh kuratiert worden, eine der führenden unabhängigen Galerien für Kunstgewerbe in Großbritannien. Im folgenden Jahr zeigte Schick Arbeiten in „USA Today" in der Londoner Lesley Craze Gallery. 1998 luden Game und ich sie ein, an unserer anlässlich der Jahrtausendwende veranstalteten Überblicksausstellung internationalen Schmucks der Gegenwart teilzunehmen – an „Jewellery Moves" (Schmuck bewegt sich, oder: Schmuck bewegt) in den National Museums of Scotland in Edinburgh, wo wir ihren atemberaubenden Halsschmuck *De La Luna/Del Sol* (Kat.-Nr. 397) an herausragender Stelle

und ohne Vitrine auf einem Podium im Zentrum der Ausstellung installiert hatten.[17] Das Museum erwarb in der Folge den Armschmuck *Edged Wave* (Kantige Welle; Kat.-Nr. 378) aus der Ausstellung für seine ständige Sammlung.[18] Erst kürzlich wurde *Ballycotton Bay* (Kat.-Nr. 431) in „The Ring" gezeigt, einer Ausstellung, welche die Mobilia Gallery aus Cambridge, Massachusetts, nach Großbritannien sandte. Im Rahmen der Wanderausstellung „Chess" (Schach) der Galerie Velvet da Vinci in San Francisco reisten Schicks meisterhaftes Schachbrett *Deception* (Täuschung; Kat.-Nr. 445) und die dazugehörigen Schachfiguren im Land umher.[19]

In Großbritannien sind die Möglichkeiten, Arbeiten amerikanischer Künstler zu sehen, begrenzt, da deren Vielfältigkeit und Stärken zum großen Teil noch nicht erkannt und nur wenige amerikanischer Schmuckkünstler ein Begriff sind. Zu diesen wenigen gehört ganz sicher Marjorie Schick. Sie ist hier seit einem Vierteljahrhundert sehr bekannt, und weil sie regelmäßig Teil des „Kanons", vor allem der 1980er Jahre, gewesen ist, könnte man versucht sein, sie mehr oder weniger zu uns zu zählen. Diesem läge jedoch ein Missverständnis zugrunde. Wie David Watkins scharfsinnig bemerkt hat, wurden „Schicks frühere [...] Körperkonstruktionen in den 1980er Jahren in Europa ‚entdeckt', als man in ihnen eine Affinität zur mit unedlen Materialien arbeitenden Schmuck-Avantgarde jener Zeit feststellte. Bald war deutlich geworden, dass es sich hier um ein zufälliges Zusammentreffen von Interessen handelte und dass sie ihr eigenes Programm hatte. Ihr Werk [...] ist in seinem eigentlichen Wesen, in seiner nach außen gewandten uneingeschränkten Zuversicht ‚amerikanisch'."[20] In Großbritannien ist sie gleichermaßen vertraut und exotisch. Wie andere große Künstler nimmt sie einen Platz ein, den sie selbst geschaffen hat und der überaus individuell ist. Mit niemals nachlassender Energie verfolgt sie beharrlich ihren Weg; immer wieder stellt sie sich neuen Herausforderungen, aus denen sie stets als Siegerin hervorgeht. Dies sind Eigenschaften, die in Großbritannien sehr geschätzt werden. Wir freuen uns auf viele weitere Besuche.

1 Diese Bewegung hatte in den 1970er Jahren in Großbritannien an Boden gewonnen, unter anderem durch Ausstellungen wie „Fourways" (Vier Richtungen), eine Wanderausstellung mit Arbeiten von Caroline Broadhead, Julia Manheim, Susanna Heron und Nuala Jamison. Sie wurde 1977/78 an zwölf Stationen in England, Schottland und Wales gezeigt.

2 Dies war auf den Versuch der berüchtigten Gebrüder Hunt zurückzuführen, den weltweiten Metallmarkt zu beherrschen, welcher 1980 spektakulär scheiterte.

3 Diese von Ralph Turner kuratierte Wanderausstellung des Scottish Arts Council/Crafts Advisory Committee wurde 1975/76 an mehreren Orten gezeigt. Schick kehrte im folgenden Jahr nach Europa zurück und besuchte Wien und London, wo sie die dritte „Loot" (Beute)-Ausstellung in der Goldsmiths Hall sah.

4 „Aspects hat sich sehr bemüht, den modernen Schmuck neu zu definieren." Newsletter der Zeitschrift *Aspects*, Januar–März 1985, S. 7. Die 1981 von Plant gegründete Galerie war ein bedeutendes Zentrum für diejenigen, die sich für wegweisenden Schmuck und andere Arten von Kunsthandwerk der Gegenwart interessierten.

5 Hierbei handelte es sich um eine von einer Jury getroffene Auswahl von 220 Arbeiten internationaler Künstler in unedlen Materialien, die aus mehr als 1.800 eingereichten Objekten ausgewählt worden waren. Die Ausstellung wurde vom 1. Oktober bis zum 13. November 1982 im British Crafts Centre in London gezeigt. Alle sieben Jurymitglieder waren maßgebliche Persönlichkeiten: Pierre Degen, Paul Derrez, Hermann Jünger, Julia Manheim, Jean Muir, Sarah Osborn

und Ralph Turner. Schick stellte drei Rundholzstab- und drei Papierbroschen aus (alle aus dem Jahr 1982). Siehe Diana Hughes, *Jewellery Redefined*, London: British Crafts Centre 1982, S. 52; Ausstellungsnummern 176–181. Schick war bei der Eröffnung der Ausstellung anwesend und nahm auch am Symposium teil.

6 James Evans macht auf die auffällige Gleichzeitigkeit von „Jewellery Redefined" mit „Pierre Degen: New Work" (Crafts Council, London, 22. September–24. Oktober 1982), „The Jewellery Project" (British Crafts Centre, London, 20. April–26. Juni 1982) und weiteren Ausstellungen aufmerksam. In: *The New Jewellery: a documentational account*, Online-Zusammenstellung, http://vads.ahds.ac.uk/ learning/designingbritain/html/tnj.html. Schick sah die Pierre Degen-Ausstellung, als sie anlässlich der Eröffnung von „Jewellery Redefined" in London war.

7 Sie erläutert ihren Grund hierfür: „Während des Studiums habe ich nie eine Teekanne gemacht, und deshalb war ich der Meinung, dass ich das nun tun sollte." (Private Mitteilung)

8 Schick zeigte den Armschmuck *White Edges* (Weiße Ecken; Kat.-Nr. 48), den sie 1985 neu bemalte. Schick und Arline Fisch waren die einzigen amerikanischen Künstlerinnen, die teilnahmen. Siehe Caroline Broadhead, *New Tradition. The Evolution of Jewellery 1966–1985*, London: British Crafts Council 1985, S. 78.

9 Peter Dormer und Ralph Turner, *The New Jewelry. Trends and Traditions*, London: Thames and Hudson 1985, überarbeitete Auflage 1994; Peter Dormer, „The Cultural Divide in new jewellery: Europe v America", in: Newsletter der Zeitschrift *Aspects*, Januar–März 1985, S. 6 f. Dormer schreibt: „Schick [...] ist heute die radikalste der amerikanischen Schmuckdesigner, und sie hat ihr Werk tatsächlich bis zu dem Punkt vorangetrieben, an dem es mehr ,skulpturenhaft' als tragbares Ornament ist."

10 Lange bevor sie sich kennenlernten, beschrieb sich Schick selbst als „Cathys amerikanisches Groupie" (private Mitteilung).

11 Schick sandte Harris „amerikanischen Schund" für ihre Collagen, zuerst Einwickelpapiere von Süßigkeiten und Kaugummi wie auch Banderolen von Dosenkost, später die Schokoriegel selbst. Harris revanchierte sich mit den Schokoladen-Doppelkeksen von Sainsbury's (private Mitteilung).

12 Schick veranstaltet heute „Cathy Harris-Tage" für ihre Studenten und erinnert an ihr Talent, indem sie Dias und Arbeiten von Harris aus ihrer Sammlung zeigt (private Mitteilung).

13 Sie hielt auch Vorträge am Royal College of Art in London und am West Surrey College of Art and Design in Farnham. An beiden Institutionen hatte sie schon vorher, 1985 bzw. 1986, Vorträge gehalten.

14 Ralph Turner, *Jewelry in Europe and America. New Times, New Thinking*, London: Thames and Hudson 1991, S. 38. Schick kam nach Europa, um diese Ausstellung zu besuchen und um an einem Workshop von Geoff Roberts teilzunehmen.

15 Am Vorbild der jährlichen Konferenzen der Society of North American Goldsmiths orientiert, führte diese Konferenz im folgenden Jahr zur Gründung der Association for Contemporary Jewellery. Einer der Rundholzstab-Halsschmuckstücke von Schick wurde von der Hauptrednerin Helen W. Drutt English besprochen.

16 Diese Ausstellungen fanden im Shipley Museum and Art Gallery in Gateshead, dem Cleveland Crafts Centre in Middlesbrough und dem Queens Hall Arts Centre in Hexham statt. Schick zeigte ihren Halsschmuck *Katella* und ihren Armschmuck *Bodega Bay* (beide 1995, Kat.-Nrn. 379 bzw. 374) in der von der Society of North American Goldsmiths veranstalteten Schau „American Revelations: new Jewellery" (Amerikanische Entdeckungen: Neuer Schmuck) im Shipley; einige ihrer Arbeiten aus der wichtigen Sammlung der Society wurden in „Jewellery Innovations" (Schmuckinnovationen) im Cleveland Crafts Centre gezeigt.

17 Wir hatten 1989 Schicks Arbeiten in der außergewöhnlichen Ausstellung „Ornamenta 1" im Schmuckmuseum Pforzheim gesehen, wo ihre faltbaren Kragen (Kat.-Nrn. 334–338) einen tiefen Eindruck auf uns machten. Schick hatte die „Ornamenta 1" anlässlich ihrer Eröffnung ebenfalls besucht. Die vier anderen Arbeiten in „Jewellery Moves" waren der Armschmuck *Edged Wave* (Kantige Welle; Kat.-Nr. 378), ein Halsschmuck aus der Serie LA/DC (Kat.-Nr. 391) sowie ein Behälter und Armschmuck aus derselben Serie (Kat.-Nr. 390). Siehe Amanda Game und Elizabeth Goring, *Jewellery Moves: Ornament for the 21st century*, Edinburgh: NMS Publishing 1998, S. 23.

18 Game und Goring 1998 (wie Anm. 17) bilden *Edged Wave* (Kat.-Nr. 378) ab. Andere Arbeiten Schicks in öffentlichen Sammlungen Großbritanniens: *Ring of Fire*

(Feuerring; Kat.-Nr. 376) im Victoria and Albert Museum, London, siehe Clare Phillips, *Jewels and Jewellery*, London: V & A Publications 2000, S. 138; zwei der drei Stücke aus dem Cleveland Crafts Centre in Middlesbrough sind in Publikationen abgebildet: ein Armschmuck in *Jewellery Innovations*, Ausst.-Kat. Cleveland Crafts Centre 1996, ohne Paginierung [S. 11], und der Halsschmuck *Dowel Necklace #1* (Rundholzstab-Halsschmuck Nr. 1; Kat.-Nr. 163) in *International Contemporary Jewellery*, Middlesbrough: Cleveland Crafts Centre, ohne Jahr [etwa 2000], lose Beilage. Diese Institution wird heute als „mima" bezeichnet.

19 *The Ring. The art of the ring*, Cambridge, MA: Mobilia Gallery 2001, Einführung; *Chess*, San Francisco, CA: Velvet da Vinci 2003, Titelabbildung und S. 8, Nr. 43.

20 David Watkins: *The Best in Contemporary Jewellery*, Mies, Schweiz: Rotovision 1993, S. 146 f.

S. 108   *Marjorie Schick*

Als ich gerade darüber nachdachte, welches Thema ich auf einem Antrag für Forschungsurlaub angeben sollte, schlug Jim eine Reihe von Arbeiten über Orte vor, an denen wir gelebt oder die wir besucht hatten. *Quetzalcoatl* und *Bound Colors* (Gebundene Farben), Halsschmuckarbeiten auf Wandreliefs, beziehen sich auf historische Schnitzarbeiten, die wir während unseres Forschungsurlaubs in Mexiko gesehen hatten. Die Halsschmuckarbeiten zu Van Gogh und Mondrian in *Double Dutch Artists* („Holländisches Künstlerdoppel" oder auch „Kauderwelschkünstler") gehen wiederum auf unsere Reisen nach Amsterdam zurück. Eine große Straße in Kalifornien, wo mein Sohn Rob lebt, sowie Zeichnungen von Palmwedeln in seinem Garten waren die Inspirationsquelle für den Halsschmuck *La Palma*. Dort, wo wir in Kansas leben, wurden früher dunkelrote Ziegelsteine hergestellt, weshalb viele unserer Straßen, Bürgersteige und sogar der offene Kamin in unserer Küche daraus bestehen. Eine Schulterskulptur, *Pittsburg Brick* (Ziegel aus Pittsburg), erinnert daran, und wenn die Skulptur nicht getragen wird, ruht sie auf einem Relief, das so bemalt wurde, dass es Schmutz und Gras ähnelt.

S. 119f.

VON INNEN NACH AUSSEN DAS TRAGEN VON MARJORIE SCHICKS SKULPTUREN
Suzanne Ramljak

Eine jede Diskussion über Marjorie Schicks tragbare Objekte führt schnell zu Überlegungen über deren skulpturale Eigenschaften. Dies ist nur angemessen, wurde Schicks schöpferisches Unternehmen doch von Überlegungen ihrerseits ausgelöst, wie es sich wohl anfühlen möge, *innerhalb* einer Skulptur von David Smith zu sein. Ähnliche Gedankengänge haben Schicks Werk während der letzten 40 Jahre stimuliert, in denen sie die vielversprechenden Möglichkeiten der Körperskulptur fortwährend erkundete.

Schmuck und Skulptur werden häufig miteinander verglichen, und in der Regel wird behauptet, dass es sich bei Schmuck um Skulptur in kleinem Maßstab oder um tragbare Skulptur handelt. Zwischen beiden gibt es in der Tat Gemeinsamkeiten, doch auch entscheidende Unterschiede. Schicks Mischkonstruktionen machen sich das Beste aus beiden Gebieten zunutze, und eine Beurteilung ihres Werkes in seiner Beziehung zur Skulptur und zum Schmuck hebt die Eigenartigkeit und sogar die Radikalität ihres künstlerischen Unterfangens hervor.

Die Skulptur ist in erster Linie ein Gebilde, das den Raum besetzt oder verdrängt. Sie ist dreidimensional. Demgegenüber ist ein Schmuckstück ebenfalls ein Objekt mit Dimensionen, doch sind sein Volumen und sein Maßstab durch seine Bindungen an den menschlichen Körper begrenzt. Die tragbaren Objekte von Schick meiden jedoch die für Schmuck übliche Größe und treiben Maßstab und Gewicht an ihre Grenzen. „Ich habe es gerne dramatisch und möchte, dass es viel Platz einnimmt", sagt sie. „Man muss schon mutig sein, um so große Objekte zu tragen."[1] Dementsprechend haben ihre Arbeiten, wie *Yellow Ladderback Chair (Body Sculpture)* (Gelber Stuhl mit Sprossenlehne [Körperskulptur]; 2001, Kat.-Nr. 434), bekanntlich oft eine Größe von mehr als einem Meter.

Neben dem Maßstab müssen sowohl Skulptur als auch Schmuck mit den Zwängen von Schwerkraft und Gewicht ringen. Bei der Skulptur werden diese Elemente indirekt durch den Betrachter erfahren, als Eigenschaften, die als vorhanden angenommen werden. Umgekehrt muss sich der Schmuck jedoch mit dem tatsächlichen Gewicht und der Schwerkraft, denen das Objekt und sein Träger ausgesetzt sind, befassen. Schicks eindrucksvolle Konstruktionen erkunden die Belastbarkeit des Körpers. Obwohl sie sich für relativ leichte Materialien wie Papier, Rundholzstäbe und Leinwand entscheidet, wiegen ihre Arbeiten oft mehr als zwei Kilogramm. „Mich fasziniert die Vorstellung, dass der menschliche Körper, physisch und auch optisch, große Objekte tragen kann", hat die Künstlerin angemerkt.[2]

Der eingenommene Raum und die Maße der meisten Skulpturen erfordern zudem ein Material, das nicht nachgibt. Hierin besteht ein Gegensatz zu vielen Schmuckstücken, die typischerweise dem Druck und der Bewegung des Trägers nachgeben. Schmuck ändert seine Lage, um dem Körper entgegenzukommen, die Skulptur aber verlangt, dass wir uns an sie anpassen. Schicks tragbare Arbeiten kehren diese Prioritäten um – der menschliche Körper wird zum Erfüllungsgehilfen des Schmucks und nicht umgekehrt. Tatsächlich trägt die Skulptur den Körper und verwandelt diesen in einen Sockel, der den Kunstgegenstand trägt.

Während Schicks Arbeiten in der Raumbeherrschung und der Materialität der Skulptur schwelgen, zehren sie auch vom wichtigsten Kapital des Schmucks, nämlich der Berührung. Zwar mögen wir im Bezug auf die Skulptur von Fühlbarkeit sprechen, doch ist die Berührung meist indirekt. Fast immer erleben wir eine Skulptur visuell, nicht taktil, insbesondere wenn es sich um eine Skulptur im öffentlichen Raum handelt. Die Berührung liegt dem Vermögen des Schmucks, eine intime Einbindung herzustellen, zugrunde, und die Wirkung von Schicks tragbaren Skulpturen wird durch diese haptische Qualität gesteigert.

Wenn Schicks aufwendig bemalte Stücke auch jeden visuellen Appetit stillen können, stürzen sie die Hierarchie der Sinne doch um. Sie unterminieren den Sehsinn zugunsten eines vielfältigen Sinneneinsatzes. Seit langem steht der Sehsinn in der abendländischen Tradition über den anderen Sinnen, wobei ihn schon Aristoteles auf die höchste Stufe seiner sensorischen Skala gesetzt hatte. Jedem Sinn ist eine andere Art der Beziehung zur Welt eigen: Der Sehsinn ist üblicherweise distanziert und analytisch, wohingegen der Tastsinn eher ganzheitlich und umfassend ist. Der Sehsinn isoliert, der Tastsinn bindet ein. Der Sehsinn platziert den Betrachter außerhalb des Gegenstandes, in einer gewissen Entfernung, während uns der Tastsinn ins Zentrum eines fühlbaren Feldes setzt. Es ist möglich, sich in die Berührung zu versenken, nicht möglich ist es jedoch, sich auf vergleichbare Weise in den Anblick zu vertiefen.

Indem sie ihre Werke so konstruiert, dass wir in sie tatsächlich eintreten und sie nicht nur anschauen oder halten, choreographiert Schick eine umfassende sinnliche Umarmung. Üblicherweise bleiben wir außerhalb der Skulptur und betrachten ihre Formen. Wenn wir Schicks Arbeiten tragen, hat die Skulptur uns ergriffen: Betrachter werden zu Aufführenden. In dieser Beziehung hat ihr Werk Gemeinsamkeiten mit der Kleidung, und wirklich nehmen einige ihrer Arbeiten die Gestalt von Kleidungsstücken wie Röcken oder Schals an.

In der heutigen Kultur wirkt so vieles zusammen, das uns von unserem eigenen Körpergefühl entfernt. Wir wandern in einem Zustand des Getrenntseins, der physischen und psychischen Entfremdung umher. Indem sie uns in ihren komplexen Strukturen wiederverkörpern, dienen Schicks Arbeiten dazu, einer solchen Trennung entgegenzuwirken. Wie in ihrem *Cocoon for Spiral Necklace* (Kokon für einen spiralförmigen Halsschmuck; 2003, Kat.-Nr. 444) werden wir in sinnlichen Reichtum eingehüllt. Anstatt Außenseiter zu bleiben, die in das Leben hineinblicken, kehren uns ihre hybriden Skulpturen von innen nach außen und platzieren uns im Zentrum unserer eigenen erlebten Erfahrung.

1 Zitiert nach: *Marjorie Schick, Body Works: Structure, Color, Space*, Ausst.-Kat. Arkansas Arts Centre, Little Rock, Arkansas 2001.
2 Äußerung der Künstlerin Anfang der 1990er Jahre, im Internet: http://www.pittstate.edu/art/marjo.html.

S. 125

MARJORIE SCHICK, ZAUBER UND GEIST
Paul Derrez

Den Arbeiten von Marjorie Schick begegnete ich erstmals im Jahr 1982, während der Auswahlphase für „Jewellery Redefined" (Schmuck, eine Neudefinition), einer Ausstellung, die sich „Schmuck in vielerlei Techniken und aus unedlen Materialien" widmete und vom British Crafts Centre in London organisiert wurde. Sie war der Höhepunkt einer alternativen Bewegung innerhalb der Schmuckkunst, die ich als Eigentümer der relativ neuen Galerie Ra voller Enthusiasmus förderte. Die Befreiung von der Tradition und von Klischeevorstellungen, die seit den 1960er Jahren zu vielen wesentlichen Veränderungen im politischen, sozialen und kulturellen Leben geführt hatte, bot auch für den Schmuck viele neue Möglichkeiten und führte hier zu Euphorie und einer wahren Explosion von Energie. Gelegentlich waren seit den 1960er Jahren Schmuckstücke großen Maßstabs gefertigt worden, unter anderem von Arline Fisch und Marjorie Schick in den Vereinigten Staaten und auch von Gijs Bakker und Emmy van Leersum in den Niederlanden. Anfang der 1980er Jahre erlebte das „tragbare Objekt" durch die freie und uneingeschränkte Verwendung aller Arten von Materialien schließlich seine wahre Hochphase. Es entstanden die Tapetenbroschen von Otto Künzli, die Halsschmuckstücke aus Laminat von Gijs Bakker, die Schmuckstücke von Lam de Wolf, die „Hüte" von Susanna Heron und die „Rahmen" von Julia Manheim sowie die aus Schichten bestehenden Halsschmucke von David Watkins, die tragbaren Collagen von Pierre Degen und auch mein eigener gefalteter Kragen, der von den großen Spitzenkragen in den Gemälden holländischer Meister des 17. Jahrhunderts inspiriert worden war. Solche Stücke waren bis dahin oft als Nebenprodukte entstanden, möglicherweise für das Theater, doch in der ersten Hälfte der 1980er Jahre wurden umfangreiche thematische Kollektionen entworfen. Die Fotografie wurde zu einem wichtigen Mittel, diese Schmuckkreationen auf Modellen oder in einem besonderen Umfeld festzuhalten. Der Umzug der Galerie Ra in ein größeres und eigens für diesen Zweck errichtetes Gebäude im Jahr 1983 machte es möglich, diese Entwicklungen bestmöglich zu präsentieren.

Die erste Einzelausstellung von Marjorie Schick in der Galerie Ra zeigte 1983 Arm- und Halsschmuckstücke aus hölzernen Stäben, die ausdrucksvoll und bunt bemalt waren. Die Galeriebesucher wurden von der Explosion von Form und Farbe überwältigt. Einige reagierten skeptisch auf diese Werke, andere waren extrem enthusiastisch und erwarben auch ihre Arbeiten. Die Stücke wurden kaum getragen, doch zumeist erhielten sie als visuelles Statement im Zuhause der Käufer einen Platz.

Marjorie Schick stellte dann regelmäßig in der Galerie Ra aus. Ihr Werk entwickelte sich weiter und wurde immer vielfältiger. Im Laufe der Jahre veränderte sich die offensichtliche Linearität ihrer Arbeiten, sie wurden kompakter und in stärkerem Maße malerisch. Die Verwendung dünner Holzstäbe wich hölzernen Oberflächen, und der Gebrauch von Papiermaché brachte organische, fließende Formen hervor. Später schuf sie Arbeiten, die aus einer Art Basis bestanden, mit denen sie an einer Wand aufgehängt werden konnten, und die ein herausnehmbares Schmuckstück enthielten. Alle diese Entwicklungen konnte man anhand von Marjories Einzelausstellungen in der Galerie Ra (1983, 1988, 1993, 1998) oder den alle fünf Jahre stattfindenden Gruppenausstellungen der Galerie (1986, 1991, 1996, 2001, 2006), die jeweils eine Rückschau auf die vorangegangenen Jahre boten, nachvollziehen. Es ist spannend zu sehen, wie Marjorie sich selbst treu geblieben ist und zugleich ein wunderbares Einfühlungsvermögen für bestimmte Themen zeigt. Als ich vor einigen Jahren ihr Schachspiel (Kat.-Nr. 445) im Laden des Crafts Council des Londoner Victoria and Albert Museum sah, war ich ganz einfach platt. Die Ausdruckskraft dieser Arbeit ist atemberaubend.

Die Tatsache, dass von Schmuckkünstlern heutzutage kaum noch Objekte gemacht werden, die auch getragen werden können,

ist ein weiterer Beleg dafür, wie eigenständig sich Marjories Werk entwickelt hat. Und hinter diesem aufsehenerregend radikalen Werk steht Marjorie als Person – bescheiden, freundlich und amüsant. Dieser Kontrast überrascht alle, die sie kennenlernen. Häufig versuchen wir, unsere beruflichen Reisen – zu Ausstellungen und Konferenzen – so einzurichten, dass wir zur selben Zeit am selben Ort sind. Und wenn uns das gelingt, ist das immer etwas Besonderes und wir haben viel Spaß. Ich schätze Marjorie Schick – persönlich und auch in beruflicher Hinsicht – als warmherzigen Menschen voller Geist.

S. 131

Das Erwachsenwerden ist manchmal schwierig, vor allem als ich, die Neue in der 6. Klasse, von „klügeren und größeren" Schülern, die mir nur Angst machen wollten, von der Schule nach Hause begleitet wurde. Ich war jedoch getröstet, wenn ich den Lattenzaun unseres Gartens sah. Ihn stellt der Halsschmuck *Fences* (Zäune) dar. Als Mädchen von sechs oder sieben Jahren zeichnete ich eine Figur, die ich vor kurzem für *From Childhood* (Aus der Kindheit), eine Brosche auf einem Relief, kopiert habe. Die Lichter der Stadt, vor allem die von hohen Wohnblöcken, haben mich als Jugendliche fasziniert und zu *Chicago Windows* (Fenster in Chicago) angeregt. Der Halsschmuck *Carousel* (Karussell) erinnert daran, wie ich Rob aufwachsen sah und an die Vielzahl seiner Kindheitserlebnisse.

S. 135

EINE DAS ABENTEUER SUCHENDE SEELE
Helen Williams Drutt English

Von den Ballettkostümen Oskar Schlemmers bis zum Kinderspiel Mikado – in unserem Kopf gibt es einige Bilder von farbigen Holzstäben, die sich über den Körper hinaus verlängern. Wir sehen Krümmungen aus Gummi, die als Gegengewicht für die komplexen Konstruktionen dienen, und dann eine Farbexplosion, die in großen Halsschmuckstücken aus Papiermaché Form annimmt. Alle diese Bilder führen uns in die Welt von Marjorie Schick.

Kann eine Reihe farbenfroher gerader Hölzer sich über den Körper hinaus verlängern oder von der Schulter in die Luft abheben und dem Begriff Brosche eine weitere Bedeutungskomponente hinzufügen?

Kann ein Hut, konstruiert wie ein komplexer linearer Käfig, zum Tee im Four Seasons oder im Brown's Hotel in London getragen werden? Eine Kopfbedeckung, die einem starren, aus Geraden zusammengesetzten Gehäuse gleicht, schmückt den Träger, ist ihrer Zeit aber voraus.

Kann ein Gummischlauch sich um den Hals legen und sein starrer Halbkreis durch die üblichen kleinen Stangen zusammengebunden werden?

Kann eine das Abenteuer suchende Künstlerseele, die sich hinter dem Anschein von Unschuld versteckt, im Mittleren Westen ihr kreatives Glück finden? Kann eine faszinierende Künstlerin inmitten von Feldern und Weizen ihr Potenzial über das Übliche hinaus entwickeln? Durch ihre Arbeiten wissen wir, was sich im Geist von Marjorie Schick verbirgt.

Schicks schöpferische Kraft hat die Papiermaché zu einer Form erweitert, die uns umschließt, als ob Elisabeth I. im 21. Jahrhundert herrschen würde. Der Hals ist verborgen, und der Kopf tritt aus einer farbigen Quelle hervor. Hierdurch gelangen wir auf majestätische Art und Weise zu einer neuen Auffassung von Schmuck.

Liberty Torch (Fackel der Freiheit; Kat.-Nr. 395) aus dem Jahr 1997 war ein Beitrag für die Ausstellung „Brooching It Diplomatically: A Tribute to Madeleine Albright" (etwa: Diplomatie durch die Brosche: Eine Hommage an Madeleine Albright), deren Vorliebe für symbolhaften „Gesellschaftsschmuck" sie auf ihrer diplomatischen Pilgerfahrt durch die ganze Welt begleitete. Anstatt der üblichen, mit farbigen Steinen besetzten amerikanischen Flagge oder einem kühnen, aus Gold gegossenem Adler auf einer Perle entwarf Marjorie eine Freiheitsfackel für das späte 20. Jahrhundert. Ihre kräftigen Formen preisen die amerikanische Geschichte; sie führen uns, wie die an Fackeln erinnernden akrobatischen Figuren der Cheerleader, zu einem großartigen Sieg oder erleuchten unseren Weg in die Freiheit.

Im Jahr 2000 erging an Künstler eine einfache Anfrage: Schaffen Sie für die Ausstellung „Commemorative Medals: The Politics of History" (Gedenkmedaillen: Die Politik der Geschichte) eine Medaille, die an ein wichtiges historisches Ereignis erinnert. Marjorie antwortete nicht mit dem üblichen Anhänger oder Medaillon! Ein Gitter aus Bundesstaaten, einer über dem anderen, aus einem Element, das die Form eines Staates wiedergibt und gezielt in die Umrisse der USA eingesetzt wurde, ergab die *Fifty States* (Fünfzig Staaten; Kat.-Nr. 423) genannte, als Kleidungsstück dienende doppelte Leinenbahn. Man fragt sich, ob diese mühevolle und viel Überlegung erfordernde Arbeit in einem Atelier an der Ost- oder Westküste hätte geleistet werden können, wo die Verlockungen der städtischen Kultur so zahlreich sind.

Aus einer Anzahl von Symbolen und technischer Neuerungen, die das Werk der früheren Pariser Modezarin Elsa Schiaparelli rühmen, trug Schick unterschiedliche Elemente aus grellem Rosa für die Ausstellung „Challenging the Châtelaine!" (Eine Herausforderung an die Châtelaine!; Kat.-Nr. 459) zusammen. Aus all den Dingen, die Schiaparelli fasziniert hatten, bezog Marjorie Elemente ein, darunter Insekten aus dem *Bug Necklace* (der Insekten-Halskette) von 1937/38, die enghalsige Flasche für das Parfum Shocking! wie auch gefaltete Kanten, die an ein Kleid Schiaparellis aus dem Jahr 1936 und das 1950 entstandene Kostüm für Schwanensee erinnern – eine Châtelaine! Viele Schiaparelli-Objekte – Scheren, Bürsten, mit künstlichen Fingernägeln bestickte Handschuhe – sind an der aufwendigen Halspasse aus grellem Rosa befestigt, die durch lange Ranken gehalten wird. Es scheint sich um Beine zu handeln, doch sind sie aufgehängt wie eine umgekehrte Marionette.

Schick stellt profunde und detaillierte Nachforschungen an und dem entsprechen ihre Werke. Hinter ihrem engelhaften Gesichtsausdruck verbirgt sich eine unermüdliche schöpferische Persön-

lichkeit, deren Beitrag zur Schmuckkunst der Gegenwart Amerika und Europa verbindet.

S. 196

NACHWORT
EINE FRAGE DER DIMENSION UND DEFINITION
Fritz Falk

Die Frage, was Schmuck denn eigentlich ist, muss immer wieder aufs Neue gestellt werden. Soziologen, Anthropologen, Kultur- und Kunsthistoriker haben sich ebenso wie Ethnologen mit der Thematik befasst. Sie haben versucht, das Phänomen zu erkennen und zu erklären: Warum schmückt sich der Mensch?

Sie finden Definitionen und geben Antworten, die in ihrer Vielfalt und Unterschiedlichkeit aufschlussreich und verwirrend zugleich sind. Die Wissenschaftler fragen nach und analysieren, welche magischen, materiellen oder auch rein ästhetischen Gründe die Zierde des menschlichen Körpers veranlassen.

Vorrangig und zwangsläufig steht der Mensch im Zentrum jeglicher Beschäftigung mit Schmuck – ob er nun Angehöriger früher oder „primitiver" Kulturen war, ob er Mitglied einer adeligen, bürgerlichen, bäuerlichen oder einer Punk-Gesellschaft war oder ist. Nicht nur der Nutzer – der Träger, die Trägerin – ist Gegenstand entsprechender Untersuchungen. Auch derjenige, der den schmückenden Gegenstand erfindet und schafft, wird betrachtet und bewertet in seiner handwerklichen und gestalterischen Tätigkeit, die aus althergebrachter Tradition stammen mag, aus Konventionen abgeleitet sein kann oder – losgelöst von allen gesellschaftlichen und kommerziellen Zwängen – ausschließlich der eigenen, ganz persönlichen Kreativität verpflichtet ist.

Noch heute gibt es den Kunsthandwerker im Stammesverband seines afrikanischen Dorfes, es gibt noch den traditionell und eher konservativ arbeitenden Goldschmied und Juwelier, für den der materielle Wert des von ihm geschaffenen Schmuckes im Vordergrund steht. Darüber hinaus gibt es, als bemerkenswerte Erscheinung seit der zweiten Hälfte des 20. Jahrhunderts, den Schmuckkünstler, die Schmuckkünstlerin, die wie bildende Künstler, Bildhauer und Maler, auch wie manche Architekten, aus innerem Bedürfnis und mit ausgeprägt individueller Gestaltungskraft Schmuckstücke im eigentlichen Sinne und andere den menschlichen Körper schmückende Gegenstände schaffen.

Und nun ist es wirklich die Frage der Definition! Eine Brosche, ein Armreif, ein Anhänger, die zwar als Unikate die gestalterische Eigenart ihres Schöpfers in spezifischen Ausdrucksformen der Moderne dokumentieren, bleiben dennoch eine Brosche, ein Armreif oder ein Anhänger. Es gibt aber auch die Überwindung solcher trotz aller künstlerischer Aktualität letztlich uralten Traditionen verpflichteter Schmuckformen, durch die wie schon immer einzelne Partien des menschlichen Körpers hervorgehoben und ausgezeichnet werden. Als faszinierende Alternative hierzu wird die ganze

Figur mit großformatigen Gegenständen geschmückt, die sich innerhalb der üblichen Schmuckkategorisierungen nicht mehr eindeutig definieren lassen. Es gibt nun einen Körperschmuck, der den Menschen in seiner ganzen Körperlichkeit zu einem „Gesamtschmuckwerk" werden lässt.

Es entsteht so eine neue, faszinierende Dimension des Schmückens, die von Wissenschaftlern, vornehmlich von Ethnologen, mit Sicherheit eingeordnet werden könnte in ihnen aus fernen Kulturen bekannte Erscheinungsbilder, die dort aber in magischen und rituellen Zusammenhängen stehen. Hier jedoch steht der künstlerische, der ästhetische Aspekt im Vordergrund.

Das Oeuvre von Marjorie Schick steht nun im Blickfeld! Beispielsweise ein großformatiger, kragenartiger Gegenstand aus bemaltem Holz, der mit anderen Körperskulpturen Marjorie Schicks auf der „Ornamenta 1" des Jahres 1989 im Mittelpunkt des Interesses stand (Kat.-Nrn. 334–338). Obwohl um Hals und Nacken gelegt, ist er kein Halsschmuck im üblichen Sinne, kein bloßes dekoratives Accessoire. Dieses Objekt von Marjorie Schick ist wie alle anderen Kreationen der Künstlerin ein Kunstwerk an sich, mit dem und durch das der Träger, die Trägerin selbst zum lebenden Kunstwerk wird. Wie fantasievoll schafft Marjorie Schick Assoziationen zum Schaffen anderer Künstler, wenn sie zum Beispiel mit einer ihrer Körperskulpturen – *Chagall's Circles* – ihrer Verehrung für diesen Künstler Ausdruck verleiht (Kat.-Nr. 474)! Andere Schmuckgestalter würdigt sie geistreich und vielleicht auch ein bisschen ironisch, wenn sie eines ihrer Werke *Tribute to Elsa Schiaparelli* nennt (Kat.-Nr. 459).

Marjorie Schick ist sicherlich nicht die Einzige, die den ganzen Körper des Menschen schmückt. An vorderster Stelle stehend gehört sie jedoch zu den Künstlerinnen und Künstlern, für die der Mensch – ob Mann oder Frau – nicht nur Konsument ist, sondern integraler Bestandteil ihrer Kunst. Und so fordert uns Marjorie Schick, die den Schmuck und das Schmücken auf spannende Weise in neue gedankliche und formale Dimensionen führt, zu eigenen Stellungnahmen heraus! Und sie fordert uns gleichermaßen auf, die Frage, was Schmuck denn eigentlich ist, erneut zu stellen, um eine ihrem Schaffen entsprechende Definition zu finden.

S. 198ff.

„SIGNIFIERS"
Repräsentative Statements zu meiner Arbeit zu verschiedenen Zeitpunkten in meiner Laufbahn

Wenn ich auf die Versuche zurückblicke, meine künstlerischen Bestrebungen über die Jahre hinweg zu erklären, bin ich erstaunt, wie sich bei meinen Anliegen ein Kerninteresse für plastische Formen herauskristallisiert hat, welche den Körper einbeziehen, doch davon unabhängig als Kunstwerke existieren. Dies war meine Absicht, als ich 1966 das Statement für meinen Master of Fine Arts-Abschluss an der Indiana University schrieb, und sollte über die Jahre hinweg die Essenz meines künstlerischen Schaffens bleiben,

wie ich es auch in meinen Künstlerstatements der Jahre 1975, 1985 und 1999 erläutert habe.

Zusammengenommen erklären diese vier Statements, was in meiner Arbeit konstant geblieben ist und wie sich meine Absichten im Lauf der Zeit entwickelt haben. Sie zeigen – wie die auf den Seiten dieses Buches dokumentierten Kunstwerke und die Texte, welche diese Arbeiten begleiten –, wo ich begonnen habe und wohin ich in einem der Kunst gewidmeten Leben gelangt bin. 1966 konnte ich nicht wissen, was ich erreichen sollte. Es hätte mich sicher überrascht, zu erfahren, dass das, was ich damals in meiner Arbeit sah, bleiben sollte. Überrascht hätte mich auch die Tatsache, dass dieses Interesse an der Skulptur für den menschlichen Körper ein so vielfältiges Werk hervorbringen würde.

STATEMENT DER ABSCHLUSSARBEIT ZUR ERLANGUNG DES MASTER OF FINE ARTS, 1966
Schmuck ist ein Gegenstand zur Zierde des Körpers, der seinen Träger aufwerten soll. Seit jeher zeigt der Mensch das Bedürfnis bzw. den Wunsch nach Schmuck und Verzierung, doch muss dieses Verlangen nicht notwendigerweise mit Gegenständen von ganz alltäglicher Bedeutung gestillt werden. Stattdessen kann ein Schmuckstück sowohl seine schmückenden Funktionen erfüllen und Freude schenken als auch zugleich als eigenständige Kunstform existieren.

Der vorrangige Zweck meines Schmucks ist, sowohl seinen Träger als auch den Betrachter innerhalb einer kleinen fantasievollen Welt zu stimulieren und zu erfreuen. Ich möchte, dass der Betrachter diese plastischen Formen untersucht, alle ihre Teile wahrnimmt und irgendwie mit dem Gegenstand in Beziehung tritt. Meine Schmuckstücke sind eine Interpretation meiner Gefühle und Ansichten. Es ist nicht zu vermeiden, dass sich darin auch meine augenblickliche Umgebung spiegelt. So sind meine Schmuckformen Teil der gegenwärtigen Welt.

Wenn ich ein Schmuckstück beginne, habe ich kein vorgeformtes Bild davon, wie das Endprodukt aussehen wird. Vorläufige Ideen ergeben sich in erster Linie aus Zeichnungen von Naturobjekten und aus experimentellen Arrangements von Stücken aus Metall, Stein und anderen Materialien. Ich meine, dass kein Material ohne einen besonderen Grund nicht in Betracht gezogen werden sollte. Ich baue auf der anfänglichen Idee auf, überarbeite und verfeinere sie und schneide meine Arbeit sogar auseinander, bis ich zu einem Schmuckstück gelange, das visuelles Gleichgewicht, miteinander harmonierende Positiv- und Negativformen, eine aussagekräftige Silhouette und Einheit zwischen dem Ganzen und kleineren Teilen zeigt. Die von mir verwendeten Techniken sind zwar nicht neu, doch versuche ich, eine dreidimensionale Form zu schaffen, die einzigartig ist.

Die Anregungen für meine Schmuckstücke erhalte ich aus verschiedensten Quellen. Die Idee für den großen Silberhalsschmuck (*Continuous Form* [Sich fortsetzende Form; Kat.-Nr. 27]) entwickelte sich aus einer Zeichnung. Ich habe das Objekt begonnen, indem ich eine Linie der Zeichnung in Metall wiederholte, dann aber davon abwich. Dann konstruierte ich das Objekt Stück für Stück, wobei ich jedes Teil mit den zuvor geschaffenen Linien, Formen und Räumen in Beziehung setzte. Inspiriert wurde der Halsschmuck auch durch die Idee, einen modernen Brustharnisch herzustellen. Es war meine Absicht, ein ernstzunehmendes Kunstobjekt zu schaffen, das zugleich das Gefühl eines Fantasiebildes vermitteln sollte.

Mein letztes Werk (*Wheatfields* [Weizenfelder]; Kat.-Nr. 59, im Vorfeld der Ausstellung für die Abschlussarbeit entstanden), der große Halsschmuck aus vielen Linien und vier braunen Steinen, zeigt den derzeitigen Stand der Entwicklung, was das Experimentieren mit Gruppierungen linearer Formen betrifft. Diese wurden durch die kleine bronzene Anstecknadel mit sich ausdehnenden eisernen Linien eingeleitet (*Small and Mighty* [Klein, aber fein]; Kat.-Nr. 9). Der Halsschmuck wurde auch von Vincent van Goghs *Weizenfeld mit Krähen* (1887) angeregt: Hier wurde eines der drei horizontalen Bänder, aus denen das Gemälde besteht, aus unzähligen langen feinen Linien zusammengesetzt, welche in kurzen Pinselstrichen enden, die sich im rechten Winkel von den Stielen wegbewegen. Die Dichte und Intensität dieser Linienmasse, die in Van Goghs Gemälde den Weizen darstellt, ermunterte mich, ein Schmuckstück zu schaffen, das sich an die Wirkung dieser Linien annähert.

Ich glaube, dass diese letzten beiden Stücke in meiner Arbeit einen Übergang darstellen: von Objekten, die lediglich schmückende Gegenstände sind, zu solchen, die sowohl beim Träger als auch beim Betrachter eine emotionale Reaktion auslösen. Ich möchte nicht, dass mein Schmuck eine passive Kunstform ist, er muss beim Betrachter und beim Träger etwas bewirken. Mein Schmuck mag den Betrachter überraschen und, falls nötig, auch verstören, doch vor allem muss er aggressiv sein – er muss auffallen.

In meiner Arbeit geht es mir darum, die Beziehungen zwischen Linien, Ebenen und Räumen durch die Konstruktion dreidimensionaler Formen zu erkunden. Ich berücksichtige auch Farbe, Textur, Bewegung, Klang, Balance sowie Gewicht und natürlich, wie das Objekt dem Körper passen wird. In meinen letzten Arbeiten war ich mehr an der Handhabung von Formen im Raum interessiert und an der Projektion dieser Formen in die direkte Umgebung des Trägers. Ich beabsichtige mit meinen künftigen Arbeiten, diese Erkundungen dreidimensionaler Schmuckformen fortzusetzen.

STATEMENT, 1975

Ich schaffe Körperskulpturen, die man tragen kann, und versuche hierbei, jene Intimität zu erreichen, die sich einstellt, wenn man Kleidung oder Schmuck an den Körper anlegt. Meine Arbeiten haben ein großes Format, und weil sie in ihrer theatralischen Erscheinung die Aufmerksamkeit auf den Träger lenken, verlangen sie, dass er sich ganz einbringt. Diese Objekte erfordern ebenfalls, dass der Träger sich seines Körpers stärker bewusst ist, und zum Bespiel weiß, wie seine Arme am Körper anliegen oder wie man sich durch den Raum bewegt.

1966, als ich mich auf die letzte Beurteilung für meinen weiterführenden Abschluss an der Indiana University vorbereitete, warf ich einen Blick in eine Ausgabe der Zeitschrift *Art in America*, die einen Artikel über den Bildhauer David Smith brachte. Beim Betrachten seiner Skulpturen, die auf den Feldern von Bolton Landing fotografiert worden waren, kam es mir in den Sinn, dass man diese Formen besser erfahren würde, wenn man zu ihnen hingehen und einen Arm oder den Kopf durch ein Loch in ihnen stecken könnte. Auf diese Weise könnte der Betrachter der Skulptur zum Teilnehmer und tatsächlich zum Teil der Skulptur werden. In diesem Moment wusste ich, dass das Schaffen von tragbaren Skulpturen das war, was ich tun wollte.

Mein Metallschmuck war zu dieser Zeit skulpturenhaft, aber erst später in jenem Jahr, in meinem ersten Jahr als Lehrerin, begann ich, mit Papiermaché zu arbeiten. Die ersten sechs Armschmuckstücke waren nicht besonders groß, doch als ich weitere Arbeiten schuf, stellte ich fest, dass sich das Material perfekt zur Konstruktion großer Formen für den Körper eignete, da es relativ leicht war. Auch war für mich die Tatsache, dass ich die Arbeiten bemalen konnte, außerordentlich attraktiv. Mein Ziel war es, Formen zu schaffen, die tragbar waren, doch wenn sie nicht am Körper getragen wurden, von allen Seiten als fertige Skulpturen Bestand hatten.

Der menschliche Körper ist groß, und er ist, sowohl visuell als auch physisch, in der Lage, ein beträchtliches Gewicht zu tragen. In anderen Kulturen werden große Schmuckstücke getragen und können einen großen Teil des Körpers bedecken. Dieses Wissen nahm mir die Angst davor, Körperskulpturen jeglicher Größe zu bauen, auch wenn sie nur für einen kurzen Zeitraum getragen werden konnten. Einige meiner Arbeiten machen den Körper größer, andere scheinen einen Arm oder den Hals oder sogar den ganzen Körper zu umfassen.

Wenn man eine Blume als Schmuck oder ein Ballkleid trägt, muss man sich recht vorsichtig durch den Raum bewegen, sich sowohl großer als auch kleiner Bewegungen bewusster sein und auch dessen, wie man durch eine Tür geht und wie man in ein oder aus einem Auto steigt. Normalerweise führt das Tragen von Schmuck nicht dazu, dass Menschen anders gehen oder sich bewegen, doch warum eigentlich nicht? Mein Ziel ist, ein größeres Bewusstsein der eigenen körperlichen Präsenz zu schaffen. Diese Objekte schaffen neue Erfahrungen für den Träger, ob für ein paar Minuten oder für einige Stunden. Wenn das Objekt entfernt wird, bleibt die Erinnerung, wie es sich am Körper und wie sich der Körper im Objekt anfühlte.

STATEMENT, 1985

Momentan arbeite ich an tragbaren skulpturalen Aussagen, die aus bemaltem und naturbelassenem Holz, Gummiröhren, Plastikstäben und durchstochenem Papier bestehen. Technik interessiert mich nur insofern, als dass sie dazu dient, eine Form zu schaffen. Unabhängig von ihrer Größe sollen meine Werke Präsenz vermitteln. Außerdem sollen meine Arbeiten etwas Zeitloses haben, so dass ihre Formen jetzt wie auch in 100 Jahren noch ästhetisch überzeugen. Mein Ziel ist, zwischen den Richtungskräften und Farbbeziehungen visuelle Spannung zu schaffen. Mir ist es lieber, dass der Betrachter schockiert oder sogar abgestoßen wird als dass er passiv bleibt.

Der menschliche Körper ist der Grund für meine Arbeiten, doch ihre Formen sind, auch wenn sie nicht getragen werden, vollständig. Sie sind keine Maquetten für größere Arbeiten. Sie sind in Verbindung mit dem Maßstab des menschlichen Körpers erdacht und geschaffen worden. Zwar sollen sie getragen werden, doch sollen sie auch ungetragen fertige Skulpturen sein.

Der reinen Freude am nächsten bin ich im Atelier, wenn ich gerade mit einer neuen Arbeit begonnen und das Radio laut gestellt habe, wenn die vor mir liegenden Herausforderungen noch bewältigt werden müssen. Zur Zeit ist es mein Ziel, gerade Linien mit Krümmungen zu kombinieren und die Kontraste zwischen beiden hervorzuheben, indem ich gerade Rundholzstäbe mit naturbelassenen Birkenstöcken kombiniere. Es zeigt sich auch in den Arbeiten aus geraden Plastikstäben und gekrümmten Formen aus durchstochenem Papier.

Als Lehrerin versuche ich, meinen Schülern Engagement und Faszination für ihre Arbeit sowie Selbstdisziplin zu vermitteln.

STATEMENT, 1999

Ich schaffe Schmuck und Körperskulpturen, die, auch wenn sie nicht am Körper getragen werden, fertige Skulpturen sind. Die Größe meiner Arbeiten und ihre Skulpturenhaftigkeit führen dazu, dass sich der Träger seines Körpers und auch des Raums um das Objekt herum in höchstem Maße bewusst und so zu einer sich bewegenden Skulptur wird. Wenn die Arbeit abgenommen und als Skulptur betrachtet wird, entweder an einer Wand, in einem Gemälde oder auf einem Sockel, bleibt dem Träger die Erinnerung, wie sie sich anfühlte und seine Beweglichkeit beeinflusste, wie sie das Bewusstsein von seinem Körper erhöhte und welche Reaktionen sie bei denjenigen, die ihr begegneten, hervorrief.

Meine Überlegungen gelten vor allem dem Ästhetischen und der Tragbarkeit. Dreidimensionale Strukturen und aufgetragene Farben sind in meinen Arbeiten gleich wichtig. Diese aus unkonventionellen Materialien hergestellten Gegenstände sind persönliche Studien über Form, Farbe, Raum, Muster und Rhythmus. Die Materialien, wie z.B. zusammengeheftete und gepolsterte Leinwand oder Sperrholz, sind Mittel zum Zweck. Leinwand wähle ich oft, weil dieses Material auch Maler benutzen, und in meiner Arbeit geht es ebenso um die bemalten Oberflächen wie um die dreidimensionale Struktur. Holz wiederum wähle ich wegen seines Gewichts und seiner Härte. Es eignet sich gut für das Zusammenbauen der Formen, zudem kann es ohne Schwierigkeiten bemalt werden.

In meiner Arbeit resultiert die Innovation aus einer fortwährenden experimentellen Annäherung an Form und Materialien. Größe und Dreidimensionalität treiben die Grenzen des Tragbaren absichtlich bis zum Äußersten. Letztendlich nähere ich mich ästhetischen Problemen auf dieselbe Weise, wie es jeder andere bildende Künstler tun würde.

S. 201 ff.

BIOGRAFIE

1941 Am 29. August in Taylorville, Illinois, geboren.

1957–1959 Samstags- und Sommerkurse für Highschool-Schüler an der School of the Chicago Art Institute.

1959 Abschluss an der Evanston Township High School, Evanston, Illinois (Unterricht in Modedesign bei Frank Tresise).
Beginn des Studiums an der University of Wisconsin, Madison.

1963 Bachelor of Science in Kunsterziehung (mit Auszeichnung), University of Wisconsin (Unterricht in Schmuckdesign bei Arthur Vierthaler).
Heiratet James B. M. Schick.
Beginn des weiterführenden Studiums an der Indiana University, Bloomington.

1966 Master of Fine Arts (mit besonderer Auszeichnung) in Schmuckdesign und Metallbearbeitung, Indiana University (Unterricht bei Professor Alma Eikerman).

1966/67 Lehrt Schmuckdesign an der University of Kansas, Lawrence, unter Professor Carlyle H. Smith.
Erste Papiermaché-Arbeiten.
Reist nach Bloomington zu Professor Eikerman und nach New York. Trifft dort Paul J. Smith im American Craft Museum (heute: Museum of Arts & Design), um ihm die neuen Armschmuckstücke aus Papiermaché zu zeigen.

1967 Beginn der bis heute andauernden Lehrtätigkeit an der Pittsburg State University, Kansas. Zu den Unterrichtsfächern zählen Schmuck, Kunsthandwerk, Weben, Visuelle Erkundungen, Design, Kunsterziehung, Ausstellungstechnik für höhere Semester und Absolventen, Seminare für Studenten im Hauptstudium und Absolventen, Spezialkurs zum Thema Körperbedeckung.

1970 Geburt des Sohnes Robert M. Schick.

1975 Vortrag am Philadelphia College of Art, eine der ersten Präsentationen außerhalb des Campus.
Besuch der Helen Drutt Gallery, Philadelphia.

1976 Während eines Forschungsurlaubs viermonatige Reise nach Europa, besucht dort Museen, Schmuckateliers und Schmuckschulen.

1978 Nimmt Prüfungen in einem Keramikkurs ab und fertigt selbst Keramikschmuck.
Ring aus dicklagigem Karton und Rundholzstäben.

1979 Schreibt sich in einen Plastiklehrgang an der Pittsburg State University ein und macht Plastikschmuck.

1981 Erste Rundholzstab-Brosche.
Erste „Fadenzeichnungen"; diese inspirieren Schmuck aus Papier und Draht wie auch aus Papier und Faden.

1982 Eine Einzelausstellung am Coffeyville Community College erfordert die Herstellung zweier neuer Werkgruppen – sechs Broschen aus bemalten Rundholzstäben und sechs Broschen aus Papier und Draht. Das Fehlen von Vitrinen und das Vorhandensein nur einer Ziegelwand verlangt nach einer Lösung, bei der die Broschen auf bezogenen Sperrholzbefestigungen aufgehängt werden. Aus dieser Ausstellung ergeben sich die sechs Arbeiten, die für die Ausstellung „Jewellery Refined" eingereicht werden.

Besuch der Eröffnung von „Jewellery Redefined: First International Exhibition of Multi-Media Non-Precious Jewellery" (Schmuck – eine Neudefinition: Erste internationale Ausstellung von Multimedia-Schmuck in unedlen Materialien) im British Crafts Centre und des anlässlich der Ausstellung veranstalteten Symposiums in London.

Einrichtung der Schick-Schmucksammlung an der Pittsburg State University.

Einladung, in der Galerie Ra in Amsterdam und in der Galerie Aspects in London auszustellen.

1983 Forschungsurlaub, um ein Trimester lang Metallbearbeitung an der Sir John Cass School of Art (heute: Department of Art, Media and Design, London Metropolitan University) in London zu studieren.

Besuch der Eröffnung der neuen Galerie Ra in Amsterdam.

Rückkehr nach Amsterdam anlässlich einer Einzelausstellung in der Galerie Ra (mit Mutter).

1984 Im Sommer Artist in Residence an der Sir John Cass School of Art.

1985 Kuratiert für das Visual Arts Center of Alaska in Anchorage „Body Works and Wearable Sculpture" (Körperarbeiten und tragbare Skulptur), eine Ausstellung, zu der Künstler aus dem In- und Ausland eingeladen werden.

Erhält in Alaska Stäbe aus gestreifter Birke geschenkt, Inspiration für eine Serie von Broschen, Armschmuckstücken und einem Halsschmuck sowie für andere Arbeiten aus schwarzen und unbemalten Rundholzstäben.

1986 Erstmalige Verwendung von Sperrholz, nachdem ihr das Bedürfnis bewusst wird, zusätzlich zu den Rundholzstabreihen in ihren Arbeiten Ebenen zu schaffen.

Erstmalig Konzentration auf größere Formen für den Körper.

Einzelausstellungen in der VO Galerie in Washington, D. C. und der Helen Drutt Gallery in Philadelphia.

1987 Erkundung einer Vielzahl von Pinselstrich-Arten, Farbschichtungen und bemalten Geweben.

Beginnt die erste Arbeit in einer Werkgruppe von Rückenskulpturen.

Die Einzelausstellung bemalter Rundholzstabarbeiten unter dem Titel „Jewelry: Marjorie Schick" in der Alexander Hogue Gallery der Unversity of Tulsa zieht neue Überlegungen nach sich, wie die eigenen Arbeiten bezeichnet werden sollten. Sofort nach ihrer Einrichtung geht ein Besucher durch die Ausstellung, betrachtet jedes Objekt eingehend, dreht sich um und fragt: „Wo ist der Schmuck?"

1988 Konstruktion des ersten Wandreliefs, das einen Armschmuck aufnimmt.

Erstes „Gemälde", das drei Halsschmuckstücke aufnimmt.

Einzelausstellung „Transition", Galerie Ra, Amsterdam.

Reise nach Südkorea mit amerikanischen Metallschmieden (Organisation: Komelia Okim).

1989 Besucht Eröffnung der Ausstellung „Ornamenta 1" in Pforzheim, Deutschland.

Einzelausstellung im Nordenfjeldske Kunstindustrimuseum, Trondheim, Norwegen.

1990 Retrospektive an der Indiana University anlässlich der Auszeichnung mit dem School of Fine Arts Distinguished Alumni Award 1990.

Auftrag für einen faltbaren Wandschirm in Utrecht, Niederlande.

1991 Forschungsurlaub für einen Aufenthalt als Artist in Residence am Middlesex Polytechnic und an der Sir John Cass School of Art in London.

Lehrt im Rahmen eines Fakultätsaustauschs der Pittsburg State University an der Silapkorn University in Bangkok, Thailand.

1992 Besuch der Eröffnung von „Design Visions Triennial" in Perth, Australien; Vortrag auf der Jewelers and Metalsmiths Group Conference.

1993 Åkersvida-Addenda, zehntägiger Workshop in Hamar, Norwegen, unterstützt von der Kulturabteilung des Organisationskomitees der 1994 in Lillehammer stattfindenden Olympischen Winterspiele.

1994 Einladung, in der Galerie Mobilia in Cambridge, Massachusetts, auszustellen, wo Libby und JoAnne Cooper zahlreiche Ausstellungen zu bestimmten Themen kuratieren, die Stücke inspirieren wie Yellow Ladderback Chair (Gelber Stuhl mit Sprossenlehne) für eine Stuhlausstellung, Variations on a Theme (Variationen eines Themas) – ein aufklappbarer Buch-Halsschmuck/Schärpe – für eine Buchausstellung, Spiraling Discs (Sich in die Höhe schraubende Scheiben), die eine Gefäßform ergeben, für „Basket (R)evolution" (Korbrevolution bzw. -entwicklung) und zahlreiche tragbare Teekannen für Teekannenausstellungen.

1996 Erstmalige Verwendung von Leinwand, dem Material von Malern.

Schafft drei Gruppen von Ohrringen, die auf einem Relief befestigt sind, für „Earrings: Classic and Wild" (Ohrringe: klassisch und wild) in der Galerie Electrum, London.

1998 Forschungsurlaub für eine Reise nach Mexiko; Besuch von acht historischen Stätten zur Erforschung von Farbe.

Lebt und arbeitet für sechs Wochen in London.

Einzelausstellung „Sense of Place" (Gefühl für den Standort) in der Galerie Ra, Amsterdam.

Ausstellung „Time, Color, Place" (Zeit, Farbe, Ort) in der Galerie Mobilia, Cambridge, Massachusetts.

2000 Ernennung zum Fellow des American Craft Council.

2002 Beginn der Arbeit an Progression, einer Folge von Halsschmuckstücken, welche eine Reihe biografischer Werke inspiriert, darunter It's a Boy Named Rob (Es ist ein Junge, und er heißt Rob), Fences (Zäune), Carousel (Karussell) und Ode to Clothespins (Ode an die Wäscheklammer).

2004   Interviewt von Tacey Rosolowski für das Archives of American Art Oral History Program der Smithonian Institution, Bestandteil des Nanette L. Laitman Documentation Project for Craft and Decorative Arts in America.

2007   Erste Stationen der Retrospektive „Sculpture Transformed: the Work of Marjorie Schick" (Die Verwandlung der Skulptur. Das Werk von Marjorie Schick), kuratiert von Tacey Rosolowski und organisiert von International Arts and Artists of Washington, D. C.

Stationen der Retrospektive:

San Francisco Museum of Craft + Design, San Francisco, Kalifornien, Juni–September 2007

Indiana University Art Museum, Bloomington, Indiana, Oktober–Dezember 2007

Marianna Kistler Beach Museum of Art, Kansas State University, Manhattan, Kansas, Januar–März 2008

Fuller Craft Museum, Brockton, Massachusetts, Mai–September 2008

Muskegon Museum of Art, Muskegon, Michigan, Dezember 2008–Februar 2009

S. 216

AUTORENBIOGRAFIEN

TACEY A. ROSOLOWSKI, Ph. D., hat als freie Autorin zahlreiche Artikel und Katalogbeiträge zu zeitgenössischem Schmuck veröffentlicht und zum selben Thema viele Vorträge gehalten. Sie ist Kuratorin der Retrospektive und Wanderausstellung „Sculpture Transformed: The Work of Marjorie Schick" (Die Verwandlung der Skulptur. Das Werk von Marjorie Schick; 2007–2009). 2003 war sie James Renwick Fellow in American Craft an der Renwick Gallery der Smithsonian Institution in Washington D. C., ein Stipendium, das ihr für ihre Forschungen zu Schmuckdesign gewährt worden war. Sie machte ihren Ph. D. in Vergleichender Literaturwissenschaft an der State University of New York in Buffalo und ihren Master of Science im Fachbereich Umweltgestaltung der Cornell University in Ithaca, New York. Sie lebt in Buffalo im Bundesstaat New York.

GLEN R. BROWN, Ph. D., ist Professor für die Kunstgeschichte des 20. Jahrhunderts und der Gegenwart an der Kansas State University und Autor vieler Beiträge zum Schmuck der Gegenwart, welche in *Metalsmith* und *Ornament* erschienen sind. Er wurde zum Mitglied der International Academy of Ceramics in Genf gewählt und ist Associate Fellow des International Quilt Study Center in Lincoln, Nebraska.

PAUL DERREZ, international renommierter Schmuckkünstler und Inhaber der Avantgarde-Galerie Ra in Amsterdam, ist als Redner, Autor und Jurymitglied für Kunstgremien und -preise im In- und Ausland sehr gefragt. Nach seiner Ausbildung zum Goldschmied an der Vakschool in Schoonhoven zog er nach Amsterdam und gründete dort 1976 die Galerie Ra. Seine Werke befinden sich in diversen öffentlichen Sammlungen, z.B. im Stedelijk Museum in Amsterdam, in der Neuen Sammlung in der Pinakothek der Moderne in München und im Powerhouse Museum in Sydney.

HELEN WILLIAMS DRUTT ENGLISH ist die Gründerin der Helen Drutt Gallery in Philadelphia. Sie hält Vorträge weltweit und hat mehrere Auszeichnungen erhalten. Ihre praktische Arbeit setzt sich in den wegweisenden Ausstellungen, die sie für internationale Museen organisiert, und den Beiträgen zu zahlreichen Monografien fort. Vor kurzem wurde sie zur Beraterin des Museum of Fine Arts in Houston ernannt, das ihre Schmucksammlung erworben hat. Zudem ist sie als Beraterin für das Designmuseo in Helsinki, Finnland, tätig. 1979 stellte das *American Craft Magazine* fest, dass die Bedeutung ihrer Galerie für das Kunsthandwerk vergleichbar sei mit derjenigen von Alfred Stieglitz' Gallery 291 für die Fotografie zu Beginn des 20. Jahrhunderts.

FRITZ FALK, promovierter Kunsthistoriker und Goldschmiedemeister, war von 1971 bis 2003 Direktor des Schmuckmuseums Pforzheim. Unter seiner Leitung, die die Sammlung des Hauses maßgeblich geprägt hat, fanden dort mehr als 100 Ausstellungen zu unterschiedlichsten Themen der internationalen Schmuckkunst statt.

ELIZABETH GORING, Ph. D., ist Kuratorin, Autorin und Schmuckhistorikerin. Sie ist Hauptkuratorin an den National Museums of Scotland in Edinburgh, wo sie von 1983 bis 2004 die Sammlung für modernen Schmuck einrichtete und weiterentwickelte. Sie ist Honorary Research Fellow am Institut für Kunstgeschichte der University of Glasgow und am Edinburgh College of Art.

SUZANNE RAMLJAK, Autorin, Kunsthistorikerin und Kuratorin, ist die derzeitige Herausgeberin der Zeitschrift *Metalsmith*. Zuvor gab sie die Zeitschriften *Sculpture* und *Glass Quarterly* heraus und war Mitherausgeberin von *American Ceramics*. Ramljak hat Beiträge für Bücher und Kataloge verfasst und zahlreiche Vorträge zur Kunst des 20. Jahrhunderts gehalten.

HELEN SHIRK (Master of Fine Arts, Indiana University, 1969) ist emeritierte Professorin für Kunst an der San Diego State University. Ihre Metallarbeiten finden sich in vielen öffentlichen Sammlungen, so im Victoria and Albert Museum in London, im Schmuckmuseum Pforzheim, in der National Gallery of Australia in Canberra, im Houston Museum of Fine Arts, im Mint Museum of Art and Design in Charlotte, North Carolina, und im Cooper-Hewitt National Design Museum in New York.

PAUL J. SMITH, von 1963 bis 1987 Direktor des American Craft Museum (heute Museum of Arts & Design) in New York, hat durch seine ideenreiche Vermittlung von Kunst und seine internationalen Aktivitäten, die einen wichtigen Beitrag zur öffentlichen Wertschätzung von Kunsthandwerk und Design leisteten, große Anerkennung erlangt. Er ist seit 1957 Vorstandsmitglied des American Craftmen's Council. Heute arbeitet er als freier Kurator und Berater.